DICTIONARY OF ORIENTAL LITERATURES

VOLUME II
SOUTH AND SOUTH-EAST ASIA

General Editor
JAROSLAV PRŮŠEK

Volume Editor
DUŠAN ZBAVITEL

London
GEORGE ALLEN & UNWIN LTD
RUSKIN HOUSE MUSEUM STREET

First published in 1974

ISBN 0 04 890005 2

Printed in Great Britain
in Times New Roman Type
by William Clowes & Sons, Limited
London, Beccles and Colchester

ADVISORY EDITORIAL BOARD

ACKNOWLEDGEMENTS

The editors would like to express their heartiest thanks to the members of the Advisory Editorial Board who have helped, with great willingness and uncommon care, to improve the general level of this dictionary. In the present volume they were Mrs Anna J. Allott of the School of Oriental and African Studies, University of London, who revised the parts concerning South-East Asia, Professor John Brough, of the University of Cambridge, our Advisor on the literature of Ancient India, and Mr Ralph Russell of the School of Oriental and African Studies, University of London, who not only revised the New Indian literatures and those of Pakistan, Bangladesh, Ceylon and Nepal, but also gave many a general word of advice. Most of the Czech contributions were translated into English by Mrs Iris Urwin, to whom our warmest thanks are due.

In conclusion the editors would like to thank UNESCO for the grant towards the financing of this dictionary, and the publishers for their sympathetic awareness of the difficulties involved.

The Editors

CONTENTS

CONTRIBUTORS

AJA	Mrs Anna J. Allott; Lecturer in Burmese, School of Oriental and African Studies, University of London
AKR	A. K. Ramanujan; Professor of Linguistics and Dravidian Studies, University of Chicago
AKW	Dr A. K. Warder; Professor of Indian Studies, University of Toronto
AS	Prof. Dr Annemarie Schimmel; Harvard University, Cambridge, Mass.
BhK	Dr Bh. Krishnamurti; Professor of Linguistics, Osmania University, Hyderabad
BKM	Dr Bimal Krishna Matilal; Professor of Indian Philosophy, University of Toronto
BSM	Mrs Barbara Stoler Miller; Barnard College, Columbia University, New York
CBS	Clinton B. Seely; Instructor in Bengali, University of Chicago
CHBR	Christopher H. B. Reynolds; Lecturer in Sinhalese, School of Oriental and African Studies, University of London
CS	Christopher Shackle; School of Oriental and African Studies, University of London
CV	Dr Charlotte Vaudeville; Professor of Modern Indian Studies, University of Paris III, Sorbonne; Directeur d'Études, Ecole des Hautes-Études, IV, Sorbonne, Paris
DA	Dr Dagmar Ansari; Oriental Institute, Prague
DB	Mrs Dagmar Bečková; Oriental Institute, Prague
DBt	Mrs Denise Bernot; Ecole des Langues Orientales Vivantes, Paris
DJM	David J. Matthews; Lecturer in Urdu and Nepali, School of Oriental and African Studies, University of London
DZ	Dr Dušan Zbavitel; Oriental Institute, Prague
ECD	Edward C. Dimock Jr; Professor of Bengali and Bengal Studies, University of Chicago
EH	Miss Eva Horáková; Oriental Institute, Prague
EM	Dr Eliška Merhautová; Oriental Institute, Prague
EV	Dr Eva Vaníčková; Research Assistant, Indonesian Department, The Australian National University, Canberra
HP	Dr Hla Pe; Professor of Burmese, School of Oriental and African Studies, University of London
IF	Prof. Dr Ivo Fišer; Institut for Indisk Filologi, University of København
IR	Dr Ian Raeside; Lecturer in Marathi and Gujarati, School of Oriental and African Studies, University of London
IZ	Dr.phil. Irene Zahra; Dingli, Malta

CONTRIBUTORS

IZb	Miss Iva Zbořilová; Oriental Institute, Prague
JB	Dr John Brough; Professor of Sanskrit, University of Cambridge
JBe	Dr Jiří Bečka; Oriental Institute, Prague
JG	Dr J. Gonda; Professor of Sanskrit and Indology, University of Utrecht
JLM	Dr John L. Masson; Associate Professor of Sanskrit, University of Toronto
JM	Dr Jan Marek; Oriental Institute, Prague
JME	John M. Echols; Professor of Linguistics and Asian Studies, Cornell University, Ithaca, New York
JMJ	Mrs Judith M. Jacob; Lecturer in Cambodian Studies, School of Oriental and African Studies, University of London
JRM	Dr John R. Marr; Lecturer in Tamil and in Indian Music, School of Oriental and African Studies, University of London
JV	Dr Jaroslav Vacek, Assistant of Indology, Charles University, Prague
KW	Klaus Wenk, Dr.iur., Dr.phil.; Professor of Southeast-Asian Studies, Head of the Department, University of Hamburg
KZ	Prof. Dr Kamil Zvelebil; Instituut voor Oosterse Talen, Utrecht
LL	Dr Lothar Lutze; Department of Modern Languages and Literatures, South Asia Institute, University of Heidelberg
MED	Mrs Margaret Esmé Derrett, MA; London
MO	Dr Miroslav Oplt; Prague
PG	Dr Peter Gaeffke; Associate Professor in Hindi, University of Utrecht
REA	Dr R. E. Asher; Reader in Linguistics, University of Edinburgh
RR	Ralph Russell; Reader in Urdu, School of Oriental and African Studies, University of London
RSM	Dr R. S. McGregor; Lecturer in Hindi, University of Cambridge
SY	Sitanshu Yashaschandra; Gujarati poet and critic, Ford West European Studies Fellow, France
US	Dr Ute Sodemann; Research Fellow, South Asia Institute, Department of Political Science, University of Heidelberg
VV	Dr Ivo V. Vasiljev; Prague
WOF	Mrs Wendy Doniger O'Flaherty; Lecturer in the Ancient History of South Asia, School of Oriental and African Studies, University of London
WRR	Professor William R. Roff; Department of History, Columbia University, New York

ABBREVIATIONS USED FOR BOOKS AND JOURNALS

ABSLP	Alessandro Bausani, *Storia delle letterature del Pakistan* (Milano 1959)
AFMH	D. Ansari, *Frau im modernen Hindi-Roman* (Berlin 1970)
AS	J. E. Abbott, *Stotramālā, A Garland of Hindu Prayers.* A Translation of prayers of Maratha poet-saints, from Dnyāneshvar to Mahipati. The Poet-Saints of Mahārāshtra, No. 6 (Poona 1929)
BBV	*A Book of Bengali Verse*, compiled and edited by Nandagopal Sengupta (Calcutta 1969)
CEIWE	*Critical Essays on Indian Writing in English*, edited by M. K. Nair, S. K. Desai and G. S. Amur (Dharwar 1969)
CNI	T. W. Clark (ed.), *The Novel in India, its Birth and Development* (London 1970)
DHSL	S. N. Dasgupta and S. K. De, *A History of Sanskrit Literature: Classical Period* (Calcutta 1947)
DHSP	S. K. De, *History of Sanskrit Poetics* (Calcutta 1960)
DMINE	M. E. Derrett, *The Modern Indian Novel in English* (Brussels 1966)
DNILVN	M. M. Durand et Nguyen Tran Huan, *Introduction à la littérature vietnamienne* (Paris 1969)
GHEH	P. Gaeffke, *Hindiromane in der ersten Hälfte des zwanzigsten Jahrhunderts* (Leiden-Köln 1966)
GLUTR	Ute Glockner, *Literatursoziologische Untersuchungen des Thailändischen Romans in XX. Jahrhundert* (Freiburg 1967)
GPC	*The Glass Palace Chronicle of the Kings of Burma*, transl by Pe Maung Tin and G. H. Luce (London 1923)
GSML	K. M. George, *A Survey of Malayalam Literature* (London 1968)
HIL	J. Rypka and collaborators, *History of Iranian Literature* (Dordrecht 1968)
HOS	Harvard Oriental Series (Cambridge, Massachusetts)
IWE	D. McCutchion, *Indian Writing in English* (Calcutta 1969)
JAOS	Journal of the American Oriental Society
JHTL	C. Jesudasan and Hephzibah Jesudasan, *A History of Tamil Literature* (Calcutta 1961)
KHSL	A. B. Keith, *A History of Sanskrit Literature* (Oxford 1928)
KMBP	M. Kirkman (transl), *Modern Bengali Poems*, edited by D. Chatterjee (Calcutta 1945)
KSD	A. B. Keith, *The Sanskrit Drama in its Origin, Development, Theory and Practice* (Oxford 1924)
KSHS	Khushwant Singh, *A History of the Sikhs*, Vol. I (1963)

MHABD	Maung Htin Aung, *Burmese Drama* (Oxford University Press 1937)
MPMS	Nicol Macnicol, *Psalms of Marāṭhā Saints.* One hundred and eight hymns translated from the Marathi (Calcutta–London 1919)
MSHUL	Muhammad Sadiq, *A History of Urdu Literature* (London 1964)
MSR	M. A. Macauliffe, *The Sikh Religion*, 6 vols. (Oxford 1909); reprinted as 6 vols. in three (Delhi 1963)
NHML	M. K. Nadkarni, *A Short History of Marathi Literature* (Baroda 1921)
PEB	*Poems from East Bengal*, transl by Yusuf Jamal Begum (Pakistan P. E. N. Publication, 1954)
PLJ	Theodor Pigeaud, *Literature of Java: Catalogue Raisonné of Javanese Manuscripts in the Library of the University of Leiden.* Bibliotheca Universitatis, Vol. I (Leiden 1967)
PNHML	P. K. Parameswaran Nair, *History of Malayalam Literature* transl from the Malayalam by E. M. J. Venniyoor (New Delhi 1967)
PTS	Pali Text Society
RITMP	Ralph Russell and Khurshidul Islam, *Three Mughal Poets* (Cambridge 1968)
RKPSP	L. Rama Krishna, *Pañjabi Ṣūfī Poets, A.D.* 1460–1900 (London 1938)
RMBB	Lila Ray (transl), *Broken Bread. Short Stories of Modern Bengal* (Calcutta 1957)
RPML	R. D. Ranade, *Pathway to God in Marathi Literature* (Bombay 1961)
RSHUL	Ram Babu Saksena, *A History of Urdu Literature* (Allahabad 1927)
SBE	Sacred Books of the East (Oxford University Press)
SDUN	Shāista Akhtar Bānū Suhrawardy, *A Critical Survey of the Development of the Urdu Novel and Short Story* (London 1945)
SHBL	Sukumar Sen, *History of Bengali Literature* (New Delhi 1960)
SHBLL	Dinesh Chandra Sen, *History of Bengali Language and Literature* (Calcutta 1911)
SMB	*Sajak-Sajak Melayu Baru: Modern Malay Verse* (1963)
SMBP	*Studies in Modern Bengali Poetry*, edited by N. Ghose (Calcutta)
SWS	*The Sacred Writings of the Sikhs*, transl by Trilochan Singh *et al* (London 1960)
TMIL	A. Teeuw, *Modern Indonesian Literature* (The Hague 1967)
VISNM	Verghese Ittiavira, *Social Novels in Malayalam* (Bangalore 1968)
WHIL	M. Winternitz, *History of Indian Literature*, Vol. 1–2 (Calcutta 1927, 1933), Vol. 3 (Delhi 1963)
WIB	A. K. Warder, *Indian Buddhism* (Delhi 1970)

VOLUME II

SOUTH AND SOUTH-EAST ASIA

A

'Abbās, Khvāja Aḥmad (b 1914 Panipat), Urdu and English writer, journalist and film-director. He was an early member of the Progressive Writers' Association (see progressive writing), and a first volume of short stories appeared in 1937. Since then he has continued to produce both stories and novels. He draws his themes from contemporary Indian middle- and working-class life, and his work, besides expressing his social and political views, portrays the love experience and the frustrations of the younger generation. He is a master of reportage, but his journalism adversely influences the language and style of his fiction. He also writes in English. *Outside India* (1940); *Tomorrow is Ours* (1945); *Rice and Other Stories* (1945). *Inqilab* (1954) depicts the history of the Indian freedom movement. JM

'Abd ul-Karim, Master (b 1908 Utmanzay, d 1961), Pashto writer in what is now Pakistan. He went to one of the Free Schools (*Āzād skūl*) set up in the Pashto areas to improve the level of education among the Pashtuns. He then studied in Delhi, where his favourite authors were Premcand (qv) and L. N. Tolstoy. Returning to his home region he taught at a Free School, and wrote for the patriotic periodical of the thirties, *Pashtūn*, to further the cause of Pashtun independence. He set a new line in Pashto literature, often taking the hero of his short stories from the lower social strata, with whom as a writer he sympathized. His chief work is the volume of stories entitled *Dzōley gulūna* (An Armful of Blossoms, 1957). JBe

'Abdu'l-karim of Bulrrī, Shāh (1536–1624), the first Sindhi mystic poet, whose collected verses (*risālō*) have been preserved. In his 93 short verses in popular Indian metres and rhythms he touches upon the traditional topics of Sufism, uses Sindhi folk-tales in his meditations, and takes images from the daily life of villagers and fishermen. He is thus a forerunner of his great-grandson Shāh 'Abdu'l-laṭīf (qv).

Motilal Jotwani, *Shah Abdul Karim* (New Delhi 1970), with trans.; ABSLP 278, 283–4. AS

Abdullah bin Abdul Kadir, Munshi (b 1796 Malacca, d 1854 Jeddah), Malay biographer and translator. Though writing as a Malay, Abdullah was primarily of mixed Tamil and Arab descent, and in addition had a close association (as language teacher, scribe, and assistant) with many leading European scholar-officials, merchants, and missionaries, from Raffles to the Rev. Alfred North. These circumstances together conferred upon him a certain distance from his own society, and it was the resulting detachment that, in a journalistic sense (and he was above all a reporter), gave his best known writings much of their clarity and sharpness. He was far from being uninfluenced by traditional Malay literary style, as witnessed for example in his *Hikayat Galilah dan Daminah* (translated 1835 from a Tamil version of the *Pañcatantra*, qv).

However, his real contribution to new directions in Malay literature lay in the two autobiographical works which have so frequently appeared in Malay, English, and other languages: *Kisah Pelayaran Abdullah* (Tale of Abdullah's Voyage [to the East Coast of Malaya in 1838], completed 1838 or 1839), and the *Hikayat Abdullah* (Abdullah's Autobiography, completed 1843 and published 1849). Quite apart from their originality and value as a Malay historical record, the lively and colloquial language of these narratives, and their personal and idiosyncratic commentary on the times, mark them as a fresh departure in Malay letters. Abdullah's criticisms of his own society, and his eagerness to embrace standards set by the West, have caused him to be treated with some caution by a more recent generation of nationalists; however, few question the vitality and directness of his writings, or his position as 'the father of modern Malay literature'. The *Hikayat Abdullah* has been reprinted in Malay many times, the most complete and reliable version being that edited by R. A. Datoek Besar and R. Roolvink (1935); there are several translations into English (eg, J. T. Thomson, 1874; W. G. Shellabear, 1918), the only complete one, however, being that edited and annotated by A. H. Hill (1955, reprinted 1971). The best Malay edition of the *Kisah Pelayaran Abdullah* is that edited and annotated by Kassim Ahmad (1960), which includes also the uncompleted *Kisah Pelayaran Ka-Judah*; and there is an English translation of the former A. E. Coope (1949). Among his other original works (now extremely scarce) should be noted the narrative poems *Shaer Singapura Terbakar* (Ballad of the Singapore Fire [of 1830]) and *Shaer Kampong Gelam Terbakar* (Ballad of the [1874] Kampong Gelam Fire). WRR

'Abdu'l-laṭif Bhitā'i, Shāh (b 1689 near Hala, d 1752 Bhit), Sindhi mystic, poet and musician. After keeping company with a group of yogis, he settled in Bhit where his mausoleum is still a centre of pilgrimage. His *risālō* (collected verses) is the classical work of Sindhi poetry; the old legends and tales of the Indus valley are the starting point for his mystic meditations. The language is beautiful but sometimes abstruse; traditional Indian metres are used. The ingenious web of mystical ideas is partly influenced by Jalālu'd-dīn Rūmī (see Vol. III). The soul is always represented by the woman, who, longing for her beloved or her husband, is eventually united with him in death, like Sassui, Sohni, Lila, Marui, and others. This symbolism is closer to the Indian than to the Islamic mystic tradition. In their simplicity and intensity the songs of these loving women are unforgettable. In spite of praise of the yogis, his mystical poetry is Islamic in outlook and culminates in praise of the Prophet Muhammad and acknowledgement of the all-embracing Unity of Being; wherever the lover turns, there is the manifestation of God. The *risālō*, some of whose melodies the poet himself invented, is popular among the Sindhis, and furnishes imagery even for modern progressive writers.

Trans.: Elsa Kazi, *Risālō* (selections, Hyberabad 1965).

T. Sorley, *Shah Abdul Latif of Bhit* (Oxford 1940, 1968), with trans.; ABSLP 286–8. AS

Abdul Muis, Indonesian writer, see **Muis**

abhaṅga, Marathi short lyrics, see **Jñāneśvar, Nāmdev, Tukārām.**

Abhidharma, see **Tripiṭaka.**

Abhinavagupta (10th century AD), Indian philosopher and literary critic. To followers of the religious system known as Kashmir Śaivism, he is the final authority on all matters of doctrine. The legends that have grown up around his name survive to the present day: Kashmirians claim that he died by entering a cave with a large following of disciples without returning. The breadth and profundity of his intellect and the originality and brilliance of his critical insight entitle him to a distinguished place in the ranks of philosophers of aesthetics of all lands and all periods of history. Two works on literary criticism survive, both commentaries: the *Dhvanyālokalocana*, a commentary on Ānandavardhana's *Dhvanyāloka* (see *dhvani*) and his commentary, extant only in part, on the *Nāṭyaśāstra* (qv) of Bharata.

R. Gnoli, *The Aesthetic Experience according to Abhinavagupta* (Banaras 1968); J. Masson and M. V. Patwardhan, *Śāntarasa and Abhinavagupta's Philosophy of Aesthetics* (Poona 1969); J. Masson and M. V. Patwardhan, *Aesthetic Rapture* (two volumes, Poona 1970); K. C. Pandey, *Abhinavagupta—An Historical Study* (Banaras 1966); DHSP I, 110–2; II, 176–80. JLM

Abrō, Jamāluddīn (b 1924 Sangi), Sindhi prose writer. After studying law he joined government service and the practice of the law. In his realistic short stories (eg *Pishu Pasha*, 1959) he tries to show the solution to various social problems. He is the best narrative writer of modern Sindhi. JM

Abū'l-Ḥasan, *Miān* (d 1711), Sindhi religious poet, author of the first religious treatise in Sindhi verse (1700), dealing with 130 questions of ritual practice in Islam. He used the simple device of filling up the rhyme with a long *ā* to conform to the Arabic *qaṣīda* (see Vol. III) form used for didactic purposes and strongly influenced his younger contemporaries. AS

Abū Tālib Kalim Hamadāni, Indo-Persian poet, see **Kalim Kāshāni.**

Ācārya, Bhānubhakta (1814–69), the first great Nepali poet, whose version of the *Rāmāyaṇa* (qv) became popular, chiefly because of the colloquial flavour of its language. Before Bhānubhakta, Nepali poetry, such as it was, had been greatly influenced both in language and style by Sanskrit models. Bhānubhakta was born and educated in a village of western Nepal. The legend is that he was inspired to begin a Nepali translation of the *Rāmāyaṇa* by a conversation he had with an old grass cutter. He is the author of three other poetical works, two of which, *Praśnottarī* (Questions and Answers) and *Vadhūśikṣā* (The Training of the Bride) are also translations into colloquial Nepali from Sanskrit and one, *Bhaktamālā*, is an original composition. A few letters written to his son are among the first extant examples of Nepali prose. DJM

Achdiat Karta Mihardja, Indonesian novelist, see **Mihardja.**

Ādi Granth (the 'Original Book'), the Sikh scriptures, written in the Gurmukhi script. They consist of about 6,000 hymns and poems by various authors, largely composed in the religious *lingua franca* of mediaeval northern India known as *Sant Bhāśā* or *Sādhukkaṛī*, with a varying admixture of distinctively Panjabi forms. The original version of the *Ādi Granth*, called the *Kartārpur-vālī bīṛ*, was composed by the fifth Sikh *gurū*, Arjan, with Bhāī Gurdās (see Gurdās) as his amanuensis, and completed in 1604. In 1704 a revision of the *Ādi Granth* was undertaken by the tenth *gurū*, Gobind Singh (1666–1708), and this expanded version (the *Damdame-vālī bīṛ*) is in standard use among Sikhs to-day. After the death of the last *gurū*, Gobind Singh, the *Ādi Granth* became the centre of the Sikh community's religious devotion, and is normally referred to by the honorific title of *Gurū Granth Sāhib*; the recitation of its hymns forms the most significant part of Sikh religious observances. Of the ten Sikh *gurūs*, the first five and the ninth are represented in the *Ādi Granth* as follows: I Nānak (1469–1539), with 974 hymns: II Angad (1504–52), 62 hymns; III Amar Dās (1479–1574), 907 hymns; IV Rām Dās (1534–81), 679 hymns; V Arjan (1563–1606), 2,218 hymns; 115 hymns by the ninth *gurū*, Tegh Bahādur (1621–75), were included by his son Gobind Singh (see *Dasam Granth*). The most important contributors are Nānak, the founder of the Sikh religion (particularly his *Japjī*, a summary of his theology standing at the beginning of the *Granth*, and his *Āsā-kī Vār*), and Arjan, the largest contributor, whose best known hymn is the long *Sukhmanī*. A second category of contributors, the so-called 'Bhagats', includes some of the most important representatives of the Sant tradition of north and central India, notably Nāmdev (qv, 61 hymns), Ravidās (39 hymns) and Kabīr (qv, 226 hymns).

While the versions of these writers' hymns in the *Ādi Granth* often differ markedly from those preserved among their own followers, in theology as well as language, their catholic inclusion by Gurū Arjan give the *Granth* a quite distinctive quality as a scriptural book; even more remarkable is the inclusion of poems by a Panjabi Muslim mystic, Farīd (qv). A third category of hymns consists of eulogies of the *gurūs* by the Bhaṭṭs, bards attached to their entourage. The community rejected the suggestion of Bhāī Manī Singh (d 1738) that the hymns should be grouped by author. The present traditional arrangement reflects the fact that the *Ādi Granth* is a collection of hymns designed to be sung rather than read through methodically. According to this arrangement the hymns are first arranged under the 31 *rāgs* in which they are to be sung, within each *rāg* the classification is by metrical form, and only within each poetical genre is there a division by author, the compositions of the *Gurūs* preceding those of the *Bhagats*. A modern standard pagination obviates some of the difficulties of reference ensuing from this system. While there can be no doubt of the superb quality of its finest hymns, whether considered as literature or spiritual expressions, the *Ādi Granth* is so varied in content that a comprehensive critical estimate is a virtually impossible task in the present state of knowledge.

Sri Guru-Granth Sahib, complete English trans. by Gopal Singh in 4 vols. (Delhi 1962). C. H. Loehlin, *The Sikhs and their Book* (Lucknow 1946); and *The Sikhs and their Scriptures* (Lucknow 1958); W. H. McLeod, *Gurū Nānak and the Sikh Religion* (Oxford 1968); MSR; SWS. CS

Aḍiga, Sopalakrishna (b 1918), probably the most influential, stirring and complex poet of contemporary Kannada. His cultural-literary criticism, *Maṇṇina Vāsane* (1966) and his poetry have led to imitations and a wide following among the young. His early poetry (*Bhāvataraṅga*, 1946, and *Kaṭṭuvevu Nāvu*, 1948), is chiefly memorable romantic song and rhetoric. Since *Naḍedu Banda Dari* (The Road We Have Walked, 1952), and in volumes like *Caṇḍe Maddale* (1954), and *Bhūmigīta* (Song of Earth, 1959), his work has attained an unparalleled passion, complexity, irony, an unflinching attention to bitter contemporary reality, and a sinewy ranging language of music and discord. He edits the important Kannada literary review, *Sākṣi* (Witness). *Āyda Kavanagaḷu* (Selected Poems) was published in 1968.

Trans.: A. K. Ramanujan, Krishnamurthi *et al.*, *Song of the Earth* (Calcutta 1968). AKR

Adwani, Sir Bheeromal Mehrchand (1876–1953), Sindhi linguist, historian, critic, translator and dramatist. He was for a while lecturer in Sindhi at Bombay University, hence his *History of the Sindhi Language* (1941). His interest in Sindhi led him to compose *Qādim Sindh* (History of Pre-Islamic Sindh, 1957). He wrote a number of studies on literature, adapted Sir Walter Scott's *Talisman*, and *Uncle Tom's Cabin* to Sindhi, and wrote some comedies. AS

Āgarkar, Gopāl Ganeś (1856–95), Marathi essayist, journalist and social reformer. He was the first editor of *Kesarī* (see *Cipalūṇkar*), but left in 1887 to found his own paper *Sudhārak* (The Reformer) after quarrelling with his more politically activist colleagues, especially Ṭiḷak (qv). IR

Agyey, Hindi poet, see **Ajñeya.**

Aḥmad, 'Azīz (b 1914, Hyderabad, Deccan), Urdu novelist, critic, and translator, and, in later years, scholar and leading authority on Islam in India and Pakistan. His novels marked an appreciable advance in craftsmanship and frankly portrayed hitherto forbidden areas of personal relationships. *Gurez* (Flight, 1945) tells of the experiences of an Indian student in London and Paris in the late 1930's. *Āg* (Fire, 1946) shows the rise of political consciousness in Kashmir, and *Aisī bulandī, aisī pastī* (Such Height, Such Depth, 1948) is set in the upper-class society of Hyderabad.

Trans.: R. Russell, *The Shore and the Wave* (London 1971). RR

Aḥmad Khān, Sir Sayyid (b 1817 Delhi, d 1898 Aligarh), Urdu prose writer, historian, social reformer and educationalist. In 1838 he entered British service and later studied education in England. A great admirer of the British, he urged his fellow Muslims to take to Western education. In 1875 he founded what later became Aligarh Muslim University. His literary career began with an archaeological history of Delhi buildings, which helped to lay the foundations of a simple style in Urdu prose for subjects of this kind. Later works refuted the charge that the Muslims were behind the 1857 revolt. In 1870 he started the Urdu monthly *Tahẕību'l-akhlāq* (Amendment of Morals), attempting to modernize Muslim society along Western lines and applying reasoned criticism to Islamic theology. By assimilation of Western culture he inaugurated a new era in Urdu literature and established Urdu as a language capable of disseminating a wide range of new ideas. The reform movement he led is known as the Aligarh movement.

Trans.: Garcin de Tassy, *Description des monuments de Delhi en 1852* (Paris 1861).
G. F. I. Graham, *The Life and Work of Syed Ahmad Khan* (London 1909); J. M. S. Baljon, *The Reforms and Religious Ideas of Syed Ahmad Khan* (Leiden 1949); MSHUL 248–63; RSHUL 269–72. JM

Aḥmad, Mawlavī (b second half of the 19th century, Tangi in Hashtnagar), pioneer of modern Pashto prose in what is now Pakistan. He based his work on folk literary tradition and wrote verse ballads (*qissa*). In 1867 he wrote *Ghal aw qāẓi* (The Thief and the Judge) and in 1872 published *De Ādamkhān aw Durkhāney qissa* in Peshawar; in prose and verse, it told of Adamkhan's and Durkhaney's tragic love. Later he began to write prose stories (*hikāyat*) and in 1873 published a collection of 49 of them in Lahore; entitled *Ganji pakhto* (Pashto Treasures), it included humorous and satirical short pieces. Aḥmad is also the editor of the *Dīwān* of the Pashto classic poet 'Abd ur-Raḥmān (see Vol. III).

Trans.: G. O. Ross-Kappel, *Ganj-e-Pashtu* (Lahore 1905). JBe

Aḥmad, Naẕīr (b 1836 Rohar, d 1912 Delhi), pioneer of the Urdu novel, writer of educational books for children, translator, Islamic scholar, lecturer, and one of the masters of modern Urdu prose. A modernist, and strong, though critical supporter of Sayyid Aḥmad K͟hān (qv), he entered the British educational service, where his translation of the Indian Penal Code, and later his moral tale *Mir'ātu'l 'Arūs* (The Bride's Mirror, 1869), written originally for his daughter, attracted attention. This was the first of a series of didactic tales (1872–1892), which treat successively of the upbringing and education of girls (*Banātu'n-Na'sh*), the importance of religion in life (*Taubatu'n-Naṣūḥ*), the evils of polygamy (*Fasāna-e Mubtalā*), the inappropriateness of adopting English dress, food and manners (*Ibnu'l-Vaqt*), the desirability of widow remarriage (*Ayāma*), and the correct application of Islam to modern problems (*Rūya-e Ṣādiqa*). In these, realism, descriptive power, characterization and prose style bring them close to the novel. He translated the *Qur'ān* into Urdu (1896) and wrote *Al-Ḥuqūq va'l-Farā'iẓ* (The Rights and the Duties [of modern Muslims], 1906).

Trans.: M. Kempson, *The Repentance of Nussooh* (London 1884); G. E. Ward, *The Bride's Mirror* (London 1903); Khaja Khan, *Mubtala or a Tale of Two Wives* (Madras 1934). CNI 117–22; SDUN 41–65; MSHUL 316–25. RR

Aḥmadjān Khān Bahādur, Munshī (b 1882 near Kelat, d 1951), Pashto writer in what is now Pakistan. He went to the mission school in Peshawar and became a *munshi*, teaching Pashto to British officials and officers. One of the writers who worked for the revival of Pashto culture and national feelings, he also translated English works (eg the *Utopia* of Sir Thomas More), collected and published folk legends and anecdotes, and wrote short stories. Anthologies: *Hagha dagha* (This and That, 1929); anecdotes: *De qissakhaney gap* (The Teller of Legends, 1930). JBe

Aiṅkuṟunuṟu, classical Tamil anthology, see **Eṭṭuttokai.**

Aiyar, Swaminatha, Tamil philologist, see **Cuvāmināta Aiyar.**

Aiyar, V.V.S., Tamil writer, see **Cuppiramaṇiya Aiyar.**

Ajñeya, or **Agyey,** Saccidānanda Hīrānanda Vātsyāyan (b 1911 Kasiya), Hindi poet and writer (Hindi Literature Award 1965), leading theorist of *nayī kavitā* (qv). He is probably the most cosmopolitan of living Hindi authors. In his writings, in which the recurrent theme is 'the integrity of the human individual' (*Ajñeya*), he attempts, and often achieves, an ideal synthesis of Indian and Western patterns of thought. He has published numerous works, including novels: *Śekhar: ek jīvnī* (Shekhar,

A Biography, 1, 1941, 2, 1944); *Nadī ke dvīp* (Islands in the River, 1952); *Apne-apne ajnabī* (To Each his Stranger, 1961); short stories (*Ajñeya kī kahāniyā̃*, Stories by Agyey, 1, 1954, 2, 1957, 3–4, 1961); a play (*Uttar priyadarśī*, 1967) and criticism (*Hindī sāhitya: ek ādhunik paridṛśya*, Hindi Literature, A Modern Panorama, 1967, ao), although poetry has remained his main medium (*Ityalam*, 1946; *Ā̃gan ke pār dvār*, Doors across the Courtyard, 1961; *Kyõki mãi use jāntā hū*, For I Know Him, 1970 ao). LL

akam, classical Tamil erotic poetry, see **Eṭṭuttokai.**

Akanāṉūṟu, classical Tamil anthology, see **Eṭṭuttokai.**

Akbar Ilāhābādī (b 1846 Bara, d 1921 Allahabad), Urdu poet. He was born in a poor family, but entered the legal profession and rose to be a judge. His humorous verse attacks the westernized products of the new educational system, accusing them of having no ideals beyond a career in British government service, and exchanging their own traditions for a 'modernism' which imitates the mere externals of the English style of living, and an education sufficient only for the needs of their employment. He ridicules their sanguine hopes of the British, arguing that the British rule in their interest alone, and that only superior force could make them yield substantial gains to Indians. He urges instead the importance of religion in the conduct of life, pride in the Muslim cultural tradition, and recognition of the realities of power.

RSHUL 227–38; MSHUL 304–15. RR

Akho, Gujarati poet, see **Premānanda.**

Akustia, Klara, Indonesian poet, see **Dharta,** A.S.

Alagiyavanna (16th–17th centuries), Sinhalese poet who flourished in the time of King Rājasiṃha I of Sītāvaka, near modern Awissawella (1581–92). He held the office of court secretary. W. Geiger refers to him by the name of Mohoṭṭāla, which is properly a title of office. Works: *Sævul Asna* (or *Sandesa*), sometimes considered the last of the classical *sandesa* (qv) poems, was written c1585. *Dahamsoňḍakava* is a non-canonical *jātaka* (qv) poem. *Kusadākava*, another *jātaka* poem, is his most famous work. Dated 1610, it sets out to be a *mahākāvya* (see kāvya). It is based on the same story as the best known Sinhalese *mahākāvya*, King Parākramabāhu II's (qv) *Kavsilumina*, but the treatment is more popular and less purely literary, so that the work is still widely known today. *Subhāṣitaya*, apparently dated 1611, is a set of 100 traditional Indian moral maxims derived from various sources, including Tamil. Many of these are proverbial. *Kustantinu Haṭana*, a ballad poem usually attributed to Alagiyavanna, describes the rebellion in 1619 of a Sinhalese against the Portuguese, and his suppression by the governor Constantine de Sa.

Trans.: Edmund P. Wijetunge, *Dahamsonda Jataka Kavya* (Colombo 1954); Thomas Steele, *Kusa Jatakaya* (London 1871); Edmund P. Wijetunge, *Alagiyavanna's Subhasitaya* (Colombo 1930); S. G. Perera and M. E. Fernando, *Alagiyawanna's Kustantinu Hatana* (Colombo 1932). CHBR

alaṃkāraśāstra, literary criticism in Sanskrit. The tradition in India is long and rich. It begins with Bharata's *Nāṭyaśāstra* (qv) towards the beginning of the Christian era and ends with Jagannāthapaṇḍitarāja's *Rasagaṅgādhara* in the 17th century. While it is true that certain authors emphasize specific elements in literature, it is artificial to divide the tradition (as standard textbooks do) into different schools, such as the school that emphasizes figures of speech, the one that emphasizes suggestion, and the one that emphasizes *rasa* (for the latter is in any case hardly antithetical to the school of suggestion). More realistic is the traditional division into *prācīna* (old) and *navya* (new). The former refers to the works written before Ānandavardhana (ie before the 9th century AD) and include the following authors; (those authors whose works have been translated are marked with a star): *Bhāmaha (qv, c600 AD), *Daṇḍin (qv, c650), *Ubdhaṭa (qv, c700), *Vāmana (c700) and Rudraṭa (c800). These works concern themselves primarily with what later came to be regarded as the externals of poetics; grammar, verbal qualities, style and figures of speech.

The 'new' school refers to the works that come after Ānandavardhana, whose great work, the *Dhvanyāloka* (see *dhvani*) marks a turning point in the concerns of Sanskrit rhetoricians. The major authors are: Rājaśekhara (qv, who really falls outside both schools, 925), Abhinavagupta (qv, 980), Dhanañjaya and his brother Dhanika (who wrote on dramaturgy, 980), Kuntaka (in certain respects a critic of Ānandavardhana, though his book, the *Vakroktijīvita* never engendered much enthusiasm in the later tradition or indeed modern scholarship, 980), Bhoja (qv, 1000), *Mammaṭa (who marks the beginning of the total acceptance of Ānanda's theories and who is the most popular and widely read of all critics, 1074), Mahimabhaṭṭa (qv, a more open critic of Ānandavardhana and a forbiddingly acute logician, 1050), *Viśvanātha (whose *Sāhityadarpaṇa* became the textbook in the field, undistinguished though it is by new insights, 1350) and finally Jagannāthapaṇḍitarāja (who applies the techniques of 'modern logic' to poetics, 1645). Both Ānandavardhana and Abhinavagupta were concerned with what we would today regard as important areas of literary criticism, the nature of aesthetic experience, suggestion, poetic imagination, the relationship between drama and poetry, the treatment of love in literature, etc. The writers who come after them are generally content to synthesize; they accept the major insights achieved by these two towering figures, yet they also seek a place for the purely technical side of poetics, figures of speech, grammar, etc.

DHSP; P. V. Kane, *History of Sanskrit Poetics* (New Delhi 1961); J. L. Masson and M. V. Patwardhan, *Aesthetic Rapture* (2 vols, Poona 1970). JLM

Ālāol (b ?1597 Fatehābād, d ?1673), Bengali poet. His father, a court official, was killed, and Ālāol probably taken prisoner, by Portuguese pirates (c1612). He arrived in Rosānga, the capital of the Mag kingdom of Ārākān, c1613, and joined the royal cavalry. He wrote under patronage of court officials from c1645. Probably in 1660, he was falsely accused of conspiracy and imprisoned. After being released, he continued to write under several patrons until death. Ālāol's writings are mainly Bengali translations or adaptations, in verse, of Hindi and Persian compositions. Like Daulat Kāzī, the other major Ārākān poet, Ālāol was probably a Sufi. His major work, *Padmābatī*, though replete with religious elements, is a lengthy narrative in ornate Bengali about a beautiful princess and an heroic king. Other works: *Sayphul Muluk Badiujjāmāl*, *Satī Maynā* (Faithful Maynā, completion of a work started by Daulat Kāzī), *Tophā* (The Gift), *Hapta paykar* (The Seven Castles), *Sekandarnāmā* (Stories of Alexander),

Trans.: PEB.

Md. Enamul Haq, *Muslim Bengali Literature* (Karachi 1957); SHBL 153–6; SHBLL 622–37.

CBS

Al-Hadi, Sayyid Shaykh bin Sayyid Ahmad (b 1867 Malacca, d 1934 Penang), Malay journalist and novelist. Co-founder and frequent contributor to the first Islamic reform journal in South-East Asia, *Al-Imam* (Singapore, 1906–8). Active literary career in Penang in the 1920's after starting the Jelutong Press, contemporary centre of Malay letters. A transitional figure, largely responsible for introducing the novel to peninsular Malay literature through adaptations of Arabic originals with Egyptian or other Middle-Eastern settings, notably the extremely popular love stories *Faridah Hanum* (1925–26) and *Puteri Nur al-'Ain* (Princess Nur al-'Ain, 1929), in which a variety of contemporary social situations and changing mores were explored, not without didactic intent. Three other translated stories appeared in the serial *Angan-Angan Kehidupan* (Life's Thoughts, 1927–1929), and he published also the first Malay detective stories (*Cherita Rokambul*, from the French to the Arabic, 7 vols, 1928–34). Possibly his most important contribution to Malay literature and thought lay, in the long run, in the numerous vigorously polemical articles written by him for his monthly magazine *Al-Ikhwan* (1926–31) and weekly (later bi-weekly) newspaper *Saudara* (1928–41). WRR

Ali, Ahmed (b 1912 Delhi), Pakistani writer in Urdu. In the thirties he came to prominence as a writer of Urdu short stories, but has since then written mainly in English. His two novels *Twilight in Delhi* (London 1940) and *Ocean of Night* (London 1964) are nostalgic, but realistic, pictures of Muslim life in old Delhi and Lucknow respectively, the two great traditional centres of the Muslim culture of the subcontinent. RR

'Ali Sikandar, Urdu poet, see **Jigar Murādābādi.**

Alisjahbana, Sutan Takdir (b 1908 Natal, north Sumatra), Indonesian novelist, teacher, editor, philosopher, scholar and publisher. He grew up in Bancoolen, southwest Sumatra. He studied law at the University of Indonesia, taught at a school in Palembang, was an editor with Balai Pustaka (Government Bureau for Popular Literature) in Djakarta and in 1933 founded with Armijn Pané (qv) and Amir Hamzah, the famed cultural journal *Pudjangga Baru* (The New Writer). During the Japanese period he served as secretary of the Indonesian language commission. In 1948 he established a journal called *Pembina Bahasa Indonesia* (Builder of the Indonesian Language) and also a popular scientific monthly *Ilmu, Teknik dan Hidup* (Knowledge, Technology and Life). From 1946 to 1948 he served as professor of Indonesian at the University of Indonesia and for some years was head of the National University of Indonesia where he also taught philosophy and published several works in this field. For several years he was head of the Department of Malay Studies at the University of Malaya in Kuala Lumpur but has since returned to Indonesia. He is the author of a standard grammar of Indonesian and of numerous essays on the national language.

As a publisher (Pustaka Rak-jat, Djakarta) Takdir's influence on Indonesian intellectual life has been tremendous. He has travelled widely both in the East and the West, has lived abroad over extended periods and possesses a cosmopolitan outlook with a strong Western orientation. He is considered by some to be the founder of the so-called Generation of '33 with his *Pudjangga Baru* and with his novels and their messages for the Indonesian people. As a poet he has been much influenced by the Dutch poets of the Generation of '80. With his many and diverse talents, he possesses a firm position in Indonesian intellectual history.

Works: *Ta' Poetoes Diroendoeng Malang* (Endlessly Dogged by Bad Luck, 1929); *Dian jang ta' Kundjung Padam* (The Everburning Lamp, 1932); *Tebaran Mega* (Scattered Clouds, 1935); *Lajar Terkembang* (With Sails Unfurled, 1936); *Anak Perawan Disarang Penjamun* (A Virgin in a Robbers' Nest, 1941); *Dari Perdjuangan dan Pertumbuhan Bahasa Indonesia* (On the Struggle and Growth of the Indonesian Language, 1957); *Indonesia in the Modern World* (1961); *Kebangkitan Puisi Baru Indonesia* (The Emergence of Modern Indonesian Poetry, 1969); *Grotta Azzurra; kisah chinta dan chita* (Grotta Azzurra; a Story of Love and Ideals, 1970).

TMIL 31–41 and passim. JME

Allama Prabhu, Kannada poet, see **vacana.**

āḻvār, twelve Tamil Vaiṣṇava poets, exponents of *bhakti* (qv). The term *āḻvār* is etymologically connected with Tamil *āl*, 'to sink, plunge, be absorbed, immersed'; hence *āḻvār* are those who are 'immersed' in meditation on, and devotion to, god. The most important were *Āṇṭāḷ* (qv), Nammāḻvār, Periyāḻvār (qv) and Tirumaṅkai Āḻvār. KZ

Amānat, Sayyid Āg͟hā Ḥasan (b 1816 Lucknow, where d 1859), Urdu poet and playwright. He was a pious Shiite, famous for two Urdu *vāsūk͟ht* (poems in which the lover complains to his mistress and threatens to break with her); the second of them was published in 1846 and has been reprinted many times. His most famous work, the musical drama *Indarsabhā* (The Court of Indra, 1849), was written for the court of Lucknow. This romantic story, interspersed with lyrics, transforms the Hindu deity Indra into a king of fairies and, in the tradition of Urdu romances, parted lovers are eventually united, after numerous adventures with demons, princes and singing girls. *Indarsabhā* is a charming blend of Indian and Muslim elements and is still dear to the Indian public. It inspired the German operetta by P. Lincke, *Im Reiche des Indra.*

Trans.: F. Rosen: *Die Indarsabha des Amanat* (Leipzig 1892).
RSHUL 350–3; MSHUL 393–4. AS

Amaru, Sanskrit poet; date uncertain, but earlier than 9th century AD, when he is named by Ānandavardhana (see *dhvani*); c600 AD is conjectural, but not implausible. Author of a 'century' (*śataka*) of verses on the theme of love, each verse being an independent poem in miniature. Four different recensions of the *Amaru-śataka* have been recognized, varying between 96 and 115 verses, and only 51 are common to all the recensions. Compare in this respect the *śatakas* of Bhartṛhari (qv). Obviously, interpolations and omissions have occurred; but the majority of the extant verses show a homogeneity of style and treatment of subject-matter, and it is not possible to determine which are original. Amaru's miniatures contain some of the finest love-verses in Sanskrit, and describe many varied aspects of the love-relationship. Especially noteworthy is the author's acute perception of feminine psychology.

KSHL 183 ff; DHSL 156 ff; WHIL III, 126–9. JB

Ambikātanayadatta, Kannada poet, see **Bendre,** Dattātrēya Rāmacandra.

Amir Khusraw Dihlavi, Indo-Persian poet, see Vol. III.

Amir Minā'i, Munshī Aḥmad (b 1928 Lucknow, d 1900 Hyderabad), Urdu lyric poet. Related to the Muslim saint Mīnā, he studied at Lucknow and from 1858 held a high position in the Rampur state administration. He wrote formally perfect poems on philosophical, mystical and religious topics, particularly on the life of Muhammad. His *dīwān* of conventional erotic *ghazals* and *qaṣīdas* (see Vol. III), *Mir'ātu'l-ghaib* (Mirror of the Invisible) abound in word-play and verbal associations; the style is artificial. Another volume of love verses *Ṣanam-khāna-e 'ishq* (Idol-shrine of Love) became popular because of the simplicity and directness of thought and diction.

RSHUL 180–6; MSHUL 208.

JM

Amman Dihlavi, Mīr (b c 1745 Delhi, d 1806 Calcutta), one of the founders of modern Urdu prose. From 1800 he was employed in Fort William College, Calcutta, as a translator. His most important work is *Bāgh-o-bahār* (1802), a fairy-tale narrative of the love stories of four princes travelling through the East in disguise. Imitating the framework of the 16th century Indian folk tale about four dervishes, preserved only in later Persian and Urdu versions, Amman writes in a flowing colloquial language without rhetorical encumbrances. His realistic picture of life overrides the supernatural elements of the story; his characters are singularly alive, their dialogues life-like and the plot well-rounded.

Trans.: L. F. Smith, *The Tale of the Four Dervesh* (Madras 1825); E. B. Eastwick (Hertford 1852, London 1857); D. Forbes (London 1862, 1891); W. Quentin (Calcutta 1901).
SDUN 15–18; RSHUL 243–4; MSHUL 210–1.
JM

Anand, Mulk Raj (b 1905 Peshawar), Indian author writing in English, Mother tongue Panjabi. Educated Panjab, London, and Cambridge. Sometime Tagore Professor of Art and Literature at Chandigarh. Visiting Professor of Art, Indian Institute of Advanced Study, Simla. Anand is an exponent of the sociological approach to literature. He was at the height of his powers in the 'thirties. He dealt with the Panjabi peasantry in his books, capturing the extrovert fellow-feeling, the broad humour, the simplicity and the attachment to land rather than to country or nation of the Panjabi peasant. Anand tries to present rustic speech in English and makes literal translations of Hindi and Panjabi idioms. This language can appear very mannered. His characters fall into three types, the sufferer, the oppressors, and the good men. Anand transfers his own ideas and convictions directly to his protagonists and they therefore lack the necessary background, and appear rootless and unnatural. Main works: *Untouchable* (1935), *Coolie* (1936), *Two Leaves and a Bud* (1937), *Persian Painting* (Essays, 1938), *The Village* (1939), *The Big Heart* (1945), *The Story of India* (1948), *Seven Summers* (1951), *The Private Life of an Indian Prince* (1953), *The Old Woman and the Cow* (1960), *The Road* (1961). Many of his novels have been translated into other Indian languages.

Minakshi Mukherjee, *Beyond the village: an aspect of Mulk Raj Anand* (CEIWE 192–202); DMINE. MED

Ānandavardhana, Indian writer on poetics, see **dhvani.**

Ananta Thuriya (?1112–73), Burmese courtier in the reign of Narapatisithu (1173–1210), who fell a victim to royal suspicion. He composed a soul-stirring poem of four stanzas a few minutes before he was executed. Too late, the king pardoned him. Most Burmese scholars accept the poem as the earliest standard type of Burmese verse, with lines of four syllables and 'climbing' rhymes; and tradition has invested it with 'immortality' because of the dramatic circumstances of its composition. But internal and external evidence suggest that it was written in or after the 14th century by an unidentified poet.

Trans.: GPC 138–40. HP

āñcalik upanyās, modern Hindi regional novel, developed out of the village scenes of Premcand's (qv) novels as a protest against escapism in fiction. The influence of the regional novel in Bengali cannot be denied. The *āñcalik upanyās* became a weapon for sharp criticism of the traditional (mostly rural) society of northern India. The term was coined after Phaṇīśvarnāth Reṇu's (b 1921) novel *Mailā āñcal* (The Dirty End of the Sari, 1954); other prominent novels of this type are *Partī, parikathā* (The Fallow Land, 1957), a religious story by the same author; *Balcanmā* (1952), *Bābā Baṭesarnāth* (1954), *Varuṇ ke beṭe* (Sons of the God of Water, 1957), and *Dukhmocan* (1956) by Nāgārjun (i.e. Vaidyanāth Miśra, b. 1911); *Sāgar, laharen aur manuṣya* (The Ocean, Waves and Man, 1956) by Udayśaṅkar Bhaṭṭ (qv); *Gaṅgā maiyā* (Mother Gaṅgā 1953) and *Sattī maiyā kā caurā* (The Altar of Mother Sattī, 1959) by Bhairavprasād Gupta (b 1918); *Būnd aur samudra* (A Drop and the Ocean, 1956) by Amṛtlāl Nāgar (b 1916) and several novels by Balbhadra Ṭhākur (b 1918), Śailés Maṭiyānī (b 1931), Rajendra Avasthī 'Tṛṣit' (b 1929) and others.

W. Ruben, *Indische Romane* I (Berlin 1964); AFMH. PG

aṅga, a term used in Indian Jain and Buddhist literature. In Jainism it covers the first and most important part of the Jain Canon, the *Siddhānta* (see Jain Literature). In Buddhism it is a general term for different types of Buddhist canonical texts of varying form and content; sermons in prose (*sutta*), sermons in prose interspersed with verse (*geyya*), commentaries (*veyyākaraṇa*), hymns (*gāthā*), inspired utterances (*udāna*), short speeches opening with the words, 'Thus spoke the Buddha' (*itivuttaka*), tales of former incarnations of the Buddha (*jātaka*, qv), reports of miracles (*abbhutadhamma*), and teachings in question and answer form (*vedalla*). See also *vedāṅga.* EM

Anīs, Mīr Babar 'Alī (b 1802 Fyzabad, d 1874 Lucknow), Urdu poet, master of the *marṣiya*, the elegiac poem on the martyrdom of Husain (grandson of the Prophet Muhammad) and his companions at Karbala in 680. The form developed to maturity in Lucknow, capital of the rulers of Avadh (Oudh) and is recited especially in the Muslim month of Muharram. The poem is composed in the *musaddas* form, ie in a series of six-lined stanzas rhyming AAAABB, often rising to a climax in the final couplet; it is usually cast in direct, forceful language which makes an immediate impact on the audience.

RSHUL 126–30; MSHUL 155–63. RR

Aṇṇāturai, C. N. (pseud. Aṇṇā, b 1909 Kanchipuram, d 1969 Madras), Indian politician, journalist and man of letters. After obtaining a Madras University degree in economics, he spent a very brief period as a teacher of English and then entered journalism, working on a succession of both Tamil and English weeklies and dailies. For several years a member and office-bearer of the Tamilnad Justice Party and its successor, the Dravidian Federation, he broke away from the latter in 1949 to form the DMK (Dravidian Progressive Federation). He was elected to the Madras Legislative Assembly in 1957 and rose to become Chief Minister of Madras State (now Tamilnad) in March 1967, a post which he held until his death. Widely recognized as one of the great Tamil orators of his time, he had a massive popular following in Tamilnad and countless imitators as a public speaker. He was also a very talented writer in a number of fields and published several volumes of short stories, novels and plays, as well as essays on political themes. In his creative writing, which also included a number of film scripts, he tended to give a prominent place to the expression of his ideas on the ills of society. His best works, nevertheless, are far from being mere social and political propaganda. Main works: *Aṇṇāviṉ caṭṭacapaiccorpoḷivukaḷ* (1960, speeches), *Iḷatciya varalāṟu* (politics), *Vāḷkkaip puyal* (1948, short stories), *Raṅkōṉ Rātā* (novel), *Ōr iravu* (1954, play).

A. P. Janarthanam (ed.), *Anna 60: the Anna Sixtieth Birthday Souvenir* (Madras 1968). REA

Āṇṭāḷ (probably 8th century AD), one of the twelve Vaiṣṇava *āḻvār* (qv). The legend states that she was found as a baby under some basil-shrubs (*tulasī*) by Periyāḻvār (qv) who brought her up. He gave her the name of Kōtai (Godā). From an early age, she showed intense devotion and love towards the god Viṣṇu, and was probably no more than fifteen when she composed *Tiruppāvai*. This refers to a festival celebrated by the cowherd-maidens in honour of Kṛṣṇa. Āṇṭāḷ's other work is *Nācciyār tirumoḻi*, and both are included in *Nālāyirappirapantam*, the Vaiṣṇava 'canon'. Her story spread beyond Tamilnad, and is featured in the Telugu *Āmuktamālyadā*, attributed to Kṛṣṇadevarāya (qv), wherein she is called Godā.

JHTL 107–11. JRM

anuṣṭubh, Sanskrit metre, see **śloka.**

Anwar, Malay novelist, see **Ishak bin Haji Muhammad.**

Anwar, Chairil (b 1922 Medan, d 1949 Djakarta), Indonesian poet. He attended junior high school and in 1940 moved to Djakarta where he first came to attention in 1943 through his efforts to get his poetry published. He was well read in such writers as Rilke, Wilde, Nietzsche, Slauerhoff, Du Perron, Steinbeck and André Gide. As far as we know, Anwar held no job in Djakarta, but seems to have subsisted on the help of relatives and friends. Once asked what his occupation was, he replied, 'I'm a poet.' And so he was until his untimely death of typhus. He has been dead more than twenty-two years now, but still no other Indonesian writer can match Chairil's influence on Indonesian literature. He is generally held to be the precursor of modern Indonesian poetry, in spite of the fact that his total writings are not large: some seventy original poems and several dozen translations or adaptations. Perhaps his most quoted poem is *Aku* (Me), a terse, direct thirteen-line poem. His poetry is characterized more by an intensity, as Teeuw points out, than by the introduction of new themes. Perhaps his greatest contribution, in the long run, will be to the development of the Indonesian language. Works: *Deru Tjampur Debu* (Noise Mixed with Dust, 1949); *Jang Terampas dan Jang Putus* (What is Plundered and Broken, 1949); *Kerikil Tadjam* (Sharp Gravel, 1949); *Tiga Menguak Takdir* (a play on words, 'Three Push Destiny Aside' or 'Three Push Takdir

Aside', 1950), a collection of poems of Chairil Anwar, Asrul Sani and Rivai Apin (qv).

Burton Raffel, *Complete Poetry and Prose of Chairil Anwar* (1970); TMIL 102–3 and passim. JME

apadāna, Pāli Buddhist stories, see **avadāna.**

Apin, Rivai (b 1927 Padang Pandjang), Indonesian poet, essayist and journalist. After studying law in Djakarta he edited cultural periodicals; now a member of the progressive organization LEKRA, he edits their paper *Zaman Baru* (New Times). At first a nihilist, he became a poet of revolution. Together with Chairil Anwar (qv) and Asrul Sani he published a volume of poetry attacking the conservative ideas of S. Takdir Alisjahbana (qv), the Nestor of the writers grouped round the paper *Pudjangga Baru* (New Writer). Apin's poetry is unconventional, breaking up the monotonous rhythm of the lines. He was a pioneer of a new form and content, in line with the founders of the Angkatan 45 group (Generation 45) headed by Anwar.

TMIL 207–9. MO

Appar (7th century), Tamil poet. With Campantar (qv), he was the principal contributor to *Tēvāram*, the collective name given to the first seven books of the *Tirumuṟai* (qv). Appar's hymns form books IV to VI. He belonged to a *Vēḷāḷa* Śaiva family but, as a youth, joined the Jains and became a teacher. He became reconciled to Śaivism, perhaps as a result of his sister's prayers and pleading, and thenceforward became an ardently proselytizing Śaivite. His hymns often allude to his regretted Jaina past. He is also known as Tirunāvukk'aracar, 'Lord of divine speech'.

JHTL 76–9. JRM

Appārāw, Gurajtāḍa Weṅkaṭa (b 1862 Rayavaram, d 1915 Vizianagaram), Telugu poet. He received his bachelor's degree in 1886 from the Maharajah's College, Vizianagaram, and worked for some time as a lecturer in the same college. He worked as an epigraphist in the service of the Vizianagaram Estate and later as Private Secretary to the widowed Princess of Rewa. He served as a member of the Vizianagaram Municipal Council and was a nominated member of the Senate of Madras University. Appārāw's contribution is to be judged more by its quality and impact than by its volume. His *Kanyāśulkam* (Bride Price, 1897), a full-length social play written in colloquial language, was a powerful exposure of such contemporary social evils as child marriage, bride-price, religious bigotry, caste, and prostitution; it was translated into English, Russian, Tamil and Kannada. He had a gift of incisive humour free of malevolence which cut without causing pain.

He is remembered today as an innovator not only of metrical forms but also for his adaptation of spoken dialects to serious literary writing. His language and imagery in poems dealing with contemporary social life were highly unconventional and spontaneous, in contrast to the pedantry of classicism which he tried and discarded. Though a visionary and a revolutionary in his views, he was not a militant reformer like his contemporaries, Kandukūri Wīrēśaliṅgam (qv) or Giḍugu Rāmamūrti. He created a new technique in Telugu drama, story, and lyric by harnessing the power inherent in the simple folk dialect. He pleaded for the use of modern spoken Telugu in textbooks and his *Minute of Dissent* (1914) is a classical document on the language issue in education. His centenary in 1962 was celebrated all over the country. His important works are: *Kanyāśulkam* (1897, trans. by S. N. Jayanty, Madras 1964); a collection of poems entitled *Mutyāla saramulu* (Garland of Pearls, 1929), and *Cinna kathalu* (Short Stories, 1929), published posthumously.

Unilit: Homage to Gurajāḍa (Secunderabad 1963); V. R. Narla, *Traditional Indian Culture and Other Essays* (Vijayawada 1969), 130–4. BhK

Āpṭe, Hari Nārāyaṇ (1864–1919), the first major Marathi novelist. He was educated in Bombay and Poona where he read widely in the popular English authors of the day, especially Scott, Dickens and Reynolds, and began to publish critical articles in *Kesarī* before he was 18. His enthusiasm for literature came in the way of more academic studies and he regularly failed his examinations at two Poona colleges; he finally gave up without achieving a degree. His first novel *Madhlī sthiti* (In the Middle), inspired by Reynold's *Mysteries of Old London*, was written and published while he was still nominally a student. In 1888 a rich uncle appointed him to a sinecure and he was able to devote himself to writing, spending the rest of his life uneventfully as a professional writer and solid citizen of Poona. In 1890 he founded his own monthly magazine *Karamaṇūk* and ran it until 1917, writing most of the contents himself and using it as a vehicle for his novels all of which, except the two earliest, first appeared serially in its pages.

His ten 'modern' novels treat many of the social problems of the time from a moderately reformist viewpoint and with sympathetic insight into the subservient position of women in Hindu society. *Paṇ lakṣāt koṇ gheto* (But Who Cares?, 1890–3) deals specifically with the evils of child marriage and widowhood. *Mī* (I, 1893–5) is the autobiography of a saintly social worker who chooses celibacy in order to be free to devote himself to the poor. Here one suspects Āpṭe of writing out his own unfulfilled dreams. The unfinished *Yaśvantrāv Khare* (1892–5) gives a remarkably vivid and realistic picture of the education and development of a group of young people in the Poona of Ṭiḷak and Āgarkar, showing how their attitudes to life are conditioned by their upbringing. The eleven historical novels are essentially romances in the Scott manner, many set in the period of Śivajī and the achievement of Maratha independence. All his novels display great inventiveness in the construction of exciting plots, much realism in his observation of Marathi manners and a capacity to create really solid characters. His faults were carelessness in construction and repetition (a consequence of serial publication) and a kind of self-indulgent laziness which arose from being his own editor and publisher. Whenever he tired of one plot he would start another and almost half the novels were never finished. Āpṭe also published, in *Karamaṇūk*, short-stories, essays of all kinds and even a few plays adapted from Western originals. Nothing has been translated into any non-Indian language.

CNI 91–2, 99–101. IR

āraṇyaka ('Forest treatises'), a comprehensive name for a number of Vedic treatises, appendices to *brāhmaṇas* (qv) which, because of their esoteric and 'dangerous' character, were intended to be studied in the forest, that is outside the villages. Their original purpose seems to have been to give secret explanations of the ritual. They constitute an important link between the ritualism of the older Vedic period and the speculative thought of later times. Their contents consist of ritual indications, symbolic or mystic interpretations of texts or rites, philosophical speculations, vague guessings after truth, subjects that are not inadequately mirrored in the harshness of their style which is essentially simple and natural, but also abrupt and elliptical, the art of constructing complex sentences being almost entirely wanting. The *Aitareya-* and *Śāṅkhāyana-āraṇyakas* belong to the *Ṛgveda* (qv). Of the former, books I–III (which were probably composed between 700 and 550 BC) are older than books IV–V. Book I, which bears a close resemblance in style and contents to the *Aitareya-brāhmaṇa*, consists of an explanation, from the ritualistic and allegorical points of view, of an important Vedic rite, the Mahāvrata; part of book II deals with the allegorical significance of ritual verses used by those who performed the Mahāvrata. Book III explains the mystic meaning of the various forms of the *Ṛgveda*. The *Taittirīya-āraṇyaka* belongs to the Taittirīya branch of the Black *Yajurveda* (see *Veda*). As to the White *Yajurveda*, it possesses an *āraṇyaka* in the last book of the *Śatapatha-brāhmaṇa*.

Trans.: A. B. Keith, *The Aitareya-Āraṇyaka* (1909, reprint 1969).
WHIL I, 225–247. JG

Arcellana, Francisco (b 1916 Manila), Filipino fiction writer and literary critic of Ilocano origin, writing in English. His first short story was published while he was still in high school and in 1939 he became the editor of *Expression*, a quarterly for experimental writing. He gave up medical studies for literature, and marrying early, had a hard time supporting his family, especially during the war years. For a time he then wrote in Tagalog. After the war Arcellana contributed to magazines, ran weekly columns and taught English at the University of the Philippines. He published more than 50 short stories, some of which are found in many anthologies (*The Mats*, *The Flowers of May*). Works: *Selected Stories* (1962).

EH

Arjan, Sikh gurū, see **Ādi Granth.**

Armijn Pané, Indonesian writer, see **Pané,** Armijn.

Arnimāl, Kashmiri poetess, see **Lol-lyric.**

Arthaśāstra, Sanskrit textbook of statecraft, see **Kauṭilya.**

Āṟumukam, Nallūr Kantappiḷḷai (pseud. Ārumuka Nāvalar, 1822–1879), Tamil writer. A native of Jaffna, Nāvalar was known in his day as one of the greatest of Śaiva preachers. He did much to spread a knowledge of Tamil literary classics through the editions of those printed at presses he owned in Jaffna and Madras. His importance in the history of Tamil, however, lies chiefly in his contribution to the development of Tamil prose through his commentaries on classical texts, his prose versions of *purāṇic* tales and his translation of the Bible.

JHTL 261–2. REA

Aruṇācalakavi (end of the 18th century), Tamil poet, author of the earliest and most successful attempt to transform a literary theme into a drama in the form of a succession of songs called *kīrttaṉai*. His *Rāmanāṭakakkīrttaṉai* is a charming dramatization of the *Rāmāyaṇa* (qv) story. KZ

Aruṇakirinātar (15th century), Tamil poet. No reliable biographical data are available. His extensive poetical works, religious, lyrical hymnody interwoven with Śaiva *siddhānta* (see cittar) doctrines, draw copiously on Aryan and Tamil mythology. The three basic types are lyrics of personal erotic and religious experience, reflective lyrics with philosophical elements, and hymns praising the god Murukaṉ. His main importance lies in the harmonious blending of Sanskrit and Tamil cultures, and the highly sophisticated command of diction, rhythm and metre. Main work: *Tiruppukaḻ* (Divine Praise) of the god *Murukaṉ*, in 1367 stanzas.

JHTL 212–3. KZ

arvācin kavitā, the modern Gujarati poetry. With the poetry of Narmadāśankar Davé (1833–86) and Dalapatrām Ḍāhyābhāi (1820–98), a new sensitivity for contemporary actuality and for literary forms evolved in mid-nineteenth century Gujarati literature. The next generation unified this sensitivity and sensibility. While a poem on his city, Surat, by N. Davé, begins; 'To what a disgrace have you sunk, Surat, my golden city!' a poem by Narasiṃharāo Divaṭiā (1858–1937) about the once-glorious city of Pāṭan expresses sorrow through an image: 'But here, once, there used to be vast waters of the Sahasralinga.' Maṇiśankar Bhaṭṭa (pseud. Kānta, 1867–1923) sculptured out of immense metaphysical anguish his archetypal poetry, while B. K. Ṭhakore (1869–1950), destroying the glossy icons of sentimentality, brought Gujarati poetic idiom nearer to the mobility of the spoken language. Nānālāl Kavi (1877–1947), a lyric poet *par excellence*, exploited folk-tunes and rhythmic phrase alike. Next was the Gandhian period. Umāśankar Jośi (qv) and T. Luhār (pseud Sundaram, b 1905) matched the feelings of bold confrontations by an integrity of poetic form. In the next decade a sensuous world emerged in the poetry of Prahlād Pārekh, Venibhāi Purohit and Bālamukund Davé, culminating in *Dhvani* (Resonance, 1948) by Rājendra Śāh.

In the 1950's a new phase began. In a

long poem, *Pravāl Dvīp* (The Coral Island) about the city of Bombay, Niranjan Bhagat created purely auditory images of the rhythm of the tired commuter's journeys. *Pratik* (Symbol) by Priyakānt Maṇiār marked the beginning of Gujarati poetry's freedom from meaning. In the 1960's both meaning and metre were shed by many. However, in *Tṛnano Graha* (The Planet of Grass, 1965) N. K. Pandyā (pseud. Uśanas) created a striking dual myth of the death and birth of 'the grass-planet' using textured metrical idiom. In *Mahāprasthāna* (1965) Umāśankar Jośi achieved archetypical dimensions in verse-play. In prose-poetry, Lābhaśankar Thākar, Prabodh Parikh, Rāvji Patel, Gulām-mahamad Śekh, Sureś Jośi and others excelled. Jhiṇābhāi Desāi (pseud. Sneharaśmi) successfully transplanted *haiku* poetry into Gujarati, while Haribhadra Davé evoked the mediaeval lyrical current in his unique poetry. SY

Ārya Śūra (probably c 4th century AD: a date in the 2nd century AD has sometimes been proposed, but this is based on legend), Sanskrit poet, author of the *Jātaka-mālā* ('Garland of *Jātakas*'). Although other works are ascribed to him (in Chinese translations: only one has survived in Sanskrit), these are of doubtful attribution. The *Jātaka-mālā* is of the type later known as *campū*, namely, prose interspersed with passages in verse; it recounts the stories of 34 *jātakas* (qv). Although entirely Buddhist in content, the work is composed in pure Classical Sanskrit, and is one of the early masterpieces. The prose is elegant and subtle, and though often elaborate, is virtually free from the turgidity of later authors of ornate prose such as Subandhu and Bāṇa (qqv). Delightful in the original, the charm of the work has almost entirely evaporated in the modern English translation.

Trans.: J. S. Speyer (London 1895); KHSL. JB

Āśān, Malayalam poet, see **Kumāran Āśān.**

Aśk, Upendranāth (b 1910 Jalandhar, Panjab), Hindi and Urdu writer. After studying law, Aśk became a journalist and writer; since 1946 he has also become his own publisher. From 1925 he wrote short stories in Urdu, but since 1935 he has turned to Hindi. His novels are among the best in modern Hindi literature. Starting from conventional episodic narrative he gave his view of modern man in India in a trilogy whose hero Cetan is a member of the depressed lower middle class of Panjab. Without a plot, innumerable vivid scenes of his life are related in clear language which conveys intimate human interactions. Aśk is also a prolific writer of short stories and very successful radio-plays. Main works: *Girtī dīvāren* (Falling Walls, 1940), *Śahar men ghūmtā āīnā* (A Mirror Moving through the Town, 1963), *Ek nanhin kindīl* (A Small Candle, 1969).

GHEH, AFMH. PG

Aśokāvadāna, see **Divyāvadāna.**

Aśvaghoṣa (c 2nd century AD), Sanskrit poet and dramatist. Later tradition associates him with the court of the emperor Kaniṣka, but this is worthless as evidence. Nevertheless, on other grounds, the date implied cannot be very far from the truth. Aśvaghoṣa is the earliest author of Sanskrit *kāvya* (qv) who is known to us directly. The well-developed *kāvya* characteristics in his works, as well as the evidence of some early inscriptions and some quotations in the *Mahābhāṣya* (see Patañjali), show that he is the inheritor of a tradition which had evolved considerably since the *Rāmāyaṇa* (qv), which in the orthodox view is the 'first *kāvya*'. Aśvaghoṣa wrote two epics; the *Saundarananda*, in 18 cantos, describes the conversion of Nanda, half-brother of the Buddha, to become a member of the Buddhist order. Nanda, reluctant to forsake his beautiful wife, Sundarī, is won over only after a visit to heaven, where the divine nymphs surpass even Sundarī in beauty; he is ultimately brought to understand that even the delights of heaven are transitory, and that the only way to salvation is complete renunciation, as a Buddhist monk. Fate has been less kind to the *Buddhacarita*, of which barely 14 cantos survive in the original Sanskrit, although the Tibetan and

Chinese translations, in 28 cantos, are complete. From these it can be seen that the poem contained an account of the whole life of the Buddha, ending with his *parinirvāṇa* and the division of the relics. The portion extant in Sanskrit brings the story only to the point where the Buddha attained enlightenment.

Manuscript fragments of three dramas were discovered in central Asia, and published by Lüders in 1911. One of these is shown by the colophon to be the *Śāriputraprakaraṇa* of Aśvaghoṣa, in nine acts. Enough of this remains to show that the plot concerned the conversion of Śāriputra and Maudgalyāyana, later to become two of the leading disciples of the Buddha. There is no conclusive evidence of the authorship of the other two dramas, but they may also be the work of Aśvaghoṣa. One of these is an allegorical drama, with personified abstracts as characters, such as Dhṛti, 'Steadfastness', and Kīrti, 'Fame'. The other, with a courtesan in the cast, appears to be a drama of everyday life. But, in both cases, the fragments are too scant to make it possible to reconstruct the plots. The so-called *Sūtrālaṅkāra*, a collection of Buddhist tales, was ascribed to Aśvaghoṣa by the Chinese translator. The title is a mistaken reconstruction from the Chinese title; and the ascription to Aśvaghoṣa is now known also to be wrong, since the discovery in central Asia of fragments of the Sanskrit original has shown that the text in question is the *Kalpanāmaṇḍitikā* by Kumāralāta. Other works (*Vajrasūci*, *Mahāyāna-śraddhotpāda*, *Gaṇḍīstotra*) which have traditionally been attributed to Aśvaghoṣa are almost certainly not his.

Saundarananda (ed. and trans., Oxford 1928, 1932); *Buddhacarita* (ed. and trans. of the extant Sanskrit portion, Calcutta 1936); *Buddhacarita, xv to xxviii* (trans. from the Chinese and Tibetan versions, in *Acta Orientalia* XV, 1937)—all by E. H. Johnston.
DHSL 69–79; KSD 80–90. JB

Atharvaveda, one of the four books of the **Veda.**

Ātish, Khvāja Ḥaidar 'Alī (b 1767 Fyzabad, d 1846 Lucknow), Urdu lyric poet, pupil of Muṣḥafī (qv) and rival of Nāsikh (qv). Educated at Lucknow in a decadent atmosphere, he never cared for patronage and lived as a dervish. He was one of the greatest *ghazal* writers (see Vol. III). His polished love verses, free of hypocrisy, use sensuous imagery to vivid effect. They take up conventional Sufi motifs, praising contentment and quietism, steeped in gloomy mystical symbolism. Their diction is idiomatic, simple and fluent; their interest lies in witty word-play and striking metaphors.

RSHUL 111–3; MSHUL 138. JM

Atre, Prahlād Keśav (1898–1970), Marathi playwright, journalist and humorous writer. *Sāṣṭang namaskār* (Complete Prostration, 1933), an uproarious comedy, was his first stage success and was followed by many other plays right up to his death. His short stories *Brāṇḍicī bāṭalī* (The Brandy-Bottle, 1933) and the autobiographical *Mi kasā jhālo* (How I Turned out Like This, 1953) were also very popular. IR

aṭṭakkatha, Malayalam 'story for dancing', see **kathakaḷi.**

Auḥadi, Ṭaqī (b 1565 Isfahan, d 1630 in India), Indo-Persian poet, writer and critic. From 1606 lived at the court of Emperor Jahangir. He wrote seven epic *masnavīs* (see Vol. III) and eleven lyric *dīwāns*; the best known is *Nuṣratu'l-'ārifīn* (Refuge of Gnostics) containing panegyrics and satires against his contemporaries. In his *tazkira* (see Vol. III), *'Arafātu'l-'āshiqīn* (Hill of Lovers), he collected biographies of 3,186 Persian poets with samples of their work. Its abridged version *Ka'ba-e 'irfān* (Sanctuary of Knowledge) became a source of many later *tazkiras*.

HIL 726. JM

avadāna(s), stories of 'heroic feat(s), great achievement(s)' of prominent Buddhist personalities, primarily members of the Order, performed in their previous lives. The word denotes either a single work or a number of works made into a collection, mostly anonymous and of varying age and literary values. They are, however, of great doctrinal importance (eg the introduction of the Bodhisattva idea), and they represent, in fact, collections of legends of apocryphal character, similar to the *jātakas* (qv) where many secular tales and fables were explained as a result of some heroic act (*avadāna*) performed in a previous existence. Their primary aim was to propagate and popularize Buddhist teachings through edifying narratives. *Avadāna* collections were popular among the Sarvāstivādins (see *Divyāvadāna*) as well as other schools (see *Mahāvastu*), including the Mahāyānins (see *Lalitavistara*). Later, greatly expanded versions in metre were compiled, with the generic title of *Avadānamālās*, where the Mahāyāna aspect assumes greater prominence. Beside the Sanskrit collections, there is a Pāli counterpart called *apadāna*, which seems to be somewhat older than that found in the Sanskrit texts, though it belongs to the youngest parts of the canon. As a literary form, it has no established connection with the Sanskrit compilations.

WHIL II, 277–94; WIB. IF

Avadānaśataka ('Hundred *avadānas*', c 2nd century AD), Sanskrit collection of *avadānas* (qv) of the Sarvāstivāda school of Buddhism, divided into ten chapters of ten components each. The stories are arranged and recorded according to a set pattern, so that many situations are reiterated in the same set of phrases. In spite of many wearisome repetitions and edifying moralities, however, the legends contain copious information of cultural interest as they preserve a conspicuous store of Buddhist folklore. A number of them reappear in other *avadāna* anthologies, and a few in the Pāli *apadāna*, though there is a great divergence between the two traditions.

Trans. into French by L. Feer (Paris 1891); WHIL II, 279–84. IF

Awbhatha, U (?1758–?1798), Burmese writer, a scholarly monk with great imaginative power and an excellent command of Burmese. He made his name by translating eight of the ten major *jātakas* (qv); *Candakumāra* and *Nārada* (1782), *Vidhura* and *Vessantara* (1783), *Mahosadha* (1784) and *Mahājanaka* (1785), and *Nemi* and *Temiya* (1786). His style is close to the original and tends to be prosaic in the narrative portions, but is much freer and poetic in the descriptive passages, especially in the *Vessantara*, which is still regarded by Burmese scholars as a model of narrative prose style.

Trans.: O. White, *Wethandaya* (Rangoon 1906). MHABD 54–6. HP

awit, Filipino folk-tales, see **moro-moro.**

Ayāz, Shaikh Mubārak (b 1922), Sindhi poet and prose writer, leader of the Progressive Writers' Association in Sindhi (see *progressive writing*). He combines in himself all the varied literary trends; besides treading modern paths in poetry he draws upon the traditional forms. His early poetry reflected his discontentment with the state of the world and manifested his radical thinking. His short stories denounced fratricidal fighting after the Partition of 1947 and called for unity between Hindus and Muslims. After 1955 he started to pay more attention to Sindhi nationalism and to urgent social problems but later, disappointed with development, turned towards formalist poetry.

ABSLP 298–9. JM

Āzād, Muḥammad Ḥusain (b 1830 Delhi, d 1910 Lahore), Urdu literary historian, critic and poet. Educated at Delhi College, in 1865 he went on a secret mission to Bukhara and later on two occasions to Iran. He was in Panjab government service, and from 1883 taught at Oriental College Lahore; after 1889 he became insane. In historical prose he retold stories from mediaeval Indian history. After his journey to Persia he published informative lectures on the Persian language and its literature *Sukhandān-e Fārs* (Writers of Persia, 1907) along with a description of Iranian manners and social conditions. His masterpiece is *Āb-e ḥayāt* (1880), the first critical history of the Urdu language and its literature on modern lines, introducing periodization of literature.

Muhammad Sadiq; *Muhammad Husain Azad, His Life and Works* (Lahore 1965); RSHUL 219–22; 274–9; MSHUL 288–302. JM

Āzāt Jamāldīnī, 'Abdu'l-vāḥid (b 1918 Nushki), Baluchi poet and short-story writer, member of the Progressive Writers' Association (see *progressive writing*), editor of the monthly *Balūchī*. Upon completion of his education at Quetta he entered the business world. His verses fought against the British colonial rule and supported the ideas of the Baluchi national revival. He is considered to be one of the original trend-setters of modern Baluchi poetry.

ABSLP 312. JM

B

Babad Tanah Djawi (Chronicle of Java, c 17th century), believed by some scholars to have been originally composed by a court poet of Sultan Agung of Mataram (1613–45). Written in verse of various styles with poetic descriptions and straightforward historical accounts, it celebrates the power and glory of 17th century Mataram and is permeated with Javanese mysticism, as usual in *babad* literature. The *babad* may have been originally a collection of verse or prose historical works written in 17th century Java, but all extant manuscripts date from the 18th-19th centuries. Two central Java traditions then developed, Surakarta and Jogjakarta, differing in language and style, but similar in content. There exist also local *babads* (eg *Babad Tjirebon*, *Babad Kediri*, *Babad Banjumas*, etc). They are valuable evidence of the nature and development of historiography in Java.

Trans.: W. L. Olthof, *Babad Tanah Djawi* (Den Haag 1943).
PLJ I, 158–72. EV

Baccan (Harivaṃś Rāy, b 1907 Allahabad), Hindi poet, critic and translator, master of the song (*gīt*), started writing when *chāyāvād* (qv) was declining. He gained great popularity with *Madhuśālā* (The House of Wine, 1935), eulogizing the joys of wine and love. Years of crisis followed: *Ekānt saṅgīt* (Songs of Desolation, 1939). In the 'sixties he introduced the rhythm and tone of folksongs into his poetry and became more concerned with social problems: *Tribhaṅgimā* (1961), *Do caṭṭānẽ* (Two Rocks, 1965, Sahitya Akademi Award), *Bahut din bīte* (Many Days Passed, 1967).

Trans.: M. Boulton and R. S. Vyas, *The House of Wine* (London 1950). IZ

Badruddin Chāchi, known as Badr-e Chāch, 'Moon of Tashkent' (d 1346 Daulatabad), Indo-Persian court poet of Sultan Muhammad Tughlaq. Because of his Turkish origin he wrote his panegyrics in a difficult style full of astrological allusions and complicated similes. His lyric *dīwān* contains descriptions of nature of a fascinating richness and dazzling vocabulary. His epic *Shāh-nāma* (Book of the King), of 20,000 verses, describes the reign of Muhammad Tughlaq.

HIL 719. JM

Bakśi, Candrakant, Gujarati writer, see **navalkathā, navalikā.**

Bālkavi (pen-name of Tryambak Bāpūjī Ṭhombare, 1890–1918), Marathi poet, celebrated for nature lyrics, his precocious talent (hence his name which means 'child poet') and his tragic early death. He was a friend and disciple of N. V. Ṭiḷak (qv). IR

Bālkṛṣṇa Sama, Nepali writer, see **Sama,** Bālkṛṣṇa.

Balmori, Jesus (pseud. Batikuling, b 1886 Manila, d 1948), Filipino poet of wealthy family, writing in Spanish. He studied at San Juan de Letran College, showed an early interest in poetry and his poems were well known while he was still in his teens. Among many literary prizes he won were those awarded by *El Renacimiento* magazine in 1908; his famous poem, *Mi Casa de Nipa*, won a prize in the first Commonwealth Literary Contest (1940). He ran satirical columns in poetry in several newspapers (*La Vanguardia, El Debate, Voz de Manila*). In his first collection of poetry, *Rimas Malayas* (1904), he carries on the nationalist themes introduced by José Rizal (qv). Among other works are poems *El Hombre y la Mujer* (1927), *El Libro de mis Vidas Manilenas* (1928), satirical verses compiled from his daily column in *La Vanguardia*; novels, *Bancarrota de Almas* (1910), *Se Deshojo la Flor* (1915); and several dramas.

In the public poetical jousts, traditional in the Philippines, Balmori was regularly challenged by Manuel Bernabe (1890–1960), another Filipino poet writing in Spanish. After studies at the Ateneo de Manila and University of Santo Tomas he worked for Spanish language newspapers, wrote poetry, translated books and was active in political life. Bernabe was a Congressman and an advisor on Philippine-Spanish relations. Works: *Cantos del Tropico* (1929), *Perfil de la Cresta* (1958).

Both authors contributed to the Filipino tradition of Spanish writing dating back to the first half of the 19th century to poets Don Jose de Vergara, Pedro A. Paterno, followed by nationalist prose writers Pedro Pelaez and Father Jose A. Burgos. Writing in Spanish was developed to a high literary standard by José Rizal. His contemporaries (Marcelo H. del Pilar, Graciano Lopez-Jaena) used Spanish mostly for political writing, as did Apolinario Mabini, Felipe G. Calderon and others. Some Filipinos of the period distinguished themselves as poets in Spanish (Fernando Ma. Guerrero, 1873–1929; Cecilio Apostol, 1877–1938), political writers and scholars (Claro M. Recto, 1890–1960; Teodoro M. Kalaw, 1908–1941, and others). The years following the Revolution (1898) are referred to as the Golden Age of Filipino literature in Spanish. The decline began soon after the introduction of English into Filipino life.

EH

Baltazar, Francisco (pseud. Balagtas, b 1788 Panginay, Bigaa, d 1862), Filipino Tagalog poet of a very poor family. He was brought up in Tondo, Manila, by a distant relative, whose name he adopted as a pseudonym. After graduating from San Juan de Letran College he worked for his relative, in his spare time writing poems and *moro-moro* plays (qv). At 42, he fell in love but was rivalled by another suitor who succeeded in getting him jailed in order to marry the girl himself. In prison Baltazar wrote his masterpiece, *Florante at Laura*, a long poem published in 1838. Full of allegory used to denounce Spanish rule in the Philippines, it opens with a dedicatory poem *Kay Celia* (To Celia), followed by a versified preface. In an imaginary place called Albania Florante, a young General, distinguishes himself against the Persian invaders. Returning from the battlefield, he is attacked by his political rival Adolfo who has incited the people to revolt against Florante. The brave General sent to meet death in the forest is rescued by a Persian General. After defeating Adolfo, Florante marries Laura and is proclaimed king.

EH

Bāṇa (Bāṇa Bhaṭṭa), Sanskrit author, under the patronage of king Harṣa (qv), who ruled 606–648 AD. Bāṇa's literary activity can therefore be placed in the second quarter of the 7th century AD. In his *Harṣa-carita*, he celebrated his patron's rise to power, in a lengthy narrative in highly ornate and complex prose. The work approximates more to an historical novel than to history. It commences with a somewhat detailed autobiography, leading up to Bāṇa's introduction to the king. In a similarly complicated and artificial prose style is written the *Kādambarī*, a romantic tale which was left unfinished; it was completed by the author's son. Both works abound in lengthy descriptions, with very long compounds and sentences, and frequent double meanings, being in these respects second only to Subandhu (qv), whose work is mentioned by Bāṇa, and in many ways formed a model for him. To Bāṇa is also attributed the *Caṇḍī-śataka*, a 'century' of verses in praise of the goddess Caṇḍī (Durgā).

Harṣa-carita: trans. E. B. Cowell and F. W. Thomas (London 1897); *Kādambarī*: trans. C. M. Ridding (London 1896), M. R. Kale

(Bombay 1924), Dutch trans. of concluding portion (*uttera-bhāga*) A. Scharpe (Leuven 1937).

KHSL 314 ff; DHSL 225 ff; WHIL III, 399 ff. JB

Banaphul (Balāicānd Mukhopādhyāy, b 1899 Manihari), Bengali writer, by profession a general medical practitioner. He began as a poet, but found his true medium in prose. His best work is in the short story form, especially in the brief, terse story with a well-rounded plot (eg *Banaphuler galpa*, 1936). He is particularly effective in the point which gives the final touch to his interesting stories, primarily concerned with the heroes' inner conflicts and the impact of their environment. Banaphul is sometimes near to caricature, but the humanist mood always prevails. He often draws on his medical experience. He has also written several novels and biographical plays.

SHBL 377–8. DZ

Bandyopādhyāy (Banerji), Bibhūtibhūṣan (b 1894 Muratipur, d 1950), Bengali writer. His father was a Hindu family priest, a good singer of traditional songs, but very poor. After taking his BA in Calcutta, Bibhūtibhūṣan worked as a teacher. He was a prolific writer, author of c50 books (novels, volumes of tales, autobiographical and travel essays). His best work, the novel *Pather pāñcāli* (Song of the Road, 1929), displays his warm sympathy for the rural poor and his feeling for the beauties of nature; the psychological treatment of the child characters is outstanding. The film version by Satyajit Rāy made the book famous. Other works: novels, *Āraṇyak* (The Wild Man, 1938); *Ādarśan hindu hoṭel* (Ideal Hotel for Hindus, 1940); *Icchāmatī* (1949).

Trans.: T. W. Clark a Tarapada Mukherji, *Pather panchali* (London 1968).
SHBL 363. DZ

Bandyopādhyāy (Banerji), Māṇik (Prabodhkumār, b 1908 Dumka, d 1956 Calcutta), Bengali writer. Born in an unimportant official's family, he got to know village and small town life in East Bengal in his childhood, and developed a strong feeling for the poor. He studied in Calcutta and became a free-lance writer there, later becoming editor of the Marxist monthly *Paricay* (Acquaintance) which, since 1931, largely helped to form the Bengali literary left-wing. Towards the end of his life he was President of the Bengali Progressive Writers' Association (see *progressive writing*) and active in political life. Māṇik developed straight from emotional humanism to Marxism, as can be seen from his work; the first novels, especially *Padmā nadīr mājhi* (Boatman of the Padma, 1936) and *Putulnācer itikathā* (Story of the Puppet-dance, 1936), express his profound feeling for the country people. During and immediately after the Second World War his work, especially the very fine stories, considered the peak achievement in this genre in Bengali literature, was forged into a weapon attacking social exploitation and fighting for political independence for his country. The heroes of his earlier works tend to be seekers and victims; those of the later works are fighters, drawn mainly from lower class life in the great city of Calcutta. Other novels: *Sahartalī* (The Suburb, 1940–1); *Sonār ceye dāmī* (More Precious than Gold, 1951–2); stories, *Pheriwālā* (The Peddler, 1946).

Trans.: H. Mukerjee, *Boatman of the Padma* (Bombay 1948); D. Chattopadhyay (ed.), *Primeval and Other Stories* (New Delhi 1958).
SHBL 378. DZ

Bandyopādhyāy (Banerji), Tārāśaṅkar (b 1898 Labpur, d 1971 Calcutta), Bengali writer. He worked free-lance, and after 1947 became active in politics. Like many progressive writers of the time, he began publishing in the periodical *Kallol* (Mountain Stream), founded in 1923 as the organ of the modernists, bringing anti-traditional trends into Bengali literature. Tārāśaṅkar has written excellent novels of rural life, drawn mainly from his native Birbhum, and fine short stories of lyrical mood with original characters. Novels include *Dhātrī debatā* (The Nursing Deity, 1939); *Kālindī* (1940); *Kabi* (The Poet, 1941); *Hāṃsuli bāṃker upakathā* (Legend of Hāṃsuli

Bend, 1947); *Manvantar* (Epoch's End, 1944).

Trans.: H. Mukerjee, *Epoch's End* (Calcutta 1945); *The Woman and the Serpent and Other Stories* (Calcutta 1971).
SHBL 376–7. DZ

bangsawan, Malayan theatrical form with live actors, speech predominating over music, singing and dancing; it originated in the late 19th century in Penang, under the influence of Malays, Arabs, Indians, Chinese and European settlers, and Indonesians from Sumatra and Java. Up to the 1950's, a brief summary of the play served as script, as in all Indonesian and Malayan forms except *sandiwara* (qv). To the traditional mythology, pseudo-historical and didactic themes new social subjects were added in the twenties. The language used is Malay. Few groups now perform traditional *bangsawan.* At its height (1900–30) *bangsawan* groups were famous in other South-East Asian countries as well. After the Malayan *bangsawan* began to decline in the 'thirties, there was a revival of the Indonesian *bangsawan* started by the Opera Dardanella. No group survived longer than 5–7 years, which made it difficult for the genre to evolve successfully.

James R. Brandon, *Theatre in Southeast Asia* (Cambridge 1967); Claire Holt, *Art in Indonesia: Continuity and Change* (Ithaca 1967). EV

Banmo Tin Aun, Burmese writer, see **Tin Aun,** Banmo.

Bantugan, Mindanao epic, see **darangan.**

Basavaṇṇa, Kannada poet, see **vacana.**

Basheer, Malayalam novelist, see **Muhammad Baśīr,** Vaikkam.

Basu (Bose), Buddhadeb (b 1908 Comilla), Bengali writer. He received his MA in English at Dacca University. He first co-edited *Pragati* magazine and later co-edited/edited *Kabitā*, poetry quarterly. He was a Visiting Professor in United States, and lectured in Europe and Japan. In 1956–63 he was the first chairman of the Comparative Literature Department, Jadavpur University, and received the Sahitya Akademi award for his drama, *Tapasvī o Taraṅginī*, in 1967. A critic, dramatist, novelist and poet, Buddhadeb has given direction to the post-Tagore period in Bengali literature. *Pragati*, along with the two other progressive journals of the 1920's, *Kallol* and *Kali-kalam*, provided the first real examples of, and outlets for, modern writings. *Kabitā* provided a standard of excellence for poetry during its lifetime, 1935–61. Buddhadeb, author of well over a hundred titles, continues to be a prolific writer in all literary genres. Books include *Kaṅkābatī* (1937); *Kāler putul* (Puppet of Time, 1946); *Bipanna bismay* (Precarious Surprise, 1969).

Trans.: KMBP, RMBB.
SHBL 368–70. CBS

Basu (Bose), Samareś (b 1923 Rajanagar), Bengali writer, regarded as the most talented writer of the left ever since his debut. His mature novels and stories usually deal with social problems of town and country, and are marked by firm, controlled style. He also wrote several books under the pseudonym Kālkut. Some novels: *B. T. Roḍer dhāre* (On the B. T. Road, 1953); *Amṛtakumbher sandhāne* (Searching for Nectar, 1954); *Gaṅgā* (1957). DZ

Batikuling, Filipino poet, see **Balmori,** Jesus.

Bāul songs, Bengali spiritual songs. The word *bāul* means 'madman', and Bāuls are mendicant singers who, consciously dressed in mixed Hindu and Muslim clothing, wander the countryside of Bengal living on whatever the householders choose to give them in return for their songs. The Bāuls believe in no ritual, either Hindu or Muslim; their songs reflect this belief and are their only form of worship. They are earthy in their imagery, speaking for example of the river of life, the ferryman who is the *guru* (religious teacher), the six senses being the drunken oarsmen who, were it not for the helmsman's steady hand, would drive the boat onto the rocks. The tunes to which these religious songs are sung are hauntingly beautiful, so beautiful that

Tagore (see Ṭhākur) set some of his own poetry, often similar in spirit to that of the Bāuls, to such music. Bāuls often accompany their songs on a simple instrument called *ek-tār* (one-stringed) made from a gourd, and sometimes with small cymbals or a drum. They often dance as they sing, carried away with religious ecstasy.

S. Dasgupta, *Obscure Religious Cults* (Calcutta 1962), pp. 157–87. ECD

Bēdi, Rājindar Singh (b 1915 Lahore), Urdu writer. He made his name as a short-story writer in the thirties and forties, and has published two collections of plays as well as three of short stories. In 1962 he published his first novel, *Ek cādar mailī sī* (A Soiled Sheet), on a marital tragedy in the setting of rural Panjab. This won the Sahitya Akademi award in 1966.

Trans.: Khushwant Singh, *I Take this Woman* (Delhi 1967). RR

Bedil, 'Abdulqādir, Indo-Persian poet, see Vol. III.

Bēdil, Qādir Bakhsh of Rohri (1814–1872), Sindhi mystic poet of the Qādirīya order. He was a typical preacher of the idea of Unity of Being and lived in complete absorption in the contemplation of his Beloved. He wrote books on Sufism in Arabic, Persian and Sindhi, and a *mukhammas* in five languages. In one book he connects a Qur'ānic verse, a *ḥadīṣ*, a verse from Rūmī's (see Vol. III) *Maṣnavī* and one from Shāh 'Abdu'l-laṭīf's (qv) *risālō* with a Persian story, a typical example of the eclectic method of later Sindhi Sufis.

ABSLP 296. AS

Bendre, Dattātrēya Rāmacandra or 'Ambikātanayadatta' (b 1896 Dharwar), a pioneer poet of modern Kannada, with over twenty-five volumes (beginning with *Sari*, 1930, to *Araḷu Maraḷu*, a collection, 1957). Compassionate, mystical and exquisitely lyrical, he draws on both folk and classical metres and sources, bridges old and new, village lore and traditional learning, intricate word-play, song and metaphysics. His use of North Kannada folk-idiom, imagery and earthy humour in both verse and drama (eg, *Sāyō Āṭa*, The Death Game, acclaimed as the first Kannada 'absurd play') is the most striking in all modern writing. AKR

Bernabe, Manuel, Filipino poet, see **Balmori,** Jesus.

Beschi, Constanzo Giuseppe (pseud. Vīramāmuṉivar, b 1680 Castiglione, d 1746 Ambalakkad), Tamil poet, writer, grammarian and lexicographer. He came to India as a Jesuit missionary. Following the example of the Italian Jesuit, Roberto de Nobili, probably the first serious European student of Tamil, Beschi learnt Sanskrit and Tamil so well that he became one of the founders of Tamil philology and prose-writing. His most ambitious work, *Tēmpāvaṇi* (1726), an epic narrative in 30 cantos (3615 stanzas) about St Joseph, excels by perfect diction; no one has handled so many metres in Tamil as Beschi in this poem. Most popular is *Paramārtta kuru* (*viṉ*) *katai*, a farce about a silly hermit and his disciples, which stimulated the evolution of Tamil prose. Other important works: *Vētiyar oḷukkam* (1727), Catholic apologetics in prose; *Grammatica latino-tamulica* (?1728, a grammar of High Tamil); *Grammatica latino-tamulica* (?1738, a grammar of Low Tamil); *Toṉṉūl viḷakkam* (c1730, a traditional grammar of Tamil); *Clavis humaniorum litterarum sublimioris tamulici idiomatici* (a grammar of literary Tamil); two dictionaries.

Trans.: B. G. Babington, *The Adventures of the Gooroo Paramartan* (London 1822).
JHTL 237–9. KZ

Bezbaṛuā, Lakṣmīnāth (1868–1938), Assamese poet, writer and journalist. Studied in Calcutta, under the influence of the modernistic trends of Bengal, at the end of the nineteenth century. One of the leading figures of the movement for the independence of Assamese culture. With some friends, he founded the magazine *Jonaki* (Firefly), in 1889, which became an instrument for propagating the romantic and patriotic ideas of the Assamese intelligentsia. In it Bezbaṛuā published many of his essays on topical and everyday subjects (collected later in *Bezbaṛuār bhāvar ber-burani*, Bubbles of B.'s Thoughts), short stories, often satires against social and religious survivals of the past, and poems marked by a language near to the colloquial speech of his time; he also introduced new forms into Assamese poetry. He was the first short story writer in Assamese and also wrote several historical plays inspired by admiration of his country's idealized past.

Trans.: A. D. Mukherjea, *Tales of a Grandfather from Assam* (Bangalore 1955). DZ

Bha Shein, U, Burmese writer, see **Maha Hswei.**

Bhagat, Niranjan, Gujarati poet, see **arvācin kavitā.**

Bhagavadgītā (c200 BC), Sanskrit sacred poem. Although the Hindus believe that their religion is based upon the *Vedas* (qv), the text which they actually use and revere most, and which forms the basis of the creed of Hindus of almost every sect, is the *Bhagavadgītā*. This text (638 verses divided into 18 chapters) forms a part of the *Mahābhārata* (qv, VI, 23–40), in which it is presented as a dialogue between the hero Arjuna and his charioteer Kṛṣṇa, the latter appearing sometimes as a human warrior and sometimes as an incarnation of Viṣṇu. It is the divine aspect which emerges in the *Gītā*, when Kṛṣṇa replies to Arjuna's questions about the immorality of war, the nature of *dharma*, and the mysteries of life and death. Kṛṣṇa's answer takes the form of a statement of the essential threads of Hindu philosophy incorporating much of the thinking of the *upaniṣads* (qv) and other ancient schools, notably the doctrines of *Sāṅkhya* (a school of philosophy which held that spirit and matter are separate, and that there is an infinity of souls) and *Yoga* (a school of practical philosophy which strove to enable the human soul to unite completely with the Supreme Spirit), as well as other concepts generally classed as Vedantic. Drawing upon this metaphysical background, Kṛṣṇa strives to resolve for Arjuna the conflict between temporal *dharma* (which required him, as a warrior, to kill his relatives), the Buddhist-influenced principle of *ahiṃsā* (non-injury to living creatures), and eternal *mokṣa* (the goal of Release, in the light of which all wordly concerns are meaningless). On another level, the conflict is manifested as the tension between the method of *karma* (ritual, action) and that of *jñāna* (meditation), which are tentatively resolved by a third path, *bhakti* (qv, devotion), the fervent spirit which, coupled with indifference towards the fruits of all actions, justifies all the conflicting demands made upon the individual. First translated into English by Charles Wilkins in 1785, the *Gītā* has been translated, commented upon, and reinterpreted by most major Hindu philosophers and numerous European students of Indian religion. In spite of its diverse sources, it is viewed by many scholars as a unified statement of a philosophy that has guided the thoughts and worship of Hindus for two millennia.

Trans.: W. Douglas P. Hill (Oxford 1928), F. Edgerton (Harvard 1944), R. C. Zaehner (Oxford 1969).
H. Zimmer, *Philosophies of India* (New York 1950); WHIL I, 365–77. WOF

Bhāgavata Purāṇa (c900 AD), Sanskrit devotional Vaiṣṇava poem, the most famous of the *purāṇas* (qv), though not the oldest. In its cosmogony and cosmology it is indebted to the older *Viṣṇu Purāṇa*, and it has incorporated many *Mahābhārata* tales, as well as portions of the *Bhagavadgītā* (qqv). Its 18,000 verses (in several metres besides the usual *purāṇic śloka*) are divided into 12 books devoted to Viṣṇu in all his aspects and incarnations, but by far the most beloved is the 10th book, which describes the childhood and youth of the cowherd (*gopa*) Kṛṣṇa. The spirit of *bhakti* (qv) is beautifully expressed in this book, which solicits from the hearer an entire spectrum of love—the maternal affection which Kṛṣṇa's mother feels for her son, the comradeship which the other young *gopas* feel for him, and finally the passion which he inspires in the *gopīs*, the wives of the cowherds. It is this latter scene which became particularly popular in later poetry and painting, though the other miraculous deeds of Kṛṣṇa's childhood are also retold with delight and reverence: how the wicked Kaṃsa tried in vain to murder the infant Kṛṣṇa, who was exchanged with another new-born boy at night; how a terrible demoness tried to kill him by giving him her poisonous breast to suckle, but was killed by the force with which he sucked; how Kṛṣṇa's mother tried to punish him (for stealing butter) by tying him up, an effort which proved in vain as the rope grew longer and longer; how he trampled the heads of the wicked serpent Kāliya until Kāliya's wives begged for mercy, which was granted; and how Kṛṣṇa's mother, inspecting his mouth for dirt which he had eaten, saw the entire universe, and herself, within him. These and other scenes are described in a style more elaborate and consciously poetic, and more aesthetically and theologically consistent, than that of the other *purāṇas*, making it the great favourite not only of the Indians themselves but, ever since its translation into French in 1840, of many Europeans as well.

Trans. into French by E. Burnouf (Paris 1840–98).
W. Archer, *The Loves of Krishna* (New York 1958); M. Singer (ed.), *Krishna: Myths, Rites and Attitudes* (Honolulu 1966); WHIL I, 464–6.

WOF

bhakti, Indian devotional religion. Early Indian religion was characterized by a formal sacrificial cult, presided over by a priest or a group of priests, and an equally formal household ritual. During the centuries preceding the Christian era, however, a more personal cult began to emerge, particularly in South India. It offered hymns of worship in the vernacular (in contrast with the Sanskrit liturgy of the earlier religion) to a more personalized, anthropomorphic god. Here, for the first time, the individual expressed his inner feelings to a god believed to reciprocate these feelings. This was the cult of *bhakti*, a Sanskrit term etymologically linked with a verb-root *bhaj*, 'participate, share', and denoting both the worshipper's intense love for the god and the god's love for his devotees, an irrational, compelling emotion as far removed from Vedantic philosophy as it was from Vedic cult (see *Veda*). *Bhakti* appears in the *Bhagavadgītā* (qv) as a third path synthesizing the earlier paths of worship, *karma* (action, ritual) and *jñāna* (knowledge, meditation).

Though particularly associated with the cult of Kṛṣṇa, *bhakti* transformed and influenced all of Hinduism. It inspired many of India's greatest works of art in the mediaeval period. In South India, *bhakti* was one of the most powerful and attractive ideas with which the renascent Hinduism from the 7th century onwards countered the more austere Jaina and Buddhist faiths. *Bhakti* literature by its very nature demanded increasing use of the vernacular languages, hence the importance of the Śaiva *Tirumuṛai* and Vaiṣṇava *Nālāyirappirapantam* (see Appar, Āṇṭāḷ) in the history of mediaeval Hinduism. The earlier portions of the *Tirumuṛai*, together with *Tirumurukāṟṟuppaṭai* (see *Pattuppāṭṭu*) and the hymns to Cevvēḷ in *Paripāṭal* are probably the earliest extant *bhakti* poetry in an Indian vernacular. *Bhakti* is extended to cover the mystical union of the soul with God, in which sense the Tamil word *aṉpu* is used, as in *Tirumantiram* (see *Tirumuṛai*). Supreme among early Tamil mystical poets was Māṇikkavācakar (qv) for Śaivism and Āṇṭāḷ for Vaiṣṇavism. In the north, an extensive *bhakti* literature was produced in mediaeval times, in Sanskrit, and especially in the Indo-Aryan vernacular languages of the period.

WOF and JRM

Bhāmaha, the earliest Indian writer on poetics proper (preceded only by the *Nāṭyaśāstra*, qv). His date is still in dispute: 6th century AD seems reasonable. The one work to come down is the *Kāvyālaṃkāra*, a beautifully written short work dealing with literary criticism in general. It would not be unjust to claim that the entire tradition of literary criticism is solidly based on Bhāmaha's work. Unfortunately no old commentary has survived. Udbhaṭa (qv) wrote a *Bhāmahavivaraṇa*, but this work has not yet been discovered, despite claims to the contrary. The relatively simple text of the *Kāvyālaṃkāra* is not without problems; some of the verses simply do not make sense and this may lie behind the surprising lack of translations.

Trans. by P. V. Naganatha Sastry (Tanjore 1927). DHSP I, 46–57, II, 32–54. JLM

Bhañj, Upendra, classical Oriya poet, of royal blood. He is considered the greatest representative of the classical poetry of Orissa which followed the aesthetic principles of Sanskrit *kāvya* (qv) literature, with main stress laid on the form of poetic expression. Bhañj wrote a number of adaptations of Sanskrit works, mostly the epics and the *purāṇas* (qv). His most important contribution is his original epic poem *Lāvaṇyavatī* on the love between the Prince of Karnatak and the Princess of Ceylon. Bhañj's verse is characterized by musical euphony, skilful use of alliteration and metrical ingenuity. By his style and language he influenced all subsequent classical poets of Orissa.

J. B. Mohanty, *Oriya Literature* (Cuttack 1953). DZ

Bhānubhakta, Nepali poet, see **Ācārya,** Bhānubhakta.

Bharata, legendary author of the Sanskrit **Nāṭyaśāstra.**

Bharathidasan, or **Bharathithasan,** Tamil poet, see **Cuppuratti<u>n</u>am.**

Bharati, S., Tamil poet, see **Pārati,** Cuppiramaṇiyam Ci.

Bhāravi (c550 AD), Sanskrit poet, author of the *Kirātārjunīya*, a court-epic (*mahākāvya*: see *kāvya*) in 18 cantos. The poem is based on an episode from the third book of the *Mahābhārata* (qv) and describes the fight between the hero Arjuna and a mountain-tribesman (*kirāta*), who is however the god Śiva in disguise. As a reward for Arjuna's asceticism and heroism, Śiva grants him the gift of divine weapons. The relatively simple theme is adorned by Bhāravi in typical *kāvya* fashion, by the insertion of lengthy digressions, descriptions of nature, of the Himālayas, of feminine beauty, and so forth. Canto 15 is famous for the use made of elaborate verbal *tours de force*. Especially in his descriptive passages, Bhāravi shows considerable poetic merit, and is not unjustly regarded by Sanskrit critics as one of the 'great poets' (*mahākavi*).

German trans., C. Cappeller, HOS 15, 1912; KHSL 109 ff.; WHIL III, 71.

JB

Bhārtendu, Hindi poet, see **Hariścandra.**

Bhartṛhari (1) (*floruit* c500 AD or slightly earlier), Sanskrit grammarian and philosopher, author of the *Vākyapadīya* ('Treatise on Words and Sentences') and a commentary, only partially preserved, on the *Mahābhāṣya* of Patañjali (qv). Bhartṛhari's grammatical works are mentioned by the Chinese traveller I-ching (see Vol. I), who gives as the date of his death c651 AD. This date was long accepted by modern scholars, but is now known to be wrong, since quotations from the *Vākyapadīya* have been discovered in the *Pramāṇasamuccaya* (extant in a Tibetan version) of the Buddhist logician Dignāga, whose date cannot be later than early 6th century, and may be earlier. Bhartṛhari was an outstanding original thinker, and the *Vākyapadīya* is much concerned with the philosophical problems of language. The work is in three parts (*kāṇḍa*), and the last and by far the longest is, at the time of writing, still in process of publication. The author must be distinguished from the poet of the same name: see following entry.

Ed. and French trans. of Kāṇḍa I with commentary; Madeleine Biardeau, *Vākyapadīya Brahmakāṇḍa, avec la vṛtti de Harivṛṣabha*, (Paris 1964); see also K. A. Subramania Iyer, *Bhartṛhari, a Study of the Vākyapadīya in the Light of the Ancient Commentaries* (Poona 1969). JB

Bhartṛhari (2) (possible c7th century AD), Sanskrit poet, traditionally the author of three *śatakas* ('centuries') of separate verses on the themes of *śṛṅgāra* 'love', *nīti* 'worldly wisdom' and *vairāgya* 'religious renunciation' respectively. The author cannot conceivably be the same person as the grammarian (see preceding entry), although it is possible that I-ching (who does not mention the *śatakas*) was misled by the identity of name, and that the date which he gave for Bhartṛhari's death might then refer to the poet. But this is mere speculation. The verses of Bhartṛhari, elegant, often moving, and showing considerable poetic power, achieved wide popularity, and spread throughout India. The unfortunate result was that numerous regional recensions developed, varying widely in their contents and the order of verses, and with plentiful interpolations and omissions. A great debt is due to the late D. D. Kosambi, who, after a study of well over 300 manuscripts, published a critical edition, *The Epigrams attributed to Bhartṛhari* (Bombay 1948). Here the stanzas are grouped strictly according to the weight of the evidence: Group I contains the 200 verses which are common to all the major regional recensions, and are therefore almost certainly genuine; Group II (201–352), verses missing from one or more of the major recensions, but with enough manuscript support to allow the possibility that a fair number may be genuine; Group III (353–852), verses from single versions and isolated manuscripts, or attributed to Bhartṛhari in anthologies. Virtually all of this last group must be spurious.

Numerous English translations, based on different recensions; most recently, Barbara Stoler Miller, *Bhartrihari: Poems* (New York 1967, a prose rendering of the 200 verses of Kosambi's Group I). JB

Bhāsa, early Indian dramatist of unknown date and place. Though often mentioned by other playwrights and theorists, none of his works was known before 1910 when ten anonymous dramas were discovered by T. Gaṇapati Śāstrī, and were attributed by him to Bhāsa. This attribution has been accepted by some scholars, and strongly disputed by others. It is probably true to say that most authorities would now agree that at least some of the plays in question are by Bhāsa. Twelve complete dramas and a fragment are extant now. Bhāsa is the earliest known Indian dramatist after Aśvaghoṣa (qv) and must have lived before Kālidāsa (qv), who has mentioned him with respect. Mentions by other authors and a few citations testify to his popularity and high esteem in ancient India.

The five one-act plays and the drama *Pañcarātra* (Five Nights) elaborate various episodes from the *Mahābhārata* (qv); *Pratimānāṭaka* (The Drama of the Statue) and *Abhiṣekanāṭaka* (The Drama of the Inauguration) are based on the *Rāmāyaṇa* (qv), and *Bālacarita* (The Adventures of the Boy) is the oldest extant drama on Kṛṣṇa. Two plays most probably retell stories from Guṇāḍhya's (qv) *Bṛhatkathā*: the fairy-tale *Avimāraka* and the love-drama *Svapnavāsavadattā* (Vāsavadattā of the Dream), considered the best work of Bhāsa by many. *Pratijñāyaugandharāyaṇa* (Yaugandharāyaṇa [true to his] Promise) is a political play about a minister defeating his rival by virtue and cleverness. The much debated *Daridracārudatta* (The Poor Cārudatta), of which only four acts are known, was recast in full by Śūdraka (qv), in his famous *Mṛcchakaṭikā*. In his dramas Bhāsa has respected the rules given by the theorists of the ancient Indian theatre, but both his language and his style are free from exaggerations and artificiality typical of the *kāvya* (qv) literature in the later phases of its development. His characters are full of life and his plots interesting, developed with a sense of dramatic tension.

Trans.: A. C. Woolner and Lakshman Sarup, *Thirteen Trivandrum Plays Attributed to Bhāsa*, 2 vols. (London 1930–1); A. S. P. Ayyar, *Two Plays of Bhasa* (Madras 1941).
M. Lindenau, *Bhāsa-Studien* (Leipzig 1918) WHIL III, 201–24. DZ

Bhaṭṭ, Udayśaṅkar (b 1898 Itava), Hindi playwright. Born in a traditional Brahmin family, he studied at the Hindu University, Banaras, and became a teacher in Lahore; from 1947 to retirement he was Hindi adviser to All-India Radio. In more than a dozen plays on *purāṇic* and historical subjects he developed the tradition of Jayśaṅkar Prasād's (qv) Hindi dramas, with skilful characterization, beautiful songs and a critical attitude towards national evils, especially in his plays *Ambā* (1933), *Sāgar-vijay* (Conquest of the Ocean, 1934), *Viśvamitra* (1935) ao. His one novel, *Sāgar, lahren aur manuṣya* (The Ocean, Waves and Man, 1956), shows his keen interest in the life of the poor and underprivileged. His poetry developed from romanticism to social commitment. PG

Bhaṭṭa, G., Gujarati writer, see **navalikā.**

Bhaṭṭa, Maṇiśankar, Gujarati poet, see **arvācin kavitā.**

Bhaṭṭa, Motīrām (b 1865 Kathmandu, d 1896), Nepali poet and writer. When still young, he went to Benares where he studied not only Sanskrit but Urdu and Persian. Among his first literary works was a verse-play in Urdu and later he tried, though without much success, to popularize the *ghazal* (see Vol. III) in Nepali. On a subsequent visit to Benares, he opened a Nepali press and published part of Bhānubhakta's (see Ācarya) *Rāmāyaṇa.* He also began the first Nepali newspaper, *Gorkhā Bhārat Jīvan.* During his stay in Benares, he wrote a number of short works, both prose and poetry, in Nepali, but is best remembered for his biography of Bhānubhakta, the first significant Nepali prose work. He fell ill while studying in Calcutta and soon after returning to Nepal died at the age of 31. DJM

Bhaṭṭa Nārāyaṇa, the author of an important Sanskrit drama, the *Veṇīsaṃhāra.* The play deals with an episode from the *Mahābhārata* (qv) story, and in the Prologue the dramatist pays homage to *Kṛṣṇa-Dvaipāyana* as the author of the *Mahābhārata.* The Prologue seems to give us another title or surname of the dramatist, viz. Mṛgarājalakṣman. However, this could have meant simply that he was a *kavisiṃha* or 'the best of poets'. The title 'Bhaṭṭa' might indicate that he was a Brahmin. And some scholars have surmised (apparently on insufficient grounds) that he was a Vaiṣṇava and probably a follower of the Pañcarātra system. Early literary critics like Vāmana and Ānandavardhana refer to the drama *Veṇīsaṃhāra,* and many citations are found in the *Daśarūpaka.* The play does not have a Vidūṣaka. The predominant *rasa* or mood in the play is *vīra* or 'heroism'. Since Vāmana flourished between 750 AD and 800 AD, Bhaṭṭa Nārāyaṇa could be placed in the 7th century AD. There is a 'Bengal legend' which claims that Bhaṭṭa Nārāyaṇa was a Brahmin from Kānyakubja who came to Bengal at the request of the king Ādiśūra. The historicity of Ādiśūra is doubtful, but if he is regarded as the founder of the Sena Dynasty, he must be placed at 650 AD. BKM

Bhaṭṭa, Śāmal, Gujarati poet, see **Premānanda.**

Bhaṭṭi (probably early 7th century AD, but on the evidence available, possibly about a century earlier), Sanskrit poet, author of the *Rāvaṇavadha,* often called the *Bhaṭṭikāvya.* The poem is a court-epic (*mahākāvya*: see *kāvya*) in 22 cantos, and has the double purpose of recounting the story of the *Rāmāyaṇa* (qv), and of illustrating the rules of the grammar of *Pāṇini* (qv) and the figures (*alaṅkāra*) of poetry. Cantos 1 to 9 illustrate miscellaneous grammatic rules, with sections devoted to special individual formations—various verbal classes, gerundives, nominal derivatives of verbs, use of nominal cases, and so forth. Cantos 10 to 13 illustrate the figures of poetry (canto 13 being so composed as to be capable of being read either as Sanskrit or as Prakrit). The remaining cantos illustrate the various moods and tenses of the verb. In spite of the artificiality of his endeavour—which was a positive merit in the eyes of his contemporaries—Bhaṭṭi is a poet of considerable stature, and much of his work can still be read with pleasure.

KHSL 116–19; WHIL III, 77–9. JB

Bhavabhūti (early 8th century AD), Sanskrit dramatist, author of the *Mahāvīra-carita, Uttararāma-carita,* and *Mālatī-mādhava.* The first and second of these are *nāṭakas* ('heroic dramas'), both in seven acts, and recount the story of the *Rāmāyaṇa* (qv). The *Mahāvīra* covers the first six books, the *Uttararāma* the last book of the *Rāmāyaṇa.*

In both, Bhavabhūti displays a dramatic inventiveness and skill superior to the great majority of Sanskrit playwrights, many of whom had little sense of the theatre as such, and whose works are worth reading more for the quality of their verses. In the *Uttararāma* especially, Bhavabhūti had the opportunity to evoke the poetic emotion of pathos (*karuṇa-rasa*), for which he was justly renowned in later centuries. In complete contrast, the *Mālatī-mādhava* is a *prakaraṇa*, a romantic drama in 10 acts, the theme of which may be inspired by a story from the *Bṛhatkathā* (see Guṇāḍhya), and other sources. In this genre Bhavabhūti is decidedly less effective in dramatic construction, although the play is not without attractiveness. As a poet, Bhavabhūti ranks high, and many critics have assessed his place in Sanskrit literature as second only to Kālidāsa (qv).

Mālatī-mādhava: ed. with English version, M. R. Kale (Bombay 1913); *Mahāvīra-carita*: trans. J. Pickford (London 1892); *Uttararāma-carita*: trans. S. K. Belvalkar, HOS XXI, 1915; French trans., N. Stchoupak (Paris 1935); KSD 186–203; DHSL 277–98. JB

Bhimnidhi, Nepali writer, see **Tivāri,** Bhīmnidhi.

Bhoja (11th century AD), a Paramāra king of Mālava, encyclopaedic scholar, creative writer and one of India's greatest critics. Though he may be suspected of buying work from the members of his literary 'assembly', there is an individual stamp of style and originality of aesthetic theory at least in Bhoja's critical and *kāvya* (qv) work, suggesting his own prolific genius. His major *kāvyas* are the *Rāmāyaṇacampū*, one of the five most popular *campūs* (see Ārya Śūra), a poetic and figurative summary of the story of Rāma, and the *nidarśanakathā Śṛṅgāramañjarī*, a collection of short novels or *gāṇikās* illustrating the varieties of love and lovers, told to Śṛṅgāramañjarī, Bhoja's favourite, to caution her through the misfortunes of their heroines. Bhoja's great contribution to aesthetics, in his *Sarasvatīkaṇṭhābharaṇa* and *Śṛṅgāraprakāśa*, begins with the idea that love is not only the most basic emotion but ultimately the one real emotion in the world. Every experience is love of something. Therefore all art must find its goal in the production of the sensitive *śṛṅgāra* aesthetic experience *rasa*, which is the aesthetic transformation of the basic instinct of love and self-assertion. Among his other works the most important is the *Samarāṅgaṇasūtradhāra* on architecture and its aesthetics.

Śṛṅgāramañjarīkathā, ed. and trans. K. K. Munshi (Bombay 1959). V. Raghavan, *Bhoja's Śṛṅgāra Prakāśa* (Madras 1963). AKW

Biag ni Lam-ang, Ilocamo epic, see **darangan.**

Bidyāsāgar, Iśvarcandra (1820–91), Bengali writer, translator, journalist and literary historian; a learned Calcutta Brahmin from a family of traditional pundits, teacher and author of texts for use in Fort William College, Calcutta. Regarded as the most learned Indian of his day, he embodied a synthesis of traditional Indian and modern European learning, but in the spirit of modern social and cultural reform. His prose texts for college use, mostly Bengali adaptations of Sanskrit and English works (*Śakuntalā*, 1854; *Sītār banabās*, Sītā's Exile, 1860; *Bhrāntibilās*, an adaptation of Shakespeare's *Comedy of Errors*, 1869), are remarkable for their purity of style and for their language, which schooled successive generations of writers. Of equal significance were his polemics directed against polygamy and the prohibition of remarriage for widows.

S. K. De, *Bengali Literature in the Nineteenth Century* (Calcutta 1919); CNI 33–6. DZ

Bihārilāl (1595–1664), Hindi poet. He was attached to the court of Śāhjahān in the early 17th century, and thereafter to that of Jaysingh of Amber. His language suggests Bundeli origin, and some connection between him and the poet Keśavdās of Orchā is likely. Bihārī's *Satsaī*, 700-odd couplets in Braj Bhāṣā, show a brilliant fusion of various literary traditions, and reflect the fruitful cultural environment of the middle Mughal period. Terse and pithy in expression, their themes and conventions are drawn from the earlier aphoristic, devotional and erotic-amatory traditions of Indian literature, and are interwoven with an air of extraordinary suggestiveness and charm. In combining a predominantly secular approach so artistically with elements drawn from devotional tradition, Bihārī reflects the composite culture of his time more fully than any other single Hindi poet, and no doubt for this reason remains one of the most popular of Hindi poets today.

G. Grierson, *The Satsai of Bihārīlal* (Calcutta 1896). RSM

Bilhaṇa (11th century AD), Sanskrit poet. Born in Kashmir, he served as court poet (*vidyāpati*) at the Chalukya court of Vikramāditya VI (1076–1127), where he composed a court epic entitled *Vikramāṅkadevacarita*. Also attributed to Bilhaṇa's authorship are the play *Karṇasundarī* and the series of lyric verses best known by the title *Caurapañcāśikā*. In all three works there are many verses which are similar in subject and style. The marriage and love-making of Vikramāditya and Princess Candralekhā is described in chapters VII to IX of the *Vikramāṅkadevacarita* with the same attention to sensuous details of the princess's beauty and love's pleasures that characterizes the verses of the *Caurapañcāśikā*; such verses also abound in *Karṇasundarī*, which deal with the marriage of a king to a fairy princess. Romantic legends attached to the *Caurapañcāśikā* relate that the poet became involved in a secret affair with a king's daughter and was condemned to death by her father when they were discovered. While awaiting execution, he recited a series of quatrains, each beginning with the phrase 'even now' (*adyāpi*), to evoke his mistress's presence. The verses worked their magic; he won his life and the princess. The legend and the verses, in two distinct recensions, are found in an old Gujarati translation of the 16th century and in Bhāratcandra Rāy's (qv) 18th century Bengali poem *Vidyāsundar*.

Trans.: E. Poway Mathers, *Black Marigolds (A free interpretation of the Chaurapanchasika)*, in *An Anthology of World Poetry* (New York 1936); S. N. Tadpatrikar, *Caurapañcāśikā: An Indian Love Lament of Bilhaṇakavi* (Poona 1966); B. Stoler Miller, *Phantasies of a Love-Thief: The Caurapañcāśikā Attributed to Bilhaṇa* (New York 1971).
DHSL 350–3, 367–9, 471–2; KHSL 153–8, 188–190. BSM

Binh-nguyen-Loc (real name To-van Tuan, b 1914 Tan-uyen, Bien-hoa province), Vietnamese writer. One of the most fertile South Vietnamese novelists and short story writers, he has also written poems, essays and scholarly works. Chief works: *Do doc* (The Governor); *Gieo gio gat bao* (They Have Sown the Wind and They Shall Reap the Whirlwind); *Khinh tam benh va sang tac van nghe* (Neurosis and the Arts).

DNILVN 182. VV

Bisaldev-rāso, Rajasthani romance, see **rāso.**

Bose, see **Basu.**

Brahman, real name Chandar Bhān (b 1574 Lahore, d 1662 Benares), Indo-Persian poet and writer. Son of a Brahmin, minister and court-historian of the Emperor Shahjahan, later private secretary to prince *Dārā Shikōh* (qv). His main prose work *Chahār chaman* (Four Meadows, 1648), partly autobiographical, describes festivities at the Mughal court, episodes from the emperor's life and expounds some religious and moral principles. He translated the questions of Dārā Shikōh about Hindu beliefs and customs into Persian from Hindi and the *Ātmavilāsa* of Śaṅkara (qv) on Vedānta philosophy from Sanskrit, under the title *Khayālāt-e nāzuk* (Fine Thoughts).

HIL 727–8. JM

brāhmaṇas, a body of prose literature attached to the Vedic *saṃhitās* and belonging to the period 850–600 BC. As 'interpretations of the *brahman*, ie the holy content of the *Veda*', they were composed in the Vedic 'schools' to explain the significance of the *saṃhitās* as used in the sacrifices, as well as the import of the ritual acts performed by the officiants. The arguments are largely based on a twofold conviction; first, that all things and events are connected with each other and that there must exist a close relationship or correspondence between phenomenal reality, a province of the universe or a section made from it (for instance the sacrificial place), and the eternal transcendent reality behind the phenomena determining or governing these; second, that beneficial relations with the supra-mundane sacred order can best be established and maintained through the rites, which, however, must be thoroughly understood to be efficacious.

In order to illustrate their ritual explanations the authors insert myths and legends, accounting for the introduction of a definite ritual practice, but they do not furnish a guide to sacrificial procedure. The many passing references in these works to contemporary life are very valuable for the historian of Indian culture. Their style is archaic and generally concise with a predilection for stereotyped phrases. To the White *Yajurveda* belongs the voluminous *Śatapatha-Brāhmaṇa* which, consisting of a hundred 'paths', ie sections, is one of the most important works of Indian antiquity. It deals with the rites of the Full and New Moon, the establishment of the sacred fires, the seasonal sacrifices, the Soma sacrifices, the construction of the great fire-place, the Horse-sacrifice and many other rites.

Of the extant *brāhmaṇas* the *Tāṇḍya* or *Pañcaviṃśa* (consisting of 'Twenty-five' chapters) and the *Jaiminīya*, both of them belonging to the *Sāmaveda*, are largely parallel in their exposition of definite rites. While the former, adhering more rigidly to the order of the sacrifices discussed, tends to focus attention on the significance of the Vedic chants, the latter disgresses. The *Ṣaḍviṃśa* ('Twenty-sixth') and the final section of the *Jaiminīya* deal with the atonements required for mistakes or evil portents that may have occurred during sacrifices. To the *Ṛgveda* (qv) belong the *Aitareya* and the *Śāṅkhāyana-Brāhmaṇas*, explaining the *agnihotra*, ie the daily morning and evening sacrifices. The former also contains an exposition of the Agniṣṭoma and of the rites connected with the installation of a king.

Trans.: J. Eggeling, *The Śatapatha-Brāhmaṇa*, 5 vols. (SBE ,1882–1900, reprinted 1963); A. B. Keith, *Rigveda Brāhmaṇas* (1920); W. Caland, *Pañcaviṃśa-Brāhmaṇa* (1931).
WHIL I, 187–225. JG

Bṛhad-Āraṇyaka-Upaniṣad, see **upaniṣads.**

Brokor, Gulabdas, Gujarati writer, see **navalikā.**

Buddhaghosa (5th century AD), exegetic philosopher and commentator of the Sthaviravāda (Pāli, Theravāda) school of Buddhism. According to tradition, he was a north Indian Brahmin who came to Ceylon during the reign of king Mahānāma (2nd half of the 5th century AD). In Anurādhapura, an ancient seat of Buddhist learning, he undertook a comprehensive study of old Sinhalese, commentaries on the Pāli Canon (called *aṭṭhakathā*, lit. 'discussions on the meaning'); he later rendered them into Pāli. Together with two other famous contemporaries, Buddhadatta and Dhammapāla, as well as later scholars, Buddhaghosa aimed at consistent and systematic exposition of Theravāda traditions. In his own work, *Visuddhimagga* (The Path of Purity), he achieved an encyclopaedic survey of essential points of the doctrine, thus eclipsing all the other authorities on exegesis. In fact, modern *Pāli* Buddhism draws predominantly on his interpretations.

Trans.: Pe Maung Tin, *The Path of Purity*, 3 vols., (PTS 1923–31); Ñāṇamoli, *The Path of Purification* (Colombo 1956).
B. C. Law, *The Life and Work of Buddhaghosa* (Calcutta 1923); WHIL II, 190–2, 196–205, 609–11. IF

Buddhist literature of India may be regarded as part of Indian literature generally, overlapping with Brahmanical, Jaina (etc), literature in form, style and content. From the standpoint of literature as an art, *kāvya* (qv), whose tradition and principles are essentially secular, along with literary criticism (*nāṭyaśāstra*, *alaṃkāraśāstra*, qqv), the distinction between Buddhist and non-Buddhist authors or subject matter is secondary to the aesthetic aim of delighting the reader or audience. Even the Buddhist *Tripiṭaka* (tradition of the teaching of the Buddha) overlaps historically and stylistically with the Vedic *brāhmaṇas* (qv); the Buddhist *śāstras* (qv) range from commentaries, stemming from the same tradition of interpretative techniques as the Vedic *Mīmāṃsā*, to treatises on epistemology, grammar and literary criticism indistinguishable in style from Brahmanical works. We are not here concerned with the problem of unhappiness and how to end it in *nirvāṇa*, but the *Tripiṭaka*, though in principle an instructive *āgama* and not *kāvya*, itself contains much of value from the aesthetic standpoint. In fact it partially makes up for the loss of most early *kāvya*, from the formative period of that secular tradition (500–100 BC). Thus the largely apocryphal (composed by later propagandists, not by the Buddha) *Kṣudraka Āgama* contains specimens of epic and lyric poetry from several centuries in its *Jātaka* (qv), *Sthaviragāthā* (Pāli *Theragāthā*, qv) and *Suttanipāta* anthologies. In the prose narratives, especially the *Mahāparinirvāṇa Sūtra* describing the last days of the Buddha, may be discerned the nascent art of the biography *ākhyāyikā* as a *kāvya* genre. The art of story-telling in prose, out of which developed the many varieties of *kathā* (including the novel), can be richly illustrated from the *Tripiṭaka*.

The first great Indian novel, the *Bṛhatkathā* (see Guṇāḍhya), clearly grew out of the same art and the same milieu. The *Kuṇāla Jātaka* is a *campū kāvya* (see *Ārya Śūra*). Certain dialogues in mixed prose and verse, mostly in the *Saṃyukta Āgama*, called *geya*, where the Buddha confronts the gods, may reflect the dramatic techniques of the 4th and 3rd centuries BC. The post-canonical (except in Burma) *Milindapañha* (qv) again seems to be based on the *ākhyāyikā* genre, though adapted, like its prototype the *Śrāmaṇyaphala Sūtra*, to present a long dialogue on Buddhist doctrine, literary rather than rigorously philosophical with its picturesque analogies. The Mahāyāna *sūtras* offer some parallels and supplements to the little remaining secular prose literature of the early centuries AD, culminating in the grand religious novel *Gaṇḍavyūha*. The 'empty' conversation of the *Prajñāpāramitā* stands closest to the old *Tripiṭaka* dialogues, dropping at every turn from superficial worldly questions into empty *nirvāṇa* answers with an appearance of paradox. This is more humorously presented in the *ākhyāyikā*-dialogue *Vimalakīrtinirdeśa*. The same philosophy underlies the fantastic *bodhisattva* stories of the great *Ratnakūṭa* and the *Saddharmapuṇḍarīka*'s drama-like presentation of an eternal Buddha.

Aśvaghoṣa (qv) seems to be the earliest known Buddhist writer who belongs unambiguously to *kāvya*, despite his secondary or ulterior aim of instruction. His two epics are among the finest achievements in that genre in Sanskrit, though stylistically archaic and obsessed with grammar in the eyes of mediaeval critics (Rājaśekhara, qv). His philosophy is hidden among the richest profusion of similes in Indian literature. His special charm derives largely from the tension between the delights of the world and the joy of freedom from it. His (probably at least) four dramas are unfortunately known only from some fragments. Mātṛceta is the most celebrated Buddhist lyric poet among hundreds of writers of *stotras* singing simply of renunciation. Ārya Śūra (qv) stood at the beginning of the fully formed classical style of Sanskrit prose and verse in his *campū Jātakamālā* and was recognized as among the greatest writers by Brahmanical critical tradition (Rājaśekhara) as well as Buddhist: Ratnaśrījñāna quotes him to illustrate the 'Southern' (*vaidarbha*) style. The philosopher Nāgārjuna (qv) meanwhile (2nd century AD) seems to have inaugurated the series of Buddhist poetic 'epistles' (*lekhas*), as well as composing philosophical *stotra* lyrics and 'tracts' (*parikathās*). Mātṛceta, Śūra and many others followed him in these special Buddhist genres. Kumāralāta's (3rd century) narratives in his *Kalpanāmaṇḍitikā* are sometimes bracketed with those of Śūra, but we now have only fragments of them. Candragomin (probably 4th century) became better known for a famous Epistle to a Pupil, called a *dharmakāvya*, and a *bodhisattva* drama *Lokānanda*, as well as some *stotras* and a tract. The best known later *stotra* writers are Triratnadāsa (?4th century), Harṣa, Jñānayaśas (both 7th century), Sarvajñamitra (8th century) and Vajradatta (9th century). The Emperor Harṣa (qv) also wrote a *bodhisattva* play, the *Nāgānanda*, which has held the stage in Kerala (almost the only country where the classical Indian theatre has survived) down to modern times. Among the little extant Buddhist literature in south Indian languages the Tamil novel *Maṇimēkalai* by Cāttaṉār (qv) is outstanding. No Buddhist novels in Sanskrit or Prakrit seem to have been preserved.

Of later Buddhist epics, Śivasvāmin's *Kapphiṇābhyudaya* (9th century) is a masterpiece, Buddhaghosa's *Padyacūḍāmaṇi* a simple expression of devotion, ritualistic and without epic movement. A number of Buddhist lyric poets, some of whom may have been dramatists, are known to us through Vidyākara's anthology of Sanskrit verse, selected with supreme connoisseurship and breadth of outlook perhaps surprising in a monk. Of the probable Buddhists here, Yogeśvara (c800 AD) is noteworthy for his realistic country scenes; of the others we may note Aparājita (9th century, a novelist), Vasukalpa (10th century) and Vallaṇa (a dramatist?).

Numerous Buddhist lyrics in Apabhraṃśa have survived from the period 8th to 12th centuries, which present the Mantrayāna or Sahajayāna 'natural' way to enlightenment through varied imagery. The poets include Saraha, Kambala, Kṛṣṇācārya, Tailapāda, Lūyipāda and Bhusuka. Based on some of the vast semi-canonical narrative literature, we may note Kṣemendra's collection of *avadānas* (qv), because the author was not a Buddhist but summarized the stories purely for their literary interest. Buddhist writers also made major contributions to literary criticism, the most important Buddhist critics known to us being Bhāmaha (qv), Ratnaśrījñāna (10th century) and Vidyākara (12th century). Ratnākaraśānti's work on metrics is extant. Something should be said of Buddhist historical writing in India, though little of it survives (compared with Ceylon, where a complete historical tradition with Buddhism survives).

Buddhist historiography began within the *Tripiṭaka*, in the *Vinaya*, as an historical record of the first 150 years after the Enlightenment, supplemented by certain *sūtra* narratives. It continued in supplements to and commentaries on the *Vinaya* (eg *Lalitavistara*, qv, Śākyaprabha), annals and chronicles (eg the Nepal Buddhist *Vaṃsāvalīs*), legendary compilations (eg the *Svayambhū Purāṇa*), accounts of the schisms and schools (eg Vasumitra, Bhāvaviveka, Paramārtha, Vinītadeva) and more general histories and collections of biographies of teachers (eg Padmākaraghoṣa; the works of Bhaṭaghaṭī, Indradatta, etc, seem to be lost, but much survives indirectly in the Tibetan histories of Bu-ston, Tāranātha, etc). The *Tantra Mañjuśrīmūlakalpa* contains an historical section in the manner of a *purāṇa* (qv) 'predicting' the events from the time of the Buddha down to the 8th century AD, when it was presumably written.

WIB; WHIL II, 1–423. AKW

Bullhe Śāh (1680–1758), Panjabi poet. Born into a Sayyid family of Kasur, became the disciple of Śāh Ināyat, a Qādirī *pīr* of Lahore. After the latter's death he returned to Kasur, where his tomb is still a centre of religious devotion. Bullhe Śāh composed some 160 *kāfīs*, mystical lyrics designed to be sung by religious minstrels (*qavvāl*). He is agreed to have been the greatest practitioner of this popular Panjabi genre. His poetry is distinguished by a mystical insight and expressiveness almost unique in Panjabi Muslim literature, being at once colloquial and highly theological, but eschewing the detailed imagery characteristic of Śāh Husain or Ghulām Farīd (qqv). Like many Sūfī poets Bullhe Śāh is often monistic in tone, but his possible indebtedness to Hindu Vedāntic ideas should not be over-stressed. Besides the *kāfīs*, Bullhe Śāh also wrote a notable *bārāmāh*.

RKPSP 40–71 CS

Bulosan, Carlos (1914 Binalonan, Pangasinan, d 1956), Filipino humorist and poet writing in English. Although he received only basic education he attained prominence, especially abroad. His collection of short stories *The Laughter of My Father* (1944) was translated into Italian, Swedish and Danish. EH

C

Cakrabarti (Chakravarty), Amiya (b 1901 Serampore), Bengali poet. He received an MA in philosophy and literature, Patna University, and a doctorate at, Oxford University; he taught at several colleges and universities in India and in the United States, Canada and Australia. In 1963, he received the Sahitya Akademi award for his book of poetry, *Ghare pherār din* (Homecoming). Presently he is professor of philosophy at State University College, New Paltz, New York. Amiya, for some time Tagore's personal secretary, was initially influenced by Rabīndranāth; both subscribe to a similar positive, mystical philosophy. But the two differ in their approach to poetry. Tagore seems to have written after contemplating; Amiya seems to write after observing. He observes and records his physical surroundings. One can follow him via poetry as he moved through Bengal or Europe or the United States, whence he continues to write today. Some books include *Khasṛā* (Rough Draft, 1938); *Pārāpār* (On Opposite Shores, 1953); *Pālābadal* (Change of Time, 1955).

Trans.: KMPB, BBV.
SMBP; SHBL 379–80. CBS

Campantar (7th century), Tamil poet, with Appar (qv) the principal author of *Tēvāram* (the first seven books of *Tirumuṛai*, qv). His work appears as *Tirumuṛai* I–III. Legend states that, when hungry as a baby, Campantar, in Cīrkāḻi, was suckled by the goddess Pārvatī, whereupon he sang his first hymn. At the request of the Pāṇṭiya queen, Maṅkaiyārkk'araci, Campantar went to the south to save the country from the Jainism professed by the king and many of his subjects. Apart from the sentiment of *bhakti* (qv), Campantar's poems, like all those of *Tēvāram*, relate to various shrines of the god Śiva, which are in consequence known as *Pāṭal peṟṟa stalam* (Shrines that have received song).

JHTL 79–82. JRM

campū, see **kāvya.**

Cāṇakya, Minister of Candragupta Maurya, see **Kauṭilya.**

Cand Bardāī, Rajasthani poet, see **rāso.**

Candar, Kriṣan, Urdu writer, see **Chandar,** Krishan.

Caṇḍīdās, Bengali poet. The same historical problems that vex the question of the identity and date of Vidyāpati (qv) apply to the great Vaiṣṇava poet Caṇḍīdās. Legend has it that he was born in the late 14th century in Birbhum district. It is certain only that a poet by the name of Caṇḍīdās ('servant of Caṇḍī') flourished before the time of the Vaiṣṇava saint Caitanya (b 1486), for it is said in biographies of the saint that he read such a poet 'with pleasure'. In fact, as is the case with Vidyāpati, it is certain that there were at least two poets who signed their poems Caṇḍīdās. One Caṇḍīdās who wrote on the Rādhā-Kṛṣṇa theme was Baṛu-Caṇḍīdās (Baṛu meaning a Brahmin temple attendant; this Caṇḍīdās served a temple of the form of the goddess called Vāsulī). His work is the long cycle now called *Śrīkṛṣṇa-kīrtan*; the name was given to the untitled manuscript by its editor, Basantarañjan Rāy, when it was first published in 1916. Linguistic evidence indicates that the text is as old as the early 15th century, though the manuscript itself may be as recent as the 18th; internal inconsistencies also suggest updating in the language of the text. The cycle concerns itself with the very earthy aspects of the love affair between Rādhā and Kṛṣṇa, set in the form of a dramatic dialogue between the lovers, and between one or the other of them and the old woman go-between, Baṛāi. In the cycle Kṛṣṇa, though frequently reminding the others of his divinity, acts very much the lusty and often cruel young man, out to satisfy his desires without regard for the consequences; Rādhā is portrayed with great sensitivity as the young girl at first tentatively, then hopelessly, in love. The poems also show such deviant characteristics of the later non-purāṇic Vaiṣṇava tradition as Rādhā being married at the time she falls in love with Kṛṣṇa. These poems have done more than any other text to set the warm, human tone of later Vaiṣṇava religious poetry.

Since the beginning of the 20th century, vast numbers of poems with the signature Caṇḍīdās have emerged, so many that scholars have wondered if it was possible for one poet to have produced them all. On textual examination, it has become clear that they are in fact from the hands of several poets. At least one of these was a Sahajiyā (Tantric) poet, whose poems are more drily doctrinal than those of the earlier Caṇḍīdās; he was from all points of view a lesser poet. The later Caṇḍīdās also lived after Caitanya, for his doctrine points to religious developments that took place only after Caitanya's life had been interpreted from the Sahajiyā point of view.

The most famous legend associated with the name Caṇḍīdās is that of his love for the washerwoman Rāmī. Because of his love, the romantic story goes, he was excommunicated from his Brahmin caste. Not only did he openly declare his love for a woman of low degree, but glorified her with the title 'Mother *gāyatrī*' (the *gāyatrī* being the most sacred ritual formula in brahmanical Hinduism). If there is any truth in the legend, it perhaps suggests that this Caṇḍīdās was a Sahajiyā, for one of the tenets of that belief is the union of high and low, and in fact the conjunction of all opposites.

Trans.: Deben Bhattacharya, *Love Songs of Candidās* (London 1967).
E. C. Dimock, Jr., *The Place of the Hidden Moon* (Chicago 1966); SHBL 70–9. ECD

Candragomin, ancient Indian writer, see **Buddhist literature.**

caṅkam, classical Tamil 'Academy', see **Eṭṭuttokai.**

Cantu Mēnōn, Oyyārattu or **Chandu Menon** (1847–99), Malayalam novelist. A member of the Madras Civil Service, he developed a passionate interest in the English novel at the age of forty and from then on began to devote all his leisure time to novel reading. After an unsuccessful attempt to translate Disraeli's *Henrietta Temple* he decided to write an original novel in his mother tongue so that fellow-speakers of Malayalam should know what a novel was. So he published *Indulekhā* (1889), the first novel of any consequence in Malayalam. It is the story of a middle-class family in south Malabar and suggests a number of ways in which the customs of that society could be changed for the better. A second novel, *Śārada* (1892), showing the perils of litigation, was never completed.

Trans.: W. Dumergue, *Indulekha* (Madras 1890, reprint Calicut 1965).
CNI 208–17; GSML 172–3; PNHML 122–5; VISNM 5–9. REA

Caryā-padas, the earliest known texts in Bengali, as that language was developing out of the earlier Indo-Aryan stage known as Apabhraṃśa. Opinions vary as to their date, but the state of linguistic development indicated by the songs would suggest the period between the 11th and 13th centuries. Scholars also debate whether or not the songs are Old Oriya, Old Assamese, or Old Maithili. In fact, they probably represent a stage of development at which there was no distinction among the four. The songs are Sahajiyā or Tantric in nature, although internal evidence also suggests the presence of the more austere varieties of Yoga. They also contain not only Buddhist elements, but elements of Śaivite (Hindu) Tantra. Like many esoteric texts, they are written in a 'twilight language', the metaphor and imagery of which deliberately cloud the meaning, to keep it from the uninitiated. The manuscript which contains the songs was discovered in Nepal in 1918 by Haraprasād Śāstrī (a manuscript of such antiquity would not have lasted in the humid heat of Bengal). A 14th century Tibetan translation, including a translation of the commentary, provides confirmation of the text, in addition to two songs not found in the Nepal manuscript.

Trans.: Md. Shahidullah, *Buddhist Mystic Songs. Aścarya-caryācarya* (The Dacca University Studies, Vol. IV, January, 1940. No. II. Pp. 1–87).
Tarapada Mukherji, *The Old Bengali Language and Text* (Calcutta 1963); S. Dasgupta, *Obscure Religious Cults* (Calcutta ²1962), pp. 1–109.
ECD

Cāttaṉār (6th–8th century), classical Tamil poet. No biographical data are available. *Maṇimēkalai*, an epic in 30 cantos, tells how the beautiful heroine, daughter of Kovalaṉ and Mātavi (see *Iḷaṅkōvaṭikaḷ*), becomes a Buddhist nun, and avoiding the attentions of Prince Utayakumāraṉ, is involved in many miraculous adventures, becoming the involuntary cause of the prince's death. As a work of art, *Maṇimēkalai* is unsuccessful. The story itself is lost in confusing details, the heroine's character is uninteresting and unconvincing, and art is sacrified to Buddhist philosophy and propaganda. It preaches detachment from the world, service to all living things, and pity for animals, but it also attacks Jains and others. There are only a few great moments in the text, mainly lovely similes and brilliant metaphors.

S. Krishnaswami Aiyangar, *Manimekalai in its Historical Setting* (London 1928).
JHTL 60–4. KZ

Caṭṭopādhyāy (Chatterji), Baṅkimcandra (b 1838 at Kantalpara, d 1894, Calcutta), Bengali writer. Son of a rural tax-collector, he was given a modern education and became the first graduate of Calcutta University. He served as a government official in various parts of Bengal for thirty years. He had a good knowledge of English and English literature, and at first wrote in English; a novel, *Rajmohan's Wife*, appeared in 1864. In 1872 he founded the literary monthly *Baṅgadarśan* (Mirror of Bengal), where most of his novels appeared. Towards the end of his life he turned to orthodox Hinduism and encouraged its traditions.

Baṅkimcandra is often called the father of the Indian novel; under the undoubted influence of Walter Scott both in structure and in the romantic approach, he introduced the historical novel into Bengali literature, his choice of themes and their treatment being in keeping with the patriotic feeling of the time and the effort to revive the former glory of India. The song *Vande Mātaram* (I sing the praise of the Mother, ie India) in the novel *Ānandamaṭh* (The Mission House of the Ānandas, 1882), about the heroic resistance of the Sanyasi hermits to the Muslims and the British, became the first hymn of the Indian movement for independence. Baṅkimcandra's rejection of certain modern trends towards social reform can be seen in his social novels, where the ideal of womanhood is presented in the spirit of the old traditions. In spite of the literary shortcomings of his novels (in the development of the plot, the vocabulary and characterization), he takes major credit for the emergence of the modern Indian novel, for popularizing good reading among the broad public and for the encouragement of Bengali journalism. Other novels (and their translations): *Durgeśnandinī* (1865; C. C. Mookherji, *The Chieftain's Daughter*, Calcutta ²1903); *Kapālkuṇḍalā* (1866; D. N. Ghosal, Calcutta 1919); *Mṛṇālinī* (1869); *Biṣabṛkṣa* (1873; M. S. Knight, *The Poison Tree*, London 1884); *Candraśekhar* (1877; M. N. Ray Chowdhury, Calcutta 1904); *Rajanī* (1877; P. Majumdar, Calcutta 1928); *Kṛṣṇakānter uil* (1878; D. C. Ray, *Krishnakanta's Will*, Calcutta 1918); *Rājsiṃha* (1881), *Debī Caudhurāṇī* (1884; S. C. Mitter, Calcutta 1946); *Sītārām* (1886; S. Mukherji, Calcutta 1903).

J. Dasgupta, *A Critical Study of the Life and Novels of Bankimchandra* (Calcutta 1937); CNI 61–74; SHBL 232–8. DZ

Caṭṭopādhyāy (Chatterji), Śaratcandra (b

1876 Debnandapur, d 1937 Calcutta), Bengali writer. Son of poor parents, he had no higher education; he spent many years outside Bengal, particularly in Bihar and Burma. He began to write stories at 17, then published nothing further for ten years. Fame came then rapidly, and he devoted himself to writing. His books appeared in many large editions, many being translated into other Indian languages, dramatized and filmed. From the outset he was influenced by Ṭhākur (qv) in style and language, but his work (almost 30 books) is more concerned with social questions. It deals mainly with the lives and problems of the middle classes, and the decadence of landlord society. He often featured the problems of women, and castigated the social inequity and family oppression of women in India. On the other hand, his work is highly emotional and often sinks to sentimentality, a quality which made him the most widely read writer in India, but prevented his work from recognition abroad. His best work, as literature, is that with autobiographical features, particularly the four-volume novel *Śrīkānta* (1915–31). Other novels: *Caritrahīn* (Bad Man, 1917); *Debdās* (1916); *Pallīr samāj* (Village Society, 1916); *Gṛhadāha* (House Afire, 1919); *Śeṣ praśna* (Final Question, 1931).

Trans.: K. C. Sen, *Srikanta* (Benares 1945); D. K. Roy, *Deliverance* (Calcutta sd).
S. C. Sengupta, *Saratchandra* (Calcutta 1945); Humayun Kabir, *Saratchandra* (Bombay 1942); SHBL 344–7. DZ

Caudhari, Raghuvir, Gujarati writer, see **navalkathā.**

Cayaṉkoṇṭār (11th-12th century), Tamil poet at court of the Cōḻa king Kulōttuṅka (1064–1113). No detailed biographical data are available. *Kaliṅkattupparaṇi* (after 1110) is a war-poem in honour of Kulōttuṅka's victory over the Kalinga. *Paraṇi* is a war-poem in honour of the Cōḻa land, the devilish havoc caused by their warrior-husbands on the battlefield, and the misery of the widows in the enemy country. It is a typical court war-poem, exploiting with great vividness sensual eroticism, the gruesome aspects of war, with occasional gory humour. A master of onomatopoeia, Cayaṉkoṇṭār has no equal in Tamil literature in depicting the nightmare of war and the grotesque and fantastic.

JHTL 185–8. KZ

Cēkkiḻār, Tamil poet, minister under the Cōḻa king Kulōttuṅka I (1064–1113) and author of *Periyapurāṇam*, the twelfth book of the *Tirumuṟai* (qv). His work is of 1286 stanzas, divided into 72 cantos, and it tells the stories of the 63 Śaiva hymnist-devotees known as *Nāyaṉmār*, that include Campantar, Māṇikkavācakar (qqv) and others. Unlike many of the Tamil *purāṇas* (qv), *Periyapurāṇam* is purely local in its source-material, and it is not based on a Sanskrit model. It is not a single story epic, but a collection of 'biographies'. Apart from those already mentioned this work includes such great devotees as the Cēra ruler Cēramāṉ Perumāḷ, Cuntarar's contemporary, and Kaṇṇappanāyaṉār. When the latter saw the eye of the Śivaliṅga bleeding, he plucked out his own eye to replace it and so stopped the flow of blood; he would have done the same for the other eye had the god not stopped him. *Periyapurāṇam* is written largely in the *viruttam*-metre.

JHTL 152–7. JRM

Cellappā, Ci. Cu. (Chellappa, C. S.; b 1912), Tamil poet, writer, critic and editor. He is the most unorthodox and modern-oriented Tamil critic. In 1959 he founded an influential journal, *Eḻuttu* (Writing), open to *avant garde* writing and modern criticism, absorbing Western influences, and striving for the creation of new prose and poetic diction and style in Tamil. In 1962 he published in Madras a pioneer collection of 63 poems by 24 poets, entitled *Putukkuralkaḷ* (New Voices), with his own programme introduction. Thanks to him, the years 1959–62 were a decisive turning-point in modern Tamil literature. The 'new' poets, gathered round Cellappā's review and publishing house, broke radically with the traditional literary past, preoccupied with contemporary and hitherto ignored subjects, they experiment with language and form but do not reject Tamil cultural heritage. KZ

Chairil Anwar, Indonesian poet, see **Anwar,** Chairil.

Chakravarty, see **Cakrabarti.**

Chandar Bhān, Indo-Persian poet, see **Brahman.**

Chandar, Krishan (b 1914 Lahore), Urdu prose writer, for some years general secretary of the Progressive Writers' Association (see *progressive writing*), later editor in Bombay. He moved from idealism and romanticism towards the critical realist method. His early short stories were not free from idealization of patriarchal village life, but later he criticized the evils of Indian society, entering fully the fight for democracy and against fascism. His first, partly autobiographical novel *Shikast* (Defeat, 1939) depicts the life of the peasants and the efforts of progressive young Indian intellectuals. His later prose reflects the hardships of life in the lower strata of Indian society.

Trans.: *Flame and the Flower* (Bombay 1951). JM

Chandogya-Upaniṣad, see **upaniṣads.**

Chandu Menon, Malayalam novelist, see **Cantu Mēnōn.**

Changampuzha, Malayalam poet, see **Kṛṣṇa Piḷḷa,** Caṅṅampuḻa.

Chatterji, see **Caṭṭopādhyāy.**

Chattopadhyay, Harindranath (b 1898 Hyderabad), Indian author writing in English; his mother tongue is Bengali. Started writing at the age of 8 and by 14 had written many plays. His *Five Plays* (1937) reveal his social consciousness and realism but are too heavily coated with purpose; eg *The Parrot* is dedicated 'to all those whose morality is not a parrot's cage'. Of his historical plays *Siddhartha: Man of Peace* (1956) is the most ambitious, portraying the main events of Buddha's life. Chattopadhyay is now an active leftist politician. MED

Chau Kambet Bantoh, Cambodian folktale, see **Thmenh Chey.**

Chaudhuri, Nirad C. (b 1897 Kishorganj), Indian author writing in English; his mother tongue is Bengali. Educated Calcutta University. Essentially a self-taught man, with almost encyclopaedic knowledge of aspects of European life and history. Journalist, later full-time writer. *The Autobiography of an Unknown Indian* (1951) shows that he is abnormally sensitive to the odour of death and decay. The major theme is the origin and death of the Indian effort to create a modern culture of the humanistic sort on the basis of an East-West cultural synthesis. It is a study of his life and times in Bengal and is now in its second edition having received worldwide acclaim as a prose masterpiece. The two basic co-ordinates of his study of Indian culture are time and space, history and geography. This thesis has special relevance to the problem of the Indian writer in English, though as part of the wider predicament of the westernized minority. He feels himself a European Aryan, enslaved by the tropical snares of the Indian subcontinent. This explains the paradoxes of his Anglophilia, his contempt for the cheaply westernized, and his ambivalence towards British rule in India. Chaudhuri was invited to England for a five-week visit in 1955 and crystallized some of his impressions in *A Passage to England* (1959). *The Continent of Circe* (1965) is a fantastic history of modern India and indology. In 1970 he was working on an account of India since partition and a biography of Max Müller.

K. Raghavendra Rao, *An epitaph for the British Raj* (CEIWE 346–58); DMINE. MED

chāyāvād, the Indian analogue of Romanticism, started in Bengal where R. Tagore (see Ṭhākur) was its leading representative.

In Hindi literature *chāyāvād* flourished from 1920–35, in an atmosphere of national awakening and patriotic movement (Gandhi). It drew inspiration from India's cultural heritage and English Romanticism. Fundamentally individualistic, it began as a kind of emotional revolt against feudal conventions and fetters, the court poetry and Mahāvīr P. Dvivedī's (qv) rationalism and classicism. The main subject of *chāyāvād* poetry was the beauty of Nature, whereby Nature was considered as an animated being, endowed with human emotions, and *Weltschmerz* was the essence of many a lyric poem. The philosophical background was *sarvcetanvād* (Panpsychism), whereas *īśvarvād* (Theism) was the philosophical basis of *rahasyavād* (qv), a mystical and pessimistic trend within the movement. Famous *chāyāvād* poets in Hindi literature were J. Prasād, S. T. Nirālā and S. Pant (qqv). M. Varmā (qv) and Rāmkumār Varmā were mainly *rahasyavād* poets. Not confined to poetry, *chāyāvād* also influenced prose, especially the historical novel and literary criticism. IZ

Chbap Kram and other didactic poetry of Cambodia. The *Chbap Kram* (Rules for Behaviour) and other *Chbap* such as *Chbap Pros* (Rules for Men) were written by Buddhist monks round about the beginning of the 18th century. They are addressed to rich and poor alike and give, in a simple, direct style, without any self-conscious use of clever words or poetic devices, sound and practical advice on social and moral behaviour. Their didactic character is relieved by frequent illustrations from nature or from the everyday life of the peasant, introduced in order to point a moral. This poetry is very dear to Cambodian hearts and is much quoted. JMJ

Chek Sorat, Cambodian novelist, see **pralom-lok.**

Chellappa, C. S., Tamil poet, see **Cellappā,** Ci. Cu.

Chughtāi, 'Iṣmat (b 1915), Urdu writer. Her first work appeared in 1938, and she has continued to write ever since. Her work includes essays, short stories, drama, and three novels, of which the best known is *Ṭeṛhī lakīr* (Crooked Line), the life-story of an Indian Muslim girl. Her best writing, especially in her short stories, is extraordinarily powerful, moving, and unsentimental. RR

Cipaḷūṇkar, Viṣṇuśāstrī (1850–82), Marathi essayist and journalist. The appearance of his periodical *Nibandhamālā* in 1874 is generally taken to mark the emergence of modern Marathi letters from the hesitant and transitional period that followed the impact of the west on traditional literature. He later founded two influential newspapers, *Kesarī* and *Marāṭhā*, which are still extant. IR

cittar (siddhas, the **siddhar,** c10th–14th century), a group of mediaeval Tamil poets. Some of the *cittar* belong to an even later age (17th–18th century), and the *cittar* tradition seems to be alive even today. They can be defined as an esoteric school of mystic poets, connected with the tantric and yogic tradition of Hinduism elsewhere in India (North Indian *siddhācāryas*). The term means 'those who have attained *siddhi*', ie 'occult, miraculous power'. In Tamil literature, the *cittar* line proper begins with Tirumūlar (7th century AD or later) in his *Tirumantiram*, and ends with Tāyumāṉavar (1706–44). Traditionally, the Tamil *cittar* trace their origin to the sage Agastya. Their work is characterized by heterodox, even anti-Brahmanic religious and philosophical views, vital interest in medicine and alchemy, social protest, and the introduction of colloquial speech into poetry. Their verses are often deliberately ambiguous and obscure: only a practising *cittar* yogi should be able to unlock the esoteric meaning. The most important Tamil *cittar* poets were Civavākkiyar, Pattirakiriyar and Paṭṭiṉattār. 527 stanzas are ascribed to Civavākkiyar, probably one of the earliest among Tamil *cittar*. He is the greatest mediaeval rebel against orthodoxy, sacerdotalism, and the Hindu establishment; as a poet, he is powerful, independent, crude and striking. The greatest poet of the school is Paṭṭiṉattār (14th century), the author of *Paṭṭiṉattār Pāṭal* (632 stanzas), the greatest relativist and pessimist of Tamil literature. According to him, life is a tragedy, man the seat of vileness and egoism, and woman the filthy temptress. A mixture of cynicism and pathetic helplessness, of abuse and appeal, is typical of his fierce and forceful stanzas. KZ

Civavākkiyar, mediaeval Tamil poet, see **cittar.**

Cjis (Chit) Maun, Burmese writer, see **Ma Ma Lei,** Djanetjo.

Cuntaram Piḷḷai, Alappuṟai Perumāḷ (1855–1897), Tamil scholar and poet. Professor of Philosophy in the Maharaja's College, Trivandrum, he published works on mediaeval Tamil literature and on the history of Travancore. He is best known for his *Maṉōṉmaṇīyam* (1891), 'a play in Tamil verse, after the Shakespearean model', the plot of which is based on 'The Secret Way', one of Bulwer Lytton's *The Lost Tales of Miletus* (which were themselves written in verse). REA

Cuntarar (9th century), Tamil poet, the third author of *Tevāram,* who composed the last book thereof (ie *Tirumuṟai,* qv, VII). He was a Brahmin from the south Arcot district, who married two women of low caste. He sang of the reciprocal love between God and man and, in an interesting passage, suggests that God does not withhold His grace from His devotees even if they sin. He considered himself as a woman in love with God as her husband. Cuntarar is said to have died at the age of 32.

JHTL 82–5. JRM

Cuppiramaṇiya Aiyar, Varakaṉēri Veṅkaṭēcaṉ (1881–1925), Tamil writer. A fervent opponent of British rule in India, V. V. S. Aiyar (as he is always known) spent ten years in exile in Pondicherry. Under Gandhi's influence he gave up his ideas of violent revolution and became a supporter of *ahiṃsa.* He wrote a number of biographies in Tamil of European revolutionary figures, including Garibaldi, Mazzini and Napoleon. For many critics, however, he is more important in the history of Tamil prose as the first writer of short stories, a collection of which appeared under the title *Maṅkaiyarkkaraciyiṉ kātal* (The Love of Maṅkaiyarkkaraci, 1916?). Among his English writings is a most perceptive study of Kampaṉ's (qv) epic, *Kamba Ramayana. A Study* (Delhi 1950). REA

Cuppurattiṉam, Kaṉaka (pseud. Bharathithasan, b 1891 Pondicherry, d 1964 Madras), Tamil poet, brought up in the French cultural atmosphere. A teacher of Tamil, he was later active in politics and became one of the main ideologists of the Dravidian movement. He wrote many poetical works, from lyrical and epic poems on classical themes and deeply intimate lyrics to radical political songs and propagandist harangues. His best work reveals great talent and independence as well as mastery of diction and form. Main works: *Pāratitācaṉ kavitaikaḷ* (3 vols. of poetry, 1938–55); *Etirpārāta muttam* (Unexpected Kiss, 1938); *Aḻakiṉ cirippu* (Smiles of Beauty, 1940); *Kuṭumpa viḷakku* (The Family Lamp, 1941); *Kātal niṉaivukaḷ* (Thoughts about Love, 1944); *Tamiḻiyakkam* (The Tamil Movement, 1945). KZ

Currimbhoy, Asif (b 1928), Indian playwright writing in English. Educated at Bombay and Berkeley, California. Oil-company executive. First recognized in America. He himself translated his works into Hindi and the regional languages. Works: *The Dol Drummers* (1961), *The Dumb Dancer* (1962), *Om* (1962), *Thorns on a Canvas* (1963), *The Captives* (1963), *Goa* (1964), *The Hungry Ones* (1966). MED

Cuvāmināta Aiyar, U. Vē. (Dr U. V. Swaminath Aiyar, 1855–1942), Tamil editor, philologist, textual and literary critic and writer. Born in an orthodox Brahmin family, he was given a traditional education and became professor of Tamil and Tamil literature (1880), first in Kumabakonam, then at Presidency College, Madras. Together with Damodaram Piḷḷai

(1832–1901), he started the work of editing Tamil classical texts (in Oct. 1880; the first to be published was *Cīvakacintāmaṇi* in 1887), and became thus one of the two 're-discoverers' of the classical literature, and the father of the Tamil renaissance. The last of his great editions was that of *Kuṟuntokai* (1937). Though he was not well-versed in Western-style textual criticism, his editions are extremely careful, with glossaries, various readings, and valuable introductions. His autobiography *En Carittiram* (1940–42 in a journal, 1950 as a book), gives a charming, often naïve, but always engaging picture of the first bloom of Tamil cultural rinascimento. Among other works, *Nāṉ kaṇṭatum kēṭṭatum* (What I Saw and Heard, 1938) makes very pleasant reading.

KZ

D

Dāgh Dihlavī, Navāb Mīrzā Khān (b 1831 Delhi, d 1905 Hyderabad), Urdu poet of love lyrics, pupil of Zauq (qv). Born in an aristocratic family, after 1857 moved from the Delhi Red Fort to the Rampur court and in 1886 to Hyderabad. His erotic poetry, based on his experiences of palace life, reflects the decadent feelings of feudal nobility, emptiness of thought and superficial emotion. His sensitive, smooth and at times frivolous *ghazals* (see Vol. III) are very musical; his use of simple words and current idioms reveals a unique power of artistic diction. He was the last classical court poet of Urdu and the most popular poet of his age.

RSHUL 186–90; MSHUL 206–7. JM

Dagoun Taya, Burmese poet, see **Taya,** Dagoun.

Ḍāhyābhāi, Dalapatram, Gujarati poet, see **arvācin kavitā.**

Dāmle, Kṛṣṇāji Keśav, Marathi poet, see **Keśavsut.**

Dāmodaragupta (8th–9th century AD), minister of king Jayāpīḍa of Kashmir, poet and author of a late *kāvya* (qv) work *Kuṭṭanīmata* (Teaching of a Bawd). It contains instructions imparted by a procuress to a concubine, concerning the acquisition of fortune from a young rich client through the application of the art of erotics. It is a scholarly work which makes abundant use of ornamental poetry and Sanskrit lexicography, and is quoted by later poets (eg Kalhaṇa, qv) as such. Dāmodaragupta treated his topic with pedantic fervour and his influence is evident in later works of the same type, such as Kṣemendra's *Samayamātṛkā* and *Kalāvilāsa* (11th century AD). All such works provide valuable material for the study of cultural and social conditions of their period.

Trans. into German by J. J. Meyer (Leipzig 1903); WHIL III, 169. IF

Damrong, Prince, Thai historian, see **Phongsāwadān** and **Prachum Phongsāwadān.**

Daṇḍin (c650 AD), wrote the *Daśakumāracarita* and, possibly, the *Avantīsundarīkakathā*, only recently discovered. His work on poetics, the *Kāvyādarśa*, runs to about 660 verses. More than 500 of these verses are concerned with figures of speech. The work as we have it is possibly incomplete: at III.71, for example, he speaks of a subject to be treated in the chapter on *kalā*, fine arts. No such chapter exists. Daṇḍin writes in a delightful, simple style and his striking ideas and lovely expressions were much praised by the later tradition. The *Daśakumāracarita* is one of the great prose works in Sanskrit. It is a charmingly irreverent collection of secular tales. Earlier generations condemned the work for its lack of moral judgement; the very quality that today justly endears it to modern readers. This work was also left incomplete.

Trans.: S. K. Belvalkar, *Kāvyādarśa* (Poona 1924); V. V. Sastulu (Madras 1952); A. W. Ryder, *Daśakumāracarita* (Chicago 1927). DHSP I, 57–72; II, 75–88; WHIL III, 388–94. JLM

daptar (record), Baluchi heroic ballads, particularly those regarding the origin of the Baluchi tribes in Arabia, their subsequent migration eastward, their tribal quarrels and divisions, their heroes and deeds of valour. The central subject of others is the 'thirty years' war' led by Mīr Chākar, chief of the Rinds, against Gvārām, leader of the Lasharis, in 1489–1511, or the war between the Rinds and the Dodais (1520–30). The *daptars* were composed by the Baluchi chieftains themselves or by unknown poets attached to their entourages. Their formal structure is more or less fixed. The minstrel starts with an introduction in prose and after the 'heading' containing the praises of God and the Prophet Muhammad he embarks upon the main subject; he concludes with some personal comment or advice to his listeners. The use of rhyme is not strict.

M. L. Dames, *Popular Poetry of the Baloches*, 2 vols. (London 1907). JM

Dārā Shikōh, Muḥammad (b 1615 Ajmer, executed 1658 Delhi), Indo-Persian mystic poet and writer, eldest son of Emperor Shahjahan. He attempted to unite Hinduism and Islam into an abstract monotheistic doctrine. He wrote biographies of both Sūfī and *bhakti* (qv) mystics, books on the ways by which ultimate spiritual fulfilment is achieved. His most important book *Majma u'l-baḥrain* (Mingling of Two Oceans, 1654) is a comparative study of Hinduism and Islam demonstrating their various points of contact. To this end Dārā translated 50 chapters of the *Upaniṣads* (qv) from Sanskrit into simple Persian. His lyric *dīwān* is a typical sample of the Persian poetry written in India during the 17th century.

Trans. and ed.: M. Mahfuz-ul-Haq, *Majma-ul-Bahrain* (Calcutta 1929).
K. R. Qanungo, *Dara Shukoh* (Calcutta 1934); Bikramajit Hasrat, *Dara Shikuh, Life and Works* (Calcutta 1955); HIL 728. JM

darangan, ancient epics of the Maranaos from Mindanao in the Philippines. Some themes can be traced to the *Mahābhārata* and *Rāmāyaṇa* (qqv) or old Malay literature. The best known is *Bantugan*, a story of a conflict between a great warrior, Prince Bantugan, and his envious brother, the king. Another popular *daragan* epic is *Indarapatra and Sulayman*, a long narrative about a mighty emperor and his brother, also a ruler, who use their strength and wisdom to make their people happy and their kingdoms prosperous. Both these epics have been translated into English. Other ethnic groups in the Philippines also preserved their old epics but only some of them have been transcribed or translated. *Hudhud* is an outstanding epic of the Ifugao people. It originated in the pre-Spanish period and in the story of an Ifugao hero, it presents the philosophy of life and the ideals of the Ifugaos and their culture. *Biag ni Lam-ang* (Life of Lam-ang) is an Ilocano epic first transcribed in the middle of the 17th century. It is the story of Lam-ang, born with the power of speech and supernatural abilities that helped him later in his adventures and his struggle to win the hand of a beautiful girl. Numerous epics have been preserved among the Bisayan people. *Maragtas*, a story of ten Malay datus who came from Kalimantan and founded the Confederation of Madya (as in Panay) and *Hinilawod*, so far the longest epic recorded in the Philippines, are the best known. Parts of *Tuwaang* preserved by the Bagobo people and fragments of *Parang Sabil* of the Tawsug people have recently been recorded. EH

Dard, Khvāja Mīr (b 1721 Delhi, where d 1785), Urdu and Persian mystical poet. Son of a mystical poet, Muḥammad Nāṣir 'Andalīb, he early took to the mystical life and succeeded his father in 1758. His order, the ṭarīqa Muḥammadīya, was a fundamentalist offspring of the Naqshbandīya. Dard was a prolific writer in Persian; his prose is beautiful, although his Persian poetry, a number of quatrains, is more traditional. He considered most of his poems as divinely inspired. His fame rests upon the small collection of mystical Urdu poetry which is of exquisite beauty and deeply felt. The afflictions which came over Delhi are echoed in his numerous verses about the instability of everything but the

Divine Essence. His main work is *'Ilmu'l-kitāb* (Knowledge of the Scripture, c1770) and four *risāla* (treatises, between 1772 and 1785).

RSHUL 55–8; MSHUL 101–5. AS

Dāś, Jībanānanda (b 1899 Barisal, d 1954 Calcutta), Bengali poet. Born and raised in East Bengal in a Brahmo family, he received his MA in English at Presidency College and Calcutta University, and studied law for three years. He taught English at several colleges. For a short period, he was an editor of the *Swarāj* newspaper. In 1955 he received posthumously the first Sahitya Akademi award for his book of poetry, *Banalatā Sen.* An obstacle in the progression of Bengali literature, as perceived by the young poets of the 20's and 30's, was the pervasiveness of Tagore's (see Ṭhākur) influence. Jībanānanda is considered the first poet to successfully break free of this Tagorian influence, in his *Dhūsar pāṇḍulipi* (Grey Manuscripts, 1936). His language is simple; he never hesitated to use what was then considered 'unpoetic language'; English words find their way freely and naturally into his Bengali poetry. The individual's (probably his own) concern with time and death, with human love or rejection and deceit, together with images drawn from lush Bengal and also from a somewhat ancient and distant West Asia comprise the substance of much of his earlier poetry. He was considered a romantic and criticized by the Marxists for his lack of social conscience. World War II, independence which brought with it partition of Bengal, and the influx of refugees which followed partition, all affected him, as evidenced in his later poetry. Never extremely popular during his lifetime, Jībanānanda Dāś is now probably the most respected and popular post-Tagore poet in West Bengal; he is becoming more and more popular in Bangladesh. Further books: *Jharā pālak* (Falling Feathers, 1927); *Mahāpṛthibī* (The Great World, 1944); *Sātṭi tārār timir* (The Darkness of Seven Stars, 1948); *Rūpasī Bāṃlā* (Bengal the Beautiful, 1957); *Belā abelā kālbelā* (Time, Un-time and Time Apart, 1961).

Trans.: *Banalata Sen, and Other Poems* (Calcutta 1962); KMBP; BBV.
SMBP; SHBL 371–3. CBS

Dās, Sāralā (14th century), Oriya poet. Farmer by origin, with no Sanskrit education, he composed an Oriyan version of the *Mahābhārata* (qv), introducing many new elements and episodes of native origin and turning the characters of the classical heroes and heroines into Oriyas. The work, told in a simple rustic language, has always been the favourite book of the masses of Orissa.

J. B. Mohanty, *Oriya Literature* (Cuttack 1953). DZ

Dasam Granth, or *Dasveṃ Pādśāh kā Granth* ('The Book of the Tenth King'), a collection of writings of the late 17th and early 18th centuries composed in a number of languages, all recorded in the Gurmukhi script. When the tenth Sikh *gurū*, Gobind Singh (1666–1708), produced the standard revised version of the *Ādi Granth* (qv), he did not include his own works, and the *Dasam Granth* purports to be a collection of these, as compiled after his death by one of his most important followers, Bhāī Manī Singh (d 1738). There is nowadays, however, a consensus of scholarly opinion that much of *Dasam Granth* is not the work of Gurū Gobind Singh himself, but that of poets attached to his court at Ānandpūr in the Sivalik hills, where local traditions of devotion to the goddess Caṇḍī (Kālī, Durgā) are doubtless responsible for the many poems devoted to her. Individual views differ as to precisely which works are to be regarded as the work of Gobind Singh. Much work remains to be done on the text itself and the history of its transmission before definite statements can be made. The contents of the *Dasam Granth*, which are for the most part in verse and some form of Hindi (usually Braj), may be summarized as follows: (i) a group of liturgical texts, which may confidently be attributed to Gurū Gobind Singh, including the prayer known as the *Jāp Sāhib*, and a number of hymns in the form of *savaīe* and *caupaīāṃ*; (ii) the *Akāl Ustat*, a long poem in praise of God; (iii) the *Bacitra Nāṭak*, a Braj poem which purports to be the autobiography of the *gurū*; (iv) a number of poems on different Hindu *avatārs*; (v) three poems on the battles of the goddess Caṇḍī against demons, based on the *Mārkaṇḍeya Purāṇa*, of which two (known as *Caṇḍī Caritra*) are in Hindi, while the third, *Caṇḍī dī Vār*, is the only work in the *Dasam Granth* to be written in pure Panjabi, and is in the form of a traditional Panjabi heroic ode; (vi) the *Zafarnāma*, a short Persian poem in the form of a letter of defiance to the Mughal emperor Aurangzeb, the chief enemy of Gobind Singh; (vii) the *Pakhyān Caritra*, some 400 prose anecdotes about the wiles of women, with which may be grouped the similar *Hikāyats*, written in Persian, and which are generally agreed not to be the work of Gurū Gobind Singh.

SWS 266–75; KSHS, vol. 1, 313–8; MSR. CS

dāstāns, Urdu prose narrative cycles of mediaeval Islamic romance, which assumed their present form perhaps in the 18th century and were transmitted orally by professional reciters until in the second half of the 19th century they were written down at their dictation. Most celebrated is the *Dāstān-e Amīr Ḥamza* (Tale of Amir Hamza), itself consisting of several cycles, in eighteen bulky volumes. It celebrates the legendary exploits of the uncle of the Prophet Muhammad in his battles for the Faith, assisted by his comic sorcerer-companion 'Amar Ayyār. The reciters claimed that their Urdu versions were translations from Persian originals, but most seem certainly to be original compositions.

CNI 106–10. RR

Datta (Dutt), Michael Madhusūdan (b1824 Sagardanri, d 1873 Calcutta), Bengali poet and playwright. Educated in an atmosphere of admiration for European culture, he became a Christian. He was of considerable learning, travelled in France and England, and led a stormy, irregular life filled with errors and extravagances. After attempts to write poetry in English (*The Captive Ladie*, 1848), he introduced a new modern spirit into his Bengali poems and plays, and successfully adapted certain European verse forms, especially the sonnet. His lyrics were subjective in mood, reflective, yet with modern ideas of social progress; they spoke for the revolt of the younger generation against ancient traditions. Although his greatest epic *Meghnādbadh* (The Death of Meghnād, 1861) draws on the *Rāmāyaṇa* (qv) it is informed with the spirit of the modern age; formally significant was the introduction of a new epic line based on that of English blank verse and more malleable than the classical Bengali line. Datta's place in the history of Bengali drama is ensured by his plays of social satire and romantic dramas.

Trans.: *Sermista* (by the author, Calcutta 1859).
SHBL 197–200, 212–24. DZ

Datta (Dutt), Sudhīndranāth (b 1901 Calcutta, where d 1960), Bengali poet and critic. After receiving his BA he studied law and for an MA in English at Calcutta University. He was associated with the literary magazine, *Sabuj patra*, and with the newspaper, *Forward.* He accompanied Tagore in Japan and the United States, 1929, and visited Europe several times. He founded and edited the literary journal, *Paricay* (see Bandyopādhyāy), and taught comparative literature, Jadavpur University, Calcutta. Sudhīn was by birth and by choice an aristocrat. He professed to be a materialist but not a Marxist. His vocabulary is Sanskritic, even archaic at times; he played with old words and coined new ones. And because he used it, the Bengali language is richer today. Some books: *Orchestra* (1935); *Saṃbarta* (Cataclysmic Clouds, 1953); *Kulāy o kālpuruṣ* (The Abode and Orion, 1957).

Trans.: *The World of Twilight* (Calcutta 1970); KMBP; BBV.
SMBP; SHBL 374. CBS

Daulat Kāzi, Bengali poet, see **Ālāol.**

Davé, Haribhadra, Gujarati poet, see **arvācin kavitā.**

Davé, Narmadaśaṅkar, Gujarati poet, see **arvācin kavitā.**

Dayārām, Gujarati poet, see **pada.**

De, Biṣṇu (b 1909 Calcutta), Bengali poet. He received MA in English, Calcutta University. He was associated with *Paricay* magazine (see Bandyopādhyāy) from its inception, and helped found and edit the literary quarterly, *Sāhitya patra.* In 1965, he received the Sahitya Akademi award for his book of poetry, *Smṛti sattā bhabiṣyat* (Remembrance, Reality, the Future). He retired as Professor of English, Maulana Azad College, Calcutta, in 1969. Biṣṇu De, an excellent poet and critic, is extremely well read in both Western and Indian literatures, classical and modern, and uses these literary traditions in his own creations. He has moved from a romantic writer of love lyrics to a poet who views the world in Marxist terms. He continues to write poetry and probably has the greatest influence of any of the senior poets on the younger Bengali writers of today. Some books: *Urbaśī o Ārṭemis* (Urvaśī and Artemis, 1933); *Sāhityer bhabiṣyat* (The Future of Literature, 1952); *Sei andhakār cāi* (I Want That Darkness, 1966).

Trans.: KMBP; BBV.
SMBP; SHBL 374–4. CBS

Desāi, Jhiṇābhāi, Gujarati poet, see **arvācin kavitā.**

Desāi, R. V., Gujarati writer, see **navalkathā.**

Dev, Malayalam writer, see **Kēśava Dēv.**

Deval, Govind Ballāḷ (1855–1916), Marathi dramatist. Author of seven plays that are mainly adaptations of Sanskrit or English originals, but one *Śāradā* (1899) has a social-reformist theme that had immense appeal and influence in its time. IR

Dēvara Dāsimayya, Kannada poet, see **vacana.**

Devarakṣita Jayabāhu Dharmakirti (14th–15th centuries), Sinhalese monk who lived at Gaḍalādeniya near Kandy, and conducted the Ordinations of 1396 as *sangharāja* ('King of the Monks'). Besides a Sinhalese work on Pāli grammar, he wrote *Nikāyasangrahaya* (finished in 1390), a history of the Buddhist monastic order in Ceylon, and *Saddharmālaṃkāraya*, a prose translation of a book of Pāli stories, Vedeha's *Rasavāhinī*, which contains lengthy semi-historical accounts of early Ceylon history.

Trans.: C. M. Fernando, *The Nikaya Sangrahawa* (Colombo 1908). CHBR

Devkoṭā, Lakṣmī Prasād (b 1909 Kathmandu, d 1959), one of the best known and most popular modern Nepali writers. His father, also a poet and scholar, greatly encouraged his first attempts at writing poetry. After studying for his BA degree, he was appointed lecturer at Trichandra College in Kathmandu. In 1947, he left Nepal with a group of young men whose aim was to overthrow the Rāṇā régime and in Benares edited the revolutionary newspaper, *Yugvāṇī.* When he finally returned to Nepal, his works were already popular. In 1951 he became Minister of Education and it was largely through his efforts that Nepali became the only medium of instruction throughout the whole of the country. As well as being the first Nepali epic-poet (*mahākavi*), he also wrote short stories, novels and plays. In his famous poem, *Munā-Madan*, he made use of the native *jyāuṛe* metre. He is also said to have composed poetry in other languages, including Newari. DJM

Dhammapada, see **Dharmapada.**

Dhammarāja, Sri (first half of the 18th century), Cambodian monarch, renowned both as a poet and as a man of letters. A religious poem by him, written on an inscription of 1701 AD, is the earliest known dated poem in Cambodian. His poetry was mainly lyrical, the chief themes being his love for a young cousin whom he could never marry and descriptions of nature.

Other members of the royal family, both male and female, wrote poetry about love and nature during his reign and from then on into the 19th century. JMJ

Dhanañjaya, Indian writer on dramaturgy, see **alaṃkāraśāstra.**

Dhanika, Indian writer on dramaturgy, see **alaṃkāraśāstra.**

Dharmapada (Pāli, **Dhammapada**), one of the shorter of the canonical or paracanonical texts of the Buddhist schools of the Lesser Vehicle (see *Tripiṭaka*). In the Pāli canon, it is one of the texts included in the *Khuddaka-nikāya* of the *Sutta-piṭaka.* In the Sarvāstivādin school, its counterpart is the Sanskrit *Udānavarga,* which, in spite of its name, is not connected with the Pāli *Udāna.* In addition to these, a manuscript of a different recension, in the north-west Prakrit (Gāndhārī) written in the Kharoṣṭhī script, was discovered in 1892 near Khotan in Chinese Turkistan. Of this latter, approximately three-eighths of the text has been lost. It is not known to which school this recension belonged. The recension of the Mahāsāṅghika school is known only from two sections (*varga*) and a few isolated verses quoted in the *Mahāvastu* (qv). The earliest Chinese version, translated in 224 AD, contains as its nucleus a recension almost identical with the Pāli *Dhammapada,* but has 13 additional chapters, some from the *Udānavarga,* and others from another text as yet unidentified, but in all probability the *Dharmapada* of yet another school. Apart from the complete canon of the Theravāda school, only portions (in some cases, mere fragments) of the canons of other schools of the Lesser Vehicle survive. It is thus possible that some of these numerous schools (traditionally 18 in number) possessed still other different *Dharmapada*-recensions.

The contents of the versions known to us are all similar in nature. They are collections of ethical and gnomic verses, grouped in chapters (*varga,* Pāli *vagga*) bearing ethical or descriptive titles, for example, *yamaka* 'twinned verses', *apramāda* 'vigilance', *pāpa* 'sin', *tṛṣṇā* 'worldly desire', *jarā* 'old age', *puṣpa* 'flowers', and so forth. What is striking, however, is the fact that the surviving recensions, while having a large number of verses and *varga*-titles in common, show great differences in length, in the inclusion or exclusion of many verses, in the order of arrangement even of the verses and *vargas* which they share, while the same verse is frequently placed under different *varga*-titles in different recensions. The Pāli *Dhammapada* has 423 verses, in 26 *vaggas*; there are good grounds for assuming that the Gāndhārī Prakrit text had approximately 540 verses, also in 26 sections; while the *Udānavarga* has over 1,000 verses, in 33 *vargas.* In view of all these differences, it is impossible to reconstruct a 'primitive *Dharmapada*' which might have been the common source of the known versions. It is equally certain that the Pāli *Dhammapada* has no claim to be the original text. In spite of the high and sometimes extravagant praise which the Pāli version has sometimes received, the poetical quality, as one might expect in didactic verses, is for the most part mediocre, with only an occasional stanza of real poetic merit.

Numerous translations of the Pāli *Dhammapada* in the main Western languages: convenient is that by S. Radhakrishnan, Oxford, 1950 (which to a large extent is pieced together from earlier English translations); *Udānavarga,* ed. F. Bernhard (Göttingen 1965, 1968); *The Gāndhārī Dharmapada,* ed. J. Brough (Oxford 1962). See the Introduction to this last for a more detailed discussion of the problems involved. IB

dharmaśāstra (300 BC–500 AD), Indian sacred treatise. This Sanskrit term refers to the science of the Hindu sacred law; it is to be compared with the sciences of the three other Hindu goals in life—*artha, kāma* and *mokṣa.* More particularly, the term denotes texts, composed for the most part in the *śloka* (qv) metre (*anuṣṭubh*), dealing with Hindu religious and social law. These texts are based in part upon the *dharmasūtras,* prose texts of an earlier period, as well as upon the general oral tradition of scriptural exegesis. Each authority disputes the views of several antecedent jurists, many of them otherwise unknown to us, and as the law continued to be expanded in this way, *dharmaśāstra* texts are difficult to date. Some include the laws of behaviour of the king (*rājadharma*) and rules for the performance of rituals. Most important, however, are the discussions of the *varṇāśramadharma*, the rules for the four classes (priest, warrior, merchant, and servant) and the four stages of life (student, householder, forest-dweller, and ascetic). See also *smṛti*. WOF

Dharmasena, Sinhalese monk who translated the 300 stories of the Pāli Commentary to the *Dharmapada* (qv) into Sinhalese prose in the mid-13th century. The style is a remarkable mixture of literary and colloquial features, which remains unique. It is especially noteworthy for similes and for punning treatment of words. CHBR

Dharta, A. S. (b 1924 Java), Indonesian poet. Leaving secondary school he worked in the youth organization, later becoming head of the information department of SOBSI (central trade union organization) and General Secretary of the progressive cultural organization LEKRA. He also uses the pseudonym Klara Akustia. The whole of his poetry is dedicated to the Indonesian working class movement and their struggle against colonialism. It is marked by profound feeling, a wealth of verbal invention and melodious verse. Chief work: *Rangsang Detik* (Exciting Moments, 1957). MO

Ḍholā-Mārū rā Dūhā, an ancient ballad in Old Western Rajasthani (OWR) which must have its origin in Marwar, but which is known under various forms all over north-western India. The *dūhā* or *dōhā* (couplet) is a very popular metrical form which OWR inherited from Apabhraṃśa. The *Ḍholā-Mārū* is a remarkable specimen of ancient folk-literature, in which the freshness and simplicity of style enhances the charm of a naïve legend. To bring back to his city, Narvar, his young bride Māruṇī or 'Mārū', to whom he was betrothed in infancy and who is waiting for him in the far-away, desert Pūgal, the hero, Prince 'Ḍholā', must overcome the stubborn resistance, wily tricks and supplications of his second wife, the proud Princess Mālvāṇī. Escaping from Narvar under cover of night, he crosses the Āṛāvalli mountains and the whole desert land of Marwar in a single day, mounted on his fast-running and wise camel. Vivid dialogues and short but suggestive descriptions of old Marwar alternate with pathetic songs on the theme of *viraha*, the torment of separation of a loving wife away from her spouse, which increases with the coming of the rains. Faithful love wins, and the hero and heroine, after surmounting terrible dangers, happily reach Narvar. This romantic ballad (with its evidently plebeian, rural background) is also a kind of hymn to Marwar. Māruṇī's victory is the victory of Marwar, a harsh, desert land, which prides itself above all on the radiant beauty and supreme charm of its gay, brilliantly clad women. Besides the ancient *dūhā* version, there are several other forms of the legend, one of them being composed mostly in prose: the *Ḍholā-Mārū ri Vāt* by Kallol (1620 AD).

K. M. Munshi, *Gujarāt and its Literature* (Bombay [2]1954); Verrier-Elwin, *Folk-songs of Chattisgarth* (Oxford 1946); C. Vaudeville, *Les Dūhā de Ḍholā-Mārū, une ancienne ballade du Rājasthān*, traduction (française) et notes (Pondichery 1962). CV

dhvani ('suggestion' or 'implied meaning') refers to the Indian theory that was first propounded in the celebrated *Dhvanyāloka* (*Kāvyāloka*) of Ānandavardhana, a Kashmiri literary critic who lived in the 9th century AD. The Indian tradition holds, and most modern scholars would agree, that this is the single greatest work on literary citicism in Sanskrit. It consists of four chapters. Each chapter contains *kārikās* (verses) with a *vṛtti* (prose explanation). The whole work contains about 115 *kārikās*. It is possible that the *kārikās* are not by Ānanda and may predate him slightly. Ānanda's theory, which he elaborates in great detail, quoting and carefully analysing a large number of Sanskrit verses, is that beside the denotative and secondary function of the words, there is a third power, which he calls *vyañjanā* (suggestivity), an element of language not previously recognized. It is through this function that one reaches the suggested meaning of a poem, so different from the 'literal' meaning. Ānanda develops three main types of suggestion:

vastudhvani, where a situation is suggested. An example of this is where a lonely wife indicates to a traveller that she is willing to spend the night with him. The second variety is where a figure of speech is suggested. The third variety, and the real heart of Ānanda's theory, is called *rasadhvani*. This is when an emotion, or an imaginative experience (*rasa*) is suggested in a poem. A successful poem awakens the sensitive reader (*sahṛdaya*) to the beauty of love without being too obvious or crude, without directly naming the emotion (*svaśabdavācya*).

By emphasizing that the central concern of literary criticism ought not to consist of mere grammatical analysis or acquiring proficiency in recognizing and categorizing figures of speech, Ānanda infused a discipline that was beginning, in its increasing preciosity, to turn away from the broader issues of literary criticism, with a fresh and vital approach. The later tradition recognized his greatness and very few authors dared to ignore the new dimensions Ānanda brought to criticism. Ānanda's theory is carefully elaborated in lucid and lively Sanskrit. One senses immediately that one is in the presence of a creative mind whose deliberations are of importance to all literary critics. But it is not only the precision of the thinking that appeals to us; the beauty of the language and the profundity of the insights compel attention.

Trans.: K. Krishnamoorthy (Poona 1956); a new translation of the *Dhvanyāloka* and Abhinavagupta's commentary by J. L. Masson is to appear in the Harvard Oriental Series.
DHSP I, 101–10; II, 139–75. JLM

Dignāga, Indian Buddhist logician, see **Bhartṛhari** (1).

Dik Keam, Cambodian writer, see **pralomlok.**

Dinkar (Rāmdhārīsinh, b 1908 Simaria), Hindi poet and critic. He started writing when *chāyāvād* (qv) was declining and *pragativād* (qv) rising. Both movements left their mark on his works: *Reṇukā* (1935), *Miṭṭī kī or* (Towards the Earth, 1946), *Dillī* (1955), *Ātmā kī ā̃khẽ* (Eyes of the Soul, 1964), *Sāhityamukhī* (On Literature, 1968), etc. *Kurukṣetra* (1946) and *Urvaśī* (1961, Nirālā Award) are masterpieces of epic poetry. They are based on themes of ancient Indian literature, such as man's moral attitude towards war (*Kurukṣetra*) and his conflicts in love (*Urvaśī*), but Dinkar treats them in the light of contemporary Indian thought.

Trans.: R. K. Kapur, *Kurukshetra* (London 1967); V. Gokak, *Voice of the Himalaya* (London 1967). IZ

Dipavaṃsa (Island's Chronicle, c4th–5th century AD), oldest known history of Ceylon in Pāli verses (interspersed with prose). *Dīpavaṃsa* is an unskilled attempt of anonymous Sinhalese authors to bring together old traditions in an epic relating the island's history up to the time of king Mahāsīha (4th century AD). It abounds in grammatical and stylistic errors and an uncritical approach to diverse traditions but, nevertheless, it preserved a bulk of valuable material which could be critically rearranged and historically appraised in *Mahāvaṃsa* (The Great Chronicle) of Mahānāma, a learned monk who compiled his work during the reign of king Dhātusena (beginning of 6th century AD). *Mahāvaṃsa* is written in polished Pāli verse, inspired by Sanskrit court epics, and it became the primary source for later Pāli and Sinhalese chronicles of the island, its prominent monasteries and places of pious interest. The original version consisting of 37 chapters has been extended by later additions.

Trans.: *The Dīpavaṃsa*, H. Oldenberg (London 1879), *The Mahāvaṃsa*, W. Geiger (PTS 1912), *The Cūlavaṃsa* (continuation of the preceding work), W. Geiger and M. Bode, 2 vols. (PTS 1929–30).
WHIL II, 210–8. IF

Divaṭia, Narasiṃharāo, Gujarati poet, see **arvācin kavitā.**

Divyāvadāna (Divine *avadāna*), collection of

Sanskrit *avadānas* (qv). Many of the tales are taken from the *Vinaya* of the Mūlasarvāstivādins, and may thus be dated c4th century AD. The redaction of these, together with other stories, into a single collection under the title *Divyāvadāna*, is probably many centuries later. It is composed of varied materials, and neither the language nor the style have been unified. Its primary value lies in those legend motifs which were lost elsewhere. *Divyāvadāna* contains some very popular legends, eg the story of Prince Kuṇāla, the Buddha's compassionate disciple and son of Emperor Aśoka, who lost his eyesight and regained it by the sheer power of his virtues. This '*Aśokāvadāna*' is preserved as a separate text in two Chinese versions.

WHIL II, 284–90; J. Przyluski, *La légende de l'empereur Açoka* (Paris 1923). IF

dīwān, collection of poems, see Vol. III.

Djanetjo Ma Ma Lei, Burmese writer, see **Ma Ma Lei,** Djanetjo.

Dñyāndev, Marathi poet, see **Jñāneśvar.**

Doan-thi-Diem (b 1705 Hien-pham, Bacninh province, d 1748), talented Vietnamese poetess, of an educated family; she took care of her mother, refusing all offers of marriage, until 37. Then she married an official who shortly afterwards led a mission to China; during this time (1743–5) she produced her most important work, the lyrical *Chinh phu ngam* (Lament of a Soldier's Wife), a translation into Vietnamese (written in *chu nom*, see *truyen*) of a poem composed 1741–42 in Chinese by Dang-tran-Con. The poem is the lament of a woman whose husband has left for the wars in troubled times. Its wealth of imagery and perfection of form make it a major work of classical Vietnamese literature, while the language is close to the vernacular. The 312 strophes comprise quatrains of 7,7,6 and 8-syllable lines (see *luc bat*).

DNILVN 84, 185. VV

dohā, verse form, see **Ḍholā-Mārū rā Dūhā.**

Dọkmai Sot (pseudonym of Mom Lūong Bubphā Nimmānhemint, b 1906 Bangkok, d 1962), Thai writer. Of a well-to-do family, she was educated in a French convent and then married. She wrote most of her novels between 1929–40, dealing mainly with upper class women in urban surroundings. Her outlook is conservative and therefore she criticizes the modern way of life, under Western influence, which clashes with the old Thai tradition. Her main theme is love, seen in a romantic but nevertheless psychologically perceptive way. Her style is elaborate and refined, and the atmosphere of the stories cheerful and bright; this perhaps explains why her books appeal so much to the Thai reading public. Some of her main works are *Khwām phit khrang rāēk* (The First Mistake, 1930), *Kam Kau* (The Old Karma, 1935), *Nī lae lōk* (This is Our World, 1935) and *Phū dī* (The Nobles, 1937).

Trans.: *The Good Citizen*, in: *SPAN, an Adventure in Asian and Australian Writing* (Melbourne 1958). US

Dong-Ho, Vietnamese poet, see **The-Lu.**

Drama in English (India). Modern Indian dramatic writing in English is neither rich in quality or quantity as the natural medium of conversation is the mother tongue and it is difficult to make a dialogue between Indians in English sound convincing. The modern Indian theatre stems directly from the West. By the time it was introduced the hold of Sanskrit over all literature was broken. The growth of modern drama has of necessity been a provincial concern.

MED

dūhā, verse form, see **Ḍholā-Mārū rā Dūhā.**

Durrak, Jām (b mid-17th century, d 1706 Kalat), founder of Baluchi lyric poetry. He lived at the court of Naṣīr Khān, Emir of Kalat, who persecuted him because of his amorous adventures with the harem ladies. Durrak introduced art poetry into Baluchi literature which consisted up to that time only of folk ballads and romances. Taking over the formal structure of the Persian lyric, he wrote melodious love *ghazals* (see Vol. III) rooted in his deep emotional experience. He used a simple colloquial language with popular expressions. His poetry was therefore very popular among the common people.

ABSLP 311–2. JM

Dutt, see **Datta.**

Dvivedi, Mahāvīrprasād (b 1864 Daulatpur, d 1938), Hindi writer. He served as a railway-employee, ultimately head clerk to the District Traffic Superintendent in Jhansi. From 1903 to 1920 he was editor of the literary journal *Sarasvatī*. After his retirement he became headman of his native village. Through his critical writings he established the standard prose of modern Hindi. He encouraged poets to abandon the traditional Braj Bhāṣā and to write in Hindi. Pointing out the ideals of modern Hindi nationalism he became a source of inspiration to many writers and poets.

R. A. Dvivedi, *A Critical Survey of Hindi Literature* (Delhi 1966). PG

E

Eṭṭuttokai (The Eight Anthologies), with *Pattuppāṭṭu* (qv) forms the corpus of classical Tamil poetry. The poems of *Eṭṭuttokai* range in length from short lyrical stanzas of 3 lines to narrative poems of several decades of verses (in *Kalittokai*). The poems are ascribed to a great number of different authors; since the language, diction and style, as well as the prosody and rhetoric are highly conventionalized, it is almost impossible to distinguish individual authors. However, traditionally, and with some justification, the poets Kapilar, Paraṇar and Nakkīrar (qv) are considered to be the most outstanding. Individual poems were anthologized into *tokais* (collections) some time in the middle of the 8th century AD if not later, and compiled into the great corpus of *Eṭṭuttokai* some time before the 13th–14th century AD. The absolute majority of the poems, however, is much earlier: internal and external evidence points to 1st century BC–3rd century AD for individual poems.

The poetry with its highly uniform, conventionalized language, style and subject matter has the characteristic features of bardic songs composed for the appreciation of fairly sophisticated listeners of the ruling aristocracy of Tamilnad. However, it is entirely secular, and deals with the total experience of man in a world which was perceived and conceived as divided between two (and only two) spheres of activities: making love, and fighting wars. Hence, the entire subject-matter (*poruḷ*) of poetry is divided into the main genres, *akam* (erotic poetry) and *puṟam* (war-poetry). In fact, the themes covered by these two terms are broader: the *akam* genre deals with many aspects of man's private, domestic life, above all with all phases and situations of love, including premarital, wedded and extramarital love; the *puṟam* poems describe not only all possible phases of warfare, but also public affairs and political life. Love, as conventionalized in this poetry, may be illmatched (*peruntiṇai* or 'mismatched' love and *kaikkiḷai* or 'one-sided affair') or wellmatched. In the latter case, love should be described within the framework of five physiographic regions (*ain tiṇṇai*), five 'landscapes' corresponding to five phases of love: *pālai* dealing with elopement and search for the girl, *kuṟiñci* dealing with (first) union of lovers, *mullai*, separation and patient waiting, *marutam*, infidelity, and *neytal*, anxious waiting. The heroes of love-poetry are fully anonymous and typified; in contrast, the heroes of the *puṟam* genre are frequently individualized as concrete, historical and quasi-historical persons. About a quarter of the total corpus are war-poems, about three quarters deal with love.

The following anthologies (in possible chronological order) belong to *Eṭṭuttokai:* (i) *Aiṅkuṟunūṟu*, '(The collection of) five hundred short (poems)', having 3–6 lines each, ascribed to five poets, and dealing with well-matched love. (ii) *Kuṟuntokai*, 'The collection of short (poems)', 400 stanzas ascribed to 205 bards, ranging from 4–8 lines, on well-matched love. (iii) *Naṟṟiṇai*, '(The collection of poems) on excellent *tiṇais*', 400 songs ranging from 8–13 lines on well-matched love. (iv) *Patiṟṟuppattu*, 'Ten Tens', a collection of panegyric poems in praise of the kings of the Cēra dynasty of Kerala. The 1st and the 10th decades are lost. (v) *Akanāṉūṟu*, 'The four hundred (poems) in the *akam* genre', also called *Neṭuntokai*, 'The collection of long (poems), 400 stanzas on well-matched love, ranging from 13–31 lines. (vi) *Puranāṉūṟu*, 'The four hundred (poems) in the *puṟam* genre', containing stanzas of different age on heroic themes, historically very valuable. (vii) *Paripāṭal*, a late classical collection, partly traditional love-poetry and partly *bhakti* (qv) poems dedicated to the gods Tirumāl and Cevvēl, and to the river Vaikai. Of the original 70 poems in the *paripāṭal* metre, 24 are extant in full. (viii) *Kalittokai*, 'The anthology in the *kali* metre', a late classical collection of 150 narrative and lyrical love-songs, dealing with well-matched and ill-matched love situations. A rather late legend, for the first time fully developed in Nakkīrar's commentary (650–750 AD) to *Iṛaiyaṉar Akapporuḷ*, ascribes the majority of classical Tamil poetry to a body of poets assembled in three 'academies' or 'colleges' (*caṅkam*), particularly to the Third Academy in Madurai. It seems that in the 5th century AD there indeed existed a 'college' of Tamil poets and critics under royal patronage in Madurai, and later some facts were mixed with much fiction, until in the age of commentators the legend of the 'Academies' received its final shape. From the purely literary point of view and as a part of the universal cultural heritage, many of the 2,381 classical Tamil poems reached the summit of excellence of Indian literature; they are definitely the best ever produced in Tamil creative writing.

Trans.: A. K. Ramanujan, *The Interior Landscape* (Bloomington 1967, the best translation of Tamil love-poetry into English).
K. Kailasapathy, *Tamil Heroic Poetry* (London 1968); Xavier S. Thani Nayagam, *Landscape and Poetry* (Bombay 1965). KZ

Ezekiel, Nizzim. (b 1921 Bombay), Indian poet writing in English. Lived in England 1948–52 where he obtained his MA. Editor of *Quest* 1955–57. Associate editor of *Imprint* 1960–67. Art critic of the *Times of India*, 1964–66. Visiting Professor, Leeds University 1964. He lectured in America 1967 and is represented in *New Poems* (1963, 1965) and in *Commonwealth Verse* (1965). He now concentrates on teaching and editing *Poetry India*, a quarterly journal which started in 1966. This has a section for poetry written originally in English. His first book of poetry was *A Time to Change* (1951), followed by *Sixty Poems* (1953), *The Third* (1959), *The Unfinished Man* (1960), and *The Exact Name* (1965). He contributed to *Indian Writers in Conference* (1963) and *Writing in India* (1965). His purpose in writing is to make a harmony out of existence. The recurrent note in his most recent poems is the hurt that urban civilization inflicts on modern man, deadening his sensibilities and dehumanizing him. The central metaphor in many poems is that of a departure, journey, sea-voyage or venture. There is a pictorial development in his verse. He has been influenced by T. S. Eliot and W. H. Auden.

M. Garman, *Nizzim Ezekiel—pilgrimage and myth* (CEIWE 106–22); IWE 370–403. MED

Ezhutchachan, Malayalam poet, see **Tuñcatt' Eẓuttacchan,** Rāmānujan.

F

Faiż Aḥmad Faiż (b 1912 Sialkot), Urdu lyric poet, Lenin Prize winner. He studied in Lahore, then lectured at Amritsar, took part in the Indian labour movement and during the war served in the Indian Army as information officer; later he edited the *Pakistan Times* and *Emrōz*, but was imprisoned on political charges. As a poet with an introspective romantic bent of mind and a keen poetic sensibility he writes love *ghazals* (see Vol. III) of traditional format and poems in more modern style. His suggestive poetry is mellow in tone and intimate in nature; it is distinguished by sincerity and seriousness of thought. Prison made him long for freedom and affirmed his faith in a better future; his verse started to draw new strength from his harsh personal experience and express his determination to fight for independence and democracy. He uses the traditional metres but sometimes abandons the old flexible system of conventional symbolic images in order to express his revolutionary ideas more precisely. His volumes *Naqsh-e faryādī* (Lamentations, 1943) and *Dast-e ṣabā* (Fingers of Breeze, 1952) contain the finest and most popular Urdu poetry of recent years.

Trans.: V. G. Kiernan, *Poems by Faiz* (Lahore 1962, Leiden 1970). JM

Faiżi, Shaikh Abū'l-Faiż (b 1547 Agra, where d 1595), Indo-Persian poet. A courtier, tolerant in religion, diplomat and poet-laureate of the Emperor Akbar, elder brother of his famous minister Abū'l-Fażl. He headed the imperial translating office and edited many Persian versions of Sanskrit literary works. He re-wrote the story of King Nala and Princess Damayantī from the *Mahābhārata* (see *Nalopākhyāna*) in the form of a Persian *maṣnavī* (see Vol. III) *Nal Daman*. In his *dīwān* he kept to the older more simple poetical style, in his love *ghazals* he followed Hāfiẓ (see Vol. III). His poetry represents a synthesis of the Iranian and Indian poetical traditions.

HIL 465, 724. JM

Fakirmohan Senāpati, Oriya novelist, see **Senāpati,** Fakīrmohan.

Farid, Panjabi poet, see **Ghulām Farid.**

Farid (d 1552), Panjabi poet, whose verse is preserved in the *Ādi Granth* (qv). The view that this verse was the work of the great Chishtī saint, Śaikh Farīd al-dīn Śakarganj (1175–1265), is now discredited, and it is attributed to his eponymous descendant and successor as head of the family shrine at Pākpaṭan, Śaikh Ibrāhīm Farīd II, who was a contemporary of Nānak, the first Sikh *gurū*; anecdotes in the *janamsākhīs* (qv) suggest that the two may have met. The 130 *śloks* and 4 hymns attributed to Farīd in the *Ādi Granth* constitute the most important Muslim contribution to the Sikh scriptures, and are of great interest as the oldest extant examples of Muslim Panjabi verse. The *ślok* (couplet) is too short a form to allow the expression of very complex thought, and the majority of those by Farīd are somewhat gloomy pictures of the transitory nature of youth and worldly success, and exhortations to trust only in God, although some are enlivened by their vivid natural imagery.

Trans.: Maqbool Elahi, *Couplets of Baba Farīd* (Lahore 1967).
RKPSP 1–12; MSR, vol. 6, 356–414. CS

Fayyāżi, Indo-Persian poet, see **Faiżi,** Shaikh Abū'l-Faiż.

Fazal Śāh, Panjabi poet, see **Hāśam Śāh.**

Fāżil, Maulānā Muḥammad (19th century), Baluchi writer, theologian and social reformer. He founded a *madrasa* (Islamic religious school) at Durkhan and waged there a literary crusade against the influence of British missionaries and the European way of life. He organized a group of patriotic writers, poets, critics and preachers and published over 600 Islamic books in Baluchi, which he made a written language. JM

Firāq Gŏrakhpurī (real name Raghupati Sahāy, b 1896 Gorakhpur), Urdu lyric poet. He was jailed early for support of the Indian freedom movement; then he served as Under-Secretary in the Indian National Congress and later taught at Allahabad University. He is a master of the Urdu *ghazal* (see Vol. III) and quatrain; his early poetry reflects his nationalist and revolutionary feelings. In his numerous volumes of lyrics, eg *Ramz-o-kināyāt* (Mysteries and Metaphors, 1947), he fills the traditional *ghazal* form with novel ideas on women, love and beauty; he sings of a woman who enjoys equal rights with men. His erotic quatrains *Rūp* (Shapes, 1947) are a synthesis of Western and Islamic culture and of ancient Hindu and Buddhist motifs. They enriched Urdu from Sanskrit. JM

G

Gāḍgīḷ, Gangādhar Gopāl (b 1923), the leading Marathi short-story writer of the post-war era. Doyen of the 'new short-story' he has published many collections including *Kabutareṃ* (Doves, 1952), *Taḷāv-ātīl cāndaṇeṃ* (Moonlight on the Lake, 1954). A few of his stories have been translated into English.

Trans.: I. Raeside, *The Rough and the Smooth* (Bombay 1966). IR

Gaḍkari, Rām Ganeś (1885–1919), Marathi playwright (especially *Ekac pyālā*, Just One More Glass, 1917) and lyric poet under the pen-name of Govindāgraj. A short selection of his poems have been translated into English. IR

Trans.: S. and S. Namjoshi, *Poems of Govindagraj* (Calcutta 1968).

Gaṇḍavyūha, ancient Indian novel, see **Buddhist literature.**

Gaṅgeśa (13th century AD), Indian logician, author of the *Tattva-cintāmaṇi.* This work marked the beginning of a new critical approach to the doctrines of the Nyāya school of philosophy, and was followed by numerous commentaries and sub-commentaries as well as original works by later authors. This school, known as the Navya-Nyāya ('the New Logic'), flourished in Mithila and Bengal until about the 18th century, and produced many important philosophers, among whom Raghunātha Śiromaṇi (*floruit* early 16th century) deserves special mention. The Navya-Nyāya has been stigmatized as 'scholasticism of the worst description' (A. B. Keith); but this is a mistaken judgement. In reality, the contribution of the New School was of outstanding philosophical significance. It developed a new technical Sanskrit apparatus which, though at first sight extremely complex and cumbersome, represents an effort to formalize the expression of philosophical concepts in a rigorous and unambiguous terminology. In many ways, Navya-Nyāya can be compared with the development of modern Western symbolic logic in the 19th and 20th centuries, and did in fact discover several important theorems of logic some centuries before they were known in Europe.

D. H. H. Ingalls, *Materials for the study of Navya-Nyāya logic* (HOS 40, 1951); B. K. Matilal, *The Navya-Nyāya doctrine of negation* (HOS 46, 1968). JB

Gaṅgopādhyāy (Ganguli), Nārāyan (b 1918 Baliadangi, d 1970 Calcutta), Bengali writer, literary historian and critic. He came of a country family and studied in Calcutta. After teaching at secondary schools he became Reader of Bengali Literature at Calcutta University. Beginning with short prose forms, Nārāyaṇ went on to write novellas and novels. The earlier short pieces were mostly drawn from a rural environment and were marked by uncompromising criticism of superstition and backwardness, and of the repressive policy of the British colonial authorities. After India gained independence he turned more to city life for his themes, to the lower middle class and their problems. His work betrays a passionate concern for human suffering and the vain struggle to resist unbearable conditions and pressures. His favourite theme is the suffering caused by the division of Bengal in 1947, and the refugees from East Pakistan. Chief works: *Śreṣṭha galpa* (Best Tales, 1952); novels *Upanibeś* (Colony, 1943); *Śilalipi* (Writing on the Rock, 1949); *Nīl diganta* (Blue Horizons, 1958); *Megher upar prāsād* (Castles in the Air, 1963). DZ

G͟hālib, Mirzā Asadullāh K͟hān (b 1797 Agra, d 1869 Delhi), Urdu and Persian poet and writer. He moved to Delhi in his teens, and apart from a journey to Calcutta in 1827–29 lived there almost continuously for the rest of his life. He began writing Urdu and Persian verse in his childhood, and compiled his first Urdu collection in 1821; but for the next 30 years or so he wrote almost wholly in Persian. His Persian prose is in the poetic, rhythmical, rhyming idiom prevalent in his day, but this does not impair its power and effectiveness. His Persian letters, published as a model to others, are his best and most interesting prose work of this period. In 1850 he gained regular access to the court of the last Mughal king, Bahādur Shāh Ẓafar (qv), and was commissioned to write a Persian prose history of the Mughal dynasty; but only the first part of this was ever completed. The later Mughals favoured Urdu as the medium of poetry, and under Ẓafar's patronage Ghālib wrote much of his best Urdu verse. In 1857 came the great revolt initiated by the sepoy mutiny. The rebel sepoys occupied Delhi in May and held it until September, when it was retaken by the British, under whose renewed occupation its citizens experienced long-continued hardship and distress. Ghālib was there throughout, and a Persian prose work *Dastanbū*, written, as he said, in old Persian, without the use of Arabic words, records his experiences from May 1857 to August 1858.

For the remaining 11 years of his life he carried on from Delhi a vast correspondence with his absent friends, in a style which he claimed 'transformed correspondence into conversation'. At first opposed to the publication of his letters, he later helped gather them together for a first collection published just before his death and entitled *'Ūd-e hindī*. A second larger collection *Urdū-e mu'allā* followed (Part I, 1869; Part II, 1899). They were very popular, and helped finally to turn the scales in favour of the colloquial as the basis of literary prose. Other major collections were published as late as 1937 (*Makātīb-e Ghālib*) and 1949 (*Nādirāt-e Ghālib*). His Urdu verse acquired its present immense popularity only from about the beginning of the 20th century. Its expression is often difficult, but it is perhaps its striking modernity which put it largely beyond the reach of his contemporaries, so that, as he once prophesied, it would, 'like wine that has grown old', win fame only after his death. An appealing humour, irony, and clear-sighted detachment pervades the whole collection, and finds expression in his view of God, the universe, his fellow-men, his beloved, and himself. He carries forward the strong humanist tradition of the Urdu *ghazal* (see Vol. III), often with a proud audacity which endears him to his readers, claiming that he himself is the most outstanding of mankind. His Persian verse, which shows the same qualities, is only now beginning to receive the attention it deserves.

Trans.: K. A. Faruqi, *Dastanbūy* (London 1970).

R. Russell and K. Islam, *Ghalib: Life and Letters* (London 1969); M. Mujeeb, *Ghalib* (Delhi 1969); Sardar Jafri and Qurratulain Hyder, *Ghalib and his Poetry* (1970). RR

Ghavvāsī (17th century Golkonda), Dakkhini Urdu epic poet, panegyric of Sultan 'Abdullāh Quṭb Shāh at Golkonda. He was the first romance writer in Urdu poetry. His *Qiṣṣa-e Ṣaifu'l-mulūk va Badī'u'l-jamāl* (1625) of 14,000 lines, narrating the love of the Egyptian prince Ṣaifu'l-mulūk for the Chinese princess Badī'u'l-jamāl, derives from a story in the Arabian Nights. His *maṣnavī* (see Vol. III) *Ṭūṭī-nāma* (Tales of a Parrot, 1639) is derived from a Persian rendering of the Sanskrit *Śukasaptati* (qv).

RSHUL 37–8; MSHUL 51. JM

ghazal, see Vol. III.

Ghulām Ahmad Mahjūr, Kashmiri poet, see **Mahjūr,** Ghulām Ahmad.

Ghulām Farīd (1845–1901), Panjabi poet. His family were *pīrs* of the Chishtī order, and he spent his life as *pīr* at the family shrine of Chachran in the former Bahawalpur State, where he enjoyed a great reputation during his lifetime as a poet, scholar and saint. His poetry is written mostly in the south-west Panjabi dialect known as Multānī or Sirāikī. It consists of 272 *kāfīs*, short mystical poems designed for musical recitation. His work is distinguished from the verse of his predecessors, such as Śāh Husain or Bullhe Śāh (qqv), by its greater indebtedness to the style of the Perso–Urdu *ghazal* (see Vol. III). However, Ghulām Farīd's poetry is also noteworthy for its local colour, in particular the vivid pictures it gives of life in the '*rohī*', the desert to the south of Bahawalpur, where he spent many years in ascetic seclusion.

ABSLP 271–4. CS

Girhōri, Makhdūm 'Abdu'r-raḥīm (1739–1778), Sindhi religious writer and didactic poet, a Naqshbandī mystic of strict ascetic attitude. He sought martyrdom by destroying a Shiva idol. Besides some works in Persian and an Arabic commentary on the sentences and Sindhi verses of his masters, he wrote Sindhi religio-didactic poems, containing commentaries on Qur'ānic *Sūras*. His hymns on the Prophet are a typical expression of the Sindhi religious feeling found in more popular songs.

ABSLP 289–90. AS

Gitā, see **Bhagavadgitā.**

Gitagovinda, see **Jayadeva.**

Gobind Singh, Sikh gurū, see **Dasam Granth** and **Ādi Granth.**

Gokhale, Aravind Viṣṇu (b 1919), Marathi short story writer. With Gāḍgīḷ (qv) one of the founders of the post-war, realistic short story. He has published numerous collections.

Trans.: *The Unmarried Widow and Other Stories* (Bombay 1957); I. Raeside, *The Rough and the Smooth* (Bombay 1966). IR

Gonsalves, Jacome, a Konkani Brahmin from Goa, who came to Ceylon in 1705 as a Roman Catholic priest and lived in the Kandyan kingdom. He started a school of Sinhalese Christian literature, written in a particular linguistic style.

S. G. Perera, *Life of Father Jacome Gonsalves* (Madura 1942). CHBR

Gonzalez, Nestor Vicente Madali (b 1915), Filipino writer and poet writing in English. Born on the island of Romblon into a teacher's family, he studied law in Manila but switched to journalism and later to creative writing, which he studied in the USA. At home he continued writing and worked for several magazines. On a second Rockefeller grant he made a tour of South-East Asia. He now teaches at the University of the Philippines. Works: novels, *The Winds of April* (1940), *A Season of Grace* (1956), *The Bamboo Dancers* (1960); collections of short stories, *Children of the Ash-Covered Loam* (1954), *Look, Stranger, on This Island Now* (1963); tales, *Seven Hills Away* (1947). EH

Gosvāmi, Hemcandra (b 1872 Gaurangsatra, d 1928 Gauhati), historian of Assam and Assamese literature, editor of texts and poet. Son of a poor family, with both traditional Brahminic erudition and a modern education obtained in Calcutta, he became a teacher, later a government official. Gosvāmī greatly helped to preserve and edit many works of Assamese classical and folk literature. He was entrusted by the government with the task of collecting manuscripts, many of which he then edited with erudite commentaries. His *Asamiya Sahityar Chaneki, or Typical Selections from Assamese Literature* (Calcutta 1923–29), in seven volumes, comprise, in a sensitive compilation, the best samples of Assamese literature, from the beginnings up to modern times. These activities were a strong impetus to the Assamese nationalist movement at the beginning of the present century. DZ

Govindāgraj, Marathi poet, see **Gaḍkari,** Rām Ganeś.

Granth, Sikh scriptures, see **Ādi Granth** and **Dasam Granth.**

Gṛhyasūtra, see **vedāṅga** and **sūtra.**

Guerrero, Wilfrido Ma. (b 1917 Ermita, Manila), a prolific Filipino playwright writing in English. Author of 13 *Plays* (1947), 8 *Other Plays* (1962), 7 *More Plays* (1963). EH

Guṇāḍhya, ancient Indian author of the lost work *Bṛhatkathā* (Great Narrative). His time cannot be decided, but he must have lived (probably much) earlier than the 6th century AD. The book written in a Prakrit called Paiśācī was obviously a collection of fairy-tales and stories presented within a frame-narrative on the life and adventures of the Vatsa king Udayana. Though the tradition mentions several recensions of the *Bṛhatkathā*, only two are known nowadays, both in Sanskrit, one from Nepal and the other from Kashmir, considerably different from each other in conception and contents. The Nepal recension is represented by the partially preserved *Bṛhatkathāślokasaṃgraha* (Verse-summary of the Great Narrative) of Budhasvāmin, of unknown but relatively late date; it presents a vivid picture of certain aspects of life at the author's time. The Kashmiri recension is known in two versions, the *Kathāsaritsāgara* of Somadeva (qv) and the *Bṛhatkathāmañjarī* (composed probably in 1037) by Kṣemendra; the author of the latter was renowned as an exceptionally fertile, but not particularly original, versifier and author of numerous epic poems and plays, delighting in erotic motifs.

F. Lacôte, *Essai sur Guṇāḍhya et la Bṛhatkathā* (Paris 1908).
WHIL III, 346–52. DZ

Gupta, Bhairavprasād, Hindi writer, see **āñcalik upanyās.**

Gupta, Maithilīśaraṇ (b 1886 Cirganv, d 1964), Hindi poet. He established himself as a poet under the guidance of Mahāvīrprasād Dvivedī (qv) while writing *Bhāratbhāratī* (1912), a poem of Hindu nationalism, which earned him the title of National Poet (*rāṣṭrakavi*). His devotion to Rāma, an incarnation of God, led him to write the epic poem *Sāket* (1932), a modern *Rāmcaritmānas* (see Tulsīdās), in which he depicted his ideal Hindu society. He was the first generally accepted poet who wrote in modern Hindi and became later the poet of Gandhi's ideas to the Hindi speaking world.

P. Gaeffke, *Sāket*, Kindlers Literatur Lexikon VI (Zürich 1971). PG

Gurdās Bhallā, Bhāī (d 1637), Panjabi poet. Converted to Sikhism in 1579, was first posted as a missionary to Agra, from where he was later recalled by Gurū Arjan to act as his amanuensis when he was compiling the original version of the *Ādi Granth* (qv). After the death of Arjan in 1606, he became an important leader of the Sikh community during the troubled period which followed. Gurdās' own Panjabi compositions, although not included in the *Ādi Granth*, have an established place in the Sikh canon and are described as the 'key to the *Granth*'; they consist of 39 *vārs*, the form used for Panjabi heroic verse, consisting of a number of rhymed stanzas (*pauṛī*). While valuable evidence of contemporary Sikh beliefs, the *vārs* are somewhat crude when viewed as literature, although they contain much vivid homely imagery. Gurdās also composed 566 Braj *kabitts*.

KSHS, vol. 1, 310–12. CS

Gurulugōmi (c1200), lay author. He provides the earliest examples of connected Sinhalese prose in *Dharmapradīpikāva*, a learned Sanskritic Buddhist treatise, and *Amāvatura*, a set of narrative stories from the life of the Buddha, constructed from a judicious mixture of Pāli texts and written in a non-Sanskritic '*Elu*' style. This style does not appear in later prose works. CHBR

Gurūprasād, Nepali writer, see **Mainālī,** Gurūprasād.

Gyanagyaw Ma Ma Lei, Burmese writer, see **Ma Ma Lei,** Djanetjo.

H

Haba Khotūn, Kashmiri poetess, see **Lol-lyric.**

Ḥaidar, Qurratu'l-'ain (b 1927 Aligarh), Urdu novelist, short-story writer and translator, daughter of the Urdu writer S. H. Yildarim. She was educated at Lucknow and after partition left for Pakistan, but in recent years returned to India. Her first short stories appeared in 1947, and were followed by two other collections, and by three novels. Her novel, *Āg kā daryā* (River of Fire, 1959) expressing in symbol and allegory the development of Indian history, has won the greatest acclaim. JM

Hāla (?2nd century AD), Indian anthologist, a Sātavāhana emperor, apparently Puḷamāyi II. He collected the *Gāhāsattasaī* (Seven Hundred Songs) in Māhārāṣṭrī in the musical *āryā* metre; they portray village life, perhaps round a nucleus of actual folk songs in the spoken dialect of Mahārāṣṭra, as contrasted with the archaic administrative language of the inscriptions. Their vernacular allusiveness, expressible only by intonation, was appreciated by the critic Ānandavardhana as the most sophisticated flight of *dhvanikāvya* where the whole meaning lies in the implication (see *dhvani*). The viewpoint is usually that of the woman as lover, either described or speaking.

Trans. by A. Weber (reprint 1966).
A. K. Warder, *Indian Kāvya Literature*, Vol. II (in the press). AKW

Ḥāli, Khvāja Alṭāf Ḥusain (b 1837 Panipat, where d 1914), Urdu romantic poet, biographer and critic. He studied in Delhi and served in Indian administration; later he taught in Delhi and Hyderabad. He wanted to arouse the Indian Muslims from the lethargy which followed the defeat of the revolt of 1857, and to induce them to loyal cooperation with the British. His major poem in six-verse stanzas, known as *musaddas* (1879; see Anīs) was a moving lament for vanished Islamic glory, urging Muslims to emulate their past greatness. Influenced by English literature, he introduced political themes into poetry and composed verses vividly describing nature. his *dīwān* with the critical Urdu *Introduction to Verse and Poetry* (1893) is remarkable for its simplicity and frankness. He wrote also biographies of Sa'dī, Ghālib (qv) and Aḥmad Khān (qv).

Trans.: *The Quatrains of Hali*, G. E. Ward (London 1904), N. C. Chatterjee (Calcutta 1918).
RSHUL 210–19; MSHUL 263–74. JM

Han-mac-Tu (real name Nguyen-trong-Tri, b 1912 Dong-hoi, Quang-binh province, d 1940), Vietnamese Catholic poet. He died young after being ill for a long time with leprosy. His poetry is full of anxiety and sorrow, but he also praised sensual love. He was one of the few Vietnamese poets to confess Christianity in his work. Chief works: *Gai que* (Village Girl, 1936), *Tho dien* (Mad Poems), *Quan tien hoi* (Gathering of the Immortals).

DNILVN 186. VV

Haqqgū, 'Abdu'l-ḥakīm (b 1912), Baluchi formalist poet and critic. He founded the Baluchi section of the West Pakistan formalist writers' association (Circle of the Friends of Taste) and in 1952 organized the Baluchi Literary Society. JM

Hariaudh (Ayodhyāsiṃh Upādhyāy, b 1865 Nizamabad, d 1941 Banaras), Hindi poet and prose writer. He was a teacher, then a clerk and later lectured at Banaras University. He wrote his verses at first in the Braj dialect, but since 1914 in literary Hindi. In the first modern Hindi epic, *Priya-pravās* (The Beloved's Exile, 1914), composed in Sanskrit metres, he used the traditional Kṛṣṇa-theme (Kṛṣṇa's stay in Mathura) to point out that the national cause is more important than personal troubles; he depicted Rādhā as a brave self-sacrificing woman. *Cokhe caupade* (Acid Couplets, 1924) is an anthology of satirical verses. The story *Devbālā* (1899) in prose criticizes the system of forced marriages. DA

Haribhadra, Indian Jain writer, see **Jain literature.**

Hariścandra, 'Bhārtendu' (1850–85), Hindi poet, dramatist, essayist and journalist. Born in a prosperous *vaiśya* family of Banaras, he travelled widely in India in his youth and was well-versed in Western and Perso-Islamic, as well as Hindu cultural traditions. He came to maturity at the moment when a sense of national identity, dominated by a consciousness of Hindu identity, was spreading to upper India. His prolific writings establish the use of modern Hindi as a vehicle for literature. They include verse in the traditional Braj Bhāṣā dialect, essays on historical, antiquarian, social and political subjects, and dramas, both original and translations or adaptations from Bengali and Sanskrit. His periodicals, *Kavivacansudhā* (Nectar of Poetry, 1868–) and *Harishchandra's Magazine* in English and Hindi (1873–), have contributed greatly to the moulding of contemporary opinion. In his best-known play, *Bhārat durdaśā* (India's Plight, 1880), he calls for a regeneration of Indian society and sees Muslim, and in part Western, influence as contributing to India's decline. RSM

Harivaṃśa, appendix to the *Mahābhārata*, see **purāṇa.**

Harṣa (Harṣavardhana, Śrīharṣa), king of Sthāṇvīśvara (Thanesar) and Kanyākubja (Kanauj), 606–648 AD, and latterly overlord of most of northern India: author of three Sanskrit dramas. The *Ratnāvalī* and *Priyadarśikā*, both *nāṭikās* in four acts, deal with episodes from the well-known cycle of legends concerning King Udayana and his queen Vāsavadattā, other parts of which had earlier been dramatized by Bhāsa (qv). In the former, the daughter of the king of Ceylon, betrothed to Udayana, is shipwrecked, and though finally brought to the latter's court, is kept anonymous and made to act as a maidservant under the name of Sāgarikā. The king sees her and falls in love, but is discovered by his chief queen Vāsavadattā. After scenes of jealous quarrel and intrigue, the maidservant is finally revealed as the princess Ratnāvalī, and is graciously accepted by Vāsavadattā as a co-wife for Udayana.

The *Priyadarśikā* has almost exactly the same plot, and except for its different heroine and minor variations in the development, might almost be another version of the same play composed in different words. Although these two dramas are by no means plagiarisms of the *Mālavikāgnimitra*, the reminiscences of Kālidāsa's (qv) play are too obvious to have been accidental. Harṣa's third drama, the *Nāgānanda*, is a *nāṭaka* in five acts. It is of interest in having as its main theme the Buddhist legend of the self-sacrifice of Jīmūtavāhana to save the Nāgas from the divine bird Garuḍa. Harṣa can hardly be placed in the first rank of Sanskrit dramatists, but his plays are attractive, and contain many excellent verses. (For the author of the *Naiṣadha-carita*, see Śrīharṣa.)

Ratnāvalī: German trans., L. Fritze (Chemnitz 1878); *Priyadarśikā*: ed. and trans. G. K. Nariman, A. V. W. Jackson and C. J. Ogden (New York 1923); *Nāgānanda*: trans. H. Wartham (London and New York 1911), and P. Boyd (London 1872).
DHSL 255–62; KSD 170–81. JB

Hāśam Śāh (probably 1735–1843), Panjabi poet. Born in Medina, but at a very young age came to a village near Amritsar, where his father settled as a *pīr* of the Qādirī (Nauśāhī) order. Hāśam followed him in this profession, administering his tomb while also practising as a *hakīm*. His reputation won him a fief (*jāgīr*) from Mahārājā Raṇjīt Singh, but the tradition that he was made a court poet is not to be relied upon. During the course of his long life, Hāśam Śāh wrote a considerable amount of poetry, including some in Hindi and Persian. His most famous poem is his handling of the popular Panjabi romance, *Sassī Punnūṃ*, which tells of the birth of Sassī to a king, the foretelling of the disgrace she will bring on her father and her consequent exposure. But she grows up to fall in love with the Baloch prince, Punnūṃ, who is eventually abducted from her side by his kinsmen. The high-point of the poem describes her anguished pursuit of her lover in the desert, and her death from heat and distress. Hāśam's handling of the story, which has always been the most popular of the many Panjabi versions, is distinguished by its brevity (it consists of only 126 four-line stanzas) and the simplicity of its language.

Hāśam was also the author of two other verse romances, *Śīrīn Farhād*, which he was the first to write in Panjabi (his original source was Persian), and *Sohṇī Mahīṃvāl*, a popular local romance. Although Hāśam was the first Panjabi poet to handle this latter tale too, the popularity of his version has been eclipsed by that of Fazal Śāh (d 1890). Hāśam is equally famous as the writer of some 270 *dohṛe*, quatrains of mystical love, which are often strikingly reminiscent of folk-songs. He is the only poet to have excelled in both the major forms of Panjabi Muslim poetry, the romance and the short mystical lyric. It is also in Hāśam's poetry that the influence of Perso–Urdu classical forms and style, which was increasingly to dominate Panjabi verse, are first apparent on a significant scale.

R. C. Temple, *The Legends of the Punjab* (1900), vol. 3, pp. 24–37; RKPSP 89–103. CS

Ḥasan Dihlavī, real name Amīr Najmuddīn Ḥasan Sijzī (b 1253 Delhi, d 1328 Daulatabad), Indo-Persian poet and writer. Though of a prominent family, he worked in a bakery, and later became court poet of the sultans of Delhi. He wrote panegyrics and satires, but above all excelled in the lyrical *ghazals*, influenced by Sa'dī (see Vol. III) in style and thought. His romantic and didactic *maṣnavīs* (see Vol. III) derive their subjects from Indian folk-tales. His prose deals with religious and mystic questions and is interwoven with maxims.

HIL 717–8. JM

Ḥasan Khān, Shabīr, Urdu poet, see **Jōsh Malīḥābādī.**

Hāshim, Makhdūm Maḥammad (1692–1761), Sindhi religious writer and didactic poet, a fighter against innovation and emotional Sufism. A *qāżī* of Thatta, he enjoyed the favour of Nādir Shāh, Aḥmad Shāh Abdālī and the Kalhōrō rulers. He was one of the first to compose didactic books about Islamic law and history in simple Sindhi verse. His commentary on the last part of the Qur'ān (1749) was invariably given to children. Sindhi religious literature really begins with him and his family, who were all strict adherents of the Naqshbandī school.

ABSLP 290. AS

Hāshimī, Ẓahūr Muḥammad Shāh Sa'īd (b 1926), Baluchi poet writing also in Urdu, Persian and English. In 1946 he founded the Baluchi Educational Society and started publishing the first Baluchi newspaper *Jadd-o-jahad* (Struggle), but was jailed for his political views. In 1959 he organized the Baluchi Language Association. He is the author of a lyric *dīwān* and of a useful Baluchi dictionary. JM

Ḥasrat Mōhānī, Sayyid Fażlu'l-ḥasan (b 1850 Mohan, d 1951 Lucknow), Urdu lyric poet and critic. After graduation at Aligarh, he took to journalism and politics. A strong supporter of the 'extremist' wing of the Indian National Congress, he was more than once jailed for his anti-British activities. In the mid-1920's, dissatisfied with Hindu communalist influence in the Congress and with Gandhi's non-violence, he began to play a greater part in the Muslim League and other Muslim organisations; at the same time he moved towards 'Muslim communism'. He disapproved of the 1947 settlement, and remained in India after independence and partition, where he was elected to the Indian parliament. He is perhaps the greatest *ghazal* (see Vol. III) poet of the 20th century. In his thirteen short *dīwāns* he speaks of his love experiences with a greater frankness than most of his predecessors, and the conventional *ghazal* themes are infused with fresh revolutionary content. JM

Hemacandra or Hemācārya (b 1089 Gujarat, d 1172), Indian Jain poet, commentator, philosopher and scholar, son of a merchant, at whose wish he became a monk. Lived mostly at the Gujarat court, where he exercised strong influence over the king. Thanks to him Gujarat was for centuries a bastion of the Śvetāmbara Jainas, and Jain literature flourished there in the 12th–13th centuries. His extensive biographical work *Triṣaṣṭiśalākāpuruṣacarita* (The Lives of the 63 Excellent Men), a great ornate epic in Sanskrit, is based on earlier writers. It is a typical Jain hagiographical work, frequently interspersed with long discussions of religion and ethics. An Appendix Section (*Pariśiṣṭaparvan*), or *Sthavirāvalicarita* (The Lives of the Series of the Elders) supplements it. Hemacandra was simple and original in his *Yogaśāstra*, one of the most important

Jain didactic poems; this gives a short survey of Jain teaching for laymen in simple *ślokas* (qv) with a commentary in ornate *kāvya* (qv) style and numerous illustrative stories. Other works: *Pramāṇamīmāṃsā* (a philosophical treatise), *Abhidhānacintāmaṇi* (dictionary of homonyms), *Anekārthasaṃgraha* (dictionary of synonyms), *Deśīnāmamālā* or *Ratnāvali* (dictionary of Prakrit words not obviously derived from Sanskrit), *Alaṃkāracūḍāmaṇi* (poetics), *Chandonuśāsana* (metrics), *Ayogavyavacchedā* and *Anyayogavyavacchedā* (hymns on Mahāvīra) and minor treatises.

English trans.: *Triṣaṣṭiśalākāpuruṣacarita*, H. M. Johnson (Baroda 1931–54); *Pramāṇamīmāṃsā*, S. Mookerjee and N. Tatia (Calcutta 1946); *Deśīnāmamālā*, M. Banerjee (Calcutta 1931). German transl.: *Abhidhānacintāmaṇi*, O. Boehtlingk and C. Rieu (St. Petersburg 1847); J. Hertel, *Ausgewählte Erzählungen aus Hēmacandras Pariśiṣṭaparvan* (Leipzig 1908).
J. G. Bühler, *The Life of Hemacandrācārya* (Santiniketan 1936); WHIL II, 505–11, 567–70.

EM

Hemcandra Gosvāmi, Assamese historian, see **Gosvāmi,** Hemcandra.

Hernandez, Amado V. (1903–1970), Filipino Tagalog poet, novelist and playwright. He lived among the poor in Tondo, Manila, to reflect faithfully the life of the lowest classes in his writing. As a trade union leader (President of the Congress of Labor Organizations) he was actively involved in political life. Charged with 'crimes of rebellion' he spent the years 1951–6 in prison, but in 1964 was acquitted by the Supreme Court. Although Hernandez began writing before World War II, his best works appeared in the sixties. These include collections of poems, *Isang Dipang Langit* (One Armstretch of Sky, 1962), *Bayang Malaya* (Free Country, 1969); novels, *Luha ng Buwaya* (Crocodile Tears, 1963), *Mga Ibong Mandaragit* (Mandaragit Birds, 1969); a collection of contributions to newspaper columns, *Pili sa Pinili* (The Best from Selected, 1964); and drama, *Muntinglupa* (1959).

EH

hikayat, in Malay prose narrative, the term used to denote a variety of kinds of story form (Arabic *ḥikāya*, story or tale) not otherwise constituting a single literary genre. Extant *hikayat*, dating from about the 15th to 19th centuries, range from popular folk-tales, fables and romances to mythic and historical accounts of the past and, in some cases, personal or familial biography. Some of the best-known *hikayat* in the categories mentioned are the *Hikayat Pelandok Jenaka* (Fables of the Wily Mouse-deer), *Hikayat Kalila dan Damina* (Story of Kalila and Damina, of Indian origin, see *Pañcatantra*), *Hikayat Iskandar Dzul'l-Karnain* (Story of Alexander the Great, from Arabo-Persian sources), *Hikayat Raja-Raja Pasai* (History of the Rulers of Pasai), and the *Hikayat Abdullah* (Life-story of Abdullah). A feature of traditional rather than modern literature, the *hikayat* have been the repositories of some of the finest Malay writing. Even when they are of foreign origin, they often say or imply much about Malay society.

WRR

Hinilawod, Filipino epic, see **darangan.**

Hīr Rānjhā, Panjabi epic, see **Vāras Śāh.**

Hitopadeśa (Beneficial Instruction), Sanskrit collection of fables and tales in prose and verse. Essentially it is a version of the famous *Pañcatantra* (qv), supplemented by 'another book', as the author himself tells us. The identity of this other book, however, is not known. The *Hitopadeśa* was written by a certain *Nārāyaṇa* of Bengal, between the 9th and the 14th centuries AD, but it differs from its model by retaining only four of its five chapters and by narrating a few stories not found in any extant version of the *Pañcatantra*. The didactic character of the book is stressed by numerous educative sentences deduced as moral points from the individual stories. The *Hitopadeśa* has been translated into many languages and has exercised a strong influence on the narrative literature of other nations.

Trans.: C. Wilkins, *The Hitopadesa* (London 1787); Sir Edwin Arnold, *The Book of Good Counsels* (London 1896); J. Hertel, *Hitopadesa* (Leipzig sd).

L. Sternbach, *The Hitopadeśa and its Sources* (New Haven 1960); J. Hertel, *Über Text und Verfasser des Hitopadeśa* (Leipzig 1897). DZ

Hla, U, Luhtu (b 1910 Pzunmyaun), Burmese journalist, publisher and writer. From 1933 he published the monthly *Tyipwayei* (Success), from 1945 *Luhtu* (*Ludu*, The People) Journal, from 1946 *Luhtu* Daily in Mandalay. He has been active in the Union of Burmese Writers since 1937, in the Union of Burmese Journalists, and the World Peace Movement, and travelled in Asia and Europe. In 1965 he joined the modernization movement, propagating Modern, instead of Classical, Burmese in writing. In 1953–57 he was jailed in Rangoon and recorded the true stories of his fellow prisoners, depicting with sympathetic realism the lives of thieves, prostitutes, waifs and strays, drawing attention to acute social problems. He was also the writer of travel-sketches, an indefatigable collector and publisher of the folk-tales of various nationalities of Burma, letters and memoirs, 19th and 20th century newspaper materials and translations. Main works: novel, *Lei-hnin atu* (With the Wind, 1957); short stories, *Htaun hnin Lutha* (Prison and Man, 1957–Sapei Biman Prize), *Hlauncjain twin hma Hngek nge mja* (Little Birds from a Cage, 1958—UNESCO Prize for Literature). DB

Hlain Hteip Khaun Tin, Burmese poetess, see **Hlaing,** Princess of.

Hlaing, Princess of (1833–75), Burmese poetess, also known as Hlaing Hteikhkaungtin. Daughter of King Shwebo (reigned 1837–46), and Queen of the Middle Palace. Her mother was executed for treason and her father died when she was quite young. Her marriage to the lively spirited Crown Prince, Kanaung, who was murdered in 1866 by one of the Palace rebels, was unhappy. An admirer of Sa (qv) and a contemporary of Kyin U and Ponnya (qqv), she wrote two court-plays (see Padethayaza) and many songs, most of which mirror certain aspects of her unhappy life and feelings. As such, they stir the sympathy and admiration of the reader. Her *bawlè* (plaintive song), an innovation of her own, are chiefly impassionate pleas to her wayward husband; her *dwegyo* (two-section song), *legyo* (four-section song) and *tedat* (six-section song) savour of disillusionment with life and a desire to renounce the world; and her classical *patpyo* (overture) dwell on the glories of her brother-in-law and guardian, King Mindon (1853–78). She was the last of the eminent court-poetesses. HP

Hmain, Thakhin Koujto (Lun, U, b 1876 Walij, d 1964 Rangoon), Burmese nationalist poet, writer, dramatist, journalist, historian and politician. He had traditional Burmese education and did not know English. From 1894 he worked in *Myanma Neisin* (Myanma Daily), Moulmein, and from 1911 in *Thuriya Neisin* (Sun Daily), Rangoon. He was a rebel writer who refused to serve the British rulers in any form; he boycotted the British court, eg by refusing to compose poems in praise of the visit of the Prince of Wales to Burma. Professor of Burmese History and Literature, National College (1920), he was a fervent nationalist, actively participating in Burma's independence movement (member of the *Doubama* association). After 1948 he became leader of the Burmese Peace Movement, both internal and external, and was awarded the International Stalin Peace Prize, 1954.

Hmain wrote often in rhymed prose, and in poetry raised the *leicjoutyi* form to a level of formal perfection. In his journalism, written in the form of literary commentaries (*tika*, *kanhti*) he reacted to contemporary political and social problems, supported anti-British actions (student strikes, the peasant revolt 1930–32), sharply mocked the Burmese Anglophiles and criticized profit-seeking politicians. He wrote more than 80 plays, historical works portraying Burma's glorious past. Main works: novel *Hmatopoum* (Message); commentaries *Daun Tika* (On the Peacock, 1919), *Mjauk Tika* (On Monkeys, 1920–22), *Khwei Tika* (On Dogs, 1923), *Galoumpjam Dipani Tika* (On the Galon Rebels, 1930), *Thakhin Tika* (On the Thakins, 1934). DB

Hmannan Yazawingyi, Burmese chronicle, see **Kala,** U.

Hoang-Dao, Vietnamese writer, see **Nhat-Linh.**

Ho-bieu-Chanh (real name Ho-van-Trung, b 1885 Binh-thanh, Go-cong province, d 1958), Vietnamese writer. Of a poor family, he was given a Chinese and later a French education at the Saigon *lycée.* 1906–37 he held various offices in Cochin China, including that of provincial governor. After 1946 he took no part in political life. He was a prolific writer, being the author of over 60 novels and many short stories, written in popular language and lively style. He is known mainly to readers in South Vietnam. Chief works: *Ai lam duoc* (Who Can Do It? 1912); *Chua tau Kim-quy* (Captain of the Kim-quy, 1913); *Cay dang mui doi* (Troubles of a Life, 1923).

DNILVN 118, 189. VV

Ho-chi-Minh (real name Nguyen-tat-Thanh, also known as Nguyen-ai-Quoc or Nguyen-the-Patriot, b 1890 Kim-lien, Nghe-an province, d 1969 Hanoi), Vietnamese revolutionary and statesman. He was the main initiator of the founding of the Communist Party of Indochina (1930), and was President of the Democratic Republic of Vietnam from 1945. From the outset of his public life, at the end of World War I, he was active as an anticolonialist, and later as a Marxist, writer. Some of his numerous speeches, letters and appeals equal the best examples of patriotic prose of Vietnam's past, eg *Thu gui tu nuoc ngoai* (A Letter from Abroad, 1941), *Ban Tuyen ngon doc lap* (The Declaration of Independence of the DRV, 1945), *Chong nan mu chu* (Against Illiteracy, 1945), *Loi keu goi toan quoc khang chien* (Appeal to Nation-wide Resistance, 1946), *Loi keu goi thi dua yeu nuoc* (Appeal to Patriotic Emulation, 1948), *Ve dao duc cach mang* (On Revolutionary Morality, 1958), *Ban Di chuc* (Testament, 1969). Written in a clear, original style and simple popular language, they won Ho-chi-Minh the reputation in the DRV of one of the greatest prose-writers of Vietnam. Other works: *Procès de la colonisation française* (French Colonialism on Trial, Paris 1925); *Nhat ky trong tu* (Prison Diary, poems written in classical Chinese in 1942–3, published 1964).

Trans.: *Écrits,* 1920–1969 (Hanoi 1971); *Prison Diary* (Hanoi 1964). VV

Ho-trong-Hieu, Vietnamese poet, see **Tu-Mo.**

Ho-van-Trung, Vietnamese writer, see **Ho-bieu-Chanh.**

Ho-xuan-Huong (end of 18th-beginning of 19th century), Vietnamese poetess of a family native in Quynh-doi, Nghe-an province, born in Hanoi. She lost her father early, and was educated by a learned mother; married twice, as 'secondary wife', and finally widowed, she then travelled widely in North Vietnam and met many literary figures. Her poems collected in *Xuan huong thi tap* (Poems of Xuan Huong) are mainly satirical, ridiculing the spurious authority of men in traditional society and attacking the moral hypocrisy of the Confucians and the Buddhist monks. Her language is fresh and popular, even vulgar at times, and full of puns and allusions. The poet's original contribution is the synthesis of the T'ang 7-syllable form usual in Chinese poetry with vernacular means of expression. There are only about 50 poems in the collection, but they are so original that the author is frequently ranked next to Nguyen-Du (qv) in histories of Vietnamese literature.

DNILVN 100–2, 189. VV

Hsaung, U, Burmese writer, see **Kyi,** U.

Hsüan-tsang, Chinese pilgrim to India, see Vol. I.

Htei Myain, U, Burmese poet, see Taya, Dagoun.

Htin, Maun (Htin Phat, U, b 1909 Laputta), Burmese writer, dramatist, translator and journalist. He studied English, Burmese literature and history at the Rangoon University, served in Subordinate Civil Service in 1936–43, edited *Yankoun Neisin* (Rangoon Daily) since 1950, and has been correspondent for *The Times*, London, since 1956. Htin started to write in the spirit of *Khitsam* (see Zodji), depicting the Burmese village and villagers in a realistic way (short stories, *Kou Daun Wuthtutou mja*, On Kou Daun, 1939). In the novel *Nga Bha* (The Peasant Nga Ba, 1947) he gives a simple yet vivid picture about the hard life of a Burmese peasant during the Japanese occupation. He also contributed to the development of modern drama, eg *Bha Ayeityihsoum le*? (What is Most Important? 1943), and *Azanij Mikhin* (Mother-Hero, 1943), and translated Maupassant, Tchekhov and Gorky. DB

Hudhud, Ifugao epic, see **darangan.**

Husain, Mādholāl, Panjabi poet, see **Śāh Husain.**

Huy-Can, Vietnamese poet, see **The-Lu.**

I-ching, Chinese pilgrim to India, see Vol. I.

Idrus (b 1921 Padang), Indonesian writer and editor. He is sometimes considered a pioneer in modern Indonesian prose just as Chairil Anwar (qv) is regarded as a renewer of Indonesian poetry. After completing secondary school in 1943 he was active for a brief time with Balai Pustaka. From 1950 to 1952 he was head of training for Garuda Indonesian Airways and for part of this time served as editor of the cultural journal *Indonesia* and of the literary periodical *Kisah*. The mid-fifties were spent in business after which he went in 1961 to Kuala Lumpur where he founded a publishing firm and edited a magazine. In 1965 Idrus went to Monash University in Australia where he teaches Indonesian literature. It was not until the Japanese period that Idrus began to write short stories, sketches and plays which could not be published at the time but were later collected in book form under the title *Dari Ave Maria ke Djalan Lain ke Roma* (From 'Ave Maria' to 'Djalan Lain ke Roma') in 1948. One of his best works is a short novelette *Aki* (1950). For more than ten years there was a hiatus, but during the Kuala Lumpur period Idrus issued a volume of short stories (*Dengan Mata Terbuka*, With Open Eyes, 1961) and a novel (*Hati Nurani Manusia*, Man's Innermost Self, 1963). These, however, do not rank with his best writing from Indonesia. The latter was direct, hard-hitting and stylistically quite different from pre-World War II writing. Idrus will occupy a permanent place in Indonesian literature for his short stories. Other works: *Soerabaja* (1946); *Kedjahatan Membalas Dendam* (Wickedness Takes Revenge, 1949).

TMIL 159–63 and passim. JME

I

Iesmaniasita, Sulistyautami (b 1933 Terusan-Modjokerto), Javanese poet and writer, a teacher in East Java. She showed interest in writing while still a student, and published in Javanese papers (since book publishing is limited). Her collection of eight romantic stories *Kidung wengi ing Gunung Gamping* (Evening Verses from Gunung Gamping, 1958) is one of the most widely-read prose works in Java today. She has an original style, simple and tight structure, and her social themes are presented with lyrical moods and idealized personal relationships. Some stories are marked by the Christian mysticism reminiscent of pre-war Indonesian writing. She uses colloquial Javanese in both poetry and prose, the latter usually dealing with contemporary themes while her poetry draws on ancient Javanese history and employs traditional forms. It has not yet appeared in collected form. Further stories: *Tjerita ditepi Brantas* (Stories from the Banks of the Brantas), *Usapan angin persil* (Caressed by the Wind from a Plot of Land). EV

Ikbal, Urdu poet, see **Iqbāl,** Muḥammad.

Iḷaṅkōvaṭikaḷ (5th-6th century AD), Tamil poet, according to tradition a prince of the

Cēra family, to whom is ascribed the earliest epic poem in Tamil literature, *Cilappatikāram* (The Lay of the Anklet). Nothing definite is known about him. The story of the poem is said to have taken place some time in the 2nd century AD, since the hero of the 3rd book, Cēra king Ceṅkuṭṭuvaṉ, and Gajabāhu I (171–193 AD) of Ceylon, mentioned in the poem, were contemporaries ('Gajabāhu synchronism'). The plot is based on a popular story. A young couple, Kōvalaṉ and Kaṇṇaki, belonging to the rich merchant class of Kāvērippaṭṭiṉam, lead a happy life, until Kōvalaṉ abandons his wife for Mātavi, a charming dancing girl. After a quarrel they part, Kōvalaṉ returns home, and, having lost his entire fortune, accepts Kaṇṇaki's anklet to raise the money on which he wants to start a new life. They travel to Madurai, where Kōvalaṉ becomes the victim of a thieving goldsmith's plot. He is put to death, upon which Kaṇṇaki sets fire to Madurai, and is reunited with Kōvalaṉ in heaven. The third book describes the establishment of the cult of Kaṇṇaki, transformed into Pattiṉi, Goddess of Chastity, in the Cēra capital. The epic in 30 cantos is a masterpiece of narrative and lyrical poetry. The story moves swiftly and dramatically, the characters are painted with supreme skill. Though the work is basically Jaina in outlook and the *karmic* interpretation of events is important, there is nothing schematic about the actions of the characters. The descriptions are vivid, often magnificent; the use of lyrical stanzas is fully functional. The work contains the essence of old Tamil culture and portrays an entire civilization. It has been translated into English, French, Russian and Czech.

Trans.: A. Daniélou, *The Shilappadikaram. The Ankle Bracelet* (New York 1965, London 1967).
JHTL 51–60. KZ

Im Chhom, Cambodian writer, see **pralom-lok.**

Im Chhou Det, Cambodian writer, see **pralom-lok.**

Indarapatra, Filipino epic, see **darangan.**

Inshā, Sayyid Inshā'llāh K͟hān (b 1757 Murshidabad, d 1817 Lucknow), Urdu poet, writer and grammarian. He was brought up in the family of a *ḥakīm* and joined the Delhi imperial court; he later moved to Lucknow, but because of his mockery incurred the displeasure of the *navāb* and died in poverty. His panegyric, sarcastic and erotic poetry, perfect in form, with musical language and vivid images and allegories, suffers from artifice and obscurity, stiff metres, intractable rhymes and frivolity. When expelled from the court, he wrote also Sufistic and philosophical verses. He is the author of *Rānī Kētakī kī kahānī* (Story of Queen Ketaki, 1803), a story in 'pure Hindi' in which no words of non-Indian origin are used, and of the first Persian grammar of Urdu, *Daryā-e laṭāfat* (Ocean of Eloquence, 1802); he also treated Urdu dialects and prosody.

RSHUL 82–8; MSHUL 125–30. JM

Iqbāl, Muḥammad (b 1873 or 1876 Sialkot, d 1938 Lahore), Urdu and Persian romantic poet and philosopher. He studied law and philosophy at Cambridge and took his Ph.D. from Munich with a thesis, *The Development of Metaphysics in Persia*, in 1907. He returned to Lahore, was knighted by the British Government in 1922 and became active in the Muslim League. In 1930 he declared the necessity of a separate Muslim State in north-west India, the core of present Pakistan. Starting from neo-Hegelian premises and more traditional Urdu aesthetics, after 1912 Iqbāl ardently advocated a philosophy of activity, to awaken the Muslims from their spiritual slumber.

To this goal his works in both Urdu and Persian are dedicated, especially the *Asrār-e k͟hūdī* (Secrets of the Self, 1915) whose egocentric character shocked the Muslim. The next Persian *mas̱navī* (see Vol. III) *Rumūz-e bēk͟hūdī* (Mysteries of Selflessness, 1917), determines the duties of the individual in the community. In admiration for Goethe he composed the Persian lyrical collection *Payām-e mashriq* (Message of the East, 1923); another book of Persian lyrics, *Zabūr-e 'Ajam* (Persian

Psalms, 1927), contains some of his finest prayer-poems. The *Lectures on the Reconstruction of Religious Thought in Islam* (1928) describes the ascent of man through the spheres, with highly illuminating political and theological discussions. Two Urdu collections of poems follow, of which *Bāl-e Jibrīl* (Gabriel's Wings, 1936) contains his most impressive hymns, while *Żarb-e Kalīm* (The Stroke of Moses, 1937) bitterly criticizes the political and social situation. A collection of Persian quatrains and some Urdu poems, published posthumously as *Armaghān-e Ḥijāz* (Gift of the Hejaz), shows his constant love for the homeland of Islam.

Iqbāl felt, as the title of his first book of Urdu verse *Bāng-e darā* (1924) shows, like the caravan bell which leads the pilgrims towards their goal, ie a life according to the ideas of the *Qur'ān* in imitation of the Prophet; this means developing one's personality to the greatest possible height and reflecting the Divine unity in daily life. Man remains man and is never united with God, but can cooperate with him and improve life by changing his own and human destiny. Satan's constant goading gives man the taste for struggle and activity. The idea of God as the greatest, all-comprehensive Ego and that of the Perfect Man are derived from Islamic mysticism. Iqbāl has rediscovered the dynamic character of early Sufism, which had been overshadowed by pantheistic thought. Poetry is for him the handmaid of prophecy, and the criterion is not its beauty but its life-giving power. Thus his poetry, though using classical imagery, is forceful and can easily be memorized. It has stimulated Pakistani thought, although Iqbāl's work is a strange blend of radical modernism and conservatism.

Trans.: R. A. Nicholson, *The Secrets of the Self* (London 1920); A. J. Arberry, *The Mysteries of Selflessness* (London 1953), *The Tulip of Sinai* (London 1947), *Persian Psalms I and II* (Lahore 1948), *Javidname* (London 1968); Shaikh Mahmud Ahmad, *Pilgrimage of Eternity* (Lahore 1961); V. G. Kiernan, *Poems from Iqbal* (London 1955).
S. A. Vahid, *Iqbal, His Art and Thought* (London ³1959); Iqbal Singh, *The Ardent Pilgrim* (London 1951); A. Schimmel, *Gabriel's Wing* (Leiden 1963, with bibliography); MSHUL 357–89. AS

Iraiyanār (probably 5th–6th century AD), classical Tamil author. No biographical data are available. He was the author of probably the most ancient of the theoretical works on the erotic *akam* genre of literature, *Akapporuḷ* (Grammar of Love) or *Kaḷaviyal* (Treatise on Secret Union). The work contains 60 *sūtras* (qv) of lucid and continuous text dealing with the physiology and psychology of pre-marital love, and with the rhetoric of ancient Tamil erotic poetry. KZ

Irāmaliṅka Piḷḷai, Svāmi (1823–74), Tamil poet, otherwise known as Irāmaliṅkasvāmi. He is the author of *Tiruvaruṭpā* (Song of Divine Grace), and some other minor works of Śaivism. From the age of 16, when he visited the Śaiva temple at Tiruvorriyūr, north of Madras, he wished to become a preacher. He set out the tenets of Śaivism, frequently employing technical grammatical terms or alternatively using various devices of word play. His verses satisfy the strictest metrical rules.

JHTL 252–4. JRM

Ishak bin Haji Muhammad (pseud. Anwar, b 1910 Kampong Saguntang, Pahang), Malay novelist and journalist. Educated in Malay and English, entered journalism in mid-1930's. He published his first novel, the satirical and anti-colonial *Putera Gunong Tahan* (Prince of Mount Tahan) in 1937, and another, *Anak Mat Lela Gila* (Son of Mat Lela the Mad), in 1941. In intervals of an active political career as a socialist, he was extremely productive in the late 1950's and again in the late 1960's, publishing in addition to short stories and other pieces some twelve novels. Often concerned with poverty and crime, and not above utilizing simplistically romantic or sexual themes he shows a frequent concern for social questions and a wry perceptiveness about urban Malay life in particular that lift his novels above the usual run of popular tales, and have made him an influential figure in Malay letters. From his lengthy bibliography may be instanced *Budak Becha* (Trishaw Boy, 2 vols., 1957), *Jalan ka Kota Bharu* (Journey to Kota Bharu, 1956), *Yang Miskin dan Yang Mewah* (The Poor and the Princely, 1966), *Anak Dukun Deraman* (Son of Deraman the Spirit-Doctor, 1967), and one of several collections of short stories, *Segar* (Quill, 1961).

WRR

Iskandar, Nur Sutan (b 1893 Sumatra), Indonesian writer and philologist. Trained as a teacher at the Bukit Tinggi College, he first taught and then worked in a publishing firm as reviser and later chief editor. He belongs to the oldest generation of writers, grouped round the Balai Pustaka publishing house. Although he follows the classical Malay tradition in questions of form, and writes in archaic language, in his novellas *Salah pilih* (A Bad Choice, 1932) and *Karena Mentua* (Because of Mothers-in-Law, 1932), he was one of the first writers to oppose conservative traditions. Chief novels: *Hulubalang Raja* (The King's General, 1934), *Djangir Bali* (The Bali Djangir, ie a children's dance, 1944), *Mutiara* (The Pearl, 1946), *Tjobaan* (The Test, 1947).

TMIL 57–8. MO

Ismail, Usmar (b 1921 Bukit Tinggi), Indonesian playwright, theatre and film producer. After secondary school in Djakarta under the Japanese occupation, he organized a theatre group, *Maya.* After the revolution he became first a journalist and then the director of the Perfini film company. One of the founders of the modern Indonesian drama, he has written many plays and film scenarios, most of which he has directed and produced himself. He has freed the Indonesian drama from many old-fashioned elements, and cut out the traditional long monologues. His themes are taken from everyday life. Chief works: plays, *Mutiara dari nusalaut* (The Pearl of the Islands, 1943), *Api* (Fire, 1948), *Liburan seniman* (The Artist's Holiday, 1948), *Tjitra* (1950).

TMIL 113–4. MO

I-tsing, ie I-ching, Chinese pilgrim to India, see Vol. I.

J

Jagannāthapaṇḍitarāja, Indian writer on poetics, see **alaṃkāraśāstra.**

Jain literature in India is both canonical and non-canonical. The core of the former is the Jain Canon, codified (according to Jainist tradition) a thousand years after the death of the founder of Jainism, the religious reformer Jina, by his proper name Vardhamāna, known as Mahāvīra (c599–527 BC, Pāvā in Bihar), of the Kṣatriya family of the Jñātṛka clan. Left home when about 30 and lived in the forests, preparing for his work as a preacher; he then taught for 30 years the principles said to have been enunciated by the Tīrthaṃkaras, 23 legendary sages, Vardhamāna himself being the 24th Tīrthaṃkara. These principles are embodied in Jainism today. It is a pluralist religion, recognizing the existence of matter and of the soul, which is reincarnated until, purified from the consequences of its actions, it attains *nirvāṇa*, eternal beatitude at the highest point of the cosmos.

All that remains of the Jina's teachings are the aphorisms which, arranged in sequence by his disciples and transmitted by oral tradition, form the basis of the Jain Canon; it was given its final form in the second half of the 5th or early in the 6th century AD. The Canon known as *Siddhānta* or *Āgama* is written in Ardhamāgadhī Prakrit and comprises 45 works dealing with the lives of the saints and with the monastic life, stressing strict asceticism and non-violence, describing the terrors of Hell, in a conglomeration of old traditions, legends and teachings, commandments and virtues, dealing with prayer, physiology, anatomy and embryology, teachers and pupils, discipline, astrology, repentance, etc. Nor is the form unified; some of the works are encyclopaedic, others in question and answer form, written in simple prose interspersed with verses, or in very sophisticated strophes in complicated metres, with numerous aphorisms, metaphors and similes. This Canon, however, belongs only to the Śvetāmbara sect, and is not recognized by the Digambaras. A wealth of commentaries grew up round the Canon, at first in Ardhamāgadhī and Māhārāṣṭrī, later in simple or classical Sanskrit, and in modern Indian languages in the modern era.

The non-canonical literature is also considerable; Jainism influenced and enriched the literatures of Gujarati, Hindi, Tamil and Kannada, particularly in ascetic poetry. Secular Jain literature is no less significant, however, headed by the humorous tales so popular in India. There are also many dramas and didactic works. The non-canonical Jain literature was sometimes written in the simple language of the people, and sometimes produced masterpieces of ornate court poetry. There were many outstanding Jain authors, of whom one of the most fertile was Haribhadra (8th century AD), traditionally reputed to have written 1,444 works, of which 88 have been found; he wrote verse and prose, systematic scientific treatises and philosophical works. Famous is the poet, commentator, philosopher and scholar Hemacandra (qv); well known are also the poets Vimala Sūri, Dhaneśvara, Bhāvadeva Sūri, Lakṣmaṇa Gaṇin, Siddharṣi, Dhaṇavāla, Amitagati; the novelist Pādalipta Sūri, the dramatist Rāmacandra, the philosopher Samantabhadra, and the poet and scholar Āśādhara.

WHIL II, 424–595. EM

Jainendrakumār (Ānandīlāl, b 1905 Kauriyaganj), Hindi writer. His family was active in Gandhi's movement and Jainendrakumār gave up his studies during the civil disobedience campaign of 1920–21. Unsuccessful as a businessman, he spent some time in jail as a political prisoner and lived on the unreliable income from his writings. In his short stories he further developed the technique of his friend Premcand (qv). His novels, *Sunītā* (1932), *Tyāgpatra* (Resignation, 1937), *Sukhadā* (1952) ao, deal with problems of the Indian middle-class. Jainendrakumār combines a psychological approach with Gandhian views. His philosophical essays show his independent way of thinking about the essential problems of India: *Samay aur ham* (The Times and Us, 1962).

Trans.: S. R. Vatsyayan, *The Resignation* (Delhi sd). AFMH. PG

Jambhaladatta, Sanskrit writer, see **Vetālapañcaviṃśatikā.**

Jānakirāmaṉ, Ti. (b 1921 Tevankuti), Tamil writer. He was educated at Madras University, became a journalist and teacher and worked in All-India Radio in Madras and Delhi. He wrote short stories, novels, dramas and travel books, drawing upon everyday life in urban middle-class families in Tamilnad. He is an honest, realistic writer without affectation, with a vivid, plastic style and rich, though temperate diction. Main works: *Mōkamuḷ* (Thorn of Passion, 1961), a long ambitious novel; *Ammā vantāḷ* (Mother Came, 1965), an excellent novel about a sinful mother; short story collection *Civappu rikṣā* (The Red Riksha, 1956); travels in Japan, *Utaya cūriyaṉ* (The Rising Sun, 1967). KZ

janamsākhi, term applied to hagiographies of Nānak, the first Sikh *gurū* (1469–1539), written in the Gurmukhi script. Their language is either Panjabi or the north Indian religious *lingua franca* known as *Sant Bhāśā* (*Sādhukkaṛī*). The *janamsākhīs* are in the form of more or less brief anecdotes known individually as *sākhī* ('evidence') or *goṣṭ* ('disputation'). These are in prose, with frequent verse quotations from the Gurū's hymns. Much the best known of the *janamsākhīs* is that traditionally ascribed to Bhāī Bālā, a disciple of Nānak, but now recognized to be a recension of earlier materials by an heretical sect of the early 17th century. Of a similar date are the so-called *Purātan Janamsākhī* and the recently published *Miharbān Janamsākhī*. Although historically unreliable, the *janamsākhīs* are important as the first significant works of Panjabi prose.

W. H. McLeod, *Gurū Nānak and the Sikh Religion* (Oxford 1968); MSR Vol. 1. CS

Jasadipura I, Raden Ngabehi (b c1729 Penggeing, d 1803 Surakarta), Javanese court poet and historian. Famed for his adaptations of Old Javanese classics and for his contribution to the history of central Java. Born and raised during the end of the Mataram period. At the age of eight he was taken to Kedu where he studied Islam and mysticism for six years. He then entered the service of the ruler of Kartasura. For a time he served as a member of the King's bodyguard but was soon appointed the ruler's secretary where his literary talents quickly became apparent. After the division of Mataram in 1755, Surakarta (also known as Solo), to which the king had moved in 1746, became a flourishing centre of learning and Jasadipura played a prominent role in this revival of Javanese letters. At an early age he had earned the title of 'court poet' and although quite late in life he was offered the post of Minister, he spent his career as court poet. He is buried at his birthplace.

Among his significant contributions to Javanese literature and history, which were many, are his adaptations of Old Javanese works of Indian origin such as *Serat Rama*, *Serat Bratajuda*, *Ardjuna Wiwaha*, *Serat Dewarutji* and *Nitiçastra.* He also wrote the very important *Babad Gijanti* which is a history of the kingdom from 1746 to 1797. Near the end of his life he composed *Serat Tjabolek*, a work which has been characterized as an example of religious syncretism in Central Java. Jasadipura looms large in the history of Javanese literature. He provided the court with many classics, thereby encouraging the flowering of literature. His many books not only provided an impetus for literary activity, but also greatly influenced the Javanese language of Surakarta. As a result this form became the accepted standard for present-day Javanese.

Soebardi, *The Book of Cabolek* (Canberra 1967). JME

Jasimuddin (b 1903 Faridpur), Bengali poet. After studying at the Calcutta University, he assisted Bengali literary historian, D. C. Sen, with collection of folk ballads. He has been a Professor of Bengali, Dacca University, and has held a high post in Pakistan government. He has visited Europe, the USA, and West Asia, and was awarded doctorate degree by Rabindra Bharati University, Calcutta. Though a contemporary of the progressive, avant-garde writers, Jasimuddin remained independent of any particular group. He contributed to progressive journals, eg *Kallol.* Much of his poetry, however, can be described as traditional, rather similar to the folk ballads he helped collect. His language is simple; he makes good use of metre and rhyme. He is affectionately known as *pallī-kabi* or the Village Poet. His poetry faithfully displays the village, villagers, and village life of Bangladesh. Some books: *Naksī kānthār māṭh* (1929, trans. E. M. Milford, *The Field of the Embroidered Quilt*, Karachi 1958); *Sojan bādiyār ghāṭ* (1934, trans. B. Painter and Y. Lovelock, *Gipsy Wharf*, London 1969); *Māṭir kānnā* (The Cry of the Soil, 1951).

Other trans.: BBV; PEB. CBS

Jassin, Hans Baguë (b 1917 Gorontalo, Celebes), Indonesian critic and essayist. He received his secondary education in Medan. From 1940 to 1946 he was an editor at Balai Pustaka and served with *Pudjangga Baru* for several years. Since World War II he has been an editor or a member of the editorial staff for numerous Indonesian cultural and literary magazines, including *Mimbar Indonesia*, *Zenith*, *Kissah* and *Sastera.* Since 1953 he has been connected with the University of Indonesia's Faculty of Letters as lecturer on Indonesian literature where he has played a significant role in encouraging younger critics to prepare theses on writers and their works. As a gadfly and as a steady contributor to all manner of publications, he has contributed greatly to the development of Indonesian literature. His control of the facts of this literature is tremendous and his own documentation virtually complete. His major writings are essays on various aspects of Indonesian literature, studies of individual authors, historical surveys, and anthologies. These works are indispensable for anyone concerned with any scholarly aspect of Indonesian literature. Works: *Kesusasteraan Indonesia dimasa Djepang* (Indonesian Literature in the Japanese Period, 1948); *Gema Tanah Air. Prosa dan Puisi* 1942–1948 (Echo of the Fatherland. Prose and Poetry 1942–1948, 1948); *Chairil Anwar, Peloper Angkatan* '45 (C.A., Pioneer of the Generation of '45, 1956); *Analisa. Sorotan Tjerita Péndék* (Analysis. A Spotlight on Short Stories, 1961); *Pudjangga Baru. Prosa dan Puisi* (The New Poet. Prose and Poetry, 1963); *Kesusasteraan Indonesia Modern dalam Kritik dan Esei* (Modern Indonesian Literature in Criticism and Essay, 1967).

TMIL 120–2. JME

jātakas ('birth stories', c3rd century BC—3rd century AD or later), Pāli collection of tales of the Buddha's former births, consisting of verses and prose narratives. Only the strophes (*gāthās*), believed to have been uttered by the destined Buddha, are considered as canonical, while the tales in prose form a commentary on them, later written in extenso. Each 'story of (the Buddha's previous) birth' (*jātaka*) is embedded in another narrative which supplies connecting links with some occurrence in the Buddha's historical existence, and which has been added much later. The collection of Pāli *jātakas* contains 547 tales arranged in 22 sections (*nipāta*) on purely formal grounds (increasing number of verses). Some *jātakas*, however, comprise more stories embedded in the main narrative, while several tales occur more than once, but with different verses. The stanzas (*gāthās*) are of varying age, but they are often composed in an archaic language and some of them may come from a pre-Buddhist period. They are sometimes no more than gnomic utterances of memorial verses that should recall a story, while at other times they present dialogues or even narratives of epic proportions. The tales in prose are said to be a translation from old Sinhalese, which is itself a translation from an earlier Pāli form. Thus, in the preserved form, they are definitely later, perhaps from around the beginning of the Christian era. The introductory tales are still later and many of them were probably written in Ceylon.

Jātakas preserved a vast amount of narrative lore illustrating the daily life of ancient Indian people; they include secular tales and fables of any kind provided that one of the characters in the tale was future Buddha. Thus, they supplement and modify the scanty picture of ancient India provided by Brahmanical sources and offer ample material for the study of narrative lore and fables which were applied here in order to illustrate Buddhist ethical ideals. The stories are preceded by an Introduction called *Nidānakathā* (1st century BC or later), which gives the Buddha's previous history both before his birth and during his last life until he attained Buddhahood. This commentatorial account provides for a comparison with canonical records for a critical appraisal of history and legend in the Buddha's biography.

The jātaka or Stories of the Buddha's Former Births, trans. under the editorship of E. B. Cowell, 6 vols. (PTS 1895–1907, repr., in 3 vols., 1957).
WHIL II, 113–56. IF

jātaka in Sinhalese. *Jātaka* stories had a profound literary influence in Ceylon. Among the earliest works of Sinhalese literature of which we have knowledge are two such stories in Sinhalese verse, now lost. The earliest (late 12th century) surviving examples of Sinhalese poetry, apart from fragments, include two *jātaka* poems, *Muvadevdāvata* and *Sasadāvata*, and not much later is *Kavsilumina*, first and principal example of a Sinhalese *mahākāvya* (see *kāvya*), attributed to King Parākramabāhu II of Daṁbadeniya (1236–70). Vidyācakravarti (qv) wrote *jātaka* stories in the 13th century, and a separate prose version of *Ummagga jātaka* belongs to this period. A complete Sinhalese prose translation of the Pāli *jātaka* book was compiled, or begun, during the reign of King Parākramabāhu IV of Kurunāēgala (1302–26). Poets continued to take *jātaka* stories as subjects down to the 19th century. The *jātaka* guise was sometimes given to stories to which it does not properly belong, as in *Mahāpadaranga jātaka*, translated from

Tamil in 1692, which is the Indian story of the *Mahābhārata* (qv) with the hero (Yudhiṣṭhira in Sanskrit) identified with the Bodhisattva under the name of Dharmabuddhi. Non-canonical *jātaka* stories were also known, including such curiosities as *Itikumāra jātaka* (18th century), where the Bodhisattva is born as a woman.

Trans.: T. B. Yatawara, *Ummagga Jataka* (London 1898). CHBR

Jayadeva (12th century AD), Sanskrit poet of Orissa, author of the *Gītagovinda.* Signature verses (*bhaṇitās*) within the poem give clues to the poet's history. Although actual names vary in manuscripts, a strong tradition makes him the son of Bhojadeva and Rāmādevī, born in Kindubilva (village near Puri in Orissa, less convincingly in Birbhum, West Bengal). He was inspired by his wife, the dancer Padmāvatī. He compares himself with the poets Umāpatidhara, Govardhana, and Dhoyī, all of whom are associated with the Bengal court of Lakṣmaṇasena (c1185–1205 AD). Traditional accounts also place Jayadeva at this court. Tradition is corroborated by the existence of *Gītagovinda* verses in Śrīdharadāsa's *Saduktikarṇāmṛta*, an anthology compiled c1205 AD. Also, a verse from the poem is quoted in an inscription in Patan dated 1292 AD.

The *Gītagovinda* is dedicated in devotion to Kṛṣṇa. Intense earthly passion expresses the complex relationship of love between Kṛṣṇa and his devotee. The poem elaborates variations on the theme of separated lovers' passion and culminates in the ecstatic reunion of Rādhā and Kṛṣṇa. The emotional drama unfolds in twelve movements of songs (*padāvalīs*), composed in rhymed, alliterative, moric metres and linked together by recitative verses in classical Sanskrit metres. They are true lyrics, meant to be sung with appropriate melodic patterns (*rāgas*) and rhythmic cycles (*tālas*). They are sung by Kṛṣṇa, Rādhā, and her friend who acts as a go-between. Interpretations of the *Gītagovinda* are numerous and varied, but none can convincingly divorce the meaning of the poem from the context of Jayadeva's unique Sanskrit songs.

Translations in European languages are too numerous to list; in English, *Light of Asia and the Indian Song of Songs*, E. Arnold (London 1875); *Śrī Jayadeva's Gīta-Govinda*, G. Keyt (Bombay 1940); *Gītagovinda*, M. Varma (Calcutta 1968); *Songs from Jayadeva's Gītagovinda*, Barbara Stoler Miller (Mahfil, a Quarterly of South Asian Literature, Vol. VII, 1971).

DHSL I, 388–95; KHSL 190–8. BSM

Jayakāntaṉ, T. (Jeyakanthan, Dandapani, b 1934), Tamil writer. A critical realist and rationalist, he went through a Marxist period and then mellowed into a committed humanist, dealing in his many short stories and novels with the life of the workers and middle classes in the towns of Tamilnad. His style is direct, simple and powerful. Main works: stories *Āṇum peṇṇum* (Men and Women, 1953); *Utayam* (Dawn, 1954); *Yukacanti* (Ages Meet, 1963); novels *Vāḻkkai aḻaikkiṟatu* (Invitation of Life, 1957); *Pārisukkuppō* (Go to Paris, 1966). KZ

Jesmanyjasita, Javanese poet, see **Iesmaniasita,** Sulistyautami.

Jigar Murādābādī (real name 'Alī Sikandar, b 1890 Muradabad, d 1960 Gonda), Urdu lyric and romantic poet. He stood half way between the old and the new poetry. He wrote simple and fluent conventional love *ghazals* (see Vol. III), rich in spiritual imagery and versatile in music, celebrating the agreeable aspects of life. In old traditional forms he expressed the feelings of modern man and his relation to contemporary life. In his best-known volume of poetry *Ātish-e gul* (Fire of Rose, 1954) he is incomparable for delicate sensibility and reflective wisdom. JM

Jñānayaśas, Indian Buddhist poet, see **Buddhist literature.**

Jñāneśvar or **Jñāndev,** the first great poet in the Marathi language. He flourished at the end of the 13th century AD, under the Yādava King Rāmadevarao of Devagiri, northern Deccan. A number of works are attributed to him, by far the most famous being a copious versified commentary on the *Bhagavadgītā* (qv), the *Bhāvārthadīpikā*, commonly referred to as *Jñāneśvarī*, which was completed in 1290 AD. Composed in the popular *ovī* metre, this work is remarkable for the elegance and fluidity of its style as well as for the loftiness of its religious inspiration. It also constitutes one of the oldest and most precious specimens of New Indo–Aryan literature. Its original form, however, is somewhat uncertain; it was edited in the second part of the 16th century by the Marathi poet Eknāth, who gave what he claimed to be the authentic version.

Though a devotee of Kṛṣṇa, Jñāneśvar, in the *Jñāneśvarī*, appears steeped in Vedāntic tradition and acquainted with Śaiva Yoga; he names as his own *guru* (religious teacher) Nivṛtti, a spiritual descendant of Gorakhnāth. Actually the principal form of *bhakti* (qv) advocated in the *Jñāneśvarī* is *guru-bhakti* (devotion to one's *guru*), Kṛṣṇa himself appearing as the perfect and infinitely merciful *Guru*.

The Maharashtrian tradition also attributes to the same Jñāneśvar a number of short lyrics called *abhangas*. However, the language, style and even contents of the *abhangas* are very different from those of the *Jñāneśvarī* and they could have been composed by another poet. Jñāneśvar is nevertheless considered in Maharashtra as the founder of the whole lineage of poet-saints who composed hymns in honour of the god Viṭhobā of Paṇḍharpūr. The devoted pilgrims of Paṇḍharpūr are known as *Vārakarīs* and 'Dñyāndev Mahārāj' is today revered as an incarnation of the supreme Lord by all *Vārakarīs*, who devoutly sing the *Haripāṭh* and the *abhangas* attributed to him on their way to Paṇḍharpūr.

Trans.: V. G. Pradhān, *Jñāneśvarī* (with Introduction by H. M. Lambert, London, Vol. I, 1967, Vol. II, 1969).

J. F. Edwards, *Dhyāneshwar, the Outcaste Brāhmin* (Poona 1941); C. Vaudeville, *L'Invocation: Le Haripāṭh de Dñyāndev* (Paris 1969); MPMS 13–15, 35–40; RPML 1–143; NHML.

CV

Joaquin, Nick (Nicodemes, b 1917 Paco, Manila), Filipino poet, essayist and journalist writing in English; studied in the Philippines and in Hongkong. An admirer of Spanish culture, he went to Spain, and also spent much time in the USA. Unknown before World War II, his short story published in 1940 (*Three Generations*) made him famous. After the success of his essay *La Naval de Manila* (1943) Joaquin was offered a scholarship from the Dominicans; he joined the order but left in 1950. Joaquin is on the editorial staff of the Philippines Free Press, regularly contributing essays under the name Quijano de Manila. A born lyricist and master of language, but a shy and inaccessible person. Together with J. G. Villa (qv) Joaquin is considered a giant of the contemporary Filipino literary scene. A great deal of his writing remains scattered among periodical publications. Other works: *Prose and Poems* (1952), including the novel *The Woman Who Had Two Navels*; drama, *A Portrait of the Artist as Filipino* (1952). EH

Jōsh Malīḥābādī (real name Shabīr Ḥasan Khān, b 1894 Malihabad), Urdu lyric and romantic 'poet of revolution'. He graduated from Aligarh and in 1924–34 was employed as a translator at Hyderabad; later he edited various literary magazines and the periodical *Ājkal* in Delhi; he now lives in Karachi. He was a rebel discontented with the state of the world. His first volume *Rūḥ-e adab* (Spirit of Literature, 1921) containing natural and love lyrics, fought also against traditional mysticism, social prejudices and conformism. His political verses, full of contradictions, manifested his radical thinking and predilection for communism. In his later numerous volumes of poetry he wrote mostly on patriotic, philosophical and humanist subjects. He is the father figure of Urdu progressive poetry. JM

Jośi, Ilācandra (b 1902 Almora), Hindi writer, of a Kanyakubja Brahmin family of a high rank. He ran away from home and lived in the slums of Calcutta. His friendship with Śaratcandra Caṭṭopādhyāy (qv) marks the beginning of his career as a successful novelist. Since 1947 he has held high posts with All-India Radio. Like

Śaratcandra he takes characters from the fringes of Hindu society, whose abnormal behaviour he sees as being due to heredity and psychological factors. Among his best novels are *Sannyāsī* (The Ascetic, 1941), *Pret aur chāyā* (The Ghost and the Shadow, 1944), *Nirvāsit* (The Exile, 1946), *Parde kī rānī* (The Queen of the Curtain, 1952), *Jahāz kā pañchī* (The Ship Bird, 1955). He has also written many short stories. PG

Jośi, Sureś, Gujarati writer, see **navalikā.**

Jośi, Umāśankar (b 1911 Sabarakantha), Gujarati poet. Born in rocky northern Gujarat, his early youth was spent in the dry district on the river Sabarmati, often reflected in the images of his early poetry. In the 1930's and 40's he fought in India's non-violent revolution, the Satyagraha movements, and was jailed. He studied at Ahmedabad and Bombay, and taught literature at Gujarat University, of which he is Vice-Chancellor. He was awarded the Bhāratīya Jnānapīth Award, 1968. No major writer has a simple, unit relation with his age. In Jośi's poetry from *Gangotri* (The Origins of the Ganges, 1934) to *Abhijñā* (Awareness, 1968), the ambiguity of an age finds its iconic expression. His artistic perception of reality necessarily involves mythic contradictions. It is not a broken multiplicity but a profound mythicality which alone can unify contradictions. In his creativity, images within a poem and poems within his poetry often clash and contradict, not to be resolved in a logical conclusion but to grow in a mythic unity. Indeed his poetry is the poetry of togetherness, in that unique way in which the best of Indian poetry has always been through the centuries. This togetherness is twice realized: as the togetherness of the 'Concrete' (*comcrescere*), which 'grows together', and as the togetherness of the 'Symbolic' (*symballein*), which is 'thrown together'. The natural configuration of reality and the utterly conscious act of creating a human universe are both unified in the mythic ambiguity of his poetry.

His relation with the Gujarati language is also complex. In *Prācinā* (The Times Ancient, 1944), his first collection of verse-plays, the sheer joy of expression dominates. In *Mahāprasthāna* (The Ultimate Departure, 1966), the second collection of verse-plays, silence overcomes speech and the short utterances of the ancient characters act as hollow caves reverberating with each other's unspoken, unexpressed being. In *Mantharā*, a verse-play about the woman who instigated Rāma's exile in *Rāmāyaṇa* (qv), Jośi stretches language to the point where it becomes inhuman, compelling yet startling order echoing through the empty, darkened palace. In *Bhārat*, a related verse-play, the poet fights back with the other, humane, potential of man's complex language. His one-act plays in prose combine the techniques of Sanskrit short plays with that of the modern Western one-act plays. His short stories and a novel mark early stages of his narrative techniques.

He is one of the most perceptive critics and aesthetes in Indian literature today. Equally interested in 'being' and 'becoming', he looks for the relation between the writer's engagement and his integrity. This is also reflected in his excellent work as an editor and translator. Early in his work, he has introduced Polish poetry (*Gulé-Poland*) to Gujarati readers, and his translations from Sanskrit drama are gracefully accurate. His poetry has been widely translated into Asian and European languages. Further books: *Niśith* (Midnight, 1934), *Viśvaśānti* (World Peace, 1931); *Kavini Sādhanā* (Poet's Process of Achieving Poetry, 1961); *Kavitā-Vivek* (Poetics, 1971), *Śaili ane Svarup* (Style and Form, 1960), *Shakespeare* (1964). SY

Jur'at, Shaikh Qalandar Bakhsh (b mid-18th century Delhi, d 1810 Lucknow), Urdu erotic poet of levity and melancholy. He was brought up at Fyzabad and entered court service at Lucknow, but early became blind; he was a skilled musician. He wrote witty and playful amatory, frivolous *ghazals* (see Vol. III) to please his pleasure-seeking patrons. In a fluent and simple, elegant style he wrote of such themes as the gay diversions of the decadent nobility, the flirtations of dancing girls, and the love intrigues of court ladies. Later his blindness called forth an undertone of melancholy and helplessness. He was master of the psychological analysis of love.

RSHUL 88–90; MSHUL 130–3. JM

K

Kabīr (d 1518), Indian poet and Hindu sectarian reformer. He was born apparently at Banaras and brought up by Muslim foster-parents. Under the influence chiefly of the sect of Gorakhnāth he came to reject the doctrine of Rāma as an incarnation of Viṣṇu, and to see Rāma as a divine principle, essentially unqualified, with which all other gods might be equated. At the same time he retains an attitude of devotionalism (*bhakti*, qv) inherited from Vaiṣṇava tradition, reinforced by Muslim Sufi mysticism. Kabīr's sect continues to the present day. It has never been large, but his teaching, in a mixed Hindi speech, is well known and was an important influence on Nānak, the founder of Sikhism; some of his verses occur in the Sikh *Ādi Granth* (qv). Works: *Granthāvalī* (Collected Verses); *Bījak* (Account Book).

Trans.: Ch. Vaudeville, *Kabīr granthāvalī* (Pondicherry 1957), *Au cabaret de l'amour* (Paris 1959). RSM

kabiwālā, a particular type of Bengali poet, latter half of the 18th and the first half of the 19th centuries. The songs (*kabi gān*) they wrote or rather composed extemporaneously are sometimes considered vulgar. The subject matter utilized included not only the religious themes, Vaiṣṇava and Śākta, but also more erotic, bawdy material. Their audience was probably more often the illiterate villager than the cultured, wealthy patron. Poetic battles (*kabi laṛāi*) took place. One *kabiwālā* would sing a verse on some subject; the opposing poet would have to 'reply' with a verse of his own. These duels could degenerate into mere exchanges of abuse. Antony Firingi, a European, is said to have bested his adversary in such a battle of the wits.

S. K. De, *Bengali Literature in the 19th Century* (Calcutta [2]1962). CBS

Kaciyappa Civāccāriyar (17th century), Tamil poet who lived in Kanchipuram. His *Kantapurāṇam* (1625) based on the Sanskrit *Skandapurāṇa* (see *purāṇa*) is an ambitious work of more than ten thousand stanzas, imitating, in style and diction, Kampaṉ's (qv) *Irāmāvatāram.*

JHTL 211. KZ

Kādar Yār (1802–c1850), Panjabi poet of whom little is known, best remembered for his poem *Pūran Bhagat*, which draws on a part of the legendary cycle of *Rājā Rasālū.* Kādar Yār's poem tells how Pūran, son of the king Salvān, was sentenced to be mutiliated and hung in a well, after being falsely accused of indecent assault by his young stepmother. After twelve years have passed, he is rescued by the great yogi Gorakhnāth, who restores his amputated limbs and gives him magical powers. After being tested by the love of another queen, Pūran returns home and forgives his stepmother, but upbraids his father for his cruelty; on being offered the kingdom he declines it in favour of his brother, Rasālū. The poem is written in a series of *sīharfīs*, an acrostic genre popular in Panjabi. Kādar Yār also wrote *Harī Singh Nālve dī Vār* (1837), in praise of Raṇjīt Singh's famous general.

R. C. Temple, *The Legends of the Punjab* (1885), Vol. 2, pp. 375–456 (contains a popular version of the Pūran Bhagat legend, somewhat different from that outlined above). CS

kāfī, Panjabi mystical lyrics, see **Bullhe Śāh** and **Śāh Husain.**

Kailasam, Indian playwright writing in English; his mother tongue is Tamil. Gave up a distinguished career in geology to write plays. They contain original recreations of the great Indian myths, chiefly inspired by the *Mahābhārata* (qv); at the centre of each play is an epic hero. *The Purpose* (1944) is about Ekalavya, whose devotion to his guru Drona is as absolute as his compassion for the poor fawns in his wolf-infested forest. His tragedy arises out of the conflict and the destruction of the wolves to which he is led by his noble act of sacrifice to preserve the honour of his guru, an act which renders him impotent against the wild beasts. *Karna* (written earlier but published in 1946), a much more ambitious play in five acts, unfolds the tragic life-story of the hero after whom it is named. In order to create a spotless image of his heroes Kailasam suppresses facts in his originals and creates new 'evidence'. Their adversaries are deprived of their traditional appeal and considerably reduced in stature. His style was greatly influenced by Shakespeare and this has helped to cause the archaism of his language. He has an uncontrollable fondness for alliteration. Kailasam was a talented actor and his plays therefore have a uniform technical excellence. The absence of a living theatre has made it impossible for him to improve on his weaknesses. Further plays: *The Burden* (1933), *Fulfilment* (1933), *Keechaka* (1949).

G. S. Amur, *Kailasam's quest for greatness* (CEIWE 1–15); IWE 188–203. MED

Kajai, Abdul Rahim bin Salim (b 1894 Setapak, Kuala Lumpur, d 1943 Singapore), 'the father of Malay journalism' and a short-story writer. Educated in Malay and for three years in Arabic at Mecca, whither he travelled frequently until the late 1920's. He became correspondent for the Penang weekly *Idaran Zaman* in 1925, and in 1929 was appointed assistant editor of the weekly *Saudara*, founded by Sayyid Shaykh bin Ahmad Al-Hadi (qv). His only novel, *Cherita Dzu'l-Ruhain*, translated and adapted from the Arabic, appeared in 1930–31. During the 1930's, he was editor or leading writer for all the major Malay dailies in turn, and an active literary supporter of Malay nationalism. From 1936, he became very widely known from a stream of short stories published in the press, dealing humorously and acutely with everyday life, making a lasting impression on this literary form in terms of both realism and style. Three collections of stories were published posthumously: *Pusaka Kajai* (Kajai's Legacy, 4 vols., 1949), *Banyak Udang Banyak Garam* (Plenty of Prawns, Plenty of Salt, 1959) and *Lain Padang Lain Belalang* (Other Fields, Other Grasshoppers, 1961). WRR

kakawin, classical Javanese poetic form, see **Kanwa.**

Kala, U (?1678–?1738), Burmese historian, son of a rich man. He wrote *Mahā Yazawingyi* (Great Chronicle), the first full-scale historical work in Burmese, covering the period from the beginning of the world to AD 1730. It marked the starting point of Burmese historiography and is a valuable bequest to posterity. *Hmannan Yazawingyi* (Glass Palace Chronicle), the official history, compiled in 1830, incorporated verbatim U Kala's work 'with slight variations in language here and there and interpolations of disquisitions on points of difference in opinion'. The Great Chronicle, like the *Yazawingyaw* (Celebrated Chronicle) by Thilawuntha (qv), 1520, is modelled on the pattern of the *Mahāvaṃsa* (see *Dīpavaṃsa*), but is cast in a Burmese mould. U Kala also wrote a Shorter and a Concise chronicle.

U Tet Htoot, *The Nature of the Burmese Chronicles*, in: *Historians of South-East Asia*, ed. D. G. E. Hall (London 1962), pp. 50–62; GPC XIII–XX. HP

Kalhaṇa (12th century AD), Sanskrit writer. He wrote the unique historical poem *Rājataraṅgiṇī*, which was a chronicle of the kings of Kashmir. Kalhaṇa's object was to offer a connected narrative of the various dynasties which ruled Kashmir from the earliest period down to his own time. He reconstructed the earliest part of this history from legends and popular traditions. The material for the middle part of this history was collected from older written records and Kalhaṇa arranged these historical data in a strict chronological order. The final part was, however, an account of the events which the author knew either through personal experience or from accounts of contemporary witnesses. The work is thus of much historical value, besides being a *kāvya* (qv) which shows the poetic talent of its author. This also shows the methods used by ancient historians in India. Kalhaṇa referred to various earlier compositions of the history of Kashmirian kings which he had used. But unfortunately none of them has come down to us. Kalhaṇa's date is fixed generally at 1148–49 AD, from both internal and external evidence.

Trans.: by M. A. Stein (Calcutta 1900); WHIL III, 95–101. BKM

Kālidāsa (c400 AD), Sanskrit poet and dramatist, by general consensus the greatest of Sanskrit poets. Nothing is known of his life, although much 'biographical' legend has accumulated in later centuries. His date has been much argued, but it is certain that he cannot be placed later than the date given above. Other arguments, including strong indications of an association with the Gupta dynasty, which saw a renaissance of Brahmanical Sanskrit learning, indicate that the date cannot be much earlier. Attempts to argue for dates as early as the 1st century BC can now be dismissed, and it seems almost certain that he flourished towards the latter part of the 4th century AD.

Nearly 30 spurious compositions have been attributed to Kālidāsa, some of which have been ingenuously explained as the work of one or more poets bearing the same name. The works generally accepted as genuine are seven in number: two shorter poems (*khaṇḍa-kāvya*), *Ṛtusaṃhāra* and *Meghadūta*; two epics (*mahā-kāvya*), *Raghuvaṃśa* and *Kumāra-sambhava*; and three dramas, *Mālavikāgnimitra*, *Vikramorvaśīya*, and *Śakuntalā*. Among these, Kālidāsa's authorship of the *Ṛtusaṃhāra* (The Seasons) has sometimes been doubted, but on insufficient grounds. At most, it may be felt that the poem shows a slightly less mature style than the others; but the simple explanation is that it was an early work. It treats in succession the six seasons into which the Indians divided the year (the fierce summer, the rains, autumn, early winter, the cold season, and the spring) and gives a vivid description of nature, of the reactions of the animals of the wild, and especially the interplay of the emotions of lovers in the various seasons.

In the *Meghadūta* (The Cloud-messenger) a certain *yakṣa* (a class of demigods) exiled from Alakā, the Himālayan abode of his master, the god Kubera, asks a thundercloud at the beginning of the rainy season to convey a message to his wife sorrowfully awaiting his return. In the first half of the poem, the *yakṣa* describes to the cloud the route to be followed, giving many striking word-pictures of the cities and countryside, of the mountains and rivers over which the cloud will pass on its journey. The second half of the poem gives a glowing account of the beauty of Kubera's divine city, and proceeds to tell with moving pathos the melancholy and despair of the lonely wife as she awaits the end of the curse of her husband's exile.

The *Raghuvaṃśa* (The Dynasty of Raghu), in 19 cantos, is in essence the story of Rāma (see *Rāmāyaṇa*), framed by an account of his ancestors and descendants. King Dilīpa of the Ikṣvāku dynasty is childless, but by humble service to the divine cow Nandinī he obtains the boon of a son, Raghu, who in due course succeeds to the throne (cantos 1–3), and conquers a great empire (4). To him is born a son, Aja (5), who is chosen in marriage by the princess Indumatī (6), and defeats his rivals in battle (7). After the death of the royal couple (8), the kingdom passes to their son Daśaratha, who while hunting accidentally kills a Brahmin boy, and is put under a curse in respect of his own sons (9). Cantos 10–15 tell of the birth and life of Rāma. While the narrative here follows in the main that of the *Rāmāyaṇa*, Kālidāsa shows his poetic genius in the manner of telling, and in the brilliance of his descriptive passages. After the reign of Rāma's son Kuśa (16), the remainder of the poem gives little more than a cursory account of several insignificant kings, the decline of the dynasty ending with the degenerate Agnivarman.

The *Kumāra-sambhava* (The Birth of Kumāra, the god of war, also called Skanda and Kārttikeya) is very different in subject matter and structure, while displaying the same poetic mastery. In one group of manuscripts only cantos 1–7 appear, while another group contains 17 cantos. Although the eighth canto has been accepted as genuine by most scholars, there is general agreement that cantos 9–17 are a later suppletion by a poet of inferior talent. It is not known whether Kālidāsa left the poem incomplete, or whether an authentic ending was lost in the early manuscript transmission. The theme is the threat to the gods by the demon Tāraka, who can only be overcome by a son born to the great god Śiva by Umā (Pārvatī). Śiva has no thoughts of marriage, but is engaged in religious meditation in his Himālayan hermitage, where Umā attends him as a handmaiden. The god of love, Kāma, is sent to cause Śiva to fall in love with Umā, but is seen and burnt to ashes by the fire from Śiva's third eye. Umā then resorts to severe religious austerities, whereby she wins the love of Śiva. Canto 7 describes the wedding, and canto 8 the love-making of the divine couple. The poem is enriched by magnificent descriptions of the Himālaya, and Umā's beauty (canto 1), the awakening of spring (canto 3), and the poignant lament of Kāma's wife Rati for her dead husband (canto 4).

Of the three dramas, the *Mālavikāgnimitra* is the least substantial, and, but for the fame of its author, would probably have won little esteem. The hero Agnimitra is an historical personage, a king of the Śuṅga dynasty of the 2nd century BC, but the play is not an historical drama. It depicts the king falling in love with Mālavikā, maidservant and dancing-girl of his chief queen Dhāriṇī. After much romantic intrigue, involving also the jealousy of Irāvatī, Agnimitra's second queen, Mālavikā is finally revealed as a princess of Vidarbha, already betrothed to Agnimitra; whereupon the two rival queens magnanimously accept her as a co-wife. Compare the use of variations on the same theme by Harṣa (qv).

The *Vikramorvaśīya* is on a higher level, showing a greater skill in dramatic technique, and a wealth of fine verses. The plot is derived from the ancient Vedic legend of the heavenly nymph (*apsaras*) Urvaśī and the mortal king Purūravas, though Kālidāsa has remoulded the old story into a gentler and more romantic shape. In Act I Urvaśī is captured by a demon, the king rescues her, and the two fall in love. In Act II Urvaśī reveals her love for the king by a message written on birch-bark, while she herself remains invisible by her divine power; she afterwards appears in visible form. She is recalled to heaven, and, playing the part of Lakṣmī in a drama before the gods, she inadvertently says that she loves Purūravas, where the script requires 'Puruṣottama' (Viṣṇu). The inevitable curse is mitigated by Indra, who permits her to live on earth with her lover until he sees their son. Act IV breaks the thread of the plot, but this is more than compensated by the sustained lyric excellence of the poetry. Urvaśī has accidentally entered a sacred grove where women are excluded, and is turned into a creeper. The king's soliloquy while, near to madness, he searches for her in the forest, contains some of Kālidāsa's finest poetry. In turn the king beseeches the various beasts and birds of the forest for news of his beloved. Finally he is guided to a magic gem, and holding this he embraces the creeper, whereupon Urvaśī is retransformed. Meanwhile their son Āyus, without the king's knowledge of his existence, has been brought up in a hermitage; but in Act V events bring him to the court. The earlier curse thus requires Urvaśī's return to heaven; but the tragic ending (almost invariably avoided in Sanskrit drama) is averted: the gods require the assistance of Purūravas in their battle with the demons, and in return are prepared to permit Urvaśī to remain on earth as his wife.

The *Śakuntalā* (*Śākuntala*, *Abhijñānaśakuntala*) is recognized as the finest of Kālidāsa's plays. It was among the earliest Sanskrit works to be made accessible to Europeans, through an English translation by Sir William Jones in 1789, followed by a German version by G. Forster in 1791. Seen only through the veil of translation, the drama was immediately recognized by Goethe as a masterpiece, and was celebrated by him in a verse of unreserved praise. The plot is based on a story in the first book of the *Mahābhārata* (qv), where the aim is to give an account of the birth of Bharata. As in the *Vikramorvaśīya*, Kālidāsa has with sensitive artistry re-shaped and embellished his source-material to produce a work of great charm and beauty. The action opens with the accidental intrusion of the king Duṣyanta (Duḥṣanta), while hunting in the forest, into the hermitage of the sage Kaṇva. There, unobserved, he sees Kaṇva's foster-daughter Śakuntalā, and falls deeply in love with her. When they meet, his love is returned, and in due course they are united in the Gandharva form of marriage (that is, marriage by mutual consent only, recognized as a valid form of marriage in Hindu legal tradition). When the king departs, Śakuntalā in her preoccupation fails to pay due respect to the arrival of the irascible sage Durvāsas, and is placed under a curse by him: her husband shall forget her, until he sees again the ring he gave her. As her pregnancy advances, she is sent by Kaṇva to the king's court; but since she has meanwhile lost the ring in the waters of a sacred bathing-place, the king does not recognize her. After a scene of much pathos, she is carried off by a divine figure. The lost ring is recovered by the city guards from a fisherman who found it in a fish which he has caught. The ring is duly brought to the king, who, on seeing it, immediately remembers Śakuntalā, and grieves that he has now lost her. But he is then summoned to assist the gods in battle against the demons, and is rewarded by being happily reunited with Śakuntalā and their son Bharata.

The above summaries cannot convey the outstanding merits of Kālidāsa's works; and the numerous translations, especially of the *Meghadūta* and the *Śakuntalā*, too frequently disappoint the reader. Hence none are cited here.

For fuller discussion and appreciation, see KHSL 74–108; KSD 141–67; DHSL 118–54.

JB

Kalim Kāshānī, Abū Ṭālib (d 1651 in India), Indo-Persian poet-laureate of the Emperor Shahjahan. Travelling through India he observed the life and customs of its people. His lyrical *ghazals* (see Vol. III) are written in simple language with Indian vernacular expressions. His romantic official chronicle *Shāhjahān-nāma* sings in an uncomplicated style the praises of Timur and the Mughal rulers.

HIL 301, 726.

JM

Kalittokai, classical Tamil anthology, see **Eṭṭuttokai.**

Kaliyānacuntaram, Mutaliyār Tiruvārūr V. (pseud. Tiru. Vi. Ka., 1883–1953), Tamil writer, critic, essayist, journalist, philosopher, orator, social reformer and politician. His essays, literary criticisms and speeches were extremely influential in modern Tamil literary, cultural and linguistic development. Originally an ardent Gandhi-ist, he adopted a form of Marxism, combined with Tamil nationalism. His many writings deal with cultural, linguistic and literary problems, trying also to solve pressing social and political needs. Main works: *Tamiḻccōlai* (Tamil Garden, 2 vols., 1935); *Intiyāvum viṭutalaiyum* (India and Liberty, 1947).

JHTL 265.

KZ

Kalki, Tamil novelist, see **Kiruṣṇamūrtti,** R.

Kallol, Rajasthani poet, see **Ḍholā-Mārū rā Dūhā.**

Kalpasūtra, Vedic handbooks of religious practice, see **vedāṅga.**

Kamaleśvar (b 1932 Mainpuri), Hindi writer for Indian television and later editor of literary papers, outstanding in *nayī kahānī* (qv). He writes on themes of lower middle class life, and is a master of suggestive atmosphere, especially the oppressive. Some stories: *Rājā Nirbaṃsiyā* (1957); *Khoyī huī diśāẽ* (Lost Directions, 1963); *Mās kā dariyā* (The River of Flesh, 1966).

DA

Kāmasūtra, ancient Indian book on erotics, see **Vātsyāyana.**

Kampaṉ (c1180–1250 AD), Tamil poet. Though a number of legends exist, not much is known about him. He was born in Tiruva*l*untūr (Tanjore district) and patronized by a chieftain named Caṭaiyappaṉ. Some consider him the greatest Tamil poet. His main work is *Irāmāvatāram* (The Descent of Rāma), a magnificent epic of about 40,000 lines, based on Vālmīki's Sanskrit *Rāmāyaṇa* (qv). Though the poem suffers from excess of rhetoric and exaggeration and from occasional padding, it is a work of supreme art and immense skill in its total command of metre and language. Kampaṉ was a learned poet, well-versed in both Tamil and Sanskrit literary sources and traditions, and his scholarship is very evident in the work. It is clearly not a translation of Vālmīki, but the main story follows the tradition rather closely. However, significant changes are introduced into minor episodes. The epic is based on the rhetoric of Sanskrit *kāvya* (qv), but Kampaṉ has utilized the classical Tamil tradition (eg the five landscapes). Thus Kampaṉ's ideal, 'Rāma's rule', the heavenly kingdom to be established, though set into an ideal environment of country and city (Ayodhyā), has a number of new, very concrete, and purely Tamil features. In some of the characters there are considerable differences between Kampaṉ and Vālmīki (eg Ahalyā, and especially Rāvaṇa). There is a tremendous difference between Kampaṉ and Vālmīki in form: Kampaṉ's poem is rather like a string of self-contained, individual stanzas. Probably the main difference is in the conception of Rāma where Kampaṉ has succeeded better than Vālmīki in portraying his hero not only as a god but as a true man with a divine mission.

Trans.: C. R. Rajagopalachari, *The Ayodhya Canto of the Ramayana as Told by Kamban* (London 1961).
JHTL 157–85. KZ

Kanakadāsa, Kannada saint and poet, see **Purandaradāsa.**

Kānhaḍade Prabandha of Padmanābh, considered by Tessitori as 'the most valuable treasure of Old Gujarati or Old Western Rajasthani'. According to some modern critics, it can easily stand comparison with the celebrated *Pṛthvīrāj-rāso* (see *rāso*). The *Kānhaḍade Prabandha* is a fairly long work (353 verses, ie 606 lines) composed in various popular metres (with two prose passages) in 1455 AD, by a Brahmin poet, Padmanābh, who belonged to the house of Akhairāj, the Cauhān Rājput prince of Jālaur in southern Marwar. The poem relates the heroic struggle of Akhairāj's ancestor, Rājā Kānhaḍade of Jālaur, against the repeated attacks of the Sultān of Delhi, Alauddīn. The struggle ends in the defeat and death of the Rājput hero, of his son Vīramdev and of all his relatives in a supreme, desperate fight. With this main theme is interwoven the romantic love of Princess Firozā, Alauddīn's daughter, for Prince Vīramdev, whom she resolves to follow in death by burning herself on the river Jamna's bank. The language of the poem is a good specimen of Old Western Rajasthani of the 15th century and the noble simplicity of its style fits the loftiness of the heroic Rājput ideals it depicts. The *Kānhaḍade Prabandha* is a perfect example of old Rajasthani *vīr-kāvya* (heroic poetry) with a historical background. CV

Kanwa (11th century, East Java), Javanese scholar and court poet. The epic *Arjuna Wiwaha Kakawin* (The Nuptials of Arjuna), probably his only work, is the oldest datable *kakawin*, the classical poetic form the style of which corresponds to the *kāvya* (qv) poetry of India. The 40 or so parts vary in number of lines. Learned in ancient Indian culture, Kanwa was inspired by *Vanaparva*, Book III of the *Mahābhārata* (qv); he was probably also influenced by Prince Airlangga, at whose court he lived from 1019 to 1049, as the story of Arjuna could be an allegory of the Prince's youth. The hero's battle against evil, personified by Niwata Kawaca, the prince of the demons, is presented with mastery. The renewed popularity of the epic today is due to the 18th century version by the Javanese poet Jasadipura I (qv). In modern Javanese literature, the epic entitled *Minta Raga* forms part of the ballad *Bīma Suci*; it is also a popular *wajang* (qv) theme. The *kakawin* in Java illustrates the impact of ancient Indian culture and the strength of the native Javanese element; the original Indian epic themes have been so completely adapted to suit Javanese ways of thought and mingled together with old Javanese legends that only the bare outline remains. It is rare for the earliest Javanese paraphrase of an ancient Indian epic to preserve the original poetic form, as in *Arjuna Wiwaha Kakawin*; in most cases, we find verse changed to prose or prose to verse.

PLJ I, 180–5 EV

Kapilar, classical Tamil poet, see **Eṭṭuttokai.**

Kāranta, Kōṭa Śivarāma (b 1902 Kota), the most important Kannada novelist and encyclopaedist (eg *Bālaprapanca*, 1937, a children's encyclopaedia). He is a world-traveller, yet remains the novelist of the south Kanara region, which he has recorded in loving, realistic, even anthropological, detail: eg *Maṛali Maṇṇige* (Back to the Soil, 1940), a novel of three generations; *Beṭṭada Jīva* (A Spirit of the Hills, 1943), a poetic evocation of nature and character; and *Kuḍiyara Kūsu* (A Child of the Kuḍiyas, 1951), an anthropological novel of hunting hill-tribes. A knowledge of modern science, ethnography, keen local and social observation, and a vigilant satiric eye are everywhere present. He has produced a constant stream, and his novels are rather loosely written and structured. Of his later novels, *Aḷida Mēle* (1960; it tells of a search for a dead man's character) is important; so is his fascinating autobiography regarding his versatile experiments with life, *Huccu Manassina Hattu Mukhagaḷu* (Ten Faces for a Wild Heart, 1948), and his study of *Yakṣagāna Bayalāṭa* (Kannada Folk-Theatre, 1957).

Trans.: A. N. Murti Rao, *Back to the Soil* (Puttur 1950). AKR

Kārnād, Giriś (b 1937), nationally acclaimed young dramatist of Kannada, known for three plays, widely translated and staged: *Yayāti* (1961) on a *Mahābhārata* (qv) theme, *Tuglaq* (1964) on the mediaeval Muslim emperor, and *Hayavadana* (1971) on the classical Indian tale of the Transposed Heads (retold by Thomas Mann). The last is marked by sophistication, spectacle, poetry, often epic breadth and a sure sense of theatre, with experimental use of the contemporary European as well as Kannada folk-theatre.

Trans.: *Tuglaq* (1971); *Hayavadana* (1971, in: *Enact*, June 1971). AKR

Kasimi, Urdu poet, see **Qāsimi,** Aḥmad Nadīm.

kathakaḷi, a dance-drama of Kerala, south India. Probably derived from a variety of earlier, more popular types of narrative dance, *kathakaḷi* took its present form in the 17th century as a unique combination of acting, dancing, music and literature. It is the task of the performers (by tradition all male) to interpret by their movements, gestures and miming the story told in the poem sung by members of a small group standing behind the main actors and including musicians who provide a percussion accompaniment. The texts used for these performances are called *āṭṭakkatha* ('story for dancing') and a large number have been composed over the past three or four centuries. Among the best is a version of the story of Nala (see *Nalopākhyāna*) by the 18th-century poet, Uṇṇāyi Vāriyar. The impressive 20th-century revival of this art is above all the result of the work of the Kerala Kala Mandalam (Academy of Kerala Arts) founded by the poet Vaḷḷattōḷ Nārāyaṇa Mēnōn (qv).

Beryl De Zoete, *The Other Mind. A Study of Dance in South India* (New York 1953), pp. 90–144; PNHML 86–101; GSML 97–107. REA

Kaṭha-Upaniṣad, see **upaniṣad.**

Kauṭilya (also called Cāṇakya or Viṣṇugupta), Minister of the King Candragupta Maurya (4th century BC), traditionally considered to be the author of the famous Sanskrit *Arthaśāstra*, a textbook of statecraft and diplomacy. The book, written in prose with interspersed summaries in verse (which may however have been added later), is in a mixed *sūtra-* (qv) and commentary-style. It is divided into 15 chapters, dealing successively with the education of a ruler, state and law administration, courts, fight against treason, methods of politics, army, aristocracy, diplomatic intrigue, conduct of war, and magic means. It is very improbable that the text which is known now should be the work of Kauṭilya, but it may be an elaboration of an original composed by him. The preserved book seems to have originated sometime during the early centuries AD, which, however, does not detract from its immense historical value.

Trans.: R. Shamasastry, *Kauṭilya's Arthaśāstra* (Bangalore 1915); J. J. Meyer, *Das altindische Buch vom Welt- und Staatsleben* (Hannover 1925); R. P. Kangle, *The Kauṭilīya Arthraśāstra* (Part I, Text; Part II, Translation; Part III, A Study), (Bombay 1960, 1963, 1965).
N. N. Law, *Studies in Ancient Hindu Polity* (London 1914), and *Inter-State Relations in Ancient India* (Calcutta-London 1920); O. Stein, *Megasthenes und Kauṭilya* (Vienna 1921); M. V. Krishna Rao, *Studies in Kautilya* (Delhi [2]1958). DZ

Kavi, Nānālāl, Gujarati poet, see **arvācin kavitā.**

Kavirājamārga (Royal Road of Poets, 9th century), a work of rhetoric and poetics. It is the earliest Kannada work (though the earliest example of Kannada is the Halmiḍi edict, ?c450), attributed by some to Nṛpatunga Amōghavarṣa (814–877). Though derived from Sanskrit works on rhetoric, like Daṇḍin's and Bhāmaha's (qqv) it contains valuable descriptions of the Kannada country, people, and dialects, and refers to earlier poets and prose-writers, otherwise unknown. AKR

kāvya is the generic name for 'poetry' in Classical Sanskrit, the work of a *kavi*, 'poet'. The term is restricted to compositions of literary merit, excluding didactic and technical works in verse, but including artistic prose. *Kāvya* may thus be *gadya-kāvya* 'prose poetry' or *padya-kāvya* 'metrical poetry'. Thus, the *Kāvyādarśa* of Daṇḍin (qv), a treatise on the theory of poetry, although written in verse, is not itself a *kāvya*, while the same author's *Daśakumāracarita*, a romantic prose novel, is accorded the status of *kāvya*. For other examples of ornate artistic prose, see Bāṇa, Subandhu. A *kāvya* with substantial quantities of verse and prose alternating was know as a *campū*.

Verse *kāvya* can be classified according to length, ranging from the single stanza (*muktaka*) which can present in four lines a miniature poetic intaglio, to the full-scale *mahā-kāvya*, which may be described as a court-epic. Intermediate in length is the *khaṇḍa-kāvya*, the shorter poem, of which the most famous example is the *Meghadūta* of Kālidāsa (qv). Such poems, though 'short' in comparison with the *mahā-kāvya*, are normally much longer than European lyrics, and indeed no genres comparable to the latter are known in Classical Sanskrit, their place being taken in effect by the isolated stanza. It has been said that, because of the compression and expressiveness of the classical language, some such stanzas, especially in the longer metres, may contain sufficient material for a European sonnet, although many others are more appropriately thought of as epigrams. The best known of such *muktakas* are the collections of verses attributed to Amaru and Bhartṛhari (qqv). Such isolated stanzas, however, do not differ in their style or metres from individual stanzas of the *mahā-kāvyas* and dramas. In the later mediaeval period, large anthologies of *subhāṣitas*, 'fine verses', were compiled, which took their verses impartially from *muktaka* collections and from *mahā-kāvyas* and dramas.

The *mahākāvya* or *sarga-bandha* ('composition in cantos') evolved features which later theorists prescribed as rules. Thus, the poem should have not less than 8 and not more than 30 cantos, each canto being in a single metre, except for a change of metre marking the end of the canto. The chief character should be a hero or a god, and the theme taken from tradition—in practice, most frequently from the older epics. The poem should include descriptions of the seasons, of cities and natural scenery, of beautiful women, of battles and statecraft.

It should make full use of the figures of poetry, *alaṃkāras* (literally, 'ornaments'), and convey appropriate poetic emotions (*rasa*), the most important being *śṛṅgāra* (love), *vīra* (heroism), and *karuṇa* (pathos). The drama is also classified as *kāvya*, being designated as *dṛśya-kāvya* 'poetry to be seen', in contrast to *śravya-kāvya* 'poetry to be heard'. Theorists recognized ten principal types and several subsidiary varieties, ranging from the serious heroic drama, *nāṭaka*, to the farce, *prahasana*. The dialogue is in prose liberally interspersed with verses. A standard feature is that Sanskrit is spoken by the male characters of high rank and female ascetics, while all other women, even of the highest rank, and men of lower social status use various types of Prakrit. An interesting peculiarity is that one of the stock characters, the *vidūṣaka*, who is the confidential friend of the hero, is portrayed as a buffoon, and, although a Brahmin, always speaks Prakrit. Approximately fifty different metres of varying length and complexity were developed in the classical period, although only a dozen or so are used frequently. The majority of these metres are based on strict quantitative principles, comparable to those of classical Greek and Latin metres. JB

Ken Angrok, Javanese chronicle, see **Pararaton.**

Kēśava Dēv, P. (b 1905), Malayalam writer. A member of the Progressive Writers' Association (see *progressive writing*) in Kerala in its early days, he has written a number of plays on political themes, but is best known as a novelist and writer of short stories. Most of these show a marked commitment to social reforms. Some, such as *Ulakka* (Pounding Stick, 1951) and *Kaṇṇāṭi* (Mirror, 1961), show sympathy with the idea of violent revolution. Others, like the large-scale *Ayalkkār* (Neighbours, 1963), aim rather to hold up a mirror before contemporary Kerala society and recent development in it.

PNHML 135–6, 144–5; VISNM 25–32; GSML 177–9, 185–6. REA

Keśavsut (pen-name of Kṛṣṇājī Keśav Dāmle, 1866–1905), the first major poet of modern Marathi. His life was short and externally unhappy, as he moved around Maharashtra in a succession of subordinate teaching posts, at odds with his father and with his superiors. His domestic life does seem to have been some compensation although very little is known about him either as a public or a private figure except through his verse. His poems display a series of anguished responses to the ills of humanity; sometimes fierce indignation, sometimes melancholy, often despair.

Trans.: P. Machwe, *Keshavsut* (rough translation of some of his poems, New Delhi 1968). IR

Khāḍilkar, Kṛṣṇajī Prabhākar (1872–1948), Marathi dramatist who often used the stage for covert anti-British propaganda (especially *Kīcakavadha*, The Slaying of Kicak, 1910). He was also a collaborator of Ṭiḷak (qv) on *Kesarī*. IR

Khai-Hung (real name Tran-khanh-Du, b 1896 Co-am, Hai-duong province, d 1947 Thai-binh province), Vietnamese writer active between the two world wars, son of a mandarinal family. He was a founding member of the *Tu luc van doan* group (see Nhat-Linh). A very prolific, and strongly Buddhist, author, he became one of the greatest Vietnamese novelists of the first half of this century. His work shows the characteristic features of the Romantic school, but the relationships between his characters are often too dreamlike and out of touch with reality. As a journalist he wrote for *Phong hoa* (1932) and *Ngay nay* (1935). In 1945 he became a leading figure in the Viet-nam Nationalist Party in Hanoi, opposing the Ho-chi-Minh Government. Works: novels, *Hon buom mo tien* (Soul of a Butterfly, Dreaming of Immortals, 1933); *Nua chung xuan* (Unfinished Spring, 1934); *Trong mai* (Showdown, 1936); *Thoat ly* (Escape, 1937); *Thua tu* (Inheritance, 1940); *Hanh* (1940); *Tieu-son trang si* (The Heroes of Tieu-son, 1940); stories, *Anh phai song* (You Must Live, 1936); *Tieng suoi reo* (Murmuring Brook, 1937); *Doi chc*

(Expectation, 1939); plays, *Dong benh* (The Afflicted by the Same Disease, 1942).

DNLIVN 157–68; 190. VV

Khāṇḍekar, Viṣṇu Sakhārām (b 1898), Marathi romantic novelist and short-story writer. With Phaḍke (qv) the most popular fiction writer of the inter-war years. His novels include *Hṛdayācī hāk* (The Heart's Cry, 1930), *Don dhruva* (Opposite Poles, 1934) and *Krauncavadha* (The Slaying of Kraunca, 1942). They have been translated into several other Indian languages but never into English. IR

Khiengsiri, Kanhā, Thai writer, see **Surāngkhanāng,** K.

Khin Hnin Ju (Khin Su, b 1925 Wakhema), Burmese writer. She studied at Rangoon University 1948–51, was secretary to Premier U Nu during the Anti-Fascist People's Freedom League government, and resumed her studies in 1959–61 (BA). Her best works are short stories; though a writer of prose, her descriptions are poetic. All aspects of nature, including human nature, are vividly depicted in her *Jauktja tou atyaun* (All about Men, 1960). The Buddhist feeling for nature and its impermanence is well expressed, through the ephemeral beauties of landscape, in *Myei ka Ye thij* (The Earth is Laughing, 1956). Her very effective sense of humour is shown in *Thu tyaun Khek te* (The Hindrance, 1955). Further works: novels *Ayain* (Wildness, 1948), *Tharaphu* (The Crown, 1953—Myawati Prize); short stories *Nweinhnaun* (Late Hot Season, 1952), *Tyeimoum Yeip thwin* (In the Mirror, 1959—Prize 1960), *Ayain ne Ajin* (Wildness and Civilisation), *Shwei Pyijto i Poumpyin mja* (Tales from the Royal City, 1961). DBt

Khitsam (Khitsan), Burmese literary movement, see **Zodji.**

Khlōng Kamsūon (also **Khlōng Nirāt Nakhọn**), poem attributed to Sī Prāt, famous Thai poet, but may be two centuries earlier (late 15th), judging from the style and ancient stanzaic metre. Dating and authorship of this poem is one of the most disputed questions in Thai literary history. As printed today it comprises 129 four-line verses in stanzaic (*khlōng*) form, introduced by a passage in running verse. The *khlōng* lines are very regular. Numerous archaisms render the poem difficult, and Laotian elements also occur. In content the poem is a *nirāt* (qv), describing the former Thai capital Ayuthayā and a journey by boat to Nakhọn Sī Thammarat in southern Thailand. Unlike many later *nirāt*, this poem expresses the poet's feelings as well as giving descriptions. KW

Khmer inscriptions (7th to 14th centuries) comprise the earliest dated Cambodian literature known to us. During the pre-Angkor period, the subject-matter was practical, recording gifts to the religious foundation and lists of serfs and their duties. Meanwhile, inscriptions in Sanskrit described historical events in more literary style. By the 11th century Khmer was used for more varied matter, for example for the text of an oath of allegiance. The modern Khmer inscriptions, chiefly of the 16th to 18th centuries and written on the Angkor buildings, fluently record, with much personal detail and Buddhist fervour, further donations to the temples. JMJ

Khun Chāng Khun Phāēn, greatest national epic of Thailand. It is probably exclusively native in theme, and quite apart from its literary value, is a valuable source for the cultural history of the country. Some 45,000 lines present an almost complete picture of ancient Thailand, in innumerable episodes centred round Khun Chāng and Khun Phāēn, competing for the favours of beautiful Wan Thọng. The heroes' lives (one a royal officer, the other a Buddhist novice), the fate of their dead parents and the execution of Wan Thọng enable the poet to depict social conditions in the early 18th century, without appearing to criticize the tyranny of monarchy and Buddhist thought. Death, tyrannical caprice, love and worldly pleasure, manly courage and wise piety, all find their place; the poet describes without reasoning. In spite of Prince Damrong's research, the history of this epic remains to be clarified; the story is certainly much older than its present form, parts of which are known to have been written by Rāma II (1809–1824: the marriage of Khun Phāēn and Wan Thọng, erotic passages in Part I, the jealous scenes between Wan Thọng and Lau Thọng), Rāma III (1824–51, while still Mahā Uparāt: Khun Chāng's wooing of Wan Thọng and her elopement with Khun Phāēn), and Sunthọn Phū (the birth of Phlāi Ngām to Khun Phāēn and Wan Thọng). No more is known as yet. The epic is the classical example of the *klọn* metre used in narrative poetry intended for recitation.

Prem Chaya, *The Story of Khun Chang and Khun Phan* (2 vols., Bangkok 1955); Kasem Chibunruang, *Khun Chang, Khun Phen, La Femme, le Héros et le Villain* (Paris 1960). KW

Kim Set, Cambodian writer, see **pralom-lok.**

Kiruṣṇa Piḷḷai, Henry Alfred (1827–1900), Tamil poet. Brought up as a devout Hindu, he was in 1853 appointed Tamil *pandit* in a school run by the Society for the Propagation of the Gospel. In 1858 he was baptized a Christian. After a successful teaching career he retired to devote himself to writing on Christian themes. Though his theological works are not without importance, it is as a poet that he is remembered, partly for his numerous short lyrics, but particularly for his epic poem *Rakṣaṇiya yāttirikam* (Journey towards Salvation, 1894), inspired by Bunyan's *Pilgrim's Progress.*

A. J. Appasamy, *Tamil Christian Poet. The Life and Writings of H. A. Krishna Pillai* (London 1966); JHTL 254–5. REA

Kiruṣṇamūrtti, R. (pseud. Kalki, b 1899 Puthumangalam, d 1954 Madras), Tamil novelist. A journalist by profession, Kalki worked on a number of Tamil magazines before founding the weekly *Kalki* in 1941. His own contributions to these journals included criticism of music and dance recitals and of dramatic performances, political writings (he was deeply involved in the movement for Indian independence and was twice imprisoned), humorous pieces and serialized fiction. His novels, of which there are fourteen, were all republished in book form. They fall into two fairly distinct groups: historical novels (*Pārttipan̲ kan̲avu*, Pārttipan's Dream, 1941–43; *Civakāmiyin̲ capatam*, Civakāmi's Oath, 1944–46; and the voluminous *Pon̲n̲iyin̲ celvan̲*, Ponni's Beloved, 1950–54) and stories with a contemporary setting. His interest in the independence movement found a place in several of his novels, most particularly in *Alai ōcai* (The Noise of the Waves, 1948–49). Kalki's continued popularity rests on his painstaking reconstruction of the Tamil past, his patriotism, his humour, his lively dialogue and his ability to make improbable events seem real. Some critics, however, find him at times over-sentimental and he may be said to have only a moderate capacity to depict the subtleties of human nature or behaviour. His importance in the development of Tamil narrative prose style is undisputed.

JHTL 265–7. REA

Kolhaṭkar, Śrīpad Kṛṣṇa (1871–1934), Marathi dramatist, the author of twelve plays which are mainly romantic and mildly social-reformist in theme. One or two are still performed today mainly because the songs in them are popular. IR

korido, Filipino verse tales, see **moro-moro.**

Kotmāi Trā Sām Dūong, Thai code of law, see **Pramūon Kotmāi Ratchakān thī nūng.**

Koujto (Kodaw) Hmain, Burmese poet, see **Hmain,** Thakhin Koujto.

Kṛṣṇa Piḷḷa, Caṅṅampuẓa (pseud. Changampuzha, 1914–1948), Malayalam poet. One of the most popular and, in spite of his early death from tuberculosis, one of the most prolific Malayalam poets of this century. While adopting the romanticism of an earlier generation, he introduced a new note by his uninhibited use of personal experiences as the theme of his poems. His love poems are filled with a tone of despair. A close friend of a number of novelists of the Progressive School (see *progressive* *writing*), he also wrote poems favouring social revolution. Main works: *Bāṣpāñjali* (Tear Offerings, 1934), *Ramaṇan* (1936), *Spandikkunna asthimāṭam* (Throbbing Sepulchre, 1945).

PNHML 239–46; GSML 169–71, 255–8. REA

Kṛṣṇadevarāya (16th century), Telugu poet and ruler of the Vijayanagar from 1509 to 1530 AD. The greatest patron of Telugu literature, and himself a poet, Kṛṣṇadevarāya composed an epic *Āmuktamālyadā*. This tells the story of the marriage of the god at Śrīraṅgam, Viṣṇu, to Gōdā, the daughter of a pious Vaiṣṇava devotee. Clearly, this story is either based on, or shares common origins with, that of the Tamil *āḷvār*, Āṇṭāḷ (qv). JRM

Kṛttibās, the best known of those Bengali writers who chose to write versions of the story of Rāma and Sītā. His *Rāmāyaṇa* (qv), however, is not a translation of the famous Sanskrit version of Vālmīki, but is a version, showing characteristics of the author's much later time and religious attitude. Autobiographical data in a very late and dubious manuscript indicate that he was born in 1398 AD. But other evidence, eg a comparison of genealogical tables in this late manuscript with other such tables, suggest a date in the late 15th century as being more probable. By all odds the most popular of the Bengali *Rāmāyaṇas*, that of Kṛttibās is closer to the heroic quality of Vālmīki's epic than is, for example, Tulsīdās' (qv) *Rāmcaritmānas* in Hindi. But like Tulsī he has allowed a religious attitude of *bhakti* (qv) to colour his recounting. Rāma, the fallible hero of Vālmīki, has become an incarnation of the high god Viṣṇu in the later writers, necessitating changes in the internal logic of the story. The demons, in Vālmīki fierce and often chivalrous enemies, but still representing the forces of evil in the cosmic struggle, have become in Kṛttibās and Tulsī devotees of Rāma the god, seeking to gain salvation by being slain by him. Still, Kṛttibās' story is beautifully told, both in conception and in language, and remains the morality tale *par excellence* in its influence on Bengali minds and manners.

D. C. Sen, *Bengali Ramayanas* (Calcutta 1920); SHBL 67–9. ECD

Kṣemendra, Sanskrit writer, see **Guṇāḍhya.**

Kula, U, Burmese historian, see **Kala**, U.

Kumāralāta, Indian Buddhist writer, see **Buddhist literature.**

Kumāran Āśān, N. (1873–1924), Malayalam poet. Though born into the unprivileged Ezhava (Īẓava) community, Āśān received a full education in Malayalam and Sanskrit. Later he continued his Sanskrit studies in Bangalore and Calcutta, where in addition he learnt much about both Bengali and English literature. His earliest compositions were erotic verses, but he later turned to the writing of devotional poems under the influence of Śrī Nārāyaṇa Guru, spiritual leader of the Ezhavas. He did not, however, really make his mark as a poet until the appearance in 1909 of *Vīṇa puuvu* (Fallen Flower), the first great poem of the Malayalam Romantic movement. Many equally original works were to follow, including the short narrative poems on the theme of love, *Naliṇi* (1911) and *Līla* (1914); Sītā's story, as seen by herself (*Cintāviṣṭayāya Sita*, 1919), calls for the removal of the injustices of the caste system, as does *Duravastha* (A Tragic State, 1923), telling of the marriage of a Nambudiri Brahmin girl and a Harijan; and philosophical poems, several with Buddhist subjects (including his last work, *Karuṇa*, 1924).

GSML 146–51, 229–32; PNHML 182–97. REA

Kumāranatunga (also called Kumāratunga), Munidāsa (1887–1944), founder of a literary school of Sinhalese writers who sought to purify the Sinhalese language and reintroduce certain obsolete words and inflexions. CHBR

Kumāravyāsa (15th century) or Nāraṇappa of Gadugu (Gadag), Kannada epic poet. He wrote 10 cantos of a *Mahābhārata* (qv, in 6-line stanzas called *ṣaṭpadis*) which is known for its great popularity, and its narrative and poetic power. It has a wealth of metaphor and racy speech, and expression of every *rasa* or mood, from heroic battle-scenes to scenes of death, love, humour and devotional tenderness to Kṛṣṇa; it is part of the repertory of professional and household reciters of sacred lore. Kumāravyāsa was a Brahmin poet devoted to Viṣṇu; his *Mahābhārata* has Kṛṣṇa for the central spirit, though the characters Duryodhana, the Pāṇḍava brothers and their wife Draupadī are stirringly portrayed. AKR

Kuñcan Nampyār (18th century), Malayalam poet. Little is known about his life and even the name by which he is known is not beyond dispute. Author of a great variety of poetic compositions, he is known above all as the greatest writer of *tuḷḷal* verses (qv). This popular art form of Kerala (which he is reputed to have invented) was especially suited to his particular talents, for it requires a sense of humour not possessed by all poets; it is also a perfect vehicle for satire, in which Nampyār excelled.

GSML 108–24; PNHML 102–8. REA

Kuntaka, Indian writer on poetics, see **alaṃkāraśāstra.**

Kuṟaḷ, classical Tamil book of poetry, see **Tiruvaḷḷuvar.**

Kuṟuntokai, classical Tamil anthology, see **Eṭṭuttokai.**

Kurup, Malayalam poet, see **Śaṅkara Kuṟuppu.**

Kuṭṭikkṛṣṇan, P. C. (pseud. Uṟūb, b 1915), Malayalam novelist and short story writer. Though he has written stories and novels set in other parts of India and drawn characters from other social groups, Uṟūb is above all the novelist who chronicles the life of the middle classes of Malabar, particularly the Muslims. His *Ummāccu* (1954) recounts the tragic consequences of the love of two Muslim boys for the same girl. In *Sundarikaḷum sundaranmārum* (Beautiful Women and Handsome Men, 1958), he broke new ground by building a novel out of seven separate but interrelated stories which form a saga of Malabar life during the first half of this century. *Kuññammayum kūṭṭukārum* (Kuññamma and Her Companions, 1957) adopts a similar technique but is in a lighter and more humorous vein and is less of a unity.

VISNM 43–8; PNHML 147–8. REA

Kuvempu, Kannada poet, see **Puṭṭapu, K. V.**

Kuy Laut, Cambodian writer, see **pralom-lok.**

Ky Beng Chhon, Cambodian writer, see **pralom-lok.**

Kyi, U (?1838–?1898), Burmese poet, headman of Thawuthti village, he served under the last two kings of Burma. Nurtured by folk, literary and musical songs that were in vogue in his time, he wrote many short charming idylls (see Padethayaza) in the form of nostalgic songs of *lungyin*, some of which have been ascribed to his fellow-writer and puppeteer, U Hsaung. He was outstanding for his portrayal of the bucolic life. HP

Kyin U, U (?1773–?1838), first Burmese playwright, Governor of Hsinbaungwè, a contemporary of Princess Hlaing and U Ponnya (qqv). He introduced to the Burmese cultural world the *pyazat* (stage-play) in the mixed style (verse and prose), and puppet drama in collaboration with an U Thaw, Minister of Music and Dance. He wrote two plays based on the *jātakas* (qv), *Mahawthahta* (No. 546) and *Wethandaya* (No. 547), and four other original or adapted plays: *Dewagonban*, *Vaṅkanta*, *Papahein* and *Kālakaṇṇī*. Many Burmese scholars claim that his works are superior to Ponnya's in plot and characterization, and in the texture of the stage language. He also composed many songs, some of which were perhaps intended to be used in his *pyazat.*

Hla Pe, *Konmara Pya Zat*, I, Introduction and translation (London 1952), pp. 4–6, 13; MHABD 56–75, passim. HP

L

Lakṣmī Prasād, Nepali writer, see **Devkoṭā,** Lakṣmī Prasād.

Lakṣmīnāth, Assamese poet, see **Bezbaṛuā,** Lakṣmīnāth.

Lal Ded (Sanskrit: Lallā), 14th century Kashmiri poetess. The only generally agreed fact about her life is that she was a contemporary of the Muslim saint Sayyid 'Alī Hamadānī (c 1380). Lal Ded was a female ascetic and follower of the Kashmiri school of Yoga Śaivism; she recorded the doctrines and teachings of this sect in her Kashmiri verses known as *vākh* (sayings). Not only are these important as records of a more popular form of Yoga Śaivism than is described in the Sanskrit sources, but they are also significant as the first extant poetry in Kashmiri which is still appreciated to-day. For while Lal's *vākh* (in form, couplets similar to the Hindi *dohā*), of which some 100 are extant, are sometimes technical in nature, their use of a wide range of every-day phenomena as imagery and their pithy proverbial quality have assured them continuing popularity. This was doubtless enhanced by their frequent expressions of mystical love, very similar to the Sūfī poetry of Kashmiri and the related literatures.

Sir George Grierson and L. D. Barnett, *Lallā-Vākyāni* (ed. and trans., London 1920); R. C. Temple, *The Word of Lalla the Prophetess* (Cambridge 1924). CS

Lalitavistara (Extensive Depiction of the Life's Play, ie of the future Buddha), an Indian book of late Sanskrit Buddhism. It depicts the Buddha's life from his decision to be reborn in his historical personality till the first explanation of his teaching in Banaras. The extant version of the *Lalitavistara* (c from the 3rd century AD) has the form of the Mahāyāna *sūtras* (qv), though both its prose and verse correspond mostly to similar passages in the Pāli canon. The work seems to have formed a part of a codex now lost. Some of its parts in verse are composed in the so-called *gāthā* dialect, also known as hybrid Sanskrit. The Mahāyāna framework of the book is of a very late origin.

Trans.: R. Mitra, *The Lalitavistara* (Calcutta 1881–86); S. Lefman, *Lalita Vistara* (Berlin 1874); P. E. Fouceaux, *Le Lalita Vistara* (Paris 1884–92).
WHIL II, 248–56. IF

Lallā, Kashmiri poetess, see **Lal Ded.**

Lallūlāl (b 1763 Gokulpur, d 1835 Calcutta), Hindi writer. Brahmin, served several Indian Rulers in Murshidabad, Nator and Calcutta. In 1800 John Gilchrist employed him as a teacher of Hindi at the Fort William College, Calcutta. His prose-adaptations of Sanskrit texts like *Baitāla paccīsī* (see *Vetālapañcaviṃśatikā*, 1799), *Śakuntalā nāṭak* (see Kālidāsa, 1802) and especially his *Premsāgar* (The Ocean of Love, after the Kṛṣṇa-legend of the *Bhāgavata Purāṇa*, qv, 1802) mark the beginning of modern Hindi literature. Because of its rather religious language and traditional attitude the religious importance of the *Premsāgar* was greater than its influence on later writers.

P. Gaeffke, *Premsāgar*, Kindlers Literatur Lexikon V (Zürich 1969). PG

Lat, U (b 1866 Rangoon, d 1921), the first prominent Burmese novelist, with English education together with Buddhist upbringing. A senior police officer, he resigned from service after a conflict with a British official and served then as translator for Burmah Oil Company. Lat had a wide knowledge of Burmese traditional culture, but also knew English novels (B. Lytton, W. Scott). He combined elements of classical Burmese drama (verse, songs, narration, moral lessons) with elements of the new genre—the novel. Skilfully using mystery and tension, he supported the main romantic plot by realistic episodes satirizing contemporary life. He depicted human relations in the divided Burma of the 19th century, the independent kingdom in the north and the British colony in the south, and defended traditional culture against foreign influences. His two complete novels, *Sapepin* (?1911) and *Shwei Pyij Sou* (1914), range among the best in Burmese literature. DB

Leang Hap An, Cambodian writer, see **pralom-lok.**

Lèdi Pandeitta U Maung Gyi, Burmese writer, see **Maun Tyi,** U Leti Pantita.

Lekhnāth, Nepali poet, see **Paṇḍyāl,** Lekhnāth.

Lekwethoundara, Burmese poet, see **Letwè Thondara.**

Le-qui-Don (b 1726 Duyen-ha, Thai-binh province, d 1784), Vietnamese poet and writer, together with Phan-huy-Cu (1782–1840) the greatest encyclopaedist of Vietnam. Very well educated, he held high offices at the royal court. His poems have survived in the collection *Que duong thi tap* (Poems of Que-duong) and elsewhere, but he is best known for his studies and commentaries on the classical books, on history, geography, customs; eg *Thu kinh dien nghia* (Explanations of the *Shu-ching*, see Vol. III), *Dich kinh phu thuyet* (Additional Commentary to the *I-ching*, see Vol. III), *Kien van tieu luc* (Concise Encyclopaedia), *Van dai loai ngu* (Compendium of Knowledge in Classified Order). Only parts of his history of Vietnam under the Le dynasty have survived (*Dai-Viet thong su*, History of Dai-Viet). His studies and anthologies of early Vietnamese literature are of considerable importance for the history of Vietnamese literature: *Toan Viet thi luc* (Complete Anthology of Vietnamese Poetry) and *Hoang Viet van hai* (Compendium of Vietnamese literature).

DNILVN 192. VV

Letwè Thondara (Myat San, U, 1723–?1799), Burmese poet, served under six kings as a minister, court-poet and judge. Author of some fifteen poems of different genres, his celebrity and immense popularity rest however on two *yadu* (qv) which he wrote in exile at Mèza, a penal settlement, in 1764. In these he lamented over the miseries of life at Mèza, and expressed his longing for the capital and his family. The poems reached the ear of the king, who at once ordered the recall of the poet. These two poems have been 'immortalized' due to the dramatic circumstances of their composition (see Ananta Thuriya). HP

linga (Sanskrit *alaṃkāra*, embellishment), a standard type of Burmese verse form, used through the whole classical and modern literature. It is probably the oldest in four-syllable lines, linked by 'climbing' rhymes, with the basic scheme 4–3–2 and its many alterations. *Linga* has often been used as a synonym for *pyo* (qv), though it is more generally applied to all kinds of verse in four-syllable lines that cannot be otherwise classified by their form or content, eg didactic poems, forest journeyings (*tawla*) etc. A *linga* is generally a short poem, containing from one stanza of five lines to several longer stanzas. HP

Lokamānya, Marathi nationalist leader, see **Ṭiḷak,** Bāl Gangādhar.

lol-lyric, a genre of classical Kashmiri poetry (*lol* = love, longing). It is a short love-poem of some 6–12 lines with frequent refrains, designed to be sung. It typically contains vivid references to the natural features of Kashmir, in particular to its flowers and trees. The *lol*-lyric is not mystical in tone, but describes in passionate terms the love of a woman for her lost lover. This general convention of Indian love-poetry is given special point in the case of the *lol*-lyric by the fact that its two most famous exponents were women: the 16th-century Haba Khotūn, wife of the last independent Muslim ruler of Kashmir, Yūsuf Śāh Cak (1579–86), overthrown and exiled by the emperor Akbar, and the almost equally famous 18th century poetess,

Arnīmāl, wife of the Brahmin Bhavānī Dās, himself a Persian poet.

J. L. Kaul, *Kashmiri Lyrics* (Srinagar 1945); N. C. Cook, *The Way of the Swan* (Bombay 1958). CS

luc bat (*luc* = six, *bat* = eight), the most typical form in Vietnamese prosody. The considerable degree of similarity between Vietnamese and Chinese prosody is due both to the structural and phonetic affinities of the two languages, and to a thousand years of Chinese influence in poetry. The basic elements in Vietnamese prosody, especially in classical and folk verse, are: a specific number of syllables in the line, rhyme, tone harmony, and parallelism in the phonetic, grammatical and semantic structure of the couplet. As in Chinese the tone serves to distinguish different words; each word is pronounced with one of six tones. In prosody these tones are divided into two groups, level (*bang*) and oblique (*trac*), two tones in the former and four in the latter group. Poetry is recited in a sing-song manner, stressing the musical quality. In the *luc bat* form, 6 and 8 syllable lines alternate, the final syllable of the preceding 6-syllable line rhyming with the sixth syllable of the 8-syllable line, while the eighth syllable of that line rhymes with the final syllable of the following 6-syllable line. The *luc bat* form, not divided into strophes, was used for the classical verse novel (see *truyen*), including the greatest work in Vietnamese literature, *Kieu* (see Nguyen-Du). The classical *ngam* (Lament) lyric, on the other hand (see Doan-thi-Diem, Nguyen-gia-Thieu), is made up of quatrains, the first two lines of 7 syllables and the last two *luc bat*. This form is known as *song that luc bat* (twice seven, six, eight). VV

Luhār, T., Gujarati writer and poet, see **arvācin kavitā.**

Luhtu (Ludu) U Hla, Burmese writer, see **Hla,** U, Luhtu.

Lun, U, Burmese poet, see **Hmain,** Thakhin Koujto.

Luu-trong-Lu, Vietnamese poet, see **The-Lu.**

M

Ma Ma Lei, Djanetjo (b 1917 Kamalu), Burmese writer, journalist, traditional physician. With her husband, U Cjis Maun, she published the *Djanetjo* (*Gyanegyaw*) journal and after World War II the *Pyijthu Histain* (People's Tribune) newspaper. In the sixties she was jailed by the military government. Before the war she wrote political articles, especially for women, and stories, influenced by her husband's progressive views, and since the forties novels. A fearless and outspoken critic and an able observer of human nature, she often depicts gifted, independent-minded women facing the problems of life. She defends traditional Burmese culture against admirers of the Western way of life. Her novel *Moun ywei mahu* (Not that He Hates, 1955) won a Sapei Biman Prize. Further works: novels *Thuma* (She, 1944), *Thu lou Lu* (Man Like Him, 1947) about her husband, *Seit* (Mind, 1951), *Kambha Myei we* (In the World, 1952); short stories *Shu manyi* (Endless Beauty, 1948), *Twei taseimseim* (Recollections, 1963). DB

Ma'āni, Urdu poet, see **Muḥammad Quli Quṭb Śhāh.**

Māḍgūḷkar, Vyankateś Digambar (b 1927), Marathi short-story writer and novelist whose plots are particularly associated with the village life of his own local region.

Trans.: Ram Deshmukh, *The Village Had No Walls* (in original, *Bangarvāḍī*, Bombay 1958); I. Raeside, *The Rough and the Smooth* (a few short stories, Bombay 1966). IR

Mādhava Paṇikkar, Kāvālam (b 1895 Travancore, d 1963 Mysore), Indian statesman and writer. After obtaining a degree in modern history at Oxford University, K. M. Paṇikkar taught for some years at the universities of Aligarh and Calcutta. Then, in 1925, he became editor of the *Hindustan Times*. Before India became independent, he held ministerial posts in the princely states of Patiala and Bikaner. Later he was successively Indian ambassador in China, Egypt and France. Outside south India he is known for his books on history and politics. He also wrote prolifically in Malayalam and published volumes of poetry, plays, autobiography and novels (eg *Kēraḷa siṃham*, 1942). His novels reflect his academic interests in that they are on historical themes. Most of them are concerned with Kerala's past. Some English writings: *Asia and Western Dominance* (1953), *Malabar and the Portuguese* (1929).

PNHML 130–2, 226–7. REA

Mādhavadeva (b 1489 Letuphkhuri, d 1596 Cooch Behar), Assamese Vaiṣṇava poet. A disciple of Śaṅkaradeva (qv) who converted him to his Vaiṣṇava religious movement, he was also famous as a singer. Mādhavadeva's devotional songs, *baragīta*, were extremely popular among the mass of the people for their musical content and sweet expression, combined with profound spiritual ideas. They are composed in Brajabuli, a mixed poetic language of east India, based on Maithili. In Assamese, Mādhavadeva composed *Nāmghosa*, mostly free renderings of Sanskrit verse, and *Bhakti ratnāvali*, based on a Sanskrit compilation of poems of a devotional character, propagating the *bhakti* (qv) attitude towards Viṣṇu.

B. K. Barua, *Assamese Literature* (Bombay 1941), pp. 22–24. DZ

Maḍiā, Cunilāl, Gujarati writer, see **navalikā** and **navalkathā.**

Māē Ong, Thai writer, see **Mālai Chūphinit.**

Māgha (late 7th century AD), Sanskrit poet, traditionally ranked as one of the 'great poets' (*mahākavi*), author of the court-epic (*mahākāvya*) *Śiśupālavadha*, in 20 cantos. The theme is taken from the second book of the *Mahābhārata* (qv), and tells of the insulting behaviour of Śiśupāla, king of the Cedis, towards Kṛṣṇa; of the forbearance of the latter on account of a vow; and finally, after the vow has been fulfilled, of the decapitation of Śiśupāla by Kṛṣṇa's discus. Like Bhāravi (qv) whom he imitates in many ways, Māgha adorns his theme by the liberal insertion of poetic descriptions of cities, beautiful women, the seasons, and so forth, in the manner accepted as befitting a *mahākāvya*. In spite of some artificialities, Māgha frequently displays considerable poetic merit.

German trans.: E. Hultzsch (Leipzig 1929). WHIL III, 72–6; KHSL 124–31. IB

Maha Hswei (Bha Shein, U, b 1900 Sagaing, d 1953 Rangoon), Burmese writer, journalist and teacher. His style of writing gratified the taste of the reading public. In his more prominent works he fought against the British colonialists. His works helped to strengthen the growth of the nationalist movement. He is the author of many articles, 600 short stories and 60 novels, eg *Pjou Taunpjoum* (Gods of Taunpjoum), *Dou Meimei* (Our Mother, 1935) and *Thupountyi* (The Rebel, 1936), and the autobiography *Maha Hswei i Maha Hswei* (1953). DB

Mahābhārata (400 BC–400 AD), Sanskrit epic. The *Mahābhārata* is a work of such vast dimension and scope that its parallel may be sought not in any other single work, but rather in other entire literatures. In origin it may be traced back to the *ākhyāna* hymns (dialogues, perhaps part of ritual plays) of the *Ṛgveda* (qv), which later developed into the mythological corpus of the *brāhmaṇas* (qv). Other strands which must have contributed to the elaborate fabric of the epic were the hero songs of the ancient period and the genealogical histories that were recited by the Sūtas, ancient bards who maintained and expanded the oral traditions of the great kings. By the time of the Buddha this mixture of myth and history was current as the literary form called *itihāsa* ('so-they-say'), the source of the *Mahābhārata* and the *purāṇas* (qv).

The kernel of the epic, from which its name is derived, concerns a great battle fought by the descendants of King Bharata. Historians have attempted, with very limited success, to extract from this tale some 'hard-core' history of the Vedic clans that lived in the sacred plain known as Kurukṣetra, where the battle is set. It is almost certain that such a war took place in the Panjab between the Kuru and Pañcāla tribes near the beginning of the 1st millennium BC, but more specific questions, especially those concerning dates, have met with unsatisfactory answers. For social history, however, and the history of religion, mythology, ritual, philosophy, and every aspect of ancient Indian culture, the *Mahābhārata* is a veritable cornucopia.

The original martial epic of approximately 20,000 verses, named the *Bhārata* or the *Mahābhārata*, was probably well established by 500 BC. It remained for several centuries in the hands of the non-Brahmin bards, who added other sagas and tales from their general repertory, such as the sub-epic of Nala and Damayantī (see *Nalopākhyāna*), or the romance of Śakuntalā and King Duṣyanta, the myth of the great flood, a brief version of the adventures of Rāma, the descent of the Ganges, and many, many more. The oral origin of this literature is indicated both by its formulaic nature and by the fact that it consists almost entirely of conversations, between the bard and his audience (the frame) as well as between the characters within the epic itself.

Then the Brahmin priests took over the epic and interpolated religious materials of far greater volume than the original battle saga, including didactic treatises (such as the 12th and 13th books, the *Śānti* and *Anuśāsana Parvans*), speculative passages (such as the *Bhagavadgītā*, qv), and numerous myths and ritual texts. In still later times, sectarian influences (glorifying Viṣṇu, Śiva, or the secondary gods such as Skanda, Gaṇeśa and Devī) began to appear in the reworkings of the poem, which by this time (c500 AD) could hardly be called an epic any longer. It had probably reached its present extent of 100,000 (mostly *śloka*, qv) verses (longer than the Iliad and Odyssey combined), divided into 18 books.

It is therefore impossible to date the epic as a whole, and extremely difficult to date any particular verse. Whereas the *Rāmāyaṇa* (qv) is thought to have originated in the Eastern part of the Ganges valley, most of the *Mahābhārata* seems to have been composed in the western part, which the Indo-Aryans inhabited before moving farther east. The three most important recensions are the Bombay and Calcutta (quite similar) and the Madras, which differs more significantly from the other two. Extending as it does over such a vast period of time, the *Mahābhārata* contains numerous and various religious concepts. Buddhism exerted an important influence, supplying many parables and fables even during the early stages of the epic. The fable of Śibi, for example, which appears here is also narrated in the Buddhist *jātakas* (qv), where it is more apt, for the king's virtue in sacrificing his body in order to save the life of another creature is more typical of Buddhism than of Hinduism. Increasing Buddhist influence may be seen in the character of the hero Yudhiṣṭhira, whose moral dilemma represents *in nuce* the transitional morality of the entire epic, the clash between the ancient sacrificial religion and the fast-burgeoning devotional religion (*bhakti*, qv), the tension between the ancient military code and the new emphasis upon non-injury, the reconciliation of the Vedic heaven and hell with the Vedāntic transmigration, the imposition of priestly values upon a warrior saga. The ancient tales are preserved but reinterpreted, rationalized and occasionally transformed almost beyond recognition in the attempt to justify behaviour that had in the course of time become retroactively unacceptable.

Many of the inconsistencies in the characters of the noble heroes (the Pāṇḍus or Pāṇḍavas), their occasionally immoral and even unheroic behaviour, have been attributed to the possibility of a complete reversal of the epic partisanship. It has been suggested that the Kurus were the original heroes and the more powerful family (as witness the name of the sacred plain, Kurukṣetra and not Pāṇḍukṣetra), and that only when the Pāṇḍus gained the upper hand were they whitewashed by bards who nevertheless felt obliged to retain within the epic, alongside the praises of their new patrons, the original records of the latter's less laudatory adventures. This is, however, an unnecessarily elaborate explanation of a phenomenon which is adequately justified by the change in moral values reflecting to the discredit of the Pāṇḍus' original heroic acts. This applies in particular to Kṛṣṇa, whose behaviour as a human prince (whose moral character was questionable even by the original rough-and-ready epic standards) became a source of embarrassment to later writers once he had been elevated to an incarnation of the god Viṣṇu.

Although it is impossible to indicate here even the scope of the incidental, encyclopaedic material which constitutes the bulk of the epic, the central tale of the gigantic pot-latch may be outlined as follows. In the city of Hastināpura in Kurukṣetra there lived two brothers descended from King Bharata. Since the elder, Dhṛtarāṣṭra, was blind, his brother Pāṇḍu ascended the throne. Pāṇḍu had five sons who were, according to one version, begotten on his behalf by five different gods: the wise Yudhiṣṭhira (fathered by Dharma, the god of justice), the noble Arjuna (by Indra, king of the gods), the impetuous Bhīma (by Vāyu, god of wind), and the twins Nakula and Sahadeva (by the Aśvins, the twin divine horsemen). Dhṛtarāṣṭra had a hundred sons, led by Duryodhana; they were known as the Kurus or Kauravas. When Pāṇḍu died in his youth due to a curse, Dhṛtarāṣṭra intended to give the throne to Yudhiṣṭhira, but the Kauravas plotted against their cousins until the Pāṇḍavas were forced to flee to Pañcāla, where they all married Draupadī and met Kṛṣṇa, who became their adviser and charioteer. Dhṛtarāṣṭra then divided the kingdom, giving Hastināpura to his sons and Indraprastha to the Pāṇḍavas.

But Duryodhana, jealous and greedy, invited the Pāṇḍavas to Hastināpura, where he lured them into a crooked dice game and won from them their entire kingdom, including even Draupadī. As a compromise, the Pāṇḍavas agreed to go into exile for twelve years, after which they would have their kingdom restored to them. Their adventures in the forest, and the stories they heard there, form the subject of the immense third book (*Āraṇyaka Parvan*). When, upon their return, they were refused their kingdom, a great battle took place for eighteen days, in which all the Kauravas and all but the five Pāṇḍavas and Kṛṣṇa were killed. Dhṛtarāṣṭra and the Pāṇḍavas were reconciled and Yudhiṣṭhira was made king in Hastināpura, where he performed a great horse sacrifice. After many years, Dhṛtarāṣṭra retired with his wife to a forest where they were burnt to death in a conflagration, while Kṛṣṇa also retired and was shot by a hunter. The Pāṇḍus and Draupadī retired, died, and went to heaven.

Upon this base was grafted every fancy of the Indian imagination, resulting in a work so rich and inventive that it more than justifies the boast, 'What is not here is not found anywhere else.'

Trans.: P. C. Roy (Calcutta [2]1927–32); partial trans.: K. S. Narasimha (Columbia University Press, 1968).

V. Fausbøll, *Indian Mythology in Outline, According to the Mahābhārata* (London 1903); E. W. Hopkins, *The Great Epic of India* (Yale 1920), and *Epic Mythology* (Strassburg 1915); G. I. Held, *The Mahābhārata, An Ethnological Study* (Amsterdam 1935); J. Dahlmann, *Das Mahābhārata als Epos und Rechtsbuch* (Berlin 1895); C. V. Vaidya, *Epic India* (Bombay 1907); V. S. Sukthankar, *Critical Studies in the Mahābhārata* (Bombay 1944); N. V. Thadani, *The Mystery of the Mahābhārata*, 5 vols. (Karachi 1931–35); WHIL I, 311–475. WOF

Mahādēviyakka, Kannada poet, see **vacana.**

mahākāvya, see **kāvya.**

Mahāparinirvāṇa Sūtra, see **Buddhist literature.**

Mahāvaṃsa, ancient chronicle of Ceylon, see **Dipavaṃsa.**

Mahāvastu (c 2nd century BC—1st to 4th century AD, rich collection of legends concerning the life of the Buddha and the beginnings of the Buddhist community. It was the work of the Lokottaravāda branch of the Mahāsāṃghika school, who included it in their *Vinaya* (see *Tripiṭaka*). The *Mahāvastu* is written in a mixture of prose and verse, in a Sanskritized Prakrit dialect; it presents a collection of traditions pertaining to the Buddha's life, which is treated like an *avadāna* (qv), with all the wonders and miracles accompanying important events in his career. The narrative is often interrupted by *jātakas* (qv) and doctrinal excursions, sometimes without any coherence. The verses, belonging probably to the 2nd century BC, often paraphrase or just repeat the story given in prose. The *Mahāvastu* became popular also with the Mahāyāna school and, in spite of its inconsistencies, it preserved valuable data on traditions unknown from other sources. Some portions of the narrative make an impression of great antiquity and a number of its *jātakas* and *avadānas* have not been preserved in the Pāli tradition.

Trans.: J. J. Jones, *The Mahāvastu*, 3 vols. (PTS 1949–56).
B. C. Law, *A Study of the Mahāvastu* (Calcutta and Simla 1930); WHIL II, 239–47. IF

Mahimabhaṭṭa, Rājānaka (c1000–1100 AD, Kashmir), Indian literary critic. He must have been slightly junior to Kuntaka and Abhinavagupta (qv). His *Vyakti-viveka* is one of the masterpieces of Indian literary criticism. He challenged the famous *dhvani* (qv) theory of Ānandavardhana from the point of view of logic and epistemology. Like most literary critics from Ānandavardhana onwards, Mahimabhaṭṭa accepted the theory that what constituted the essence of poetry or literature is *rasa* (aesthetic pleasure). But he disagreed with Ānandavardhana on the point about *vyañjanā* (the function of suggestivity) of words in literature. He advanced the theory that the 'suggested sense' in poetry is arrived at indirectly through *anumiti* (inference), not directly by a 'suggestive function' of words. Hence the title of his work *Vyakti-viveka*, 'a critical analysis of the suggestive function'. Mahimabhaṭṭa wrote another book called *Tattvoktikośa*, which is not extant.

DHSP I, 140–4; II, 195–200. BKM

Mahjūr, Ghulām Ahmad (1888–1952), Kashmiri poet. Born into a rural *pīrzāda* family of Kashmir, but he abandoned his family's hereditary calling to enter the service of the Kashmir government as a village accountant. As a young man, Mahjūr travelled in the Panjab, where he spent some time in literary circles of Amritsar, in which the Urdu *ghazal* (see Vol. III) was the chief medium of expression. Mahjūr himself wrote poetry in Urdu for some time, though with little success, and it was only in 1926 that a *ghazal* in Kashmiri won him wide renown. Mahjūr's work marks the replacement of classical Persian models by modern Urdu literary influences as dominant in Muslim Kashmiri literature; while his poetry is notable for its loving descriptions of Kashmiri scenery and life and its evocation of Kashmiri patriotism, it suffers from the rather bombastic tone characteristic of much Urdu poetry between the wars.

Collections of verse: *Kalām-e Mahjūr, Payām-e Mahjūr*. J. S. Kaul, *Kashmiri Lyrics* (Srinagar 1945), pp. 120–7. CS

Mahmūd Gōmī (Gāmī, c1765–1855), Kashmiri poet. Little is known of the circumstances of his long life. He was a prolific writer, whose work marks a turning-point in the development of Kashmiri literature. With the decline and eventual ending (in 1819) of Muslim rule over Kashmir, Persian increasingly lost ground as a medium of literary expression to Kashmiri. However, the new Kashmiri literature was heavily influenced by Persian in terms of metre, form and subject. Thus, while Mahmūd Gōmī wrote many short poems, including *ghazals* (see Vol. III) on the Persian model, his fame rests chiefly on his longer narrative poems, all free adaptations and abridgements of Persian originals. A noteworthy feature of these poems is their use of different (Persian-based) metres in the same poem, and the inclusion at appropriate places of short lyrics on the traditional model of the native *lol*-lyric (qv). His best known work is probably *Yūsuf Zulaikhā*, based on the famous version by the Persian Jāmī (see Vol. III). CS

Mainālī, Gurūprasād (b 1900, d 1971 Kathmandu), Nepali short story writer, he was born in a village of eastern Nepal. He spent most of his life in government service. His short stories which appeared from time to time in the literary magazine, *Śāradā*, from 1935 onwards, were first published in the collection *Nāso* (1963). This is his only published work. His early stories were greatly influenced by contemporary Hindi writers who had in turn been inspired by the European short story. Mainālī is at his best when describing the pathetic side of Nepali village life, with which he was intimately acquainted. The style and language of his stories are usually free from artificiality, and are typical of the people about whom he writes. DJM

Majāz, Asrāru'l-ḥaqq (b 1911 Rudauli, d 1955 Lucknow), Urdu lyrical poet. After education at Agra and Aligarh he worked in All-India Radio and later had various occasional employments in Bombay and Lucknow; he was three times attacked by madness and died of alcoholism. He expressed the moods and aspirations of the young Muslim middle class of India. At first his concept of revolution was a romantic fantasy; later he turned from romantic depiction of love and nature in traditional forms to social problems and placed his poetry at the service of the national freedom movement. His first lyrical collection *Āhang* (Melodies, 1939) has a strong social pathos. JM

Makhfī, Indo-Persian poetess, see **Zebu'n-nisā,** Makhfī.

Mālai Chūphinit (Rīemeng, Noi Inthanon and Māē Ong are the most important of his 18 pseudonyms; b 1906 Bāng Chāng, province Kamphāēnghpet, d 1963), Thai writer, from a rather poor family; his father sold wood. His early education in a temple school explains his strong leanings towards the Buddhist religion. He later came to Bangkok, working first as a teacher and then as a journalist. Mālai was very active in public life, promoting the art of journalism, language and literature, and working in charity organizations. He was a widely travelled writer, in Asia and Europe. The most marked feature of his writing is closeness and sensitiveness to the beauty of nature and country life, and he shows subtle understanding of humanity. His books sometimes require persistent effort on the part of the reader, because of their length and his literary mannerisms. The language is nevertheless flowing and elegant. *Lǫng phrai* (Drifting Wood, 1960) is a collection of novelettes; other important works are *Thung mahārāt* (The Great Field, 1964) and *Phāēn din khǫng rāo* (Our Land, 1959).

Trans.: *Rising Flood,* and *Nang Phathurat's Gold Mine,* in: *Thai Short Stories* (Bangkok 1964).
GLUTR 166–71. US

Mammaṭa, Indian writer on poetics, see **alaṃkāraśāstra.**

Mandalay Maun Khin Maun, Burmese writer, see **Maun Tyi.**

maṅgal-kāvya, a poetic genre in Bengal, poems which eulogize (*maṅgal* means 'auspicious') a popular god or goddess. Most often they celebrate a local or folk deity, rather than one of the Vedic pantheon; there are *maṅgals* of Śitalā, goddess of smallpox, Manasā, goddess of snakes, Ṣaṣṭhi, goddess of childbirth and children, etc. *Maṅgals* of pan-Indian gods, such as Śiva, show the character of the god in question to be more often like that of the Bengali farmer than the austere high god of Brahminical tradition. It is difficult to characterize these poems in terms of form. They vary widely in length, the *Ṣaṣṭhi-maṅgal* of Kṛṣṇarām Dās being only a few hundred lines, while the *Manasā-maṅgal* of Ketakādās or the *Caṇḍi-maṅgal* of Mukundarām Cakrabarti contain more than twelve thousand. They are all written in *payār*, a simple couplet form usually of 14 syllables with caesura following the first eight, and rhymed *aa*, *bb*, etc. The more lyrical parts of the poems are often in *tripadi*, three-part line, which permits more elaborate rhyme schemes: *aab*, *ccb; abc*, *abc*, etc. Some of these forms are appropriate to oral recitation. The texts also exhibit a variety of other characteristics of oral literature, such as an abundance of formulas, set patterns of lines which a singer uses while thinking of his next original sequence. The same formulas often occur in *maṅgals* of different deities. Finally, a characteristic of all *maṅgals* is imagery based on direct observation of daily life, as opposed to the conventional, stylized, and sophisticated imagery of classical and court poetry. An exception to this is the 18th century *Annadā-maṅgal* of Bhāratcandra Rāy (qv). But

Bhāratcandra was a court poet, and used the *maṅgal* form not as an explanation of how things came to be, but as a frame for a witty, elaborate, highly literate tale of love.

The *maṅgals* are explanations of how things came to be, how the worship of a particular god or goddess came to be established on earth. In the great majority the god or goddess either demonstrates power by conquering the worshippers of other deities, or by granting boons to those who worship the true deity. Some scholars read into this an historical statement of the overcoming of the Vedic pantheon patriarchy by local deities. Again, the poems vary widely in the manner in which this is stated. Some of the *Dharma-maṅgals* include elaborate cosmogenic myths. Other *maṅgals* may do no more than tell a simple story of the benevolence of the deity in question. There is difference of opinion among scholars about whether the *maṅgals* constitute an essential part of the ritual associated with the deity. Although *maṅgals* are recited during such rituals, they are also frequently recited by village singers for the amusement and edification of their rustic audiences. Many *maṅgals* include tales which are secular and independently popular, and a given singer may well include his own observations of the life around him. Unlike the texts of the Vedic tradition, the *maṅgals* are non-canonical literature. They have changed, not only with time, but with space; and the same *maṅgal* will vary according to what part of Bengal the singer comes from. The texts are thus valuable not only as religious documents, but also as historical documents. Some *maṅgals*, because of popularity, came to be written down. None of these written texts are older than the 16th century, but they undoubtedly include material far older; they are not frozen (except in the minds of scholars), and variants are still being produced.

Trans.: Sukumar Sen, *Vipradāsa's Manasā-maṅgal* (Calcutta 1953).
SHBL 49–65. ECD

Maṇi, C. (Mani, S.), modern Tamil poet. He is one of the main representatives on 'new poets', and his long poem *Narakam* (Hell), in 334 lines, is a milestone in modern Tamil poetry. Its minor theme, frustration of an unfulfilled relationship between man and woman, is set within the major theme of corruption of the city (*nakaram*) of Madras. Maṇi's extremely effective imagery and technique is influenced by T. S. Eliot. Raw naturalism blends in his poetry with surrealistic elements. KZ

Maṇiār, Priyakānt, Gujarati poet, see **arvācin kavitā.**

Māṇikkavācakar (9th century Tiruvātavūr), Tamil poet, sometimes known as Tiruvātavūraṭikaḷ. He was chief minister to the Pāṇṭiya king Arimārttaṉār, but turned aside from worldly power and became a Śaiva religious poet. The story of him embezzling royal funds for the purchase of horses and using the money for a Śaiva temple probably symbolizes Māṇikkavācakar's renunciation. His work represents the peak of Śaiva *bhakti* (qv) coupled with reformist Hindu activity against Jains and Buddhists, which characterized Tamil religious writing in the 7th to 9th centuries. He is said to have engaged in disputations with Ceylon Buddhists. Māṇikkavācakar is renowned for two works, which form the 8th book of the *Tirumuṟai* (qv): *Tiruvācakam* and *Tirukkōvaiyār*. The former stresses the love of the soul for God and His response with grace (*aruḷ*), and His immanence in all things. The latter is a mystical poem employing the imagery of the soul as the beloved enjoying the love of God. Many conventions of classical erotic (*akam*) poetry are employed.

JHTL 85–90. JRM

Manṯo, Sa'ādat Ḥasan (b 1912 Jullundur, d 1955 Lahore), Urdu prose writer and playwright. After education at Aligarh he entered government service at Amritsar and later worked in the Bombay film industry; in 1947 he went to Pakistan, but was several times attacked by madness and died of alcoholism. In his early short stories he dealt with the hypocrisy of the Indian middle class and naturalistically depicted its sexual morality. He was fond of the sensational and chose his characters mostly from the urban underworld. In some of his short stories written after 1947 he denounced the excesses committed at the time of the Partition and drew vivid portraits of small people caught up in fratricidal fighting. He never romanticized his heroes, and his work is free from sentimentalism.

ABSLP 208–11. JM

mantra, Sanskrit term for the typically Indian manifestation of the sacred word. Now invoking, then evoking, now deprecating, then again praising, the concept covers much more than prayer, praise, invocation or mere formula. *Mantra* ('a means of mental identification') is a general name for all verses or sequences of words which are considered flash-lights of the eternal truth, 'seen', in the days of yore, by those eminent men who had come into supersensuous contact with the Unseen. Containing praise, prayers, references to myths, religious truths, ritual injunctions or 'mystic' syllables, these passages (when correctly recited) are believed to call up divine power and to have religious or spiritual efficacy. The ancient *mantras* are collected and methodically arranged in the corpora of Vedic texts (*saṃhitās*), or contained in special collections for ritual purposes. The name applies also to similar post-Vedic formulas used in the cults of Hinduism and Buddhism, which have some peculiarities of their own and are traditionally considered sacred.

J. Gonda, *The Indian Mantra,* Oriens 16 (Leyden 1963), 244–97. JG

Maqbūl Šāh (d ?1855), Kashmiri poet. Born into an impoverished family of Qādirī *pīrs*, he lived the life of a hereditary saint. Aspects of this life are directly reflected in his *Gryūst-nāma*, a fiercely satirical poem on the wretched life of the peasants of Kashmir, which includes attacks upon them for their irreligiousness and failure to show due respect to their religious leaders. Apart from the *Gryūst-nāma*, Maqbūl's fame is above all due to his narrative poem, *Gulrez*, the most popular of all Kashmiri romantic *maṣnavīs* (see Vol. III). Like most other *maṣnavīs* of the kind in Kashmiri, it is based on a Persian original, but Maqbūl's *Gulrez* is distinguished by its naturalness of language and the vividness of its descriptive passages, which are clearly based on the scenery and life of Kashmir. As such it outranks the work of Mahmūd Gōmī (qv) and others, in which the adaptation of Persian subjects and forms is less successfully handled. CS

Maragtas, Bisayan epic, see **darangan.**

Marah Rusli, Indonesian writer, see **Rusli,** Marah.

Marḍhekar, Bāḷ Sītārām (1907–1956), Marathi poet whose work revolutionized verse writing after the war. Two collections: *Kāhī kavitā* (Some Poems, 1947) and *Āṇkhī kāhī kavitā* (Some More Poems, 1951) contain most of his poems. *Arts and Man* (literary essay in English) appeared in 1960.

Trans.: Dilip Chitre, *An Anthology of Marathi Poetry* (Bombay 1967). IR

Markandaya, Kamala, Indian author writing in English. In her first four novels, Markandaya presents either some aspects of life in India or the interaction of India and Britain. *Nectar in a Sieve* (1954) is a story of rural life in southern India, but one of the principal characters is the English missionary, who has the dual role of sympathetic observer of the Indian scene and representative of the finer traditions of the West. *Some Inner Fury* (1956) depicts the struggle for independence. In the novel *A Silence of Desire* (1960) the heroine's husband is a middle-class Indian whose attitude towards life is illustrative of the western influence on India. In *Possession* (1963) the conflict is both on artistic and spiritual planes. In Markandaya's estimate there has not been much understanding between East and West; the West has been self-consciously superior and the East self-consciously inferior. She is accused of being a sentimentalist.

K. R. Chandrasekharan, *East and West in the novels of Kamala Markandaya* (CEIWE 62–85); DMINE. MED

maṣnavi, see Vol. III.

Mātavaiyā, Appāvaiyā (1874–1926), Tamil novelist. An employee in the Salt, Abkari and Customs Department, Madras, he wrote prolifically in his hours of leisure and produced volumes of verse, Tamil translations of Shakespeare, an English version of the *Rāmāyaṇa* (qv), and novels and stories in both English and Tamil. His Tamil novels—*Patmāvati carittiram* (2 vols., 1898–1900), *Vijayamārttāṇtam* (1903) and *Muttumīṉākṣi* (1903)—and his English stories (*Short Stories on Marriage Reform and Allied Topics*, 1912) are concerned with propagating his ideas on social reform, particularly as regards marriage customs.

Trans.: *Muthumeenakshi. The Autobiography of a Brahmin Girl* (Madras 1915). Novel in English: *Thillai Govindan: a Posthumous Autobiography* (London 1903).
CNI 193–7. REA

Maun Tyi, U Leti Pantita (Than Sin, Maun, b 1879 Njaunphyupin, d 1939 Monywa), Burmese writer, poet, Buddhist scholar, translator, editor. He studied Buddhism, Pāli and Sanskrit and was a Buddhist monk, but became a layman from 1908. From 1912 he worked for *Myanma Alin* (New Light of Burma) magazine and newspaper, from 1918 for *Panja Alin* (Knowledge) magazine, and was chief editor of *Dagoun* magazine in 1923–33. He was the writer of the first Burmese historical novels (*Natshinnaung*, *Tapinshweihti*) and his eulogy of Burma's past glory stimulated national pride. He wrote novels and short stories under the pen name Mandalay Maun Khin Maun to avoid accusations of frivolity. Maun Tyi is a master of grandiloquent, flowery style and his fiction is largely in the traditions of poetic dramas. His works in Pāli include commentaries, treatises on Buddhism, poems and a Pāli dictionary; his works in Burmese are articles, popular handbooks, short stories and novels. With over 500 works he wielded great literary influence in the twenties and later. DB

Maung Htin, Burmese writer, see **Htin,** Maun.

Maung Wa, Theikpan, Burmese writer, see **Wa, Theippam Maun.**

mawgun, Burmese classical poem in four-syllable lines (see *linga*), mostly panegyric. It records a notable event, usually in the public life of the Burmese king. Its themes range from the completion of a canal, or the building of a religious edifice, to the arrival of foreign ambassadors or the acquisition by the king of a white elephant. The poet would use the notable events as the warp, and the power and glory of the king as the woof, to weave a poem in praise of his royal patron. Earlier *mawgun* are from ten to twenty-five pages long; later ones are longer. HP

Mayūra (c mid-7th century AD), Sanskrit poet, author of a well-known 'century' of verses, the *Sūrya-śataka*, in praise of the sun-god. These verses form a good specimen of the use of elaborate *kāvya*-style for singing the praises of a deity. While the poetic merit is not of the highest, the author shows undoubted ability in his technical mastery of the art of composing complex and often very effective verses. To Mayūra is also attributed, though doubtfully, a collection of eight erotic stanzas, the *Mayūrāṣṭaka*.

Trans.: G. P. Quackenbos, *The Sanskrit Poems of Mayūra* (New York 1917). JB

Mayūrapāda (13th century). The Sinhalese monk of the *Mahānetraprasāda Mūla* (Fraternity) who was in charge of the *Mayūrapāda pirivena* (monastic school), apparently at Vāgirigala near modern Kegalle. He wrote in 1266 a substantial prose work called *Pūjāvaliya*, consisting of stories from the life of the Buddha. The final two chapters contain a history of the kings of Ceylon. *Pūjāvaliya* is still very popular as a *banapota* or preaching book, and its language is mostly easily intelligible to-day. The same author also wrote two medical treatises, *Yōgārnavaya* and *Prayōgaratnāvaliya*. Legend says he was a lively character. CHBR

Mehtā, K., Gujarati writer, see **navalikā.**

Mehtā, Narasiṃha, Gujarati poet, see **pada** and **Premānanda.**

Meykaṇṭatēvar (13th century), Tamil philosopher and poet, whose *Civañāṉapōtam* (c1223 AD) in twelve short stanzas is probably the greatest theological work of Tamil Śaivism, revealing the essence of Śaiva *siddhānta* (see *cittar*) philosophy and the author's own mystic experience.

Trans.: Gordon Matthews, *Śivañānabōdham* (Oxford 1948), J. M. Nallaswami Pillai, *Meykanda Devar, Sivagnana Botham* (Dharmapuram 1946).
JHTL 214–15. KZ

Mihardja, Achdiat Karta (b 1911 Tjibatu, West Java), Indonesian novelist and short story writer. He attended secondary school in Solo. For a time after graduation he studied Thomistic philosopy and Islamic mysticism. From 1934 to 1941 he was a journalist and prior to World War II he served as an editor with Balai Pustaka. During the Japanese period he was connected with Radio Djakarta. In 1946 he held editorial positions with several magazines, including the renowned *Pudjangga Baru.* Prominent in PEN, he made at least one trip abroad as its Indonesian representative. He was also one of the founders of the Indonesian Writers' Association. For a period, too, he was a senior official in the Ministry of Education, and he later lectured in Indonesian literature, at the Australian National University in Canberra, where he still resides. Although the author of several successful volumes of short stories, Achdiat's fame as a writer undoubtedly rests upon his work *Atheis* (Atheist, 1949) which is generally considered to be the most significant post-war Indonesian novel. A Muslim, he attempts to depict the intellectual struggle between religious concepts, mysticism, and historical materialism. Although not a prolific writer, Achdiat's place in the history of Indonesian literature is assured. Further works: *Keretakan dan Ketegangan* (Cracks and Tensions, 1956); *Kesan dan Kenangan* (Impressions and Recollections, 1961).

TMIL 202–6. JME

Mihiripænne Dhammaratana (1768–1851), monk from the south of Ceylon who was the first Ceylonese to write numbers of short poetical compositions, as opposed to single large-scale works. He developed a habit of using Sanskrit metres in Sinhalese, a style called '*elu silō*'. CHBR

Milindapañha (questions of Milinda, c1st–2nd century AD), a work now existing in Pāli, which consists of a dialogue between king Milinda and a Buddhist monk Nāgasena (or Dhītika, according to the Sarvāstivādins) on momentous problems of Buddhist doctrine. Milinda (Graeco-Bactrian Menandros, probably 2nd century BC) is believed to have been well disposed towards Buddhism, though he did not reject other beliefs. The *Milindapañha* is a work of an unknown school close to the Sthaviravādins which strongly favoured a rationalistic approach to doctrinal problems. The Pāli version leans heavily on a lost text in Sanskritized Prakrit (see *Mahāvastu*) originating in north-west India around the beginning of the Christian era. The *Milindapañha* attained great fame in countries practising Sthaviravāda Buddhism, where it is accepted as a standard authority second only to the Canon (as in Ceylon) or even as part of it (as in Burma).

The Questions of King Milinda, trans. by T. W. Rhys Davids, 2 vols. (SBE XXV 1890, XXVI 1894), and by I. B. Horner, 2 vols. (PTS 1963). IF

Min Thuwum (Wun, U, b 1909 Kumcyamkoun), Burmese poet, writer, literary historian, lexicographer. He studied at Rangoon, Oxford, London and Yale universities and was from the 1950's head of the Department for Translation and Publication, Rangoon University. One of the founders of *Khitsam* (see Zodji), Min Thuwun wrote romantic and realistic works. He proved that lyrics of high aesthetic value may be written in simple language and style. He depicts Burmese village life, friendship, love, and social barriers hampering natural human relations. His short story hero, of a low social origin and having a hard life, often ends tragically. His songs for children became very popular and were imitated by younger authors. Works: poems in the anthology *Khitsam Kabja mja* (Khitsan Poems, 1934), *Thapyeinjou* (1941); short stories in the anthology *Khitsam Poumpyin mja 1* (Khitsan Stories I, 1934), *Thoumpwinhsain Khitsam Sapei* (Trefoil of Khitsan Literature, 1955); literary history *Sapei Loka* (On Life and Letters, 1949), *Tekkathoul Myanma Abhidhan* (The University Burmese Dictionary, 1952). DB

Minai, Urdu poet, see **Amir Minā'i,** Munshī Aḥmad.

Mīr Ḥasan (b 1727 Delhi, d 1787 Lucknow), Urdu poet. He was a good writer of *ghazals*, and more notably of *maṣnavīs* (see Vol. III), long poems in rhyming couplets. Among these, *Siḥru'l-bayān* (Enchantment of Story), a fairy-tale romance of the love of Prince Bēnaẓīr and Princess Badr-e Munīr, is one of the most popular works in Urdu literature.

Trans.: Henry Court, *Nasr-i-Benazīr* (Calcutta 1889).
RITMP 69–94; MSHUL 108–11. RR

Mīr, Mīr Taqī (b 1722/3 Agra, d 1810 Lucknow), Urdu poet, master of the *ghazal* (see Vol. III) and the short narrative poem. With Saudā (qv), he was the first great poet of Urdu to emerge in northern India after Urdu had superseded Persian as the major medium of verse. He moved in early youth to Delhi, where he spent most of his life until, in 1782, he went to Lucknow. He is perhaps the greatest Urdu poet of love, and of the deeply humanist values of Muslim mystic tradition, which he upheld amidst the general political, social and moral disintegration of his times. His favoured form is the *ghazal*, and his six *dīwāns* comprise about two-thirds of his voluminous poetical works. They have always been famed for their pathos and for their direct, simple, intimate style; and Mīr prided himself on writing them in the colloquial language of the city of Delhi. His *maṣnavīs* (see Vol. III), two of which are frank, moving accounts of his own tragic love, are among the best short realistic verse narratives in Urdu. He also wrote three works in Persian prose; *Ẕikr-e Mīr*, an account, part autobiographical, part historical, of the events of his lifetime; *Nikāt-ush-shu'arā*, an account of Urdu poets up to his own time; and *Faiẓ-e Mīr*, a book of anecdotes of Muslim mystics.

RITMP 95–277; MSHUL 94–101. RR

Mīrā Bāī, Gujarati poetess, see **pada.**

Mitra, Dīnabandhu (b 1829 Jessore, d 1874 Calcutta), Bengali playwright, became a postal official after leaving college. He made his literary debut with the drama *Nīl darpaṇ* (The Indigo Mirror, 1860), a crushing indictment of the cruelty of English indigo planters in Bengal. The play was forbidden after it had been translated into English, but it helped to abolish the indigo planters' privileges. In structure it follows the tragedies of Shakespeare, and achieves its effect primarily through its moral intensity. Of Mitra's other plays, the best known are social satires and farces, such as *Sadhabār ekādaśī* (The Married Woman's Widow's Fast, 1863), and *Biyepāglā buṛo* (A Marriage-mad Old Man, 1866).

Trans.: M. M. Datta, *Nil Darpan* (Calcutta 1861).
SHBL 200–1. DZ

Mitra, Premendra (b 1904 Banaras), Bengali writer and poet. He studied science but later turned to literature. He was research assistant to the Bengali literary historian, D. C. Sen, and joint editor of *Kalikalam*, *Kabitā*, and *Nirukta*, all three significant literary magazines; he also assisted editing *Bāṅglār kathā* and *Forward*. In 1957, he received Sahitya Akademi award for his book of poetry, *Sāgar theke pherā* (Return from the Sea). Premendra has made contributions in all the literary genres. Probably best known for his short stories and novels, he is however one of the significant Bengali poets from the 1920's on. He has written for both the stage and screen. His creations are as varied as his talents; his themes range from the struggles of the common man to the exploits of a science fiction hero. Further works: *Pāṅk* (Mud, 1926);

Benāmī bandar (Port with No Name, 1930); *Pherārī phauj* (Run-away Army, 1947).

Trans.: KMBP; RMBB; BBV.
SMBP; SHBL 366–7. CBS

Mohan Singh (b 1905), Panjabi poet. Born into a Sikh family of north-western Panjab, he received his MA in Persian before teaching at Khalsa College, Amritsar. In 1939 he began editing *Panj Dariā*, one of the first and still one of the most important Panjabi literary journals. He established a great reputation with his first collection of poems, *Sāve Pattar* (Green Leaves, 1936), which has remained the most popular book of modern Panjabi poetry. This popularity derives from its mixture of simple poems based on re-workings of folk-motifs, a genre in which Mohan Singh excels, and those in which Persian vocabulary and themes form the basis. His later verse, often marked by an overtly Marxist tone, has confirmed his position as the leading Panjabi poet of his generation succeeding Vīr Singh (qv).

J. S. Ahluwalia, *Tradition and Experiment in Modern Panjabi Poetry* (Jullundur 1960), pp. 47–69; Harbans Singh, *Aspects of Punjabi Literature* (Ferozepore 1961), pp. 37–46. CS

Mohōṭṭāla, Sinhalese poet, see **Alagiyavanna.**

Mom Lūong Bubphā Nimmānhemint, Thai writer, see **Dọkmai Sot.**

Mọm Rātchōthai, Thai writer, see **nirāt.**

Mo'min, Ḥakīm Muḥammad Khān (b 1800 Delhi, where d 1852), Urdu lyric poet. A son of a physician at the imperial court, he practised the Greek system of medicine and never asked for favours from the rich. His *maṣnavīs*, and some of his *ghazals* (see Vol. III) are frank descriptions of his love affairs, and are some of the best in Urdu. But his *ghazals* also treat all the traditional themes. Many of them show a highly sophisticated technique and a deliberate obscurity of meaning. Some of his verse expresses political sentiments, and one *maṣnavī* praises the religious reformist, so-called 'Vahhābī', movement.

RSHUL 148–50; MSHUL 172–5. JM

Monin (Mou Nin), Pi, Burmese writer, see **Pi Mounin.**

Moraes, Dom. (b 1938 Bombay), Indian poet writing in English, though his mother tongue is Konkani. He received his MA at Oxford, and became a journalist. His first book of poems *A Beginning* (1957) won the Hawthornden Prize. He produced a second book, *Poems* (1960) and a travel book, *Gone Away*; *John Nobody* (1965) followed. In 1960 he wrote an autobiography, *An Indian Journal.* His poems are 'permeated with a self-destroying exile's nostalgia'.

P. Lal, *Dom Moraes: stray notes on his poetry* (CEIWE 160–3). MED

moro-moro, form of Filipino folk drama originating in the old Spanish 'comedias' about the struggle between Spaniards and Arabs. Adapted to the Philippine situation, *moro-moro* also deals with conflicts between Christians and Muslims (*moro* = Muslim). All *moro-moro* plays are more or less the same story, celebrating the triumphal victory of the Christians over the Muslims, and they usually include a Muslim Filipino dance and a sword fight. Typical stories involve suspense, love intrigues, and heroes with supernatural powers and bravery. *Moro-moro* plays were very popular during the Spanish period, especially in the 18th and 19th centuries. Another predecessor of the Filipino drama is the *pasyon* (cf passion play), a long verse account of the life of Jesus Christ. There are several written versions of the *pasyon* besides those passed on by oral tradition since the early 18th century. In many rural areas the *pasyon* is still chanted for several nights during Holy Week, usually in local Filipino languages. In the 18th and 19th centuries the *korido* (corrido) and *awit* were also highly popular; they were metric tales in Filipino languages on themes borrowed from Spanish romances. They were either chanted or sung to a guitar. There is no definite dating of their first appearance. *Korido* is in octosyllabic verse (eg *Ibong Adarna*, Bird Adarna, anonymous) while *awit* is in dodecasyllabic quatrains (eg *Florante at Laura* by Baltazar, qv). Typical for *korido* and *awit* are sentimentality, adventure, allegory and a fairy-tale atmosphere. The second half of the 19th and especially the beginning of the 20th centuries were the age of the *zarzuela*, a musical comedy adopted from the Spanish tradition. *Zarzuela* became very popular because it was played in local languages and touched on Filipino contemporary political issues, with its subtle satire and patriotic propaganda. Particular attention was paid to the lyrics and tunes of numerous songs which specially appealed to the music-loving Filipino audience. The best-known authors were Aurelio Tolentino and Severino Reyes. EH

Motirām, Nepali poet, see **Bhaṭṭa,** Motīrām.

Muhammad Baṣir, Vaikkam (b 1910), Malayalam novelist. From the points of view of theme, treatment and style, Baṣīr is one of the most individual of the Malayalam writers of this century. Apart from an occasional play or film script, he has concentrated on what might broadly be called prose fiction. Beyond this his work is not easy to categorize. He does not, for example, show a simplistic acceptance of the novel/short story dichotomy. Concerned to write about what he knows best, Baṣīr has tended to write stories of Kerala Muslims, but by no means exclusively. The content of many of his writings is autobiographical, though the degree to which this is so varies considerably. Thus, *Pāttummayuṭe āṭu* (Pāttumma's Goat, 1959) introduces many members of his family by name. *Bālyakāla sakhi* (Childhood Friend, 1944) is largely based on a period of his own life, but there is nothing in the narrative to show this. His masterpiece, '*Nruppuppākkorānēṇṭārnnu!*' ('Me Grandad 'ad an Elephant!', 1951), has only a few links with persons or events he has known. Among the many features of Baṣīr's genius are a delightful sense of humour and an exceptional capacity to paint the subtleties of human emotions with a great economy of words. Unlike many of his contemporaries in Kerala he has no commitment to attempt to reform society through his writing, though he does allow his radical views to show through occasionally.

CNI 226–34; PNHML 136–8, 145–6; VISNM 19–24. REA

Muḥammad Quli Quṭb Śhāh (pseud. Ma'ānī, b mid-16th century Golkonda, where d 1611). He was the first Dakkhini Urdu poet of secular motifs, the fourth ruler (1580–1611) of the shī'ite Quṭbshāhī dynasty, the founder of Hyderabad, a lover of arts and science, and a patron of poets and scholars. He wrote over 100,000 simple and sweet couplets, dealing with love, Sufism, the Indian seasons, Hindu and Muslim festivals, fruits, vegetables and items of everyday life. His erotic poetry does not disguise love of woman in the garb of mystical love of God, but expresses it openly.

RSHUL 34–36; MSHUL 49. JM

Muhammad Yamin, Indonesian writer, see **Yamin,** Muhammad.

Muis, Abdul (b 1890 Bukit Tinggi, d 1959 Djakarta), Indonesian writer, journalist and politician. He studied at the Medical School, Djakarta, but began to work in the political organization, Sarekat Islam. From 1920 he was a member of the People's Council, and then a journalist. He belonged to the oldest generation of Indonesian writers, grouped round the publishing house Balai Pustaka. His novel *Salah Asuhan* (Wrong Upbringing, 1928) was for a long time an Indonesian best-seller; it deals with the problem of European education which has the effect of rendering people unfit for life in their Indonesian environment. The cultivated language of Muis' novel proved that Indonesian was not merely the language of servants and street hawkers, as many intellectuals of the time declared. Another novel by Muis was *Surapati* (1953).

TMIL 61–3. MO

Mukherji, see **Mukhopādhyāy,** Subhāṣ.

Mukhopādhyāy, Balāicānd, Bengali writer, see **Banaphul.**

Mukhopādhāy (Mukherji), Subhāṣ (b 1919 Krishnagar), Bengali poet. He received a BA, but while studying for his MA, he left Calcutta University to participate in the Communist movement. He subsequently spent a couple of years in Buxa Detention Camp as a political prisoner. He was associated with *Paricay* magazine (see Bandyopādhyāy, Māṇik) and became its editor in 1954. He received the 1964 Sahitya Akademi award for his book of poetry, *Yata dūrei yāi* (As Far as I Wander). Subhāṣ' first book, *Padātik* (Pedestrian, 1940), identified him as one of the most talented of the 'leftist' Bengali poets. His poetry carries references to Soviet Russia and China, to the people's war against the Axis powers, and to the famine and the plight of the people. He chides the bourgeoisie and urges the street procession on. His language is simple and strong; his message is explicit. He continues to be one of the major leftist poets writing today. Further poetry: *Phul phuṭuk* (Let the Flowers Bloom, 1957); *Kāl madhumās* (Tomorrow Comes Spring, 1966); *Ei bhāi* (This Brother, 1970).

Trans.: P. Nandy et al., *Selected Poems of Subhas Mukhopadhyay* (Calcutta 1969); KMBP; BBV. CBS

Mulk Raj Anand, Indian writer, see **Anand,** Mulk Raj.

Munshi, K. M., Gujarati writer, see **navalkathā.**

Murāri (probably mid-9th century, although Winternitz accepts a later dating, between 1050 and 1135 AD), Sanskrit dramatist, author of the *Anargharāghava*, in 7 acts, one of the numerous dramas based on the story of the *Rāmāyaṇa* (qv). While the work, taken as a whole, is of rather secondary importance, it contains a few noteworthy passages, and numerous elegant and well-turned verses, several of which were considered worthy of inclusion in the mediaeval anthologies.

KSD 225–31; DHSL 450–3. JB

Muṣḥafī, Shaikh G͟hulām Hamadānī (b 1750 Akbarpur, d 1824 Lucknow), Urdu and Persian poet and critic. He was educated at Amroha; in 1776 he went to Delhi, but later settled at Lucknow in search of patronage. As he was a fluent writer, driven by poverty, he used to sell his *ghazals* (see Vol. III) to other poets. He wrote eight Urdu *dīwāns* containing eloquent love *ghazals*, caustic satires and licentious lampoons against his more fortunate rival, Inshā (qv). Their language is archaic. His fame rests on his three *taẕkiras* or anthologies of Urdu poets; one of them tells of himself and his contemporaries.

RSHUL 90–3; MSHUL 124–5. JM

Mya Zedi (113 AD), the earliest dated Burmese inscription, it derives its name from the pagoda in Pagan, near which it was discovered in 1911. Its author was Prince Rājakumāra, the unfortunate but dutiful son of King Kyanzittha (1084–1112). It records a moving story of the prince's presentation of a gold image of the Buddha to his dying father and its enshrining in his own temple, Kubyaukkyi, in 1113. The same text appears on the four faces of the stone in Pyu, Mon, Burmese and Pāli. The inscription provides a key not only to the dates of the early kings of the Pagan dynasty (1044–1287), but also to the Pyu language. It also sets a pattern followed in subsequent dedicatory inscriptions: the dedicator and objects dedicated; the dedication ceremony; and prayer and curse.

Trans.: *Epigraphia Birmanica*, Vol. I, part 1 (Rangoon 1919).
G. E. Harvey, *History of Burma* (London 1925), pp. 43–4. HP

Myat San, U, Burmese poet, see **Letwè Thondara.**

Myawadi U Sa, Burmese poet, see **Sa,** U.

N

Nadim, Urdu poet, see **Qāsimi,** Aḥmad Nadīm.

Nāgar, Amṛtlāl (b 1916 Agra), Hindi novelist who portrays mainly urban middle-class life; his broadest canvas is in the novel *Būnd aur samudr* (The Drop and the Sea, 1956). He evokes in a masterly way the atmosphere of Lucknow, his home-town, especially its narrow streets, and its traditional way of life. The novel *Śatrañj ke mohre* (Chessmen, 1959) is set in early 19th century Lucknow. His volume of short stories, *Atom bomb*, was published in 1954. (See āñcalik upanyās.) DA

Nāgārjun, Hindi poet, see **āñcalik upanyās.**

Nāgārjuna (c200 AD), Indian Buddhist philosopher, one of the principal founders of the Madhyamaka school of the Mahāyāna. Among the eight or more works ascribed to Nāgārjuna (some of doubtful origin), the most important are the *Madhyamaka-kārikās* (Verses on the Doctrine of the Middle) and the *Vigraha-vyāvartanī* (Refutation of Contentious Argument). Nāgārjuna's aim is to systematize the doctrines of the *Mahāyāna-sūtras*, in particular the *Prajñā-pāramitā* (see Buddhist Literature). The pervading doctrine is the 'emptiness' (*śūnyatā*) of all the elements (*dharma*) of existence, a doctrine which is established (and thus, on its own terms, also denied) by rigorous argumentation. The device of a double standard, *saṃvṛti-satya* ('conventional truth') and *paramārtha-satya* ('transcendental truth'), renders the theory immune to logical refutation. An important work preserved only in a Chinese translation is the *Mahā-prajñāpāramitā-upadeśa* ('Treatise on the Large *Prajñā-pāramitā-sūtra*'). Although wrongly attributed by the Chinese to the great Nāgārjuna, this text is in the direct tradition of his school, and gives an encyclopaedic account of Madhyamaka doctrines.

German trans., M. Walleser, *Die Mittlere Lehre (Mādhyamikaśāstra) des Nāgārjuna*, Heidelberg 1911 (from the Tibetan version); also selected passages in E. Frauwallner, *Die Philosophie des Buddhismus* (Berlin 1956). For the *Upadeśa*, French trans., E. Lamotte, *Le Traité de la Grande Vertu de Sagesse* (Louvain 1944, 1949, 1970—in progress). JB

Nakkirar (perhaps 8th century), Tamil scholar and commentator. His commentary on Iṟaiyaṉār's *Akapporuḷ* (5th–6th century), a treatise on pre-marital love and erotic poetry, is the first Tamil commentary and the first important work of Tamil prose. It contains a wealth of psychological, sociological, literary and cultural data, and its ornate, rich prose influenced profoundly the entire development of literary Tamil.

JHTL 28–32. KZ

Nālaṭiyār (7th–8th century), an anonymous collection of four hundred four-line Tamil stanzas, each built around a central idea, probably by Jain ascetics; it reflects pessimistic, rather cynical, ethical values.

Trans.: G. U. Pope. *The Naladiyar or Four Hundred Quatrains in Tamil* (Oxford 1893). JHTL 120–2. KZ

Nālāyira[ttiviya]ppirapantam, collective name for the Vaiṣṇava devotional poems of the twelve Tamil *āḷvār* (qv). JRM

Nalopākhyāna (100 BC–100 AD), section of the *Mahābhārata* (qv). The tale of Nala is an ancient Indian sub-epic of approximately 1,000 verses incorporated into one of the oldest layers of the *Mahābhārata* (III, 50–78). The story concerns two lovers, the prince Nala and the princess Damayantī, who fall in love from afar and marry after she selects him from among her other suitors (several of them gods). Nala then loses his kingdom in a game of dice and enters the woods with his wife, who, abandoned by him, wanders back to her father's court. Nala, transformed into a dwarf, becomes charioteer and cook for a king who, after many years, rewards him with the secret of the dice, by which he regains his kingdom, his wife, and (when Damayantī recognizes him in disguise) his true form.

The great themes of the *Mahābhārata* and *Rāmāyaṇa* (qqv) are present in miniature here (the forest exile after the game of dice, the hero as charioteer, the separation of prince and princess), told with such charm and simplicity that the Nala tale has long been considered one of the pearls of world literature. It was translated into Latin in 1819 by Franz Bopp, later into German, English, French, Czech, Polish, Russian, Greek, and Hungarian, and it is the traditional text with which many students of Sanskrit begin.

WHIL I. 324–7. WOF

Nam-Cao (real name Tran-huu-Tri, b 1917 Dai-hong, Ha-nam province, d 1951), Vietnamese writer. In the late 30's and early 40's he wrote many stories and novels for the press, published in book form after the revolution. With the exception of *Song mon* (Worn Out by Life), his pre-1945 novels have been destroyed by the French censorship. Nam-Cao was active in the Vietminh from 1943, and joined the Communist party in 1948. He was killed on a mission behind the enemy lines. Being a realist writer, he was successful in describing lower middle class intellectuals living in poverty. He shows a tendency towards autobiography. His critical, nearly pessimistic view, of Vietnam's society under the French has its antipode in his admiration for the strength and tenacity of simple Vietnamese villagers he discovered during the War of Resistance. Stories: *Cuoi* (Laughter, 1946); *Chi-Pheo* (1956); *Tuyen tap truyen ngan Nam-Cao* (Selected Stories, 1960); *Chuyen bien gioi* (Tales of the Frontier, 1951); *Doi mat* (Eyes, 1956).

Trans.: Le Van Lap et G. Boudarel, *Chi Pheo et autres nouvelles* (Hanoi 1960).
DNILVN 194. VV

Nāmdev or **Nāmā,** Maharashtrian saint-poet who most probably lived in the 14th century AD and who is revered in northern India as well as in the Deccan as a great Vaiṣṇava devotee (*bhakta*). He is the author of a large number of short devotional songs called *abhaṅgas* in old Marathi. He was a low-born Śūdra, a tailor by caste, a layman, who expressed in a simple, touching manner his ardent devotion for the Name of God (ie Viṣṇu-Hari, whom he also called Rām) and his particular attraction for Viṭhobā, a form of Viṣṇu worshipped at Paṇḍharpūr. His legend, full of miraculous events, is told at length in Mahīpati's *Bhakta-vijaya.* Nāmdev seems to have been the real initiator of the practice of the *kīrtan* (devotional songs) in Maharashtra, and especially in Paṇḍharpūr. A number of Hindi stanzas attributed to Nāmdev are also found in the *Ādi Granth* (qv) of the Sikhs. Though Nāmdev is said to have travelled far and wide, it is not certain that the author of the Hindi stanzas and the Marathi *abhaṅgas* are one and the same Nāmdev.

Trans.: J. A. Abbott, *Stories of Indian Saints* (Mahīpati's *Bhaktavijaya*), I. 57–77, 187–357.
MPMS 42–8; RPML 144–64; NHML. CV

Nānak, Sikh *gurū*, see **Ādi Granth** and **janamsākhi.**

Nannaya, author of the Telugu version of the *Mahābhārata* (qv), composed in the 13th and 14th centuries. JRM

Nāraṉappa, Kannada poet, see **Kumār-avyāsa.**

Narayan, R. K. (b 1906 Madras), Indian author writing in English, whose mother tongue is Tamil. Educated at Madras and Mysore, he gained his Hon. D.Litt. at Leeds in 1967. He wrote without first-hand experience of the West, to which he was invited, like N. C. Chaudhuri (qv), after his work was recognized there. Narayan's achievements are the creative use of the ordinary, from the average to the extra-ordinary, and back again to a more poignant state of average; this seems to be the recurrent movement in terms of interacting characters in the majority of his novels. His endorsement of the commonplace of the group and of convention against idiosyncratic individualism is probably a remote acceptance of the life he knows best, that of the middle class. His achievement lies in the uncompromising way in which he forces the ingredients of limitation towards evolving a satisfying authenticity. Narayan's humour is a by-product of an ironical representation of truth. Works: *Swami and Friends* (1935), *The Bachelor of Arts* (1937), *The Dark Room* (1938), *The Astrologer's Day and Other Stories* (1947), *Mr Sampath* (1949), *Next Sunday* (sketches and essays, 1955), *The Guide* (1958), *The Man-Eater of Malgudi* (1961), *The Sweet Vendor* (1967). Many of these have been republished in the United States, and translated into French and German. His short stories appear in Indian and foreign journals.

Rajeev Taranath, *The average as positive—a note on R. K. Narayan* (CEIWE 362–75); DMINE. MED

Nārāyaṇa, author of the Sanskrit **Hitopadeśa.**

Nārāyaṇa Mēnōn, Vaḷḷattōḷ (1879–1958), Malayalam poet. The large poetic output of Vaḷḷattōḷ was throughout his life too varied to allow easy classification. It is nevertheless possible to discern a number of different (though overlapping) periods in his career. He began by writing in the classical mould and his early work included a translation of Vālmīki's *Rāmāyaṇa* (qv). *Badhira vilāpam* (1910), in which he laments the fact that he has gone deaf, marks his entry into the Romantic school. From then on his range increased and at the same time he tended more and more to use Dravidian metrical forms rather than the Sanskritic ones he had favoured earlier. Like Cuppiramaṇiyam Bharati (Pārati, qv) for the people of neighbouring Tamilnad, Vaḷḷattōḷ was for Malayalis the poet of Indian nationalism during the decades preceding independence, and he wrote an inspired poem in praise of Gandhi, *Enṟe gurunāthan* (My Master). Later he became known as the poet who fought for economic and social justice. These various changes of emphasis notwithstanding, he never lost his love for the great traditions of his homeland, and it is a feature of his verses of all periods that he lays stress on the spiritual unity of mankind, whatever their religious or political background. There is a justifiable unanimity in considering him the greatest Malayalam poet of this century.

Trans.: Erik de Mauny, *Mary Magdalene* (London 1952).
PNHML 198–212; GSML 151–7, 233–6. REA

Naṟṟiṇai, classical Tamil anthology, see **Eṭṭuttokai.**

Nāsikh, Shaikh Imām Bakhsh (b 1774 Lahore, d 1838 Lucknow), founder of the Lucknow school of Urdu poetry. He never married and never sought any service, but lived on the munificence of nobles and often had to flee into exile. As reformer of poetry he laid down definite rules for the high style of Urdu and charged it with Persian and Arabic expressions. His overornamented work is poetry divorced from reality. He tried to make his formalist erotic and philosophical *ghazals* (see Vol. III) original by the use of fantastic similes, stiff constructions and striking idioms.

RSHUL 102–6; MSHUL 133–7. JM

Nāṣir 'Ali Sirhindī (d 1697), a Persian poet of traditional bent in north-west India, later a member of the Naqshbandi order. His *maṡnavī* (see Vol. III) *Madhumalat and Manohar* (1649) follows a Hindi model. In his lyrics the involved Indian style of Persian poetry is carried to its extreme, perhaps even more than in the work of his contemporary Bedil (see Vol. III). An extremely haughty man, 'completely submerged in his phantasies' (Azād), he influenced, through Shāh Gulshan and the Delhi school, later Persian poetry in India; even Ghālib (qv) in his youth was fond of him. A number of very beautiful verses can, by a persevering reader, be disengaged from the complicated rhetorical fabric. AS

Naṣir, Gul Khān (b 1910 Nushki), modern Baluchi poet and prose writer, editor of several literary magazines. He is a representative of the older generation of Baluchi national revivalists, who combine the development of national consciousness with the defence of Islamic ideals. His poetry reflects a spirit of patriotism sparked off by the social awakening of the Baluchi intelligentsia. In his main volume of poetry, *Gulbāng* (Call, 1952), Naṣīr stresses the importance of returning to the simplicity and frankness of original Islam.

ABSLP 312. JM

nāṭaka, ancient Indian drama, see **kāvya.**

Naṭēca Cāstiri, Caṅkēnti Mahāliṅkam (1859–1906), Tamil novelist. A member of the Indian civil service, he was only a part-time writer; his literary output was nevertheless very large. His earlier works, in both Tamil and English, were mainly collections of folk-tales from southern India. Later he published Tamil prose versions of a number of Sanskrit classics and of a set of Persian stories. Of more lasting importance were his six 'Popular Tamil Novels', which appeared between 1900 and 1903 and which have very varied themes. Having tried his hand at prose fiction in the previous decade by bringing out the first set of Tamil detective stories (*Tāṉavaṉ*, 1894), he then produced a story of south Indian Brahmin family life (*Tiṉatayālu*, 1900), a piece of 'science-fiction' (*Kōmaḷam kumariyāṉatu*, The Rejuvenation of Kōmaḷam, 1902), the sentimental tale of *Tikaṟṟa iru kuḷantaikaḷ* (The Two Orphans, 1902), the rather melodramatic *Matikeṭṭa maṉaivi* (A Wife Condoned, 1903), a historical novel (*Śrīmāmi koluvirukkai*, The Mother-in-law in Council, 1903) and an adaptation of Douglas Jerrold's *Mrs Caudle's Curtain Lectures* (*Talaiyaṇai mantirōpatēcam*, 1903).

R. E. Asher, *Pandit S. M. Natesa Sastri (1859–1906), Pioneer Tamil Novelist*. Proceedings of the Second International Conference Seminar of Tamil Studies, Vol. II (Madras 1971), pp. 107–15; CNI 197–201. REA

Natshinnaung (1578–1613), Burmese poet, a prince and later ruler of Toungoo city. He has been extolled as the most famous *yadu* (qv) composer. He was obsessed with two aspirations: to be king of Burma and to win the hand of the princess he loved. He had the necessary courage and pugnacity, but fate had ordained otherwise. He was executed by the king for treason. He was frustrated in his affair of the heart, and although he married the princess in the end, she died in the same year. He wrote a *yadu* in allusive language on the impending fulfilment of his imperial ambition that brought comments from several Burmese scholars. He also composed many impassioned *yadu* on the beauty of the princess, the plighting of his troth and on the agonies of ill-requited love. In the context of his unfortunate career and love-life, these poems were bound to capture the imagination of posterity. But his *yadu* have been overrated; they are too formalized and several of them are reminiscences of those of Nawade (qv).

G. E. Harvey, *History of Burma* (London 1925), p. 188. HP

Nāṭyaśāstra of Bharata, the earliest Indian text preserved on dramaturgy, poetics, music, body gestures and temple architecture. No precise date can be assigned to the text, though the bulk of it seems to have been written in about the 3rd century AD. Additions were probably made until the time of Udbhaṭa (qv, 9th century), one of the earliest commentators, though many of the verses quoted in the text are probably much older; it is certain (from these citations) that there existed earlier works on dramatic theory now lost. Nobody has yet made a study of the verses, many of them very lovely, given as illustrations of the various meters in chapter XV. These might give some clues to the date of the work. Though pronouncements on style are notoriously subjective, the poems may seem, in their degree of complexity, to fall between Aśvaghoṣa (qv, 2nd century) and Kālidāsa (qv, floruit probably c400 AD).

The influence of the *Nāṭyaśāstra* has been enormous. Not a single playwright whose works have come down to us (with the possible exception of Bhāsa, qv) ignores the work, and many writers write in strict conformity to the suggestions and rules laid down in the *Nāṭyaśāstra*. Of the many commentaries referred to in later works on poetics, only one has come down to us: the great *Abhinavabhāratī* of Abhinavagupta (qv), the very greatness of which is probably responsible for the loss of earlier commentaries. Unfortunately this work is not complete; several chapters have never been found, notably the commentary on the important 7th chapter often referred to in earlier chapters.

In spite of the general simplicity of the language, the text is often obscure. The most famous line in dramaturgy: *vibhāvānubhāvavyabhicārisaṃyogād rasaniṣpattiḥ* ('An aesthetic experience comes from the combination of characters, the atmosphere created, the reactions of the characters and the emotions they express') was so obscure, in its implications if not in its literal sense, that each commentator used it as the starting point of elaborate theories on the nature of imaginative experiences in literature. The text is also often uncertain as in the 16th chapter, on *lakṣaṇas*, where Abhinavagupta cites two different recensions. Compared to his detailed treatment of the technicalities of drama (eg several hundred verses on hand-gestures, eye-gestures, dance steps and music), Bharata is comparatively brief on 'poetics' proper.

Trans.: M. Ghosh (Vol. I, Calcutta 1967, Vol. II, Calcutta 1961). J. L. Masson and M. V. Patwardhan, *Aesthetic Rapture* (Poona 1970); DHSP I, 18–45; II, 1–31. JLM

Nāvalar, Tamil writer, see **Ārumukam,** Nallūr Kantappiḷḷai.

navalikā, the modern Gujarati short story, is a half-century-old genre. In *Taṇakhāmandal* (A Bunch of Sparks, 1926) by G. Bhaṭṭa (pseud. Dhūmketu), the Gujarati short story, begun in 1918 by K. Mehtā (pseud. Malayānil), with his *Govālaṇi* (A Shepherdess), celebrated its resonating form for its romantic content. Soon, in *Dvirefni Vāto* (Tales by Dviref, 1929) Rāmanārāyaṇ Pāṭhak (pseud. Dviref) helped remove the emphasis in Gujarati short fiction on significant idealistic content. His, and later Jayant Khatri's, fiction displayed a keenness for formal experiments. Two poets, T. Luhār (pseud. Sundarām) and Umāśankar Jośi (qv), added to this their miniature craftmanship. In *Latā ané Biji Vāto* (Latā and Other Tales, 1935), Gulabdas Brokor explored in a new, casual, amoral style the wide, tabooed world of sex in the bourgeois world. In *Ghughavatān Pūr* (The Roaring Floods, 1945) Cunilāl Maḍiā employed energetic, primitive, imagist techniques and in *Ek Sānjni Mulākāt* (The Encounter on an Evening, 1963), Candrakant Bakśi created multi-focused, strongly evocative images, establishing the supremacy of techniques over the sex-related content and in a sense the form itself. In *Api Ca* (Furthermore, 1963) Sureś Jośi turned to pure form, devoid of any incident, appearing like a legend or fairy-tale. In the stories of the young avant-garde writers today, Madhu Rāy, Ghanaśyām Desāi, Prabodh Parikh, Ivā Davé, Sudhir Dalāl, Mahommad Mānkad and others, the movement of man's basic symbol, language, is itself directly and primarily presented in a reincarnation of the Gujarati short story. SY

navalkathā, the modern Gujarati novel, starts with *Karaṇa Ghelo* (The Idiot King Karaṇa, 1868). *Sarasvaticandra* (parts 1–4, 1887–1909) is a multi-centred novel, structured like a 'mosaic', as its author, G. M. Tripathi has pointed out in its preface. The inner crisis of the then-emerging 'modern' India was externalized through the archetypical and realistic images and symbols, and the actual and metaphysical journeys of its cultured, 'vagabond' hero. The second structure was developed by K. M. Munshi, who transformed the facts of India's past into a movement of its basic history. Thus, his *Pāṭaṇani Prabhutā* (The Supremacy of Paṭan, 1918) truly begins the Gujarati historical novel. The third structure was developed by R. V. Desāi in *Divya Cakṣu* (Eyes of the Soul, 1932), in which he employed an unassuming documentary technique to depict the sense and the essence of the Gandhian age. Its variations can be seen in the fiction of Jhavercand Meghani and M. Pancoli ('Darśak'). A new interaction between realism and symbolism turned Cunilāl Maḍiā's *Liluḍi Dharati* (The Green Earth, 1958) and Pannalāl Patel's *Mānavini Bhavāi* (The Human Comedy, 1947) into unit structures of symbol, unlike the earlier imagist novels. The novel of the 1960's displays a duality: Raghuvir Caudhari's *Amṛtā* (The Amortal, 1965) evolved a kaleidoscopic form resting on only three inter-reflecting characters, while Candrakant Bakśi's *Ākār* (Form, 1963) created a disjoined structure, juxtaposing meaningless but sensuous actualities. Both created a need to redefine 'fiction'. SY

Nawade I (?1498–?1588), Burmese poet, a courtier and soldier of exceptional literary acumen and advanced ideas. He had to serve under several masters and go on many military campaigns owing to the political instability of the time. He wrote some traditional *egyin*, but chose a secular story, the non-traditional theme of Manawhari, for his *pyo* (qv). He is recognized as the greatest exponent of *yadu* (qv), the dominant genre in the 16th and 17th centuries. Nawade introduced many new forms and themes, drawing on his experiences at court and as a soldier. He developed the genre to serve as a pattern for posterity, and left more than 300 *yadu*, some of which are echoed in those of Natshinnaung (qv). HP

nāyaṉmār, sixty-three Tamil Śaiva saints, some of them important poets, exponents of *bhakti* (qv). Noteworthy were Appar, Campantar, Cuntarar and Māṇikkavācakar (qqv). KZ

nayī kahānī (the New Story), Hindi literary movement arising about 1955 in encouraging circumstances. Its main representatives, R. Yādav, M. Rakeś, Kamaleśvar (qqv), Mannū Bhaṇḍārī, Uṣā Priyaṃvadā and Nirmal Varmā, write of their own urban middle-class environment. *Nayī kahānī* does not mean a break in the continuity of Hindi prose; the writers concerned are not agreed on all points, but linked by related or identical features in their work. The trend has absorbed the previous traditions of realistic social writing and introspective literature to a varying degree. *Nayī kahānī* primarily deals with the impact of social problems on the individual. These writers attempt to portray the variety and complexity of life, to reject sentimentality, literary clichés and traditional approaches, to introduce new themes or new angles on old themes and try to keep man himself at the real centre of literature. Attention is focused mainly on traditional institutions, the break-up of the joint family, and the position of women and young people. Many of their characters are intellectuals in conflict situations, leading to pathological states of mind. They are faithfully portrayed, particularly their loneliness and the longing for development of personality. Symbols are freely used, but without mystic nuances. They are used simply to enhance the fundamental idea and create atmosphere, being (as a rule) neither hackneyed nor in the accepted tradition. The same is true of the principles of composition. In the sixties the *nayī kahānī* gave expression to grimmer moods and the feeling of hopelessness, and symbolism accrued.

Anthology: Jai Ratan (ed. and trans.), *Contemporary Hindi Short Stories* (Calcutta 1962). DA

nayī kavitā, the New Poetry movement in Hindi literature. The first important manifestation of this movement was the publication, in 1933 (2nd ed. 1966), of *Tār saptak* (ed. Ajñeya, qv), an anthology including the biographies of, and statements and poems by, Gajānan Mādhav Muktibodh, Nemicandra Jain, Bhāratbhūṣaṇ Agravāl, Prabhākar Mācve, Girijākumār Māthur, Rāmvilās Śarmā, and Ajñeya. In 1951 Ajñeya edited *Dūsrā saptak* (Śamśerbahādur Siṃh, Nareś Mehtā, Raghuvīr Sahāy, Dharmvīr Bhārtī ao) and, in 1959, *Tīsrā saptak* (Kedārnāth Siṃh, Sarveśvardayāl Saksenā ao). The New Poets have never formed a 'school' founded on a common ideology, or a common concept of style. What they share is an intellectual curiosity, a fundamentally experimentalist (*prayogvādī*) attitude, 'a profound ethical concern, the quest for new values and searching examination of the basic sanctions or sources of value'. This, in a permanent trial of strength with the West, has led to 'a growing awareness of the unique total entity of man' (Ajñeya) and, consequently, a change of poetic sensibility.

Not only have they, in the process, questioned time-honoured taboos which heretofore restricted the choice of subject matter worthy of poetic treatment. Language itself, in particular the relation between word (*śabd*) and meaning (*arth*), has come under discussion, and this discussion has become a poetic theme in its own right. Their resultant awareness of literary craftsmanship and medium-consciousness have been promoted by what is basically a problem of communication. Whereas their predecessors still assumed, rather naïvely, that they were writing their poetry for, and reciting it to, the traditional Indian audience of connoisseurs trained for sympathetic reception, the New Poets, not ready to fall a victim to this illusion or accept self-expression as the end of poetic activity, and being aware of their social responsibility, have found that this audience no longer exists. Thus their poetry is most probably meant to be read, not listened to, by individuals unfamiliar with the poetic conventions of the past. As a consequence, they have turned away from poetic diction and, making a virtue of necessity, discovered the poetic possibilities of folk language.

V. N. Misra (ed.), *Modern Hindi Poetry: An Anthology* (Bloomington 1965); L. Lutze (ed. and trans.), *Als wär die Freiheit wie ein Stein gefallen—Hindilyrik der Gegenwart* (Tübingen-Basel 1968). LL

Naẓir Akbarābādī, Valī Muḥammad (b 1740 Delhi, d 1830 Agra), Urdu realistic poet, forerunner of modern Urdu poetry. He refused offers of service to local rulers, and earned his livelihood as tutor to the sons of a Hindu merchant at Agra. His poems were collected from his friends after his death. He was the poet of everyday life and of minute actual facts. With a sense of humour and a touch of burlesque he depicted the joys and sorrows of the common people, in which he directly participated. His *Admī-nāma* (Eulogy on Man) is a hymn to the equality of mankind. He also wrote long poems on the pleasures of love, wine and hunting, on nature, birds, flowers and vegetables. His humanism was individualist; he often looked back to his youth, was sad at the quick transience of human affairs, but never lost sight of reality.

RSHUL 140–5; MSHUL 111–16. JM

Naẓiri Nishāpuri, Muḥammad Ḥusain (d 1612 Ahmedabad), Indo-Persian poet, representing the ornate Indian style. He lived at the court of Emperor Akbar's minister, Abdur Rahim Khan, at Agra, then at Jahangir's court, and was closely connected with Sūfī circles. He wrote abstract philosophical *qaṣīdas* (see Vol. III) in the spirit of contemplative mysticism. His importancc lics in his difficult lyric *ghazals* (see Vol. III), full of sophisticated metaphors, in which he pursues a single line of thought throughout the poem. His florid verses are melodious, and some have an element of deep pathos. His popularity is based on his easily intelligible philosophical essays.

HIL 723 JM

Nazrul Islām (b 1899 Churuliya), Bengali poet. He left school during Class X to join the army in 1917 and was stationed in Karachi. He became editor of A. K. Fazlul Huq's paper, *Nabayug*, wrote for the newspaper, *Sevak*, and founded a radical political journal, *Dhumketu*, 1922. Convicted of sedition by the British government, he spent a year in prison. Then he edited *Lāṅgal*, the newspaper of the radical wing of Indian National Congress, and was convicted of sedition again but freed because of the Gandhi-Irwin pact (1931). He has been mentally ill since 1942.

Nazrul Islām was both a Bengali poet and an active nationalist. One of his earlier poems, *Bidrohī* (The Rebel), earned him the title 'The Rebel Poet'. Several of his books, both poetry and prose, were so powerful that the British government had them proscribed. While in prison he went on a hunger strike; Tagore is said to have sent a telegram to the fasting poet, 'Give up hunger strike, our literature claims you.' He contributed to leading journals of the day, for example *Kallol*, including those specifically oriented towards Muslim writers, eg *Moslem Bhārat* and *Saogāt*. Nazrul had learned Persian and rendered the *Rubāiyāt* of Omar Khayyām (see Vol. III) into Bengali. Persian and Urdu words are found in some of his own poems. He wrote many songs, *ghazals* (see Vol. III) and other types. At one time the most colourful, exuberant, rebellious poet of Bengal, Nazrul Islām today is silent. But his songs are still extremely popular and can be heard often throughout Bengal. Some books: *Agni bīṇā* (Fire Lute, 1922); *Biṣer bāṃśī* (Flute of Poison, 1924); *Pralay-śikhā* (Flame of Destruction, 1930); *Candrabindu* (Star and Crescent, 1930); *Gāner mālā* (Garland of Songs, 1934).

Trans.: Kabir Choudhury, *Selected Poems* (Dacca 1963); BBV; PEB.
Mizanur Rahman, *Nazrul Islam* (Dacca 1966); Serajul Islam Chaudhury, *Introducing Nazrul Islam* (Karachi 1965); B. Chakravarty, *Kazi Nazrul Islam* (New Delhi 1968). CBS

Ngo-tat-To (b 1894 Loc-ha, Bac-ninh province, d 1954 North Vietnam), Vietnamese writer and journalist. Given a classical Confucian education, he worked as a patriotic journalist, writer and critic before the 1945 August revolution. Later he was active in the Union of Vietnamese Writers and Artists; he joined the Communist party in 1948, and perished during the anti-colonial war. His novel *Tat den* (When the Light is Out, 1939) is considered the most important pre-revolution work of the realist school, and gives a painfully true picture of the life of the poor villagers. Ngo-tat-To was the first to introduce this theme to modern Vietnamese literature. His descriptions of village life and customs are of great documentary value. He is also known as translator of Chinese literature (*Duong thi*, T'ang Poetry, 1940). Other works: novels, *Leu chong* (Hut and Litter, 1941); *Vua Ham-nghi voi viec kinh thanh that thu* (King Ham-nghi and the Fall of the Capital, 1935); reportage, *Viec lang* (Village Matters, 1941).

Trans.: Le Lien Vu and G. Boudarel, *Quand la lampe s'éteint* (Hanoi 1959); *When the Light is Out* (Hanoi 1960).
DNILVN 195. VV

Nguyen-cong-Hoan (b 1903 Xuan-cau, Hung-yen province), Vietnamese writer, son of a mandarin's family. Working as a teacher and writing since 1926, after the 1945 August revolution he held posts in DRV Government departments and the army. Since 1957, he has been chairman of the Writers' Union in Hanoi. His best works date from 1930–45, tales and novels wittily satirizing the upper classes of the Vietnamese society under the French rule. Chief works: novels, *La ngoc canh vang* (Leaves of Jade and Gold Twigs, 1934); *Co giao Mingh* (Miss Minh the Teacher, 1936); *Buoc duong cung* (The End of the Way, 1938); *Cai thu lon* (Pig's Head, 1939); *Tranh toi tranh sang* (Dark and Bright Pictures, 1957); *Dong rac cu* (A Heap of Rubbish, 1963); stories, *Kep Tu-Ben* (Tu-Ben the Comic, 1933); *Truyen ngan chon loc I, II* (Selected Stories, 1958).

DNILVN 197. VV

Nguyen-dinh-Chieu (b 1822 Tan-khanh, Gia-dinh province, d 1888), Vietnamese poet, best-known writer of the older South Vietnam literature. Of a poor Confucian scholar's family, he fell ill and became blind on his way back from the official examinations in Hue in 1842; he set up a school in his home town, and devoted himself to teaching and writing. After the French attack on Gia-dinh in 1859 he went to the country and collaborated with the leaders of the anti-French revolt, dying of a broken heart when he learnt of the final defeat of the patriotic nobles. The French invasion divides his work into two distinct sections; characteristic of the first is the moralizing epic *Luc-van-Tien*, of 2,076 strophes, of variable literary quality; he paid more attention to the subject than to style. In his second period he wrote many patriotic poems, funeral orations and calls to action. The verse *Ngu tieu van dap* (Dialogue between a Fisherman and a Woodcutter), of 3,644 strophes of alternating form, is in fact a treatise on medicine.

Trans.: Abel de Michels, *Les poèmes de l'Annam—Luc Van-Tien ca dien* (Paris 1883).
DNILVN 98, 198. VV

Nguyen-Du (b 1765 Tien-dien, Ha-tinh province, d 1820 Hue), Vietnamese poet. Son of a high official, of an ancient family of mandarins, he received an excellent education in both classical Chinese and Vietnamese literature. He soon gave up his career as a military officer, and lived in poverty among the country people, getting to know folk literature. Called to high office under the Nguyen dynasty, he served without enthusiasm, and several times resigned, pretending ill-health. In 1814 he led a mission to the Imperial court in Peking. Although he wrote in classical Chinese as well, his greatest fame is based on his Vietnamese poetry, particularly the verse-novel, *Kieu* (*Truyen Kieu*, also called *Kim-van-Kieu* after the chief characters), considered the greatest poem in the Vietnamese language. It is a verse adaptation of a less well-known Chinese romance, superior to it in careful composition, subtle characterization and psychological insight. The poet uses the story of a young girl, beset by the troubles and disasters women are subject to in traditional oriental society, to give a picture of his own times; he lays great stress on the emotional relationships and the inner life of his characters. The novel is still enormously popular, and often recited from memory. Its wealth of poetic expression draws on folk literature; it is a long *truyen* (qv) of 3,245 lines of the *luc bat* (qv) type, regularly alternating 6 and 8 line strophes. Other works in Vietnamese which have survived include the epic *Van te thap loai chung sinh* (Prayer for Ten Wandering Souls) popularly known as *Chieu hon* (Invocation of Souls), and the lyric *Thac loi trai phuong non* (An Answer for the Young Man from Hat Street). Of the Chinese poetry collected in *Thanh-hien tien hau tap* (Complete Poems of Thanh-hien), *Bac hanh thi tap* (Notes on a Journey to the North) and *Nam trung tap ngam* (Song Written in the South), only fragments have survived.

Trans. into French: Xuan Phuc et Xuan Viet, *Kim Van Kieu* (Paris 1961); Nguyen-khac-Vien, *Kieu* (Hanoi 1965). VV

Nguyen-gia-Thieu (b 1741 Lieu-ngan, Bac-ninh province, d 1799), Vietnamese poet, also known as On-nhu-Hau, a member of the higher nobility who held important office at the Trinh regents' court from youth onwards. Besides his literary talents he was an excellent painter and architect. When official service became unpleasant to him he devoted himself entirely to poetry and philosophy. Under the Tay-son he pretended to be ill and mad. A prolific writer, his Chinese poems (c1,000) collected in *On-nhu thi tap* (Poems of On-nhu) have not survived. Best known of his Vietnamese poetry is the lyrical *Cung oan ngam khuc* (Lament of a Court Lady), a variation on a very topical theme of those times, the fate of a young woman in a king's harem, condemned to suffer there for the rest of her life after her master's interest flags. It is the emotional rather than the social aspect which interested the author. The poem comprises 356 strophes in quatrains, of 7, 7, 6 and 8-syllable lines (see *luc-bat*). The poet was influential in perfecting the forms of Vietnamese poetry.

DNILVN 85–6, 199. VV

Nguyen-Hong (b 1918 Nam-dinh), Vietnamese writer. Before the August revolution 1945 he had already written a number of stories about poor people who took up a life of crime through poverty. Since 1943 he was active in the underground Union of Cultural Workers for National Salvation. He follows the method of socialist realism and is considered in North Vietnam to be one of the novelists with great talent. He is now permanently settled in Ha-bac province. Main works: novels, *Bi vo* (The Thief, 1937); *Nhung ngay tho au* (Childhood Days, 1938); *Dem giai phong* (The Night of Liberation, 1952); *Giu thoc* (Defending the Crops, 1955); *Song gam* (The Roaring Waves, 1961); stories, *Dia nguc* (Hell, 1946); *Lo lua* (Furnace, 1946).

DNILVN 196. VV

Nguyen-huy-Tu, Vietnamese poet, see **truyen.**

Nguyen-khac-Hieu, Vietnamese poet, see **Tan-Da.**

Nguyen-kim-Thanh, Vietnamese poet, see **To-Huu.**

Nguyen-nhuoc-Phap, Vietnamese poet, see **The-Lu.**

Nguyen-Sen, Vietnamese writer, see **To-Hoai.**

Nguyen-Thien, Vietnamese poet, see **truyen.**

Nguyen-Trai (pseudonym Uc-Trai, b 1380 Nhi-khe, Ha-dong province, d 1442 Thang-long, Hanoi), Vietnamese poet and statesman, of a family close to the royal court. He received a very good education. After the Ming invasion 1406 he was arrested, and then joined the liberation army of Le-Loi, occupying important posts after victory; a close adviser of two successive kings, he was finally suspected to have plotted for regicide and executed. Many letters and pronouncements written by him and sent in Le-Loi's name to the Ming generals have been preserved in *Quan trung tu menh tap* (Letters and Commands from the Time of Military Service). His best known poem is in Chinese, the *Binh Ngo dai cao* (Great Proclamation after the Victory over the Ming). Many of his poems were written in Vietnamese using the *chu nom* script, developed from Chinese characters, used before the Latin script was introduced as the official alphabet in the late 19th century. Collected in *Quoc am thi tap* (Volume of Poems in the National Tongue), they are the earliest literature in Vietnamese language to have survived. He was also the author of the first geography of Vietnam, *Du dia chi* (Geographical Notes, 1435).

DNILVN 63–9, 202. vv

Nguyen-trong-Tri, Vietnamese poet, see **Han-mac-Tu.**

Nguyen-Tuan, (b 1910 Hanoi), Vietnamese writer. Writing since 1937, he was already well known before the 1945 August Revolution, particularly as an essayist contributing to various literary periodicals. His work includes novels, short stories, travel sketches and other essays, and reportage. His style, partly playful and partly blasé, poetical and often ironic, tinged with melancholy in pre-August 1945 writings, was met with sympathy by many readers. In 1946-54 Nguyen-Tuan was Secretary General of the Vietnamese Writers' Union in the DRV. He lives in Hanoi. Main works: novel, *Que huong* (Home, 1941), also known as *Thieu que huong* (Homeless); essays and reportage, *Van bong mot thoi* (Echoes and Shadows of an Epoch, 1940); *Tuy but* (Essays, 1941); *Tuy but khang chien va hoa binh* (Essays in War and Peace, 1955); *Song Da* (Black River, 1960); stories, *Nha bac Nguyen* (Mr Nguyen's Family, 1946); *Mot chuyen di* (On the Road, 1941); *Chiec lu dong mat cua* (The Bronze Incense Bowl the Colour of a Crab's Eye, 1941); *Toc chi Hoai* (Mrs Hoai's Hair, 1941).

DNILVN 123, 203. vv

Nguyen-tuong-Lan, Vietnamese writer, see **Thach-Lam.**

Nguyen-tuong-Tam, Vietnamese writer, see **Nhat-Linh.**

Nhat-Linh (real name Nguyen-tuong-Tam, 1906 Cam-giang, Hai-duong province, d 1963), Vietnamese writer. A leading figure in the romantic school of the thirties, and co-founder with Khai-Hung (qv) of the *Tu luc van doan* (With Our Own Strength) group in 1933. Together with Tam's brothers, the writers Thach-Lam (qv) and Nguyen-tuong-Long, alias Hoang-Dao (1907–1948), and others they launched the revues *Phong hoa* (Conventions, 1932) and *Ngay nay* (Modern Time, 1935) to propagate their ideas. Nguyen-tuong-Tam became an active leader of a right wing nationalist party in 1939. During the World War II he took refuge in China, where he joined a group of the nationalist *Vietnam quoc dan dang* party which was sharply opposed to the Ho Chi Minh government after the 1945 August revolution. In 1946 he entered the Coalition Resistance Government led by Ho Chi Minh, as Minister of Foreign Affairs, but on the outbreak of hostilities he emigrated to Nationalist China, returning in 1951 to occupied Hanoi. After the Geneva agreements of 1954 he went to South Vietnam, where he published the periodical *Van-hoa ngay nay* (Culture Today) from 1958, in Saigon. In 1961 he was elected chairman of the South Vietnam Pen Club. Like other writers of the *Tu luc van* *doan* group he criticized the traditional society and proclaimed the right of the individual to free development of his personality, especially in the emotional sphere. His heroes are in revolt against existing social conventions, but remain individualists. Main works: novels, *Doan tuyet* (Rupture, 1934); *Lanh lung* (Loneliness, 1936); *Doi ban* (Friends, 1939); *Buom trang* (White Butterfly, 1941); *Nang thu* (Autumn Sun, 1942). He also wrote novels and short stories in collaboration with Khai Hung, eg *Doi mua gio* (Tempestuous Life, 1936).

DNILVN 157–60, 206. VV

Nimmāmhemint, Mọm Lūong Bubphā, Thai writer, see **Dọkmai Sot.**

Nirālā (Sūryakānt Tripāṭhī, b 1898 Midnapore, d 1961 Allahabad), Hindi poet, novelist and translator. *Anāmikā* (Nameless, 1923), *Parimal* (Fragrance, 1930) and *Gītikā* (Songbook, 1936) established his fame as a *chāyāvād* (qv) poet. His historical poems, *Chatrapati Śivājī kā patra* (A Letter of King Sivaji, 1922), *Dillī* (1924) etc, are full of patriotic pathos. Among his romantic verse of the twenties there are very early socio-critical poems: *Bhikṣuk* (The Beggar, 1921), *Dīn* (The Poor, 1921). In the mid-thirties Nirālā and Pant (qv) became leading progressive poets (see *pragativād*). In his novels *Kulli bhāṭ* (1939) and *Billesur bakrihā* (Shepherd B, 1941) as much as in his poetry *Kukurmuttā* (Mushroom, 1942) and *Nae patte* (New Leaves, 1946), Nirālā depicted realistically the poverty and misery of the lower classes. His songs have served as models for the younger poets. IZ

nirāt (Travels, or Poems of Farewell), the most favoured genre in Thai literature, practised by all the great poets. These are probably over 100 in existence, but bibliographical analysis is lacking. A few describe military campaigns, but as a rule the poem depicts a civilian journey, regretfully far from the beloved, passing by beautiful scenery and interesting monuments; different goals and different means of transport provide variety in the *nirāt*. Some journeys are undertaken for pleasure, others to accompany the king elephant hunting, on missions to foreign courts, or in search of knowledge. An important type of *nirāt* describes Buddhist pilgrimages. During the fighting against the Burmese, under Rāma I (1782–1809), military campaigns were described. The earliest, *Nirāt Hariphūnchai* (Travelling to Lamphūn, first quarter of the 17th century), describes a journey from Chīengmai to the Lamphūn Buddhist shrine. *Khlōng Nirāt Kamsūon* and those by Sī Mahōsot (17th century) were still in the *khlōng* metre, which gave place to the *klọn* form in the later 18th century. *Nirāt* reached its peak in Sunthọn Phū (1786–1855), known for nine 'travels' including *Nirāt Phrabāt* (To the Buddha's Footprints Shrine) and the famous *Nirāt Phū Khau Thọng* (To the Golden Mountain). His work bears the mark of the poet's personality and experience. The best-known *nirāt* of the later 19th century is *Nirāt Lọndọn* by Mọm Rātchōthai, describing the diplomatic mission sent to London in 1858.

Schweisguth, *Étude sur la littérature Siamoise* (Paris 1951). KW

Noi Inthanon, Thai writer, see **Mālai Chūphinit.**

Nou Hach, Cambodian writer, see **pralomlok.**

Nṛpatunga Amōghavarṣa, Kannada writer, see **Kavirājamārga.**

Nu, U (b 1907 Wakhema), Burmese politician, writer, dramatist, translator. Rangoon University Student Strike leader (1936), he was active in the nationalist *Doubama* organization, and jailed by the British in 1940–42. He became Minister of Foreign Affairs in 1943, of Information in 1944, and, after World War II, Chairman of the Anti-Fascist People's Freedom League and the first Prime Minister of the Union of Burma. He was an ardent Buddhist and the sponsor of the World Peace Pagoda Building in Rangoon. In 1962–66 he was jailed by the military government, and since 1969 has lived in exile. U Nu was one of the founders of the Nagani Book Club, which published a political journal, translations of political works and original fiction. His novel *Yeksek Papei kwe* (Man, the Wolf of Man, 1942) exposes the British judiciary and life in jail. Play *Puhtuzinno Ummatako* (Man is Insane, 1943) criticizes hypocrisy in social and sexual relations. *Luthu Aun Tham* (The People Win Through, 1952) is an anti-Communist propaganda play. Memoirs *Nga Hnis Yathi Bama Pyij, 1941–45* (Burma in 1941–45, 1946) was translated into English as *Burma under the Japanese* (London 1954). DB

Nur Sutan Iskandar, Indonesian writer, see **Iskandar,** Nur Sutan.

O

O Bhatha, U, Burmese writer, see **Awbhatha,** U.

On-nu-Hau, Vietnamese poet, see **Nguyen-gia-Thieu.**

Outtamatjo, Shin, Burmese poet, see **Uttamagyaw,** Shin.

P

pada, a genre of mediaeval Gujarati poetry. In *Siddhahaima Vyākaraṇa* (1102 AD) the grammarian Hemacandra Suri has recorded many short poems on love and heroism written in the Gurjara Apabhraṃśa, the immediate precursor of the Gujarati language. The 14th century work *Mugdhāvabodhamauktikam,* in which 'we see Gujarati almost in the act of taking birth' (Grierson), contains instruction for the young. Maṇikyacandra Suri's *Pṛthvicandra Carit* (1432 AD) narrates the wealth and valour of a legendary king. Padmanābha's *Kānhaḍade Prabandha* (qv) is the swan-song of unvanquished India. To this literary tradition Narasiṃha Mehtā (c1414–80) and Mirā Bāi (c1403–70) gave a decisive turn through their *pada* poems, expressing with unmatched emotive power and through the techniques of sensuous images different aspects of a single and new theme: the love of Rādhā and Kṛṣṇa. This was indeed a new, trans-Indian myth, arising in the minds and senses of poets from Bengal to Gujarat, making the entire range of human reality experienceable in a novel way, and needing various literary genres for its total expression. The lyrical aspects of *pada* poetry reached its climax in the *garabi* poems of Dayārām (1763–1853), three centuries later.

H. Goetz, *Mira Bai, Her Life and Times: A Tentative Critical Biography* (Journal of Gujarat Research Society, 1959, 87–113); K. M. Munshi, *Gujarat and Its Literature* (Bombay 1953); U.S. Nilsson, *Mirā Bāi* (New Delhi 1970); G. M. Tripaṭhi, *Classical Poets of Gujarat* (Bombay 1891). SY

Padethayaza (?1683–1754), Burmese poet and minister, served under three Burmese kings and witnessed the fall of the capital, Ava, to the Mons in 1750. He was an avant-garde in the literary world. Endowed with originality, versatility, catholicity and vision, most of his works are both refreshing and revolutionary, when set against the background of centuries of the traditional regal-religious and stylized nature and love poems (see Rahtathara and Nawade). He did write *pyo* (qv), but the most delightful poems are those on secular and contemporary themes. He was a pioneer in composing court-plays, similar to Thai *lakhǭn nai,* and classical songs in praise of the king; and his most remarkable innovation was the bucolic song or *tya,* dealing with the life, work and diversions of the country people. The close of his life ushered in an era of change in the form and content of Burmese poetry. HP

Padmanābh, Rajasthani poet, see **Kānhaḍade Prabandha.**

Pampa (10th century), Kannada's *ādikavi* or First Poet, a great influence on later poets including Nannayabhaṭṭa, first poet of Telugu. He is supposed to have composed in his thirty-ninth year (941) his two great epic works: *Ādipurāṇa*, a *campū* (part-prose and part-verse), a religious poem on the first Jaina hero-saint, Purudēva, and his children Bharata and Bāhubali; and *Vikramārjunavijaya*, a secular and original retelling of the *Mahābhārata* (qv), which identifies Pampa's royal patron Arikēsari with Arjuna who is Pampa's hero. It omits the *Bhagavadgītā* (qv), tells the epic story succinctly in 14 cantos, and ends with Arjuna's coronation. With valuable historic references to the times and life of King Arikēsari, the work is known for its extraordinary blend of Kannada and Sanskrit, narrative power and poetic density.

Trans.: V. Sitaramiah, *Mahakavi Pampa* (Bombay 1967). AKR

Pañcatantra (Book of Five Chapters), Sanskrit collection of fables, stories and tales, of uncertain date. Essentially it is a didactic book, meant as a textbook (*śāstra*, qv) for young rulers. Accompanying its prose narratives are moral or educative maxims in verse, easy to be memorized. The wisdom taught in the book is mostly of a practical character, often preferring usefulness and success in life to abstract ethical principles. Each of the five chapters stresses a different aspect of human conduct. Undoubtedly many old fables and tales are to be found among the stories retold here, with motifs to be met in narrative folk-literature all over the world. However, they are elaborated in a characteristic way, always bearing in mind the didactic aim of the book.

The genesis of the *Pañcatantra* presents an intricate problem which many Indologists have tried to solve (Benfey, Hertel, R. Schmidt, Edgerton, Alsdorf, etc.). The manuscripts preserved represent a rather late stage of development, the beginning of which will hardly ever be retrieved with certainty. J. Hertel traced the origin of the text as we know it to the Kashmiri recension called *Tantrākhyāyikā* (c4th–5th centuries AD) which, however, must have been preceded by many earlier variants. Another recension, now lost, is said to have been translated into Pahlavi c570 AD and can be reconstructed according to its Syriac and Arabic translations. In India the *Pañcatantra* was rewritten many times, among the favourite elaborations being, for instance, the so-called *textus simplicior* (c9th–11th centuries), a somewhat younger *textus ornatior*, and the very popular *Hitopadeśa* (qv). The *Pañcatantra* is among the most frequently translated of Indian books. Its Persian and Arabic translations and adaptations go under the name of *Kalila and Dimna* (Karaṭaka and Damanaka in Sanskrit, the names of a pair of jackals, because of their shrewdness the real 'heroes' of many a fable in the first part of the book). An Arabic version was translated into Greek (11th century), Hebrew (by a Rabbi Joel, in the 12th century) and Latin (by Johannes de Capua, 1263–78). Today over 200 versions in more than 60 languages are known. Due to a misunderstanding, many non-Indian versions are ascribed to a certain Bidpai, which is, however, only a corruption of the Sanskrit title *vidyāpati* (Master of Knowledge).

Trans.: J. Hertel, *The Panchatantra* (Cambridge, Mass. 1915); F. Edgerton, *The Panchatantra Reconstructed.* Vol. I, Text and Critical Apparatus, Vol. II, Introduction and Translation (New Haven 1924); A. Williams, *Tales from the Pancatantra* (Oxford 1930); R. Schmidt, *Das Pañčatantram (textus ornatior). Eine altindische Märchensammlung* (Leipzig 1908).

J. Hertel, *Das Pañcatantra, seine Geschichte und seine Verbreitung*, 2 vols. (Leipzig und Berlin 1909); T. Benfey, *Pantschatantra: fünf Bücher indischer Fabeln, Märchen und Erzählungen* (Leipzig 1859); L. Alsdorf, *Pantschatantra* (Bergen 1952); R. Gelb, *Zur Frage nach der Urfassung des Pañcatantra* (Wiesbaden 1968). DZ

Pandyā, N.K., Gujarati poet, see **arvācin kavitā.**

Panḍyāl, Lekhnāth (1885–1965), Nepali poet, was born near Pokhara in western Nepal. After coming to Kathmandu, he was appointed tutor to the son of the prime-minister, Bhīm Śamśer, and later assumed the role of court poet. His early verse is, therefore, largely written in praise of the Rāṇā rulers, though poems like the famous *Pinjaṛāko sugā* (Bird in a Cage) contained veiled allusions to his desire to be free of them. The style and vocabulary of his poetry is greatly influenced by Sanskrit which he had first adopted as his medium of expression. Even so, his delightful lyrical poetry has done much to enrich Nepali literature. His works comprise seven short anthologies of verse and a number of translations into Nepali from Sanskrit, including the *Śakuntalā* (see Kālidāsa) and the *Pañcatantra* (qv). DJM

Pané, Armijn (b 1908 Muara Sipongi, North Sumatra, d 1970 Djakarta), Indonesian writer, editor and linguist. He attended Dutch-language schools in Sumatra, and in 1923 entered the Indies medical school in Surabaya. In 1927 he moved to the secondary school in Solo where he followed the Eastern languages and literatures stream. After teaching in a school for a few years he joined Balai Pustaka (Government Bureau for Popular Literature). In 1933 he founded, with Sutan Takdir Alisjahbana (qv) and Amir Hamzah, the cultural periodical *Pudjangga Baru* (The New Writer) with which he was associated throughout its existence. During the Japanese period Pané was connected with the Cultural Centre and served as editor of the annual *Kebudajaan Timur* (Eastern Culture). After World War II, he taught at a dramatic academy in Jogjakarta and edited the post-war cultural magazine *Indonesia* for a time. In 1949 he wrote in Dutch a survey of modern Indonesian literature and a year later published a substantial volume on Indonesian grammar (*Mentjari Sendi Baru Tatabahasa Indonesia*). At the beginning of the Japanese occupation, Pané published in Dutch a textbook of Indonesian. He is also author of several volumes of short stories, has written some poetry and several plays. Like many Indonesian writers he has published numerous translations into Indonesian, eg, Ibsen's *A Doll's House* (Ratna). In 1952 Pané visited the People's Republic of China.

Author of the controversial novel *Belenggu* (Shackled, 1940), Pané is regarded as a pioneer in modern Indonesian literature. His novel, refused by Balai Pustaka, and published by *Pudjangga Baru,* breaks with the traditional novel of East-West conflict and depicts rather the marital and extra-marital problems of a modern Indonesian physician and his young wife who drift apart. Its appearance created a sensation in intellectual circles and it was widely and hotly debated. Some Indonesian critics consider Pané the precursor of the Generation of '45 but younger writers dispute this strongly. His position as a significant figure in modern Indonesian literature and culture is assured. Further works: *Djinak-Djinak Merpati* (Not to be Trifled With, 1953); *Kisah Antara Manusia* (Stories Amongst People, 1953); *Perkembangan Bahasa Indonesia* (The Development of the Indonesian Language, 1953); *Gamelan Djiwa. Kumpulan Sadjek-Sadjak* (Orchestra of the Spirit. Collection of Poems, 1960).

TMIL 80–4, 110–1. JME

Panikkar, K. M., Indian statesman and writer, see **Mādhava Paṇikkar,** Kāvālam.

Paṇikkar, Rāma, Malayalam poet, see **Rāma Paṇikkar,** Niraṇam.

Pāṇini's Grammar (*Aṣṭādhyāyī*), the oldest preserved indigenous Sanskrit grammar (5th–4th centuries BC). Earlier works have been lost. It has preserved knowledge of the complicated structure of Sanskrit in condensed form. Written in *sūtra* (qv) style, it gives an exhaustive description of the formation of Sanskrit words in under 4,000 *sūtras*, to be learned by heart. This is followed by a list of verbal roots (*dhātupāṭha*) and of groups of words coming under the same *sūtra*-rule or rules (*gaṇapāṭha*). The grammatical description is based on very careful analysis of the data. General features are stated as general rules while common features to a few words are mentioned only once in a *sūtra* and referred to the appropriate group in the *gaṇapāṭha.* Pāṇini developed a system of abbreviations which can be demonstrated on the *Śivasūtras* (list of Sanskrit sounds preceding the grammar). The mute consonants interpolated between them mean that a whole series of sounds can be designated by the first sound and the final mute consonant: the beginning of the *Śivasūtras—a i u* (*ṇ*), (1) *ṛ ḷ* (*k*) (2), *e o* (*ṅ*) (3) etc. The syllable *aṇ* thus designates the vowels *a i u*; *ak*, *a i u ṛ ḷ*; *ik*, *i u ṛ ḷ*, etc. Pāṇini uses 41 such combinations (not all actually possible) in his description. It is necessary to study the *sūtras* in the order Pāṇini presents them; they cannot be rearranged since they have been carefully linked and each presupposes knowledge of the preceding rules. The conciseness of the *sūtras* called for many commentaries, and some abridgements of Pāṇini's difficult grammar have also been attempted. The easiest is Varadarāja's *Laghusiddhāntakaumudī*, which can serve as introductory reading for Indian indigenous linguistics.

O. Böhtlingk, *Pāṇini's Grammatik* (ed., German trans., Leipzig [2]1887); S. C. Vasu, *The Aṣṭādhyāyī of Pāṇini* (Allahabad 1891, reprinted Delhi 1962); L. Renou, *La grammaire de Pāṇini* (French trans., Paris 1948–54); V. S. Agrawala, *India as Known to Pāṇini* (Lucknow 1953).

Pant, Sumitrānandan (b 1900 Kausani), greatest living Hindi poet. His third volume of lyrics, *Pallav* (Shoots, 1926), established his fame as a *chāyāvād* (qv) poet, followed by *Guñjan* (Humming, 1932) and *Jyotsnā* (Moonlight, 1934). In the mid-thirties Pant became a leading *pragativād* (qv) poet and turned to a realistic and emphatically socio-critical representation of Indian urban and village life: *Yugvāṇī* (Voice of the Epoch, 1939), *Grāmyā* (Country-life, 1940). Studies of Aurobindo and his neo-humanism resulted in a new approach to life and literature as expressed in *Svarṇkiraṇ* (A Golden Ray, 1946) and *Svarṇdhūli* (Golden Dust, 1948). Pant's later poetry is mainly philosophical. His greatest work is *Lokāyatan* (The House of People, 1964, Soviet Land Nehru Award), a monumental epic inspired by ancient Indian literature, but dealing with contemporary problems from a classico-humanistic point of view. Pant has written more than three dozen volumes of poetry, lyric dramas and critical essays, eg *Cidaṃbarā* (1951, Bhāratīya Jñānpīṭh Award), *Kalā aur būṛhā cā̃d* (Art and the Old Moon, 1959, Sahitya Akademi Award), *Chāyāvād punarmūlyā̃kan* (Revaluation of Chāyāvād, 1965), *Gīt haṃs* (Swan of Songs, 1969).
IZ

pantun, Malay verse form characterized by a four line stanza rhyming a-b-a-b. The first couplet is associated with the second by patterned assonance and covert (often elusive) symbolism, the second expressing overtly the poet's meaning in the form of a wise saw, love message, pithy comment on life, or similar idea. Belonging essentially to traditional, oral folk literature, the origin of the *pantun* is unknown, though similar forms are found elsewhere in Asia (and indeed Europe). Most *pantun* were, and are, of the moment, though certain themes do recur, and written examples may be found embedded in classical Malay literature from at least the 15th century. Collections have been made in modern times by both European and Malay scholars (see, eg, R. J. Wilkinson and R. O. Winstedt, *Pantun Melayu*, Singapore 1914, and the Balai Pustaka *Pantun Melaju*, Djakarta 1920, both frequently reprinted). Of interest both to linguists (for prosodic and other reasons) and to anthropologists (for their encapsulation of societal attitudes and traditional myth and proverb), *pantun* for Malays are sometimes an accompaniment of popular ritual, more often simply a source of fun and competition and an opportunity to indulge a characteristic love of word-play.
WRR

Parākramabāhu II (reigned 1236–70), King of Ceylon who ruled from Daṁbadeniya. After expelling the invader Māgha, he restored the glories of the Sinhalese kingdom and his reign was one of great literary florescence. The king is said himself to have written the Sinhalese *mahākāvya* (see *kāvya*), *Kavsilumina*, and a long and learned commentary on Buddhaghosa's religious treatise *Visuddhimagga*. In his time also flourished Dharmasena and Mayūrapāda (qqv).
CHBR

Parākramabāhu VI (reigned 1415–67), King

of Ceylon in Kōṭṭe (near modern Colombo). His reign was the last period of classical literary glory before the disruption of the old Sinhalese kingdoms. The poets Śrī Rāhula, Vīdāgama Maitreya and Væṭṭæve (qv) belong to this period, and the classical *sandesas* (qv) were written at this time. To the king himself is attributed a Sinhalese lexicon. CHBR

Paramēśvarayyar, Uḷḷūr S. (1877–1949), Malayalam scholar and poet. Uḷḷūr, author of a voluminous history of the literature of Kerala, was also one of the most prolific Malayalam poets of his day. An admirer of the classical literature of Malayalam and Sanskrit, he was slower than his contemporaries, Āśān and Vaḷḷattōḷ, to follow the new trends of the Romantic movement. Eventually, however, he tackled subjects that had not traditionally belonged to poetry and abandoned Sanskritic metres and verse forms in favour of indigenous Malayalam ones. He is known for the philosophic content of his poems and for his mastery of the use of imagery. Main works: *Umākēraḷam* (1913, an epic set in 17th-century Travancore); *Tārahāram* (1925, collection of shorter poems); *Karṇabhūṣaṇam* (1929, poem on Karṇa, a leading figure in the *Mahābhārata*, qv).

PNHML 213–22, 263–4; GSML 157–9, 237–40. REA

Paraṇar, classical Tamil poet, see **Eṭṭuttokai.**

Parang Sabil, Tausug epic, see **darangan.**

Pararaton (Book of Kings, 15th century), chronicle in Middle Javanese prose, anonymous, probably by several authors. It is not a single unified work, but several separate narratives. The first and longest, *Ken Angrok*, tells of the mythical origin of the Singhasari Madjapahit dynasty, others record the Chinese invasion and war in Java, the founding and prosperity of Madjapahit and events up to 1478. *Ken Angrok* is reminiscent of the art of the professional folk ballad narrators in the Java-Bali literary tradition; other sections are close to the historical romances of Islamic Javanese literature. *Pararaton* is the prototype of later *babad* (see *Babad Tanah Djawi*). It was not discovered until the late 19th century, on Bali. Research suggests it is generally reliable as a historical work, with added myths of ancient date. Put into verse on the island of Bali.

Trans. and ed.: J. L. A. Brandes, *Pararaton* (Ken Arok), *Het Boek der Koningen van Tumapel en van Majapahit* (s'Gravengahe 1920).
C. C. Berg, *Hoofdlijnen der Javaansche Literatuurgeschiedenis* (Groningen 1929), and, *Het Rijk van de Vijfvoudige Buddha* (Amsterdam 1962); PLJ I, 119–23. EV

Pārati (Bharati), Cuppiramaṇiyam Ci. (b 1882 Ettaiyapuram, d 1921 Madras), Tamil poet, writer and journalist. He is a major landmark in Tamil literature and the greatest Tamil poet of the first half of the 20th century. He began as teacher of Tamil in Madurai, and in 1904–10 he was a journalist and editor in Madras. Taking part in the freedom movement, he was persecuted by the government of British India, spent the years 1910–19 in exile in Pondicherry, and in 1919–21 lived in poverty in Madras. His work is full of contradictions, influenced by classical Tamil poetry (chiefly Kampaṉ, *bhakti* poets and *cittar*, qqv), but also by Keats, Shelley and Emerson. Many writings attacked the social evils of Hindu society, and since about 1908 his passionately radical songs inspired the national movement in Tamil India. Pārati was the first to introduce contemporary political and social themes into Tamil poetry and to use simple, almost colloquial language. In vigorous and direct prose he deals with many acute problems of modern life, while writing allegorical and mystical poems, as well as short and exquisite lyrics. Main works: *Kuyilpāṭṭu* (The Song of the Cuckoo, 1923), a lovely fantasy of 750 lines; *Kaṇṇaṉpāṭṭu* (1917), a cycle of lyrical poems on Kṛṣṇa; *Tēciya kītaṅkaḷ* (1908–12), nationalistic songs and political poems; *Cantirikaiyiṉ katai* (The Story of Cantirikai, an unfinished novel); *Agni and Other Poems* (written in English, 1937); a number of essays, prose-poetry.

Trans.: A. Doraiswami Pillai, *Bharati's Poems: Kannan and Kuyil* (Madras 1966).

P. M. Sundaram, *Bharatiyar: His Life and Poetry* (Madras 1956); Prema Nandakumar, *Subramania Bharati* (Delhi 1968); Prema Nandakumar, *Bharati in English Verse* (Madras 1958).
KZ

Paricay, Bengali monthly, see **Bandyopādhyāy,** Māṇik.

Paripāṭal, classical Tamil anthology, see **Eṭṭuttokai.**

Parmānand (1791–1879), Kashmiri poet. A Brahmin by birth, Parmānand spent the greater part of his life (in succession to his father) as accountant of the village of Mattan, where he came into contact with many wandering *sādhūs* and religious teachers *en route* for the great centre of pilgrimage at Amarnath. A profoundly religious figure, he was fundamentally an adherent of the Kashmiri Śaiva school. Parmānand was also a devotee of Kṛṣṇa, as well as having contacts with both Sūfīs and Sikhs. He wrote a large number of poems on a variety of themes; although they are all permeated with the non-dualist ideas of the Vedānta, they demonstrate great linguistic and poetic virtuosity, in addition to profundity of religious insight. While Parmānand was undoubtedly the greatest Hindu poet of his time in Kashmir, his extensive use of Sanskrit and Hindi-derived words has prevented his general popularity among Muslim Kashmiris. His best-known poems are: *Sudāmā-caritar*, *Rādhā-suyambar*, and *Śiv-lagan.*
CS

pasyon, Filipino plays, see **moro-moro.**

Patañjali's Mahābhāṣya (Great Commentary), precise date unknown; not earlier than c150 BC, but possibly several centuries later; all that is certain is that the date is considerably earlier than the grammarian Bhartṛhari (qv), this follows a commentary of Pāṇini (qv) called Kātyāyana whose *Vārttikās* (Aphorisms) have been preserved in the *Mahābhāṣya.* Patañjali goes beyond Kātyāyana, developing the grammar of Pāṇini where it is obsolete, criticizing and rejecting some of Pāṇini's *sūtras.*

The *Mahābhāṣya* is written in the *bhāṣya* style, learned prose which developed in connection with the *sūtras*, reflecting discussions between educated people. The style is scholastic and dialectic; the many quotations from everyday life and various rules (*nyāyas*) make it very vivid in some points. This style is preserved in the *Mahābhāṣya* in conversational form with simple short sentences; the pupil usually asks a question and a would-be-teacher answers in a general way, leaving out some problems; the real teacher then explains all the details. The style is so vivid that much information on everyday life can be drawn from it. Certain features (relative clauses introduced by 'why, what, how' etc.) recall the inscriptions of King Aśoka. This suggests that both texts are relatively close in time and that both are close to contemporary conversational style, one in Sanskrit, the other in Prakrit. Only Pāṇini, Kātyāyana and Patañjali belong to the creative period of Indian grammar; later only commentaries, abridgements or attempts at rearrangement (especially of Pāṇini's grammar) were made. The author of the *Yoga-sūtra*, also named Patañjali, has sometimes been identified with the grammarian, but on insufficient grounds.

K. Kielhorn, *The Vyākaraṇa Mahābhāṣya of Patanjali* (Bombay 1906); *Patañjali's Vyākaraṇa-Mahābhāṣya*, trans. by S. D. Joshi (Poona 1969, to be completed); B. N. Puri, *India in the Time of Patañjali* (Bombay 1968).
JV

Patel, Pannalāl, Gujarati writer, see **navalkathā.**

Pāṭhak, Rāmanārāyaṇ, Gujarati writer, see **navalikā.**

Pāṭhak, Śrīdhar (b 1859 Jondhri, d 1928), Hindi poet. Educated up to the entrance examination of Calcutta University, he served in different Government offices and in 1901 became Superintendent of the Irrigation Commission. Retired in 1914; his home in Allahabad was a centre for Hindi writers. His translations of Goldsmith's poems *The Deserted Village, The Traveller* and *The Hermit* revived epic poetry in

Hindi. His original poems (*Kāśmīr suṣamā*, The Beauty of Kashmir, 1904; *Bhārat gīt*, Song of India, 1928, etc.) paved the way for the *chāyāvād* (qv) poets and for the national lyrics of Maithilīśaraṇ Gupta (qv). PG

Patirruppattu, classical Tamil anthology, see **Eṭṭuttokai.**

Paṭṭiṉattār, Tamil poet, see **cittar.**

Pattirakiriyar, Tamil poet, see **cittar.**

Pattuppāṭṭu (The Ten Songs), form with *Eṭṭuttokai* (qv) the corpus of classical Tamil poetry. It is composed largely in the same metres as the latter, and the poems (save one) are on secular subjects. But they are of much greater length and resemble only the Vaikai poems in the *Paripāṭal* section of the *Eṭṭuttokai.* It is generally considered that *Pattuppāṭṭu* belong to the same period as *Eṭṭuttokai*; indeed, the authors of some poems in both great collections are identical. However, there are grounds for regarding *Tirumurukāṟṟuppaṭai* as distinct in time from the other nine of the 'Ten Songs' as it is in subject-matter. Here too there is some resemblance to *Paripāṭal*, this time to the Cevvēḷ poems therein, since, similarly, *Tirumurukāṟṟuppaṭai* praises the god Murukaṉ (Subrahmaṇya). In later tradition, it is regarded as a Śaiva poem, being included in the XIth *Tirumuṟai* (qv).

There are other *Pattuppāṭṭu* called *Āṟṟuppaṭai*, a type of poem extolling to a colleague the virtues and liberality of one's patron. Thus, *Porunarāṟṟuppaṭai* exhorts War-bard (*porunaṉ*) to visit the Cōḻa king Karikāl. In a poem of 248 lines, his victory at Veṇṇi and the fertility of his country through which the Kāviri river flows are described. *Ciṟupāṇāṟṟuppaṭai* directs *ciṟupāṇar*, probably, 'players of the small harp', to the Ōy tribal chief Nalliyakkōṭaṉ, and elaborates upon his great liberality. *Perumpāṇar*, 'players on the great harp', are directed in *Perumpāṇāṟṟuppaṭai* to Kāñci, where the heroic chief Toṇṭaimāṉ rules. Its author, Uruttiraṅkaṇṇaṉār, is also credited with *Paṭṭiṉappālai*, the fifth *Pattappāṭṭu*, which extols the Cōḻa country and its capital. *Malaipaṭukaṭām* is also sometimes called *Kūttarāṟṟuppaṭai*, Exhortation to the Dancers. This poem praises Naṉṉaṉ and his country.

Maturaikkāñci is the longest of *Pattuppāṭṭu*, and contains 782 lines. Whatever the exact meaning of *kāñci*, which seems to refer to aspects of Counsel of Praise classified under the rhetoric of *puram*, Heroic poetry, *Maturaikkāñci*, as the title suggests, is a glorification of the city of Madurai. Life in this Pāṇṭiya capital is described through its daily round there. The riches brought into the city by the conquering armies of the king, Neṭunceḻiyaṉ, victor of Ālaṅkāṉam, are described. The remaining three *Pattuppāṭṭu: Neṭunalvāṭal*, *Mullaippāṭṭu*, and *Kuṟiñcippāṭṭu*, all contain a much greater emphasis on love, though it is worth noting that encomia such as *Paṭṭiṉappālai* are also formally arranged round a love-motif: the hero does not wish to leave the embrace of his lady-love for all the wealth of the Cōḻa capital. *Neṭunalvāṭai*, The Long Cool Wind, describes the cool season and rains. This season, in the rhetoric of love poetry, is associated with the patient waiting of the beloved for her lord who is absent at the wars, and we find this situation beautifully portrayed. *Mullaippāṭṭu*, the shortest of *Pattuppāṭṭu* with but 103 lines, carries a similar theme. Lastly, *Kuṟiñcippāṭṭu* avails itself of love-poetry rhetoric, telling a love story with the background of the hilly region of Tamilnad. A young hero rescues a girl threatened by an elephant and in danger of being swept away by a mountain stream. They fall in love, and in due course promise to marry. *Kuṟiñcippāṭṭu* is attributed to Kapilar, one of the most renowned of classical Tamil poets, whose work figures extensively in the *Eṭṭuttokai* (qv). JRM

Pavaṇanti (12th–13th century), Tamil grammarian. His great work, the *Naṉṉūl* (Excellent Treatise), c1205 AD, in 461 stanzas, is the standard grammar of Tamil, in which the Jain scholar laid down the rules codifying literary Tamil. It is observed to this day. KZ

payār, Bengali metre, see **maṅgal-kāvya.**

Pedanna, Allasāni (16th century), Telugu poet-laureate at Kṛṣṇadevarāya's (qv) court, and author of one of the five principal Telugu epics. Entitled *Svarociṣa-manusaṃbhavamu,* this tells a story from the *Mārkaṇḍeyapurāṇa* (see *purāṇa*). In the Himalayas, a nymph, Varudhinī, falls in love with a strictly pious Brahmin youth, Pravara, who, with the help of a magical plant, had gone there to see the god Śiva. Pravara rejects Varudhinī, but a celestial youth whose affection she had spurned wins her by impersonating Pravara. To them is born Svarociṣamanu. JRM

Penḍse, Śrīpad Nārāyaṇ (b 1913), leading Marathi novelist of the post-war era. His reputation is based on novels set in his own Konkan region of Maharashtra, notably *Elgār* (Attack, 1949), *Gārambicā Bāpū* (1952) and *Rathacakra* (The Chariot Wheel, 1962). The second is translated as *Wild Bapu of Garambi* (New Delhi 1969). IR

Periyāḻvār, Tamil poet. Born in Villiputtūr, he contributed 473 hymns to the *Nālāyirappirapantam* (qv), the Vaiṣṇava 'canon'. Sixteen Vaiṣṇava shrines figure in Periyāḻvār's poem, which are embodied in the first section of *Nālāyirappirapantam* entitled *Tirumoḻi.* His hymns describe the adventures in the life of Kṛṣṇa. In contrast to some of the Śaiva poets, Periyāḻvār is singularly free from proselytizing in his hymns. According to legend, he was the adoptive father of Aṇṭāḷ (qv).

JHTL 101–7. JRM

Pétrus Ky, Vietnamese writer, see **Truong-vinh-Ky.**

Phaḍke, Nārāyaṇ Sītārām (b 1894), copious Marathi novelist, short-story writer and essayist. Among his more than thirty novels, *Jādūgār* (Magician, 1928), *Daulat* (Wealth, 1929) and *Aṭakepār* (Beyond the Limit, 1931) were enormously popular. He is still writing actively.

Trans.: *The Whirlwind* (Bombay 1956). IR

Pham-juy-Thong, Vietnamese poet, see **The-Lu.**

Phan-huy-Cu, Vietnamese encyclopaedist, see **Le-qui-Don.**

Pham-Quynh (1892–1945), Vietnamese scholar, translator and journalist, equally versed in Chinese, French and Vietnamese. In his political work he actively implemented French colonial policy particularly in the fields of education and culture. 1932–45 he was Education Minister in the Imperial government of the Annam protectorate in Hue. He was well known as the founder and chief editor of the influential cultural review *Nam-phong* (South Wind, 1917–32). He made many translations from French literature and wrote studies of French writers and philosophers (Pierre Loti, Descartes, J.-J. Rousseau, Auguste Comte, Voltaire, Anatole France, etc.). His work exercised a strong influence on the vocabulary of modern Vietnamese, in particular by introducing many words from the Chinese.

DNILVN 208ff. VV

Phan-boi-Chau (pseudonym Sao-Nam, b 1867 Sa-nam, Nghe-an province, d 1940 Hue), Vietnamese writer and revolutionary, active in the anti-French struggle from youth onwards, later organizing it. In 1905 he set up a school in Japan for young Vietnamese who were not able to study in their own country; expelled in 1908, he worked in China and Thailand. In 1925 he was arrested on his way to Shanghai, and sentenced by a French court in Hanoi to life imprisonment. This was commuted under pressure of public opinion to house arrest in Hue, where he remained in complete isolation until his death. His Chinese poetry and prose, political articles and pamphlets were very influential among young patriotic intellectuals. In Japan he wrote *Viet-nam vong quoc su* (History of the Loss of Vietnam [to the French], 1905) and *Hai ngoai huyet thu* (Letters from Abroad Written in Blood, 1906), in Chinese. In Kwang-tung prison he wrote *Nguc trung thu* (Letters from Prison, 1914). He described his life's work in *Phan-boi-Chau nien* *bieu* (Phan-boi-Chau's Life, 1937–40), also known as *Tu phe phan* (Self Criticism). He also wrote in Vietnamese, *Phan Sao-nam quoc am thi tap* (Phan Sao-nam's Poems in the Native Tongue), the *Story of Le-thai-To*, a play about the Trung sisters, etc.

DNILVN. IZb

Phongsāwadān (Historical Sources) comprises all the original Thai historical sources among the manuscripts which survived the destruction of Ayuthayā in 1767. They make it possible to trace Thai history from the beginning of the first kingdom, even if some periods can only be seen in broad outline. It presents a brief chronicle of events, sometimes barely mentioned, with no expression of the chronicler's opinion at all. The most important sources are:

1 *Phongsāwadān Chabap Lūong Prasōēt* (History, Book of Lūong Prasōēt), a short text which is probably the most important source for early Thai history, based on a manuscript written in 1679 under King Phra Nārāi. Apart from inscriptions and some chronicles in Pāli, it is the oldest authentic work on Thai history, called after Lūong Prasōēt who discovered the manuscript. Of the two copies in Bangkok National Library one dates from Ayuthayā times (1350–1767), the other was copied for King Tāksin (1767–1782). The text covers Thai history 1350–1605, in brief, condensed form, and later works on the Ayuthayā period are based on it.

2 *Phongsāwadān Chabap Çhamlong* (Historical Sources Renewed), also known as *Phongsāwadān Khūam Kau* (Ancient History) and *Chabap Chulasakarāt* 1136 (Volume for the year 1136 of the Chula era, ie 1774), is as important a source as the preceding. The text is based on a manuscript copied under Bǫromakōt (1733–1759) and 'renewed' (or rediscovered?) under Tāksin. It is only a fragment, dealing in detail with the end of the reign of Phra Mahāchakraphat (c1529–1552/55). In the main outlines it agrees with the *Phongsāwadān Lūong Prasōēt*.

3 *Phongsāwadān Chabap Mǫ Bretlē, Phrarātcha* (Royal History, Book of Dr Bradley), published by an American medical missionary, comprises 57 manuscripts in the Bangkok National Library. It opens with the establishment of Ayuthayā (1350) and goes up to the reign of Rāma III (1824–1859). Bradley's edition differs from some other sources in details.

4 *Phongsāwadān Chabap Phrarātchahatlēkhā* (History, Book of the Royal Manuscript), a detailed work of c2,000 printed pages. The present edition is probably based on the same sources as the preceding, with additional material as yet unidentified. It covers the period from the establishment of Ayuthayā to the end of the reign of Rāma II; the treatment of the years 1782–1809 agrees literally with the *Phrarātcha Phongsāwadān Ratchakān Thī Nüng* of Thiphākarawong.

5 *Phongsāwadān Yōnok* (History of Northern Thailand). From the 12th to 19th centuries Northern Thailand, with the main town Chiengmai, formed a second centre to the main kingdom. The region, with its Thai, Laos, Shan, Burmese, Karen and many Austro-Asian ethnic groups, is one of the most fascinating Thai territories, with an equally varied history. Up to c1800 Thai and Burmese rule alternated. The author Phrayā Prachakitchakǫrachak gives Thai, Burmese, Laotian, Chinese and Mon sources for his work.

6 A number of important historical works, all called *Phongsāwadān*, appeared after 1860, among them the 'History of the Reigns of Rāma I to Rāma IV' (4 vols.) by Thiphākarawong, and numerous studies by Prince Damrong; these form the basis for the history of Thai under the Bangkok dynasty (from 1782). The former writer still uses the chronicle style, giving a detailed chronological account with no personal comment, and paying full attention to royal and Buddhist ceremonies and royal family events. The social background and the literary efforts of the aristocracy are not mentioned. Damrong on the other hand introduces social aspects, is more critical of his sources, and often takes a personal stand. His most outstanding books are *Phongsāwadān Ruong Thai rop Phamā* (History of the Wars between Thailand and Burma), *Phongsāwadān Ratchakān thī*

sǫng, *Phongsāwadān Ratchakān thī sī* (History of Rāma II and Rāma IV).

Vella, *Siam under Rama III* (New York 1957); K. Wenk, *The Restoration of Thailand under Rama I* (Tucson 1968). KW

Phra Aphaimanī, Ruang (Story of Phra Aphaimanī), Thai epic, c52,000 lines, by Sunthǫn Phū (1786–1855). The first part may have been written (according to Prince Damrong) in prison, sections being sold to provide the poet with food. An alternative assumption (Yūphō) is that Sunthǫn Phū began writing under Rāma III (1824–51). It can no longer be definitely dated, 1821 at the earliest, 1828 latest. Sunthǫn Phū was definitely not the only author, but others have not yet been identified. It is one of the few Thai narratives not traceable to foreign models.

Sent out to learn wisdom, Phra Aphaimanī learns to play the flute and send his hearers to sleep; his father the king, angered at this waste of time, sends him and his brother into exile. A sea ogress captures him and forces him to marry her, but unable to requite her passion, Phra Aphaimanī escapes together with their son, Sin Samut. He falls in love with a mermaid, who bears him another son. At sea again, he is pursued by the ogress who wrecks the boat when he refuses to return to her. Finally her heart breaks and she turns to stone. Meanwhile his first son is also saved, along with a princess, by English pirates. To rid her of the captain's unwelcome attentions, Sin Samut seizes the boat and saves his father's future bride. All ends well for all the heroes, after innumerable fantastic adventures described with mastery of suspense. This has made the epic a truly popular work despite its poetic and artistic refinement.

Prem Chaya, *The Story of Phra Abhai Mani* (Bangkok 1952). KW

Phra Mahā Montri, Thai poet, see **Raden Landai.**

Pi Mounin (Pi Monin, b 1883 Thoumhse, d 1940 Rangoon), Burmese writer. Of humble origin, he was educated in English and Latin at Catholic missionary schools; at 19, he abandoned preparing for the priesthood and plunged back into Burmese society and literature. Always a rebel, he led an unsettled, impecunious life as a teacher, labourer, translator, journalist (from 1914 with *Thuriya*, Sun, newspaper), novelist (his first two pen-names were Maung Kyaw, Paikhsangyi), and film producer. Opposed to the tyranny of tradition and superstitution, his writings show a constant preoccupation with the individual—his freedom of choice and responsibility for his own prosperity. The many popular short stories and novels that he wrote in the 20's and 30's show a new interest in the psychology of characters; his numerous books (adapted from English) of practical advice on careers, money and sex stress that achievement in life depends on one's own efforts. (In his own life, the bohemian and artist always triumphed over commonsense.) He abandoned the traditional flowery literary style, and evolved a clear, concise prose both for fiction and scientific works. His best-known novel is *Nei Yi Yi* (1920). Autobiography *Pi Mounin i Pi Mounin* appeared in 1940. AJA

Piḷḷai, Damodaram, editor of Tamil texts, see **Cuvāminātа Aiyar.**

Poetry in English (India). For over a century poetry has been written by Indians in English, but only since Independence (1947) has it been written and received entirely on its own merits and only now are the first anthologies and balanced criticisms appearing. There is an absence of a tradition, as no major creative personality in India chose to use English as his medium (Rabindranath Tagore's Bengali poems being so much superior to their English equivalents). Early poetic writing in English was a *tour de force*, an accomplishment perhaps politically induced, and there was unnatural pressure on the use of the language. The modern poetry is the expression of certain attitudes and values of an urban or cosmopolitan middle-class familiar with the European or American world. Most of the poets were educated in, or have lived in, the West at some point. The main source of the formal imagery which used to depict tranquil rural landscape and life no longer fits. Today the Indian finds expression in his own self-realization and individual identity. MED

Polotan-Tuvera, Kerima (pseud. Patricia S. Torre, b 1925 Jolo, Sulu), Filipino prose writer in English publishing mostly in magazines. Main works: *The Hand of the Enemy* (1961, a novel); *Stories* (1968); *Imelda Romualdez Marcos* (1969). EH

Ponnya, U (1812–1867), Burmese poet and playwright, a monk for part of his life, then a court poet, who met with a tragic ending. He was a prolific writer, and the greatest rhymester, with pungent wit and sardonic humour. He left four *mawgun* (qv), of which *Ratanā nadī* (the name of a canal in Mandalay) is a masterpiece. He achieved his fame, however, through his *pyazat*, *myittaza* (epistles) and sermons, and *tedat* (songs). He wrote at least five plays: three based on the *jātakas* (qv)—*Paduma* (No. 193), *Wethandaya* (No. 547) and *Yethè* (No. 421); and two more—*Wizaya* and *Kawthala*, all of which are said to have cryptic references to contemporary affairs in the Court. His *myittaza*, especially those dealing with personal matters, are still popular with intellectuals; his sermons, full of pathos as well as bathos, have been a model for monk- and lay-preachers alike. His *tedat*, a source of delight to the people, include one 'immortal' song, allegedly composed a few minutes before he was put to death by a minister.

Hla Pe, *Konmara Pya Zat*, I, Introduction and translation (London 1952), pp 4–6, 13–15; MHABD 76–108, passim. HP

Pōtana, Bammēra, Telugu poet of uncertain date. He composed the Telugu version of *Bhāgavata Purāṇa* (qv), which includes the famous story of Viṣṇu's Man-lion incarnation, Narasiṃha, destroying the unbelieving demon-king Hiraṇyakaśipu.

JRM

Prachum Phongsāwadān (Collection of Historical Sources) comprises works on the culture and history of Thailand and neighbouring territories formerly ruled by her, published at irregular intervals from 1914 onwards, at the instigation of Prince Damrong, the greatest Thai historian. The 77 volumes (1971) are of varying value, from great works like Damrong's *Thai rop Phamā* (The Wars between Thailand and Burma) to translations of readily accessible works by French, English and Dutch writers included to further Damrong's didactic aim. Many important works have not been included; the choice was made by Prince Damrong and later by the *Krom Sinlapakọn* (Office of the Fine Arts), bearing in mind that the edition was often financed by wealthy families in honour of some deceased member, whose life provided the theme. The volumes published include the oldest preserved chronicle of Thailand, that of Lūong Prasōēt (see *Phongsāwadān*); original historical works, like Damrong's *Thai rop Phamā*, *Tamnān Wang Kau* (On Old Palaces), *Tamnān Wang Nā* (On the Front Palace), *Tamnān Kān Lōēk Bọnbīe lae Lōēk Hūi* (On the Abolition of Gambling and Gambling Houses) and others; compilations of official and private correspondence; translations; and oral accounts. Damrong wrote introductions to many of the volumes, adopting a critical attitude to the text concerned. The series is invaluable as source material for historians, and assessment has only begun.

K. Wenk, *Prachum Phongsāwadān* (Oriens Extremus, Vol. IX, 1962), pp 232–57. KW

pragativād, literally 'progressivism' (inexact, but much used), Hindi literary movement arising c1935, influenced by Marxism, and connected with the formation of the Progressive Indian Writers' Association (see *progressive writing*). Its followers turned away from the romantic ideas of *chāyāvād* (qv) and aimed at realistic treatment of contemporary social problems demonstrated on characters of working people. The main representatives in prose were Yaśpāl, A. Rāy, R. Rāghav (qqv) and Rāhul Sāṅkṛtyāyaṇ; in poetry S. Pant and Nirālā (qqv) in their later work, S. Suman, N. Śarmā and others.

Pragativād writers were deeply committed; the anti-colonial line also attracted writers who were not at all Marxist. The movement culminated in the early forties. DA

prahasana, Sanskrit dramatic genre, see **kāvya.**

pralom-lok, the modern prose novel of Cambodia, which has been developing since the 1940's. Several works have an historical theme, eg *The Great War at Angkor* by Sot Sarun, *Phnhea Yat* (a post-Angkorian king) by Kuy Laut, and *Preah Reach Samphea* (an 18th century king) by Leang Hap An. The Japanese occupation is featured in the story of Dik Keam's *Due to the Call-up.* Opposition to the traditional arranged marriage looms large among themes of a social nature. In *Bondaul, Father's Girl* by Im Chhou Det, a rebellious daughter fortunately falls in love with the very young man whom her father intends her to marry. In *The Faded Flower* by Nou Hach, the couple whose marriage is arranged love each other but unfortunately the family of one is reduced to poverty and so the alliance is broken. Family feuds also have their role to play. In *Miss Ren Net* by Im Chhom, a daughter is cast off by her father, never to see him again, for a deed she did not commit.

Most of the novels have a love-story in them somewhere. Some, such as *Helpless Heart* by Ky Beng Chhon, are almost exclusively love-story. The degree of romanticism is striking to a 20th century Westerner. This derives perhaps partly from the tradition of the Cambodian verse-novels in which heroes and heroines were constantly separated and reunited, and partly from the romantic novels known from France. Heroes write love-poems, heroines waste away with consumption and an unbelievable series of coincidences reunite the characters. Detailed descriptions of love-scenes are sometimes attempted, as in *A Girl with More than One Love* by Kim Set. A scene of violent fighting and rapid action is described in *Three Lives Transform an Old Hut* by Chek Sorat. While some authors indulge in descriptive passages using elevated, literary words, most use a clear, simple style introducing very natural, colloquial conversation. JMJ

Pramūon Kotmāi Ratchakān thi nüng (Collection of Laws from the First Period of the Bangkok Dynasty). Over nine-tenths of the Ayuthayā laws (1350–1767) were lost when the old Thai capital was destroyed (1767). After the founding of Bangkok (1782) and the restoration of Thailand under Rāma I (1782–1809) the surviving laws were recodified. Called upon to decide a divorce case in which the culpable wife would have her property restored to her by law, the king decided that the text of the law must be corrupt. All valid laws were recodified, and all changes approved by the king himself, not in order to introduce a new system, but to clear away distortions accrued through 'dishonest officials and judges'. The work took about a year, and the new code was presented to Rāma I in 1805. Known as *Kotmāi Trā Sām Dūong* (Laws of the Three Seals) it was later enlarged to include laws passed in Rāma's own reign. The code covers many different aspects: constitutional law, the aristocratic hierarchy, family law, inheritance, slave-owning, debtors, and many points of criminal law. This code remained valid until a new legal system, based mainly on the European model, was introduced from 1900 onwards. Legal history has shown that the Ayuthayā laws came from the Mon-Burmese version of the Code of Manu, which seems to have reached Thailand in the 12th century. The form it assumed there differs considerably, however, from the Indian original. The 1805 code is of immense value for the study of Thai culture and legal history; much research remains to be done in this field.

Quaritch-Wales, *Ancient Siamese Government and Administration* (London 1934); K. Wenk, *The Restoration of Thailand under Rama I* (Tucson 1968); Lingat, *L'Esclavage Privé dans le Vieux Droit Siamois* (Paris 1931).

KW

Prapañca (14th century Madjapahit), Javanese court poet under King Rajasanagara (Hayam Wuruk, 1350–89), from a family of

Buddhist scholars. He wrote one of the last pure *kakawins* (see Kanwa), one of the finest epics of the Madjapahit period. Originally entitled *Desa Warrana* (Report about the Country), the book is a panegyric on the king, but reveals social structure, customs, cultural, political and religious life in Madjapahit. It could be called a travel book in verse. It is known by the later title *Nāgarakṛtāgama* (Book of Learning on the Order of the Realm, 1365); in extent and form it is one of the group of great *kakawins*, but differs from them in cultural and historical content. Prapañca initiated Javanese historical-legendary literature, later written in prose (see *Pararaton*), but differs from most 11th–15th century authors in not using the *kakawin* primarily to present ancient Indian mythological themes. The manuscript of *Nāgarakṛtāgama* was not discovered until 1894, on Lombok island.

T. Pigeaud, *Java in the 14th Century. A Study in Cultural History. The Nagara-Kertagama by Rakawi Prapanca of Madjapahit, 1365 AD* (The Hague 1960–5); PLJ I. EV

Prasād, Jayśaṅkar (b 1889 Banaras, d 1937), Hindi poet, dramatist and novelist. The enlarged second edition of *Jharnā* (Waterfall, 1927) and *Ā̃sū* (Tears, 1931), both full of romantic imagination and mystical associations, established his fame as a *chāyāvād* (qv) poet. His *Kāmāyanī* (1935) is a famous epic based on a theme of ancient Indian literature, but dealing allegorically with contemporary problems of Indian society. Prasād was equally outstanding as a dramatist. He wrote 13 dramas, mostly historical plays, patriotically glorifying India's past, such as *Viśākh* (1921), *Skandagupta Vikramāditya* (1928), *Candragupta Maurya* (1931) and *Dhruvsvāminī* (1934). IZ

Premānanda (b c1636, d c1734), Gujarati poet. *Ākhyāna, prabandha, rāsā* and *padya-vārtā* are the long narrative classes of mediaeval Gujarati poetry, Śāmal Bhaṭṭa's (18th century) *Siṃhāsan Batrisi*, narrated fictionally by 32 statues, shows how a *padya-vārtā* interposes between the mind and reality a world of adventures of kings, but also of merchants, carpenters and women. *Prabandha* and *ākhyāna*, however, as in Lāvanyasamaya's *Vimalaprabandha* (1505 AD), were structured teleologically, towards a preconceived religious conclusion. But *ākhyāna* poetry, originating in clusters of *pada* (qv) poems like Narasiṃha's *Rāsa Sahasrapadi*, retained emotive ambiguity even in narration. In Premānanda's *ākhyāna* poems, based on themes from the *Rāmāyaṇa*, the *Mahābhārata* (qqv) and, significantly, the life of Narasiṃha Mehtā (see *pada*), the possibilities of the genre and the language itself were fully developed. Abandoning 'action' and 'instruction' alike to express the grace of a mother, Jasodā, scolding her child, Kṛṣṇa, and the sweetness of small talk between friends, Kṛṣṇa and Sudāmā, meeting after years (in *Daśamaskandha* and *Sudāmācarit*), Premānanda has created maximally non-telic aesthetic forms. Investigating forms within and outside literature was Akho (c1591–1656), whose destructive-creative brilliant intelligence was disinterestedly fascinated by the actuality of *māyā*. He created concrete images of his metaphysical search, not leaving unturned a single foundation stone of the socio-religious frontiers of Gujarati poetry.

K. M. Munshi, *Gujarat and Its Literature* (Bombay 1935); G. M. Tripaṭhi, *Classical Poets of Gujarat* (Bombay 1891). SY

Premcand (Dhanpatrāy Śrīvāstav, 1880–1936), Hindi and Urdu novelist and short story writer. Born near Banaras, he spent most of his life in the United Provinces. He worked as schoolmaster and sub-inspector until 1921 but left the education service during Gandhi's non-cooperation movement, and devoted the rest of his life mainly to writing and publishing in Hindi, and to a lesser extent in Urdu. His earlier literary activity had, however, been chiefly in Urdu, through which he had acquired most of his literary background. Premcand was the first writer of real importance to use Hindi as a vehicle for prose fiction, and his contribution to the development of Hindi in establishing the genres of short story and novel on a genuine literary level is inestimable.

His strength is, on the whole, in the short story rather than the novel. Here he depicts a wide cross-section of north Indian life, often with great sensitivity; he displays gifts of character portrayal and realistic observation far surpassing those of his predecessors. His themes and treatment tend, however, to reflect an uncritical idealism which clashed with the realism and insight of his best work and detracts from its effectiveness. This tendency is more marked in his novels, which deal with social and political questions. The last of his twelve complete novels, *Godān* (The Gift of a Cow, 1936), is his best, with its magnificent evocation of the atmosphere of village life and fine portrayal of the peasant Horī. The novels have a collective value in presenting a comprehensive picture of the life and temper of the north India of Premcand's day. Some further works: *Mānsarovar* (The Holy Lake, 8 vols.), *Kafan* (The Shroud, short stories), *Sevāsadan* (The Hall of Service, 1918), *Raṅgbhūmi* (The Field of Strife, 1924), *Karmabhūmi* (The Field of Action, 1932).

Trans.: D. Rubin, *The World of Premcand* (London 1969); G. Roadarmel, *Gift of a Cow* (London 1958); Madan Gupta, *The Secret of Culture and Other Stories* (Bombay 1960); Gurdial Mallik, *Short Stories of Premcand* (Bombay 1946).
Madan Gopal, *Munshi Premchand. A Literary Biography* (New York 1964); Robert O. Swan, *Munshi Premchand of Lamhi Village* (Durham 1969). RSM

progressive writing in India. Writing influenced by the Progressive Writers' Association founded on leftist initiative in 1936 but extending to other shades of opinion. In some literatures (eg Urdu) the progressives were a major, and even a dominant, trend in the decade preceding independence, after which, though many continued as leading writers, they declined in relative importance. See also *pragativād*. RR

Prose fiction in English (India). Since 1947 there has been a great development of Indian writing in English, coinciding with a growing interest both in India and the West. Serious study is taking place and balanced criticism is gradually appearing in journals such as *The Literary Criterion.* Authors seek through these works to reach a wider public than would be possible in any one Indian language; they draw their readers not only from the urban Indian middle-class but also from the West, with which most of them have contact. While these authors have met with adverse criticism in India, where they are regarded by many as virtually a caste of their own, with only superficial links with genuine Indian culture, they have nevertheless won a substantial audience in their own country as well as in the West, and the best of them are as authentically Indian as writers who write in the Indian languages. MED

Pṛthvirāj-rāso, Rajasthani romance, see **rāso.**

Pukaḻēnti (13th century), Tamil poet. His only preserved work is a narrative poem, *Naḷaveṇpā,* in 378 stanzas, based on an episode in the *Mahābhārata* (see *Nalopākhyāna*), a charming, tender, colourful tale in excellent style.

Trans.: M. Langton, *The Story of King Nala and Princess Damayanti* (Madras 1950).
JHTL 205–7. KZ

Punya, U, Burmese poet, see **Ponnya,** U.

puṟam, classical Tamil war-poetry, see **Eṭṭuttokai.**

purāṇa (400 BC–1400 AD), Sanskrit sacred text. *Purāṇa* literally means 'ancient'. The *purāṇas* contain a great variety of ancient subjects—rules of caste, rituals, ceremonies, histories of sacred places, philosophy, mythology, hymns of praise and dynasties of kings. The *Mahābhārata* and *Rāmāyaṇa* (qqv), and in particular the appendix to the *Mahābhārata* known as the *Harivaṃśa* (The Dynasty of Viṣṇu), are considered *purāṇas* in the broad sense of the term, but 18 works are usually regarded as *purāṇas* rather than epics: the *Brahma, Padma, Viṣṇu, Vāyu, Bhāgavata, Bṛhannāradīya,*

Mārkaṇḍeya, Agni, Bhaviṣya, Brahmavaivarta, Liṅga, Varāha, Skanda, Vāmana, Kūrma, Maysya, Garuḍa and *Brahmāṇḍa Purāṇas*. These are said to be characterized by the 'five marks of the *purāṇas*' (*purāṇapañcalakṣaṇa*), the five essential topics: *sarga* (creation of the universe), *pratisarga* (subsequent destruction and recreation), *vaṃśa* (dynasties of gods and sages), *vaṃśānucarita* (dynasties of the solar and lunar kings), and *manvantarāṇi* (the ages of the primaeval Manus, progenitors of the human race).

In fact, not all of the *purāṇas* cover all five 'marks', which are anyway usually submerged in a mountain of incidental material of a different nature. Even the shorter *purāṇas* cover a bewildering range of subjects; the *Agni Purāṇa* contains information on the cult of the *liṅga*, astronomy, astrology, marriage, omens, house-building, politics, poetics, law, medicine, and grammar, in addition to the usual *dharmaśāstra* (qv), *stotras* (hymns of praise), *tīrthas* (tales illustrating the sanctity of particular holy places, with descriptions of the miracles wrought there), and mythology.

The *Skanda Purāṇa*, a collection of texts more extensive than the *Mahābhārata*, exists in several entirely different recensions, all calling themselves the *Skanda Purāṇa*. A further complication is introduced by the fact that the texts, very loosely constructed and minimally consolidated, borrow freely from one another and constantly reinterpret their own material. The dating of any particular *purāṇa*, therefore, is extremely difficult, though parts can be placed with reasonable accuracy and some (such as the *Bhāgavata, Brahma, Bhaviṣya, Brahmavaivarta*) exhibit a general character clearly later than others (such as the *Mārkaṇḍeya* and *Vāyu*). Yet the core of the *purāṇa* corpus is very old indeed, originating in the period of the Nandas and Mauryas when genealogies were sung and praised by the non-Brahmin court bards known as *sūtas*, who in their turn certainly drew upon a tradition extending back to the Vedic period. Most of the older *purāṇas* were well known by the Gupta age, but at that time the Brahmin priests took them over, reworked them; they often composed entirely new works, retaining only the name of the original *purāṇa*. At this time, also, the *purāṇas* began to assume the highly sectarian character which now distinguishes them. Because of their encyclopaedic nature and the impossibility of dating them, the *purāṇas* shade off into the 'sub-purāṇas' (*upapurāṇas*), from which they do not in fact differ significantly. Several of the different versions of the list of the 18 'Great *purāṇas*' (*mahāpurāṇas*) include a few *upapurāṇas* in place of some of the *mahāpurāṇas*. Such so-called *upapurāṇas* as the *Śiva, Mahābhāgavata, Bṛhaddharma, Devībhāgavata, Kālikā, Sāmba, Saura*, and *Viṣṇudharmottara* contain much valuable and ancient information.

In spite of several worthy efforts, the *purāṇas* have not proved fertile ground for political historians, but as source books for the study of social and religious history they are extremely useful. The style in which they are composed (consisting primarily of *ślokas*, qv) varies considerably according to the place and date of composition; however, it is generally degenerate, exhibiting a tendency toward extreme, rococo exaggeration and a complete disregard for the niceties of Sanskrit grammar. In addition, most *purāṇas* have come down to us in extremely corrupt manuscripts. Despite these laxities of form, the content of the *purāṇas* reveals a rich imagination and an extraordinary diverse oral tradition.

Trans.: *Agni Purāṇa* (M. N. Dutt, Chowkhamba Sanskrit Series LIV); *Garuḍa Purāṇa* (M. N. Dutta, ditto LXVII); *Mārkaṇḍeya Purāṇa* (F. Pargiter, Calcutta 1904); *Vāmana Purāṇa* (A. S. Gupta, Benares 1968); *Śiva Purāṇa* (J. L. Shastri, New Delhi 1970), *Matsya Purāṇa* (S. Vidyārṇavā, Sacred Books of the Hindus XVII), *Viṣṇu Purāṇa* (H. H. Wilson, Calcutta [3]1961). R. C. Hazra, *Studies in the Purāṇic Records on Hindu Rites and Custom* (Dacca 1948); R. C. Hazra, *Studies in the Upapurāṇas* (Calcutta 1958–63); A. D. Pusalker, *Studies in the Epics and Purāṇas of India* (Bombay 1955); WHIL I, 440–84. WOF

Puṟanāṉūru, classical Tamil anthology, see **Eṭṭuttokai.**

Purandaradāsa (c1550), with his contemporary Kanakadāsa, the best known of

Kannada Vaiṣṇava saints (*haridāsas*, ie servants of Hari, or Viṣṇu). He was a composer of devotional songs (*kīrtane*) set to Karnatic music, widely sung all over Southern India, in concerts, religious gatherings and at home. A rich miser and merchant before the 'leap of faith', he gave away all he had and became a *haridāsa*, a wandering mendicant singer-saint. His songs (*pada*), composed in simple folk-idiom, convey social criticism, moral teaching, and intense feeling of *bhakti* (qv) and praise for his favourite form of Viṣṇu, Purandara Viṭṭhala. They are a landmark in Karnatic musical tradition. AKR

Puskar Śamśer, Nepali lexicographer, see **Sama,** Bālkṛṣṇa.

Puṭṭapu, K. V., or **Kuvempu** (b 1904 Kuppali), modern Kannada poet of nature, love, idealism, and yearning for god. He has written over 50 books of poems, stories, verse plays; some poetic, yet earthy, regional novels (*Kānūru Subbamma Heggaḍiti*, 1936, and *Malegaḷalli Madumagaḷu*, Bride in the Mountains, 1967); and has adapted Shakespeare's *Hamlet* and *The Tempest*. He has been influenced by Western poets like Milton and Dante, as well as by the Sanskrit and Kannada traditions, by Sri Ramakrishna as well as Sri Aurobindo. His most acclaimed work is *Śrī Rāmāyaṇa Darśanam* (A Vision of the Rāmāyaṇa, 1955) a modern version of the epic in 23,000 lines of sonorous Miltonic verse-paragraphs and Homeric similes. Kuvempu received the prestigious Jñānapīṭha prize for poetry in 1967. AKR

Putumaippittan̲ (Viruttācalam, C., 1906–1948), Tamil writer and poet. After unsuccessful studies of law, he became a writer and journalist in Madras. He died a very poor man and a consumptive. He was a prolific writer (he wrote more than 200 short stories, a number of poems and essays, a few short plays) and some of his short stories are bound to survive as excellent literature. Among his early writings (1925–1928) there are imitations and even plagiarized stories (from Maupassant, Chekhov etc), but later he probed with fearless, ruthless frankness into the failings of modern Hindu society, which he described as a truly critical realist. There is also humour and pathos in his writings, but more often biting satire and much distress and harshness. His syntax is frequently rather involved, and his style strange and unbalanced, but, in the best of his stories, he is always forceful and expressive. His influence in the field of Tamil prose was decisive between 1930 and 1950. Main works: *Putumaippittan̲ kataikaḷ* (The Stories of Putumaippittan, 1940); *Āṇmai* (Manliness, 1947); *An̲ṟu iravu* (The Night, 1952); *Putumaippittan̲ kaṭṭuraikaḷ* (The Essays of Putumaippittan, 1954).

JHTL 267–8. KZ

pyo, Burmese classical verse-form of four-syllable lines (see *linga*), usually religious in theme and didactic in tone. A few later *pyo* deal with secular subjects, but the majority narrate an episode from the Buddha's life or re-tell a *jātaka* (qv) story. The narrative parts are usually in a fairly simple style based on the Pāli text. The poet reserved his skill for, and was judged by, the parts of the poem which expanded and embellished the thoughts contained in the Pāli verses (*gāthā*), or which contained elaborate descriptions and praise of the Buddha, the king, the royal capital, etc. (The eulogies are called *bwè*.) The greatest *pyo* of the Ava period (15th–16th centuries) are generally considered unsurpassed by later ones (written up to the beginning of the 20th century). The *pyo* are divided into stanzas of varying lengths (average 30–35 lines), with a complete poem containing 200–300 stanzas, from 20 to 200 pages. A few *pyo* merely enumerate precepts for virtuous conduct. HP

Q

Qādi Qādan of Sehwan (d 1551), Sindhi mystic poet and religious scholar. He was a disciple of the followers of the Mahdi of

Jaunpur (d 1505). Some of his short mystical verses in Sindhi are still popular.

ABSLP 282. AS

Qādir Yār, Panjabi poet, see **Kādar Yār.**

Qalich Bēg, Mīrzā (b 1853 Hyderabad, where d 1929), Sindhi prose writer, dramatist, poet and translator. Of Turco-Caucasian family, he studied in Bombay and entered British service; he devoted his life to Sindhi prose, which existed only in a few school books and newspapers. His translations include Shakespeare (whom he cleverly adapted to the Indian milieu), Sherlock Holmes, Ghazzālī (see Vol. III), Roger Bacon, a handbook of gardening, biographies of the famous women of Islam; they move from the German War to Babylon and Niniveh. He found time to write dramas and novels, of which *Zīnat* (1890) deserves special praise; dealing with the education of Muslim girls, this novel reveals an amazingly modern outlook. He wrote also on Sindhi history, on Shāh 'Abdu'l-laṭīf (qv) and composed Sindhi poetry in the classical Persian metres, together with an introduction to Persian prosody. His prose style is simple, clear and somewhat dry, but makes pleasant reading.

ABSLP 296. AS

Qāni', Mīr 'Alī Shīr (b 1717 Thatta, d 1789), Indo-Persian writer, mystical poet and the most important historian of Sind in the 18th century. His *Maqālātu'sh-shu'arā'* (Articles on Poets, 1759) contains biographies of all the poets who ever touched the soil of Sind. His *Tuḥfatu'l-kirām* (Gift of Eminent Men, 1767) deals with scholars and historical personalities of the country. *Maklī-nāma* is an account of the famous Makli Hill near Thatta, allegedly containing the tombs of 125,000 saints. Most of *Qāni'*'s *maṣnavīs* (see Vol. III) on mystical subjects and his poems are still in manuscript.

H. I. Sadarangani, *Persian Poets of Sind* (Karachi 1956), pp. 124–34. AS

qaṣida, see Vol. III.

Qāsimi, Aḥmad Nadīm (b 1916 Agra), Urdu poet and short-story writer. After graduation from Lahore he held positions in government service and edited literary journals. He was jailed as leader of the Pakistan Progressive Writers' Association. His first volume of sensitive and sincere poetry *Jalāl-o-jamāl* (Grandeur and Beauty, 1946) comprised impressionist verses on love and nature, steeped in romanticism. Later he wrote verses on social subjects, at times wrapping them in philosophical garb. His short stories depict the grey life of the lower social strata in Panjab towns and villages and protest against colonial oppression, social injustice, superstition and prejudice. JM

Quijano de Manila, Filipino poet, see **Joaquin,** Nick.

Qurratul Ain Haidar, Urdu writer, see **Ḥaidar,** Quarratu'l-'ain.

R

Raden Landai (Prince Landai), Thai poem by Phra Mahā Montrī under Rāma III (1824–51), which made the poet's fame, is remarkable both in subject and language. It is the first Thai poem on a petty-bourgeois theme, to which the language is suitably adapted, even to vulgarity. Landai, the Hindu, was a beggar musician in Bangkok, wandering about the town improvising words and tunes. He fell in love with the wife of another Hindu, the dairyman Pradū; Landai sang about his love affair, always ending with the words: 'Don't tell anyone, don't tell anyone.' Pradū was thus the only person to remain ignorant of his wife's infidelity. One day Landai went begging before Pradū's house, and was given her husband's food by the faithless wife, who thus gave herself away, was beaten and confessed. The affair ended in a general riot in the Hindu quarter, which had to be quelled by the police. The poem is written in *klọn* metre. KW

Rāghav, Rāṅgey (b 1923 Agra, d 1962), Hindi poet, novelist and short-story writer, from south India. His social novels on contemporary themes show changes in the mentality of people of different classes, and the receding force of tradition: *Gharaunde* (Doll's Houses, 1941), *Sīdhā sādhā rāstā* (A Straight Direct Road, 1957), *Kab tak pukārū̃* (How Long Must I Call? 1957). The most important of his several pseudo-historical novels is *Murdŏ kā ṭīlā* (Hill of the Dead, 1948). DA

Raghunātha Śiromaṇi, Indian philosopher, see **Gaṅgeśa.**

Raḥam 'Ali Marrī (19th–20th century), Baluchi epic poet. He strongly opposed the repression of colonial domination and set up a revolutionary trend in Baluchi poetry. He wrote over 50,000 verses, all full of fiery sentiments against the British rule and in praise for the national heroes. His lofty style and passionate tone ranks him with the greatest epic writers of Iran and India. He has been accorded the status of a national poet. JM

rahasyavād, trend of Hindi *chāyāvād* (qv). *Rahasyavād* poetry which expresses the mystical yearning of the Individual Soul for union with the Universal Soul or Supreme Deity, and grief and despair at their separation. This yearning is inspired by spiritual love, frequently with undertones of erotic love. IZ

Rahtathara, Shin Maha (1468–1530), Burmese poet, a monk of royal descent, with great human understanding, and a model for later writers. His poems cover all but one of the five major genres in four-syllable lines: *pyo*, *mawgun*, *yadu* and *linga* (qqv); like other monk-poets, he did not write *egyin* (historical ballads). He composed *Bhuridat Lingagyi* (*Jātaka* No. 543) in 1484, the oldest *pyo* on record, and its sequel *Bhuridat Zatpaung Pyo* on 1494, but his *tour de force* is said to be *Kogan Pyo* (*Jātaka* No. 509), 1526, which however does not match up to *Thanwara Pyo* (*Jātaka* No. 462), 1529, his last work, in the way the human interest is woven into the Buddhist theme. Most of the *pyo*-writers of successive ages looked to him, and not to Thilawuntha (qv) as their guide. His *Tada uti Mawgun* (1496) was taken as a model by many subsequent composers of panegyric poems, and his charming *tawla* (forest journey) *linga*, which abounds in human qualities rarely found among monk-poets, appeals to the ordinary people more than the *tawla* of Uttamagyaw (qv). HP

Rāhula, Śrī (15th century), the best known of classical Sinhalese poets. He was connected with the royal family of Kōṭṭe, but accounts of his personal life are only legendary. He resided as a monk at Toṭagamuva, on the coast north of Galle, whence he is sometimes referred to by the name of Toṭagamuve. King Parākramabāhu VI (qv) appointed him *sangharāja* ('King of the Monks') of Ceylon, but after the King's death he backed an unsuccessful candidate for the throne, and his influence faded before that of Vīdāgama Maitreya (qv). His reputation rests principally upon *Kāvyasēkharaya* (1449), a *mahākāvya* (see *kāvya*) versification of a *jātaka* (qv) story, written with a sensitivity considered by some to be improper for a monk, and *Sælalihini Sandesa* (The Starling's Message, 1450), the most famous and shortest of all Sinhalese *sandesas* (qv). His other works are *Parevi Sandesa* (The Dove's Message) and *Pancikāpradīpaya* (1457), a grammatical work in prose. *Pærakumbāsirita*, a well written panegyric on Parākramabāhu VI, is sometimes attributed to him, though it contains no indication of authorship.

Trans.: Jayasinghe and Van Geyzel, in *Anthology of Sinhalese Literature*, ed. C. Reynolds (London 1970); W. C. Macready, *Sella Lihini Sandese* (Colombo 1865). CHBR

Rājakōpālāccāri, Cakkaravartti (pseud. Rājāji, b 1878 Hosur, d 1972 Madras), Indian statesman and writer. A close associate of Gandhi and a leading figure in Indian political life for most of the present century, Rājāji served as Prime Minister of Madras in pre-independence days (1937–39) and as Chief Minister of the state after independence was won (1952–54). Before the latter period of office he was successively Governor-General of his country and minister in the Central Government. Rājāji's English works include books on aspects of Hinduism and a translation of part of Kampaṉ's (qv) *Rāmāyaṇam*. In Tamil he has published prose versions of the *Mahābhārata* and the *Rāmāyaṇa* (qqv), and collections of short stories (*Kataikaḷ* and *Kaṟpaṉaikkāṭu*), most of which have a social or didactic purpose.

Trans.: *Mahabharata* (Bombay 1955); *Ramayana* (Bombay 1962): *Stories for the Innocent* (Bombay, [2]1967).
Monica Felton, *I Meet Rajaji* (London 1962).
REA

Rājam Aiyar, B.R. (1872–98), Tamil novelist. A lawyer by training, Rājam Aiyar devoted most of his life to writing, in both English and Tamil. For the last two years of his life he edited *Prabuddha Bharata*, a monthly journal concerned with religion and philosophy. In most of his writings, including an uncompleted novel in English (*True Greatness, or Vasudeva Sastri*) and his one Tamil novel (*Kamalāmpāḷ, or the Fatal Rumour*, first published in a Tamil monthly between 1893 and 1895) Rājam Aiyar aimed to popularize the Vedānta. He did not allow his philosophizing, however, to get in the way of his telling of a story, and his *Kamalāmpāḷ* is an interesting narrative, spiced with humour and having the benefit of more subtle characterization than had so far been seen in the Tamil novel.

Selection in English: *Rambles in the Vedanta* (Madras 1905).
CNI 189–93.
REA

Rājaśekhara (b c860 AD Mahārāṣṭra, d c930 AD Kānyakubja), Indian poet, dramatist and critic. He is most appreciated by anthologists for the lyric gems scattered throughout his major works, and most readable because of his lively imagination and humour, and terse style in both drama and criticism. His *Karpūramañjarī* is a *saṭṭaka* in Prakrit and his *Viddhaśālabhañjikā* a *nāṭikā*. Both these plays are comedies of palace intrigue. The ten act *nāṭaka*, *Bālarāmāyaṇa*, though immensely long (dramatizing practically the entire Rāma epic) is effective through the dramatic presentation of incidents often imagined by Rājaśekhara, for example, the confrontation of Rāvaṇa and Sītā in Act I where the tyrant is unable to bend Śiva's bow (see *Rāmāyaṇa*). Of the parallel *Bālabhārata* only two acts are available. The epic *Harivilāsa* is apparently lost. Of Rājaśekhara's great critical work *Kāvyamīmāṃsā* (Investigation of Literature) we unfortunately have only the first of eighteen 'books' and a few quotations. In amusingly pedantic prose, a parody of the *Arthaśāstra* (see Kauṭilya), Rājaśekhara first elevates Literature and his consort Criticism with a myth of their origin and marriage in the stylish city of Vatsagulma. The critic legislates luxury with palaces and gardens for writers, but a disciplined timetable and preparedness to jot down ideas at all times.

Trans.: *Karpūramañjarī*, Lanman (HOS 4, 1901, reprinted Delhi 1963); *Viddhaśālabhañjikā*, Schuyler (JAOS 1906); *Kāvyamīmāṃsā*, Stchoupak and Renou (Paris 1946). AKW

Rakeś, Mohan (b 1925 Amritsar), Hindi writer, lecturer in Hindi in Jalandhar, Bombay and Simla and, since 1957, a freelance writer. He is one of the main authors of the *nayī kahānī* (qv), psychological stories and novels of urban middle-class life; a frequent theme is that of gradual or sudden disillusionment. His best and biggest novel is *Andhere band kamre* (Dark, Closed Rooms, 1961). Stories: *Naye bādal* (New Clouds, 1957); *Ek aur zindagī* (A Different Life, 1963).
DA

Rāma Paṇikkar, Niraṇam (15th century), Malayalam poet. He is generally considered to be the greatest of a family of poets living in Niraṇam in central Travancore in the late 14th and early 15th century. Works of two other members of the family have come down to us; Mādhava Paṇikkar's *Bhagavadgītā* and Śaṅkara Paṇikkar's *Bhāratamāla*, a very condensed version of the *Mahābhārata* (qv). Most important among Rāma Paṇikkar's poems is his *Rāmāyaṇam*, which follows Vālmīki's poem (see *Rāmāyaṇa*) quite closely but contains a number of original variations. The work of the Paṇikkars represents an important stage in the history of Malayalam literature in that with it the influence of Sanskrit became clearly marked.

PNHML 38–41; GSML 38–41. REA

Rāmakien, Phrarātcha niphon nai ratchakān thi nüng (The Glory of Rāma, Royal Poem of the First Reign [of the Bangkok dynasty]), the longest and most famous epic of ancient Thailand. It tells of the love of Rāma for the beautiful Sīdā, and his struggle against Thotsakan (ie Rāvaṇa), ruler of the demons on Lanka Island. Based on the Indian *Rāmāyaṇa* (qv), but probably modelled on a Javanese version, *Rāmakīen* is considerably longer than the *Rāmāyaṇa*; under the first two Chakrī kings, Rāma I (1782–1809) and Rāma II (1809–1824), the then extant fragments were given their present form of 70,000 lines. The history of the texts has not yet been completely clarified. The poem is amazingly diverse, arranged in a series of episodes. The *Rāmakīen* 'proper', a folk poem universally known in Thailand, ends with the death of Thotsakan. It has often been illustrated by painters and carvers, eg the marble bas-relief in the Wat Phra Chētuphon, Bangkok.

Trans. (in prose) Ray A. Olsson, *The Ramakien* (Bangkok 1968); Chalermint, *The Thai Ramayana* (Bangkok 1965). KW

Rāmāmirtam, Lā. Sa. (Ramamirtham L. S., b 1916), Tamil writer. He is one of the most prominent short-story writers, and probably the best stylist, in modern Tamil. Influenced by Tolstoy, Hamsun, Joyce and Hemingway, he began writing in English. He has published over a hundred short stories and a novel (*Putra*, Son, 1965). His stories probe deep into the inner life of his heroes, mostly middle- and lower-class men and women. He combines a very contemporary psychological approach and introspection with Hindu orthodoxy and traditional views. The greatest achievement of his writing is the use of an immensely rich, rather Sanskritized diction, and an exquisite style, often experimental, full of alliteration, of haunting rhythm and difficult syntax. Short-story collections: *Jaṉaṉi* (1957); *Itaḷkaḷ* (Petals, 1959); *Paccaikkaṉavu* (Green Dream, 1961); *Kaṅkā* (1962); *Añcali* (Gesture of Worship, 1963); *Alaikaḷ* (Waves, 1964); *Tayā* (1966). KZ

Rāman Piḷḷa, C. V. (1858–1922), Malayalam novelist. A member of the teaching staff of the Maharaja's College, Trivandrum, he wrote a number of farcical comedies, some of which were produced by the students of the college. His reputation today, however, rests on his three historical novels which are set in different periods of the history of Travancore: *Mārttāṇḍavarmma* (1891), *Dharmmarājā* (1913) and *Rāmarājabahadūr* (1918). The first such novels in Malayalam, they remain unsurpassed. A fourth novel on a contemporary theme was less successful.

PNHML 125–30, 153–5; GSML 174–5. REA

Ramanujan, A. K. (b 1929 Mysore), Indian poet writing in English; his mother tongues are Kannada and Tamil (bilingual). Educated in India, and, post-1959, in the USA. Now professor of Dravidian studies and linguistics at the University of Chicago. Ramanujan has published work in linguistics, folklore, mythology and comparative literature and translated from Kannada, Tamil and Malayalam into English. He is now engaged in translating the poetry of classical Tamil, and mediaeval Kannada religious lyrics. Works: *The Striders* (1966), *The Interior Landscape* (1967), *Relations* (in the press). MED

Rāmāyaṇa or **Vālmīki-Rāmāyaṇa,** Sanskrit epic. The fuller title is necessary to distinguish the Sanskrit poem, attributed to the authorship of Vālmīki, from the numerous adaptations and translations in New Indian languages. In contrast to the *Mahābhārata* (qv), the *Rāmāyaṇa* is sufficiently homogeneous in plan and execution to justify the attribution to a single poet (except for the last Book and the greater part of the first, which are generally agreed to be later additions; the first Book in particular is greatly inferior in poetic merit). The epic hero, Rāma, belongs to the line of Ikṣavāku kings who ruled the Gangetic Plain kingdom of Kosala from their capital in Ayodhyā in the 6th and 5th centuries BC. Legends surrounding the royal house and the adventures of the Ikṣavāku hero Rāma form the basis of the epic. It is likely that the poet gathered the scattered material of oral tradition to compose a court epic. The epic itself shows the blending of two distinct themes, historical saga and nature mythology.

The main narrative of the first part of the epic, as presented in Book II (*Ayodhyākāṇḍa*), concentrates on events at the court of Rāma's father, Daśaratha, and their consequences. Daśaratha has four sons—Rāma, Bharata, Śatrughna and Lakṣmaṇa—by his three wives. Rāma is married to Sītā, daughter of the king of the Videhas, whom he wins by the trial of bending a magical bow. Rāma is appointed heir-apparent, but the intrigues of Queen Kaikeyī to place her son Bharata on the throne result in the exile of Rāma with Sītā and Lakṣmaṇa. Bharata succeeds to the throne, but only agrees to rule as regent for Rāma until he returns from exile.

The narrative character of the second part of the epic, Books III–VI (*Āraṇyakāṇḍa*, *Kiṣkindhakāṇḍa*, *Sundarakāṇḍa*, and *Yuddhakāṇḍa*), is very different. Related to older Indian myths, the main story is full of the fantastic. After various episodes in which Rāma combats the *rākṣasas* (demons) who infest Daṇḍaka forest, the demon-chief Rāvaṇa, king of the island of Laṅkā, vows revenge. He has Rāma and Lakṣmaṇa lured away from their forest home and abducts Sītā. In order to recapture her, Rāma allies himself with the monkey chief Sugrīva and his minister Hanuman. They depose Sugrīva's powerful brother Vāli and prepare to invade Laṅkā. Meanwhile, Hanuman crosses over the ocean from the mainland to Laṅkā in a single bound and searches for Sītā. He finds her a prisoner in Rāvaṇas pleasure grove, still rejecting his suit and despairing of Rāma's ever coming to save her. Hanuman consoles her, wreaks havoc in Laṅkā, and returns to report to Rāma. The monkeys build a fabulous bridge and Hanuman carries Rāma at the head of the army to attack Rāvaṇa's rich city. The demons are routed, Rāma kills Rāvaṇa and liberates Sītā. After Sītā is made to justify her chastity by an ordeal of fire, Rāma returns with her and Lakṣmaṇa to reign in Ayodhyā.

The significance of this second part of the epic has been interpreted in allegorical and mythological terms. Allegorically, Rāma's journey and victory over the demons is said to represent the spread of Aryan culture to Southern India and Ceylon (Laṅkā); this idea is suggestive, but there is little textual evidence to support it. The mythological interpretation seems less speculative. Many *Rāmāyaṇa* characters represent basic mythological types which are traceable to Vedic and non-Vedic sources. For example, Rāma's conflict with Rāvaṇa and other *rākṣasas* parallels the complex of *Ṛgveda* (qv) myths of Indra's conflict with Vṛtra and other demons. Sītā, meaning 'furrow', is personified in the *Ṛgveda* and invoked as a goddess. Hanuman, the son of the Vedic Wind-god, Vāyu (hence also called Māruta-sūnu), flies hundreds of leagues through the air and aids Rāma in ways reminiscent of the Vedic Storm-gods, Maruts, in their alliance with Indra. On another mythological level, Sītā is related to the prototype of prehistoric tree and fertility goddesses, while Hanuman is the theriomorphic figure who embodies forms of demonic and divine powers combined into a spontaneous creative energy, which Rāma needs to accomplish the task of restoring order in the world. Rāma himself is the incarnation of order, duty and controlled power (*dharma*). He embodies the pure duty of ritualized life, in contrast to his arch-enemy Rāvaṇa, who is passion incarnate.

In the final Book (VII, *Uttarakāṇḍa*), generally agreed to be a late addition to the *Rāmāyaṇa*, public scandal concerning Sītā's chastity during her captivity in Rāvaṇa's palace forces Rāma to have Sītā abandoned in the forest. She gives birth to twins in the hermitage of Vālmīka on the bank of the Ganges, where she finds refuge. It is from Vālmīki that the twins learn the epic, which they later sing in their father's presence. On hearing the story, Rāma begs Sītā for forgiveness, but she invokes Earth from which she was born and her mother receives her. Rāma's sons are named Kuśa and Lava, and tradition has it that the epic was passed down from them by professional rhapsodists called *kuśīlavas*, who recited it all over India.

By the addition of the first and last books Vālmīki's epic was transformed in time into a poem meant to glorify the Hindu god Viṣṇu. The story is introduced that Rāvaṇa, by his austerities, obtained from Brahmā a boon of invulnerability to gods, demons, and demigods, but being arrogant he ignored humans. His abuses of his status led the gods to ask Viṣṇu to incarnate himself as a man to destroy Rāvaṇa. So, as he had done at six other crucial moments in the world's history, Viṣṇu assumed the form of an incarnation (*avatāra*), this time of the Ikṣvāku prince Rāma, to accomplish the task of restoring order by his actions in the world. The recasting of the *Rāmāyaṇa* into this Vaiṣṇava frame has served to make the epic a sacred text of Hinduism.

The language of the *Rāmāyaṇa* is a form of Sanskrit which is characterized by grammatical peculiarities that distinguish it from the standard language established by Pāṇinean grammar. The epic represents a more popular form of Sanskrit of the period preceding Pāṇini's work. The style as well as the language of the epic shows a uniformity of composition. Attention to formal considerations and ornaments of style are evident. When the character of *kāvya* (qv) style is compared with that of the legend (*ithihāsa*), the preoccupation of *kāvya* with form is apparent. The *Rāmāyaṇa*, with its elaborate descriptions and use of poetic ornaments, shows stylistic refinement of the legends and myths that are its content. Within Indian literary tradition, Vālmīki's work is considered to be *Ādikāvya*, or the first artificial poem; this in contrast to the *Mahābhārata*, which is called *Jñānakoṣa*, or encyclopaedia. According to the evidence of its Critical Edition, the fact that the *Rāmāyaṇa* was considered *Ādikāvya* profoundly affected the transmission of the text in centres of Sanskrit learning, where the original text was revised to bring it into accord with the formal standards of later court epics. Such revisions are most numerous in versions of the Northern Recension.

The popularity of *Vālmīki-Rāmāyaṇa* is attested to in many ways. For example, its story provides the inspiration for a *Mahābhārata* episode entitled *Rāmopākhyāna*, a Buddhist *jātaka* (qv) entitled *Dasaratha Jātaka*, Kālidāsa's (qv) court epic *Raghuvaṃśa*, the *Bhaṭṭikāvya* (see Bhaṭṭi), and Bhavabhūti's (qv) dramas *Mahāvīracarita* and *Uttararāmacarita*. The original epic has also been variously adapted and translated into Indian vernacular languages. The most important of these are the Tamil version by Kampaṉ, the Hindi version by Tulsīdās, and the Bengali version by Kṛttibās (qqv). The epic has also been widely transmitted to other parts of Asia. Versions are known in Java, Malaya, Vietnam, Cambodia, Laos, Thailand, where identification of the story's origin is lost; in China and Tibet, the story is still identified with India.

Trans.: H. P. Sastri, 3 vols. (London 1952–59); M. L. Sen, 3 vols. (Calcutta 1955); M. N. Dutt, 7 vols. (Calcutta 1891–94). Abridged trans.: R. C. Dutta (London 1935); C. Rajagopalachari (New Delhi); children's version by E. Seeger (New York 1969).
H. Jacobi, *Das Rāmāyaṇa* (Bonn 1893, in English Baroda 1960); E. W. Hopkins, *Epic Mythology* (Strassburg 1915, reprint New York 1969); Macdonell, *A History of Sanskrit Literature* (London 1900, reprint Delhi 1961), pp. 304–319; WHIL I, 475–517. BSM

Ramayana Kakawin (Epic of Rama, c9th century, East Java), the earliest surviving Old Javanese epic. It is anonymous, written in Old Javanese (*kawi*) probably under King Dyah Balitung. Inspired by Vālmīki's *Rāmāyaṇa* (qv), it is not an adaptation of it but may have been modelled on a shorter Sanskrit or south Indian version. The form is the *tembang gede* (great verse) brought to perfection by Kanwa (qv) in the 11th century and dominating Javanese literature up to the 15th. The story of Rama is known in many versions in Indonesia, in prose and verse, and is a popular *wajang* (qv) theme. Its language, style and philosophy make the *Ramayana Kakawin* one of the loveliest Old Javanese epics; like most of the *kakawins* it has been translated into Dutch

(1920–40). Jasadipura I (qv) paraphrased it in modern Javanese. The Malayan version (*Hikayat Seri Rama*) differs in many respects.

C. Hooykaas, *The Old Javanese Ramayana Kakawin* (Amsterdam 1958); W. F. Stutterheim, *Rāma-Legenden und Rāma-Reliefs in Indonesien* (Munich 1925); PLJ I, 176. EV

Rāmdhārisinh, Hindi poet, see **Dinkar.**

Rangācārya, Ādya or Śrīraṅga (b 1904 Agarkhed), major Kannada playwright of all-India status, with over 25 plays (*Harijanvāra*, 1932; *Kēḷu Janamējaya*, *Śōka Cakra*, *Kattale Beḷaku*, etc) and over ten novels (*Viśvamitrana Sṛṣṭi*, 1934; *Prakṛti*; *Puruṣa*, 1957, etc). He has been known for over 40 years for his wit, iconoclasm, and experiment in problem plays, satires, and tragi-comedies, using the theatre for a ceaseless criticism of life. He blends the techniques of classical Sanskrit and modern Europe, and is concerned not only with folly but evil, in Indian family, society and politics. AKR

Ranggawarsita, Raden Ngabei (b 1802 Surakarta, d 1873 Klaten), Javanese poet and writer, given an Islamic education in Ponorogo, East Java. He wandered all over Java for several years. Through the influence of the poet Jasadipura II, to whom he was related, Ranggawarsita became court poet in Surakarta. Although he wrote more prosometric works, his best known and appreciated work is a didactic poem *Serat kalatida* (Time of Doubt). His poetic style is traditional, the language still marked by archaisms. He was the first writer to attempt purely prose forms, mainly on history and mythological themes. He collected old tales, traditional sources of *wajang* (qv) stories in 19th century. Ranggawarsita introduced a new trend into Javanese literature, proving as well as preaching that prose literature is of no less value than poetry; he was followed by younger writers, eg Ki Padmasusastra and Purwalelana. His work remained largely unknown outside Indonesia until the mid-20th century. His biography was written by Padma Warsita and printed in Surakarta by a local printer between 1930–40. Other books: *Cemporet* (1856), *Pustaka Raja* (Books of Kings, 5 vols., 1884–92), *Parama Yoga* (Introduction to Cosmogony), *Jitapsara* (Cosmogony).

PLJ I, 109–110, 170. EV

Rangin, Sa'ādat Yār Khān (b 1757 Sirhind, d 1835 Lucknow), Urdu erotic poet, originator of *rēkhtī* (verse in which the poet writes as a woman and uses the characteristic language of women). He travelled widely as a soldier, artillery officer and horse-dealer, but later settled at the Lucknow court. His frivolous and sensual poetry mirrors the profligacy of debased aristocratic society. His suggestive *ghazals* (see Vol. III) embrace the entire life of court ladies and reflect his sexual intimacy with courtesans and dancing girls. His prose is a source of history.

Trans.: D. C. Phillot, *Faras-nāma or the Book of the Horse* (London 1911).
RSHUL 93–5; MSHUL 142. JM

Rao, Raja (b 1909), Indian author writing in English; his mother tongue is Kannada. Educated in Paris. The very purity of the English of the Victorian novelists became a disability to the Indian writer in fiction, so that it was fortunate that Rao received his further education in France. As a south Indian Brahmin, Rao has brilliant intellectual powers and a great sensitivity. His first novel is *Kanthapura* (1938), the story of a small village in southern Bombay caught up in the nationalist movement in the early thirties. In 1947 came a book of short stories, *The Cow of the Barricades and Other Stories*, and in 1960 *The Serpent and the Rope*, the most important piece of prose fiction by an Indian to date. He wrote it in 29 days, after many years' gestation. It is a statement of Rao's understanding of India and Europe and of their attitudes and values. Its pro-Indian attitude forms an interesting contrast to N. C. Chaudhuri (qv). In it he successfully blends elements in Indian and western forms of writing. His style comes close to that of the *purāṇas* (qv). He uses Indian idiom, speech rhythms, phraseology and proverbs. The story-teller is Rama, a south Indian Brahmin, who goes to France to do historical research. He meets Madeleine, a French teacher of history, and they marry. His four years' stay in Europe and the failure of this marriage reveal his 'Indian-ness' to him. The novel contains many autobiographical elements. In 1965, it was followed by *The Cat and Shakespeare.*

M. K. Naik, *The Serpent and the Rope; the Indo-Anglian novel as epic legend* (CEIWE 214–49); C. D. Narasimhaiah, *Raja Rao's Kanthapura—an analysis* (CEIWE 270–96); DMINE. MED

rasa, basic term of Sanskrit poetics, see **kāvya** and **dhvani.**

rāso (12th–16th century), versified romance of a popular character, mostly from Rajasthan and Gujarat. Also a prosodic metre, used in such compositions besides other metres like *dūhā*, *caupāī* etc, so that works of this type are often found under the name of *Dūhā*, *Caupāī* etc. The prototype is said to be a lost *Muñjarāsa* in Apabhraṃśa, whose fragments are quoted in the Prakrit Grammar of Hemacandra (1132). From the 12th century onwards, an abundant *rāso* literature develops in an Indo-Aryan vernacular known as Old Western Rajasthani (OWR) or Old Gujarati, also called Ḍingal. The most ancient specimen of the OWR *rāso* is said to be the *Bharateśvarabāhubali rāsa* (1185 AD) composed by a Jain author, Śālibhadra Sūri.

The theme of the *rāsos* is either heroic, centring on the warlike prowess of some Rājput hero, or romanesque and sentimental, centring on some love-affair between a Rājput prince and princess, entailing long and painful separations between the lovers which lend themselves to lyrical development. The *Kānhaḍade Prabandha* (qv) is a typically 'heroic' *rāso*, whilst the *Bīsaldev-rāso*, whose date is uncertain, represents an archaic type of 'sentimental' *rāso*: it is a simple love-ballad composed in a mixture of OWR and Pingal, ie an old Braj dialect. In fact, most of the non-Jain *rāsos* are composed in that mixed language.

By far the most famous is the *Pṛthvīrāj-rāso* attributed to Cand Bardāī, a long composition in Pingal, mixed with OWR and some archaic Apabhraṃśa words. As Cand Bardāī (sometimes given as the first great 'Hindi' poet) appears to have been the contemporary and principal adviser of the hero, king Pṛthvīrāj of Amber (defeated by Shāhāb-ud-dīn Ghorī in 1192 AD), the poem is supposed to have been composed in the first half of the 13th century. But there are no ancient manuscripts, and the poem, which has come down to us under various forms, seems to have been very largely interpolated. Both the heroic and romanesque elements are present, yet some modern critics are of the opinion that the primitive *Pṛthvīrāj-rāso* ended at the brave hero's conquest of the fair Rājput princess Saṃjogitā: it might have been originally a lyrical exaltation of Rājput chivalry, rather than the all-embracing folk-epic we know. All critics agree however in considering the *Pṛthvīrāj-rāso* as the most remarkable specimen of the whole *rāso* literature. No translation of any *rāso* in any European language has been attempted so far.

Tod, *Annals and Antiquities of Rajasthan* (2 vols., 1829–32, reprinted London 1957); Forbes, *Rās-mālā* (London 1856); G. Grierson, *Modern Vernacular Literature of Hindustan* (Calcutta 1889). CV

Ratnākaraśānti, Indian writer on metrics, see **Buddhist literature.**

Ratnaśrijñāna, ancient Indian critic, see **Buddhist literature.**

Rāy, Amṛt (b 1921 Kanpur), Hindi writer, son of Premcand (qv); editor of literary papers in Allahabad. His themes are social conflicts, religious fanaticism and the struggle against tradition. His best novel, *Bīj* (Seed, 1953), is the story of a young couple and of woman's road to equality. In the late fifties, Rāy wrote psychological stories, influenced by *nayī kahānī* (qv), eg *Gīlī miṭṭī* (Damp Earth, 1959). Stories: *Tiraṅge kafan* (Tricoloured Shrouds, 1948); *Kaṭghare* (Cages, 1956). DA

Rāy (Roy), Bhāratcandra (b 1712 Burdwan

District, d 1760), the most famous Bengali poet of the 18th century. An early student of both Sanskrit and Persian, he was in his youth the manager of his family's estates but, when they were confiscated, he made his way to the court of Kṛṣṇacandra Rāy of Krishnagar, a noted patron of the arts, especially of poetry. Bhāratcandra's poetic talent there earned him the title *guṇākar* (the incarnation of excellence). Bhāratcandra's most famous work is the long trilogy *Annadā-maṅgal*; the first part consists of a retelling of the purāṇic legend of Śiva and Pārvatī, the second is a historically-oriented romance about the conflict of the Hindu Rājā of Jessore with the Mughal emperor Jagangir, and the third, by far the most famous part, is the love-story of Vidyā and Sundar. Bhāratcandra is noted for the grace, sophistication, and wit of his writing. As a scholar of Sanskrit he was able to adapt the elaborate Sanskritic metrical system, aesthetic viewpoint, and even language to the Bengali.

Trans.: Edward C. Dimock, Jr., The Thief of Love (Chicago 1963), pp. 19–132.
SHBLL 662–78; SHBL 164–9. ECD

Rāy, Harivamś, Hindi poet, see **Baccan.**

Rāy (Roy), Rāmmohan (b 1772 Radhanagar, d 1833 Bristol), Bengali religious thinker and social reformer. Son of a Brahmin family, he was highly educated and had considerable knowledge of Hinduism, Islam and Christianity. He was a higher official of the East India Company and an emissary of the Great Mughal. Rāmmohan is justifiably called the Father of Modern India; he endeavoured to modernize religious and social life and to revive Hinduism by introducing elements from other religions. He fought against idolatry, polytheism and sectarianism in religion, and against child marriage, the enslavement of women, and *suttee.* In his pamphlets, articles and lectures he laid the foundations of modern Bengali prose; founded and edited several periodicals; and wrote a Bengali grammar which set the standards for the written language. He set in motion the movement known as the Bengali Renaissance, aimed at all-round modernization of thought and the way of life in Bengal.

S. K. De, *Bengali Literature in the Nineteenth Century* (Calcutta 1919); Amit Sen, *Notes on the Bengal Renaissance* (Bombay 1946); SHBL 182–4. DZ

Ream Ker, the Cambodian version of the *Rāmāyaṇa* (qv). The Rāma epic has held a high place in Cambodian culture at least since, if not before, the Angkor period. Favourite scenes have formed, and still form, the subject of bas-reliefs on temple walls, paintings in monasteries, performances of song and dance by peasant troupes and presentations of the wayside shadow-theatre. Nevertheless, the text which has come down to the present day, and which the Buddhist Institute has published, consists of only Books 1–10 and 75–80. Books 1–10 tell the story of Rāma from the contest of the bow and his departure to the forest with Sītā and Lakṣmaṇa as far as over the bridge to Laṅkā. Various individual fights of generals in Laṅkā are described in Books 9 and 10. Books 75–80 tell of the drawing of Rāvaṇa by Sītā and of her subsequent banishment; of the boys, Rāmalakṣmaṇa and Jupalakṣmaṇa, encountering Hanuman and Rāma; and of Sītā's flight to the Nāga country following her appearance at Rāma's pretended funeral.

The Cambodian text is clearly divided into scenes and was intended as the song accompaniment to theatrical, mimed performances such as one may still see today in Cambodia, either at the court's Royal Ballet or in local gatherings. It is written in several different metres which change from scene to scene. The style is elevated, as befits a tale in which heroic actions are applauded by the gods and terrible trials are acknowledged by a trembling of the earth. The language is characterized by the use of fixed epithets, similes and alliteration. The manuscripts from which the Buddhist Institute took its text are undated but the internal evidence of the language shows that the first ten books are much older than the last six and may well go back to the Middle Khmer period or even earlier.
JMJ

Ṛgveda ('Veda of the sacred verses recited in praise of a deity'), the first of the four *Vedas* (qv). In a narrower sense, it is the *Ṛgveda-Saṃhitā*, ie the collection of 1028 'hymns' (about 10,600 stanzas), and in a wider sense those prose texts which belong to it or depend on it. The *Ṛgveda-Saṃhitā* is divided into ten books, called 'circles' (*maṇḍalas*). Of these, books II to VII are ascribed to, and were handed down in, individual families of inspired poets (*ṛṣis*, 'seers'); generally speaking, they contain the earliest hymns. Book IX is a separate collection of hymns dedicated to the divine draught and god Soma. Book X is not only a later addition, but also contains much material of a different character which probably originated in different milieus. In books II–VII the hymns are arranged according to three principles, viz, the gods addressed, the metres used and the length of the hymns.

The composition of these poems may have covered several centuries and even the earliest of them (which may date from the 12th century BC) must be the product of a long tradition. Owing to the obscurity of many allusions, the archaic character of the language and the many difficult expressions, many passages are not fully understood. There are many recurrent phrases and verses and it is clear that the poets, generally speaking, must have borrowed from their predecessors, followed settled literary conventions and drawn on the same poetical tradition. Their products were for a long time, even after their fixation in written form, handed down orally. The arrangement and 'codification' of the extant recension, ascribed to Sākalya, must have taken place at a considerably later date. After that the text was preserved with meticulous accuracy.

The *Saṃhitā* contains eulogies praising the gods, commemorating their achievements and benevolence, invoking their aid and protection; it also refers to myths in which they play a part and to rites associated with their worship. There are, however, also texts of a more or less magical character, dialogues ascribed to divine or mythical persons, cosmogonic poems and some texts dealing with various subjects which are often wrongly regarded as secular, for instance the famous 'Gamester's lament' in book X, which in fact seems to have been intended to accompany an exorcism to free a gambler from the demon of dice. Although many hymns refer directly to rites (especially to the Soma cult) some of them have only a distant connection with the sacrifices. Yet many hymns and verses were, either from the beginning or from a later date, used for liturgical and consecratory purposes (see *Veda*, *mantra*).

Although the *Ṛgveda* is an incomparable source of linguistic and religious information, the aesthetic value of its component parts varies. Some hymns evince a considerable degree of poetical inspiration and careful competence, the diction following the lofty flight taken by the imagination of the authors; others strike us as patchwork. The literary importance of this old document of oral poetry is of course beyond dispute. The structure of the hymns and stanzas, the many stylistic devices (parallelism, anaphora, alliteration, rhyme, assonance, concatenation), the abundant use of metaphors and similes, the harmony of diction and contents, the often-emphatic style, the many more or less esoteric allusions and the peculiarities of their phraseology have, on the one hand, much in common with the archaic poetry of other peoples, and on the other many specific qualities of their own.

Trans.: R. T. H. Griffith, *Translation of the Ṛgveda*, 3 vols. (1896–7—antiquated); K. F. Geldner, *Der Rigveda übersetzt*, 3 vols. (HOS 33–5, 1951).
L. Renou, *Études védiques et pāṇinéennes*, 17 vols. (Paris 1955–69); WHIL I 57–119. JG

Riemeng, Thai writer, see **Mālai Chūphinit.**

Rivai Apin, Indonesian poet, see **Apin,** Rivai.

Rizal, José (b 1861 Kalamba, d 1896 Manila), Filipino national hero and writer, writing in Spanish. One of a large family, he studied at the Ateneo de Manila. Suspected of complicity in the anti-Spanish movement, he fled to Europe and completed Arts and Law studies in Madrid, 1882.

Rizal spoke many European and Oriental languages, and tried his hand at ethnography, painting and sculpture. In Spain and later in the Philippines he worked for reforms, and was imprisoned and exiled in Dapitan for political reasons. While on the way to Cuba as a medical volunteer, he was accused of instigating armed rebellion and executed in Manila. His early verse praised the Spanish conquerors, but soon began to express the nationalist feeling of the rising middle class. In 1887 his first novel appeared in Berlin: *Noli me tangere* is passionately patriotic, full of poetic imagination, humour and delicate irony, and gives a colourful picture of his country. It was prohibited by the censor and any copies found in the Philippines publicly burned. His second novel, *El filibusterismo* (London 1891), is full of philosophical and political discussion, sharply critical of the colonizers but less successful as writing. By his works (which include poetry) and his anticolonialist views Rizal helped on the revolutionary movement which culminated in the formation of the Philippine Republic in 1898. EH

Roesli, Indonesian novelist, see **Rusli, Marah.**

Roy, see **Rāy,** Bhāratcandra, and Rāy, Rāmmohan.

Rudraṭa, ancient Indian writer on poetics, see **alaṃkāraśāstra.**

Rusli, Marah (b 1889 Padang, Sumatra, d 1968 Bogor). Indonesian novelist. He early migrated to Java to attend veterinary school in Bogor. One of his earliest assignments upon completion of his studies was to the island of Sumbawa in east Indonesia. His novel *La Hami* is based on his experiences from this time. Much of his professional life was spent in Semarang in central Java. Upon retirement he returned to Bogor. His first work was *Sitti Nurbaja* (1922) which was also the first original novel in the Indonesian language. It appeared early in Rusli's career and is a description of the conflict between traditionalism and modernism in Minangkabau life. It has been and continues to be very popular with Indonesian readers. After a long hiatus a second novel, *La Hami*, appeared in 1953 and in the following year a third, *Anak dan Kemanakan* (Child and Cousin). His first novel assures him of an honoured place in the history of Indonesian literature.

TMIL 56–7, 219–20. JME

Rusvā, Muḥammad Hādī (b 1858 Lucknow, d 1931 Hyderabad), scientist, inventor, theologian, and first true novelist in Urdu. *Umrāo Jān Adā* (1899) paints a vivid picture of the society of Rusva's native Lucknow in the mid-19th century, in the form of the autobiography of a courtesan. The semi-autobiographical *Sharīfzāda* tells how a poor boy of good family succeeds by his own efforts, while the contrasting *Ẕāt-e sharīf* shows the ruin of a young aristocrat unable to adapt to new conditions. Rusvā regarded these novels as a 'history' of his times, but *Umrāo Jān Adā* is markedly superior to the later two.

Trans.: K. Singh and M. A. Husaini, *Courtesan of Lucknow* (Calcutta 1961).
CNI 132–9; SDUN 167–74. RR

S

Sa, U (1766–1853), Burmese poet, minister of Myawadi fief, near the Thai border, distinguished himself in the First Anglo-Burmese War (1824–6). He attained great heights as a composer of classical songs, and was admired by the Princess Hlaing (qv). U Sa was able to look beyond the limits of Burmese cultural traditions: he was ready and capable of assimilating foreign cultures to Burmese. Essentially a musician, he translated the Thai drama, *Inaung*, into Burmese and wrote into it appropriate songs. He also adapted many Thai and Mon tunes into Burmese music and could sing some English hymns. No Burmese scholar has done so much for the Burmese classical music as U Sa and Prince Pyinsi (?1813–1862).

MHABD 45–9. HP

Ṣābir, Qāżī 'Abdu'l-raḥīm (b 1919), Baluchi lyric poet writing also in Urdu. His favourite genre is the traditional love *ghazal* (see Vol. III), but he also writes verses on modern patterns of the patriotic spirit. JM

Sachchal Sarmast (b 1739 in northern Sindh, where d 1826), Sindhi and Siraiki mystic poet writing also in Persian and Urdu. Like Shāh 'Abdu'l-laṭīf (qv), he used classical Sindhi tales for meditation, but his poetry is more ecstatic and uses daring expressions; he was called 'the 'Aṭṭār (see Vol. III) of Sindh'. His Sindhi and Siraiki poetry in particular praises the Unity of Being, and Manṣūr Ḥallāj, describing in long chains of anaphora how the beloved reveals himself in contradictory forms. His Persian poems are more traditional in form and expression. His pen-name, meaning 'intoxicated', is very apt.

H. S. Sadarangani, *Persian Poets of Sind* (Karachi 1956); ABSLP 293–4. AS

Śāh Husain, also called Mādholāl Husain (1539–93), Panjabi poet. The son of a weaver of Lahore, he became an antinomian (*malāmatī*) mystic, notorious for his love of singing and dancing. His tomb on the outskirts of Lahore is the centre of the city's annual spring fair. Śāh Husain is the first Panjabi poet whose *kāfīs* (short mystical lyrics designed to be sung by religious minstrels) are still extant and popular. His poems are characterized by a wealth of imagery drawn from the activities of spinning and weaving, and by frequent references to the romance of Hīr, subsequently immortalized in the narrative poem of Vāras Śāh (qv). While Husain's *kāfīs* are often of the most attractive simplicity, they cannot compare with the intellectual and stylistic refinement of those of the later Bullhe Śāh and Ghulām Farīd (qqv).

Trans.: Ghulam Yaqoob Anwar, *Kafian Shah Hussain* (Lahore 1966); RKPSP 12–26. CS

Sahāy, Raghupati, Urdu poet, see **Firāq Gōrakhpuri.**

Sale U Pon Nya, Burmese poet, see **Ponnya, U.**

Sama, Bālkṛṣṇa (b 1899 Kathmandu), Nepali writer, of an eminent Rāṇā family. His father had been a poet and his brother, Puskar Śamśer, was a famous lexicographer, grammarian and translator. At the age of 31, Bālkṛṣṇa became the first president of the *Nepālī Bhāṣā Prakāśinī Samiti* (Society for the Propagation of the Nepali Language) and later was for two years editor of the Nepali newspaper *Gorkhā Patr.* He has distinguished himself in many spheres, as a poet, artist, sculptor and musicologist, but is best known for his dramas of which so far seventeen have been published. At present he is Vice-Chancellor of the Royal Nepal Academy. DJM

Samad Said, A[bdul] (b 1935 Malacca), Malay novelist, short-story writer and poet. Educated in both Malay and English, he has spent most of his working life as a journalist, becoming a member of the literary movement *Angkatan Sasterawan 50* (see Usman Awang) while on the staff of *Utusan Melayu* in the 1950's. Much of his writing at this time was in the form of short stories, most demonstrating the same concern for social and political change manifested by his contemporaries in *Asas 50,* and poetry, the latter occasionally more personal in impulse. His first major work, for which he received a national literary prize in 1958, was written while he was still in his early twenties, the novel *Salina* (1961). Dealing with the lives of Malays (and others) inhabiting a decrepit shanty town, Kampong Kambing, in Singapore immediately after World War II, it remains one of the outstanding Malay novels written in the peninsula. In essence the depiction of personal integrity and struggle amid urban destruction, it is remarkable for its rounded, though always compassionate, portrayal of the lives of the Malay poor. Stylistically it is characterized by fine balance and economy of plot, together with communication of character and development of situation by means of naturalistic dialogue rather than description, to a degree seldom approached by earlier writers, and never in such sustained fashion; the novel, of some 500 pages, is one of the longest written in Malay.

Although Samad did not repeat the artistic success of *Salina* in his *Bulan ta' Bermadu di Fatehpur Sikri* (No Honeymoon in Fatehpur Sikri, 1966), a brief and rather facile work, or in the more considered *Sungei Mengalir Lesu* (Sluggish Flows the Stream, 1967), set in the war years, his considerable talent seems certain to yield further fruit. In addition to his novels he has published four collections of poems and stories, *Debar Pertama* (First Heartbeats, 1964, being early stories, 1955–58), *Liar di-Api dan Di-Tepi Jalan* (Mild in the Fire, and By the Roadside, 1961); *Daun-Daun Bergugoran* (Early Fallen Leaves, 1962, with his wife Salmi Manja, also a writer of note); and *Ka-Mana Terbang-nya Si-Burong Senja?* (Whence Has Flown the Bird of Twilight?, 1966). He has also produced a number of other works, among which should be noted the play *Di-Mana Bulan Selalu Retak?* (Why is the Moon Always Cracked?, 1965); a collection of letters to his wife from overseas, *Warkah kepada Salmi Manja* (1965); and, in cooperation with Usman Awang, a series of reprinted essays on modern Malay literature, *Tema dan Tugas delam Kesusasteraan Melayu Moden* (1963).

Trans.: SMB. WRR

Sāmaveda, one of the four books of the **Veda.**

sandesa, Sinhalese term for a type of poem of which Kālidāsa's (qv) *Meghadūta* is an example. In Sinhalese these poems all follow the same general pattern: a chosen messenger (in the classical *sandesas*, this is invariably a bird) is first appealed to; then follows a detailed description of the route, occupying most of the poem, and finally a relatively unimportant message. The scene is always set in Ceylon, and hence these poems provide considerable data about the geography and history of Ceylon. The form was established before 1200, but the earliest surviving example, *Tisara sandesa*, was written about 1350. During the following century six other classical *sandesas* were written, namely *Mayūra sandesa*, *Parevi sandesa*, *Sælalihini sandesa*, *Kōkila sandesa*, *Haṃsa sandesa* and *Girā sandesa*. The form continued to be practised up to the early 20th century, and until then made up virtually the only purely secular genre in Sinhalese poetry.

CHBR

sandiwara, Indonesian literary drama and theatrical form, which arose in 1920's; it is influenced by European drama. Written and played in Indonesian, it contributed to the emergence of Malayan *sandiwara* (before World War II) and Javanese (after 1960). It was preceded by *tonel* and *komedi* in Indonesia and *bangsawan* (qv) in Malaya. *Sandiwara* symbolized the struggle for independence, a uniform language and modern society. It resembles European drama, free of the traditional Asian structure which is so marked in *bangsawan* and still visible in *tonel.* Social and pseudo-historical themes predominate; the traditional figure of the clown is missing. *Sandiwara* is based on literary drama. This has brought about a shift in emphasis in the acting (away from improvisation), a simplification of structure and a modernization of the stage. Dramas are still published in Indonesia and Malaya largely in the form of stories written up from the cyclostyled plays on which performances are based. U. T. Sontani followed by younger Indonesian writers (eg W. S. Rendra) publishes his plays as short tales. Far more plays were published in Malaysia after 1960, but they still often appear in short story form (see Usman Awang). Indonesian plays by Rustam Effendi, Andjar Asmar, Usmar Ismail, U. T. Sontani, A. and S. Pané (qv) are adapted direct for Malayan *sandiwara*, or Malayan editions are used. In Indonesia the modern literary drama, stabilized by Armijn Pané (qv) and Sanusi Pané, appears more frequently as broadcast drama than on the stage; radio and television contribute to the modernization of *sandiwara* both as a theatrical form and as a literary genre.

Claire Holt, *Art in Indonesia: Continuities and Change* (Ithaca 1967); James R. Brandon,

Theatre in Southeast Asia (Cambridge 1967); TMIL. EV

Śaṅkara (8th–9th centuries), Indian philosopher and theologian, the greatest Monist commentator and interpreter of the Vedānta. An orthodox Brahmin from Southern India, he believed in the absolute authority of the *Veda* (qv) and attempted to explain the contradictions in what is taught by the existence of two truths (a lower truth for the ordinary believer and a higher truth for the initiated) and by illusion (*māyā*), which hinders recognition of the highest reality (*brahma*); this is close (in his conception of it) to the *nirvāṇa* of Mahāyāna Buddhism. Śaṅkara's chief work is his extensive commentary on Bādarāyaṇa's *Vedānta-sūtras* (*Śārīrakamīmāṃsābhāṣya*) and his commentaries on the earliest *upaniṣads* (qv) in which he does not explain the text itself, but bases on it an exposition of his own teachings. In form, too, his work is more of an interpretation than a commentary, with long sentences, involved constructions, etc. The most popular of his works is still his commentary on the *Bhagavadgītā* (qv), again more of an independent treatise, drawing evidence in support of the author's teachings from the text it purports to comment on. Devotional *stotras* (hymns of praise to the various gods of the Hindu pantheon) are also traditionally attributed to Śaṅkara. He is still considered the highest religious authority for Hinduism; he is far more of a theologian than a philosopher. His works exerted a profound influence on the literature of his successors, followers of the Advaita (ie, non-dualist) philosophy. This influence is shown in particular through the stress he laid on the emotional aspects of religious expression, the need to assimilate alien elements into Hinduism, and the propagation of religious principles suited to the level and the position of the faithful.

Trans.: G. Thibaut, *Śārīrakamīmāṃsābhāṣya* (Oxford 1890 and 1896); W. Norman Brown, *The Saundaryalaharī or Flood of Beauty* (HOS 43, 1958); P. Deussen, *Die Sūtra's des Vedānta* (Leipzig 1887). S. Dasgupta, *A History of Indian Philosophy*, 2 vols. (Cambridge [2]1932), I, 406–94, II, 1–227. IF

Śaṅkara Kuṟuppu, G. (b 1901), Malayalam poet. A schoolteacher and later professor of Malayalam, he started writing poetry at an early age. His first works were nature poems and largely imitative of the work of Kerala's Romantic poets. As he developed, mysticism and symbolism became prominent features of his verse. A patriot, he was inspired by the work of Gandhi to turn his poetry to the service of the movement for Indian independence, a movement which he saw as offering benefits not only for his country but for all mankind. The attainment of this goal did not diminish his interest in the world around him and he has continued to write poems both on social and political themes and on the implications of the advance of scientific knowledge. He has also translated poetry into Malayalam, including Tagore's (see Ṭhākur) *Gītāñjali.* Main works: *Sūrykānti* (The Sunflower, 1946); *Muttukaḷ* (Pearls, 1946); *Ōṭakkuḻal* (The Flute, 1950); *Nimiṣam* (The Moment, 1945); *Viśvadarśanam* (Vision of the Universe, 1960).

GSML 161–6, 241–7; PNHML 232–8. REA

Śaṅkaradeva (b 1449 Alipukhuri, d 1569 Cooch Behar), Assamese poet and Vaiṣṇava reformer. Of aristocratic family, he was given a thorough education in Sanskrit, which he used in some of his writing; he completed his education at the age of 22. He made long journeys through northern and southern India, visiting places of pilgrimage and discussing religious matters with many Vaiṣṇava teachers of various trends, such as Caitanya. Śaṅkaradeva wrote about 30 books, mostly in Assamese, to make his Vaiṣṇava teaching accessible to the uneducated. He was strongly influenced by the *Bhāgavata Purāṇa* (qv), a part of which he also translated into Assamese, in an interpretative way. This book provided him with subjects for many original writings, such as *Nimi nava saṃvāda* (Nimi's Nine Discussions), on doctrinal points, *Guṇamālā* (Garland of Praises), hymns to Viṣṇu and Kṛṣṇa,

Kīrtana, a collection of 26 poems propounding the doctrine of *bhakti* (qv), to be recited at religious gatherings, and *Līlāmālā*, 107 stanzas recounting incidents of Kṛṣṇa's life.

Another source of Śaṅkara's inspiration was the *Rāmāyaṇa* (qv), the last canto of which (*Uttara kāṇḍa*) he also freely rendered into Assamese, introducing many native folk elements. Besides his epics, Śaṅkaradeva's lyrical *Baragīta* (Devotional Songs) and one-act plays were influential among the mass of the people. The plays deal with subjects similar to those in his epics, eg *Kāli-damana* (Subjugation of Kāli) retells a Kṛṣṇaite story, and *Rāma-vijaya* (Victory of Rāma) an incident from *Rāmāyaṇa*. In these plays, verse greatly predominates over prose; the descriptive parts are related by the director of the play (*sūtradhāra*). Śaṅkaradeva is rightly considered the greatest representative of mediaeval Assamese literature. Innumerable successors were directly influenced by his ideas and poetic style, characterized by novelty of expression, rhythmic fluency and good characterization. No less valuable is his contribution to the formation of the Assamese literary language.

B. K. Barua, *Studies in Early Assamese Literature* (Nowgong 1953), pp. 1–59. DZ

Santos, Lope K. (b 1879 Pasig, Rizal, d 1963), one of the first Filipino fiction writers in Tagalog. Although highly praised by literary critics, he devoted more time to public life than to pursuing a literary career. His themes are social justice, the best example being *Banaag at Sikat* (Rays and Sunrise, 1906), considered the first social novel in Tagalog. Santos also wrote poetry, mostly sentimental in character. A philologist, he specialized in the Tagalog language; his Tagalog grammar is still popular. During the Japanese occupation he was the head of the Institute of the National Language. Other works: novels, *Kundangan* (Respect, 1927), *Alila ng Kapalaran* (A Slave to Fate, 1932); collections of poetry, *Puso at Diwa* (Heart and Soul), *Sino ka? Ako'y Si* (Who are You? I am . . .), *Mga Hamak na Dakila* (The Humble Who are Great), *Ang Panggingera* (A Card-Player). EH

Santos, N. Bienvenido (b 1911 Manila), Filipino writer of fiction and poetry using English. Author of two novels: *Villa Magdalena* (1965) and *The Volcano* (1965); collections of short sories: *You Lovely People* (1955) and *The Day the Dancers Came* (1967); poems: *Wounded Stag* (1956). EH

Sao-Nam, Vietnamese writer, see **Phan-boi-Chau.**

Sarabhai, Bharati (b 1912), Indian playwright writing in English; her mother tongue is Gujarati. Educated at Bombay university, she is principal of Shreyas College, Ahmedabad. The only woman playwright in English who has had some success. *The Well of the People* (1943), a poetic pageant (there are no changes of scene) is symbolic, a contribution to the Gandhian social order. It arose from the author's visit to the Haridwar Kumbhamela in 1938 (she was an active member of the Indian National Congress) and a true story that appeared in *Harijan* (ed. Gandhi) of an old lady who, unable to go to the Mela, spent her hard-won savings in digging a village well for the benefit of the poor. *Two Women* (1952) is realistic, written in clipped prose. The political touches are real and even the spiritual atmosphere is associated with visible objects in the drawing-room of Kanak Raya. One part of the room is modern, decorated with imports from the West, the other corner is marked by a figure of the god Kṛṣṇa and flowers. Sarabhai has been influenced by W. B. Yeats and T. S. Eliot.

Prema Nandakumar, *B. Sarabhai's English Plays* (CEIWE 249–70); IWE 188–203. MED

Sarmad Kāshāni, Sa'īd (d 1661 Agra), Indo-Persian mystical poet, son of an Armenian Jewish merchant. He was one of the free-thinkers round Dārā Shikōh (qv) and was condemned to death for heresy. Several hundred of his mystical quatrains have come down to us. They are of a pantheistic nature and attempt a rapprochement between Islam and Hinduism.

HIL 728–9. JM

Sarsgār, Ratan Nāth (b 1846 Lucknow, where d 1902), Urdu writer, journalist, and pioneer of the novel. His most famous work is *Fasāna-e Āzād* (The Tale of Āzād), which first appeared serially in the weekly paper which he edited, and then (1880) in four large volumes totalling about two million words. It owes much to the *dāstāns* (qv), but its hero is the champion of the New Light of Westernization, and the overtly supernatural element is discarded. There are vivid, realistic pictures of the 19th century scene in Lucknow, and much broad humour.

CNI 110–17; MSHUL 326–38; SDUN 31–40. RR

Sarūr, Rajab 'Alī Beg (b 1787 Lucknow, d 1867 Benares), Urdu writer of the rhyming, rhythmical prose which in his day still contested with that of Mīr Amman (qv). His most famous work is *Fasāna-e 'Ajā'ib* (Tale of Wonders, written 1825/6, published 1845/6), a short tale of love, enchantment, adventure and romance in the tradition of the *dāstāns* (qv), but in more sophisticated style and language.

CNI 105–6; SDUN 27–30; RSHUL 257–62. RR

Sarvajña (c1700), most popular of Kannada gnomic poets, comparable to Tiruvaḷḷuvar (qv) in Tamil, and Vēmana in Telugu. He composed hundreds of lovingly-quoted proverbial wisdom-poems in *tripadis* (3-line Kannada folk-form) each carrying his name. They are witty, simple, wise, often bitter or crude, always memorable aphorisms, on good and evil in kingship, society, family, and individual character; they attack injustice and hypocrisy in caste and class. AKR

Sarvajñamitra, ancient Indian poet, see **Buddhist literature.**

śāstra (500 BC to the present), Indian scientific treatise. In its broadest sense, this Sanskrit term denotes a science of any nature, mathematics, iconography, astrology, etc. By extension, it refers to a treatise on that science, usually composed in Sanskrit verse or a combination of verse and prose. *Śāstras* are characterized by a tendency to classify, categorize, and enumerate topics in a highly artificial manner, often postulating non-existent possibilities for the sake of symmetry. Important *śāstras* exist on the subjects of *dharma* (qv), law, grammar (by Pāṇini, qv, and others), erotics (the *Kāmasūtra* by Vātsyāyana, qv), poetics (the science of *alaṃkāraśāstra*, qv), drama (the *Nātyaśāstra*, qv, of Bharata), and politics (the *Arthaśāstra* of Kauṭilya, qv), as well as medicine, magic, palm-reading, and hundreds of other topics. *Śāstras* are still composed, often in Sanskrit, in India today, and a learned man is a *śāstrī*, one who knows the *śāstras*. WOF

Śatapatha-Brāhmaṇa, see **brāhmaṇa** and **Veda.**

Sathāpanawat, Srirat (b 1918 Suphanburī, central Thailand), Thai writer. He began to study law at the Thammasat university, but did not finish because of financial difficulties. Before settling down as a writer, he tried forestry, tobacco farming, tin mining and other jobs in the south as well as in the far north of Thailand. This brought him into close contact with the working class, and the plight of the poor in the country far from Bangkok. For ten years he has been working as a journalist on a local Thai daily. Srirat made good use of his deep understanding of poor people in his novels and short stories. His aim was to make the rich and well-to-do understand the life of the socially underprivileged. An impressive figure often portrayed in his books is the mother in her relation to her child, especially in short stories like *Māē ca nū hiu* (Mother, I am Hungry) and *Māē ca . . . phọ pai nai* (Mother . . . Where is Father ?). The language in these short stories is strong and pregnant, catching the heart of the reader. The weak position of women exploited by men, husband or rich 'protector', is the main subject of some of his best novels, eg *Phrung nī tọng mī arun rung* (Tomorrow Will Be Another Sunrise, 1959) and *Cāk nan . . . con nirandon* (From Now on to Eternity, 1962). The plot is serious, the atmosphere sad and the language straightforward and simple. Srirat also shows talent for satirical description, criticizing human characteristics he does not approve of, as in *Müeng thāt* (A City of Slaves, 1955) and *Thāt chīwit* (The Life of a Slave, 1965).

GLUTR 125, 132–41. US

Satyanārāyaṇa, Wiśwanātha (b 1895), Telugu writer and poet. No Telegu writer of the 20th century has excelled Wiśwanātha in creative writing either in quality or quantity. He may be said to be the most outstanding writer in Telugu today. There is no literary genre to which he has not abundantly contributed in his own inimitable style. Holding views frequently running counter to those of contemporary society, he is known as one of the most controversial figures among modern Telugu writers. His disciples are spread all over Andhra, adoring and admiring him more as an institution than as an individual. His earlier writing is marked by a lyrical spontaneity which is lacking in his later works. His writing has an evocative quality of great depth which has brought him a large number of imitators. His translation of the great epic *Rāmāyaṇa* (qv) in conventional (verse and prose) style reads like an original poem of excellent craftsmanship. Main works: *Wēyipaḍagalu* (A Thousand Hoods, 1932), a social novel translated also into Hindi; *Kinnerasāni pāṭalu* (Songs of the River Kinnerasāni, [4]1956), one of the greatest lyric poems of the 20th century in Telugu; *Rāmāyaṇakalpawṛkṣamu* (Rāmāyaṇa, the Celestial Tree, 1953–59), which won the Bhāratīya Jñānapīṭha award, 1971.

V. R. Narla, *Traditional Indian Culture and Other Essays* (Vijayawada 1969), pp. 135–8. BhK

Saudā, Mirzā Rafī' (b 1707 Delhi, d 1781 Lucknow), Urdu poet. He left Delhi in adult life for Farrukhabad, and ultimately for Lucknow. With Mīr (qv), he was the greatest poet of his time, and a master of many forms, but while Mīr excelled in the *ghazal* (see Vol. III), Saudā's greatest achievement was in other forms. He is famed for the panegyric ode (*qaṣīda*), a form in which he and Ẕauq (qv) alone among Urdu poets are generally held to have equalled the great Persian masters. To modern taste his most significant work is his satire, boisterous, ribald, biting poetry which gives a vivid picture of the conditions of his age. He assails his targets without any inhibition, often refusing to disguise their identity in any way, and castigating meanness, avarice, gluttony, sanctimoniousness, false pretension to learning or poetic skill, and every other kind of false or ungenerous conduct. Prominent officials and ministers, and even the Emperor himself are not spared; two sustained and savage poems survey the whole political, social and cultural scene of mid-18th century Mughal India.

Trans.: Henry Court, *Selections* (Simla 1872). RITMP 37–68; MSHUL 82–93; RSHUL 50–66. RR

Sedah (12th century, east Java), Javanese court poet, author of the epic *Bharata Yuddha Kakawin* (The Battle of the Bharatas), completed by the poet Panuluh. A paraphrase of the ancient Indian *Mahābhārata* (qv), it deals only with the last battle between the Pāṇḍus and the Kurus. The remaining parts of the *Mahābhārata* occur in Old Javanese as prose works (*parwa*). Like the *Ramayana Kakawin* (qv), the *Bharata Yuddha Kakawin* has inspired several generations of writers. Names and characters from old Javanese *kakawins* (see Kanwa) are found even in modern Indonesian prose, poetry and drama. The *Bharata* has 52 songs, in style comparable to the epic *Arjuna Wiwaha Kakawin*, but much more Javanese in its originality; it is still popular today in *wajang* (qv) and in a modern Javanese version (18th century) entitled *Serat Bratajuda*, by Jasadipura I (qv).

P. J. Zoetmoelder, *Kawi and Kakawin* (Amsterdam 1958); PLJ I, 178–9. EV

Sein Tin, U, Burmese writer, see **Wa,** Theippam Maun.

Seintatjothu U O, Burmese poet, see **Seinda Kyawthu.**

Seinda Kyawthu (Aw, U, 1736–1771), Burmese poet. Regarded as a child prodigy in his early years, he later became poet-laureate to Alaungpaya (1752–60), the founder of the new Konbaung dynasty, and it fell to him to write panegyrics for his master. He also composed several traditional poems, but his fame stemmed from his *yadu* (qv): he started where Nawade and Natshinnaung (qqv) left off, and he has been greatly underrated. His *yadu* are couched in simple and concise words which are at once emotive and evocative, eg two poems on the Maha Nanda Lake, and 'The Crow', 'A Dream', and 'A Military Campaign' describing the harrowing experiences of the Upper Burman soldiers in the wet, stormy and mosquito-infested delta region. HP

Sejarah Melayu (Malay Annals), probably the oldest of Malay historical works, it appears in the form in which it has gained principal currency (Raffles Ms. 18) to have been written in 1612. There is still scholarly argument over the possibility of an earlier date for the nucleus of this version (?1482, 1536), and, in consequence, concerning the probable nature of its predecessors (cf. R. W. Roolvink's introduction to the 1970 reprint of C. C. Brown's English translation of Raffles Ms. 18). The *Sejarah Melayu* is of both literary and historiographical importance, for though its authorship is uncertain it is written in general in a clear, vivid, narrative style, with much wit and colour; it clearly deals for most of its length with real historical persons. After early sections depicting in largely mythic terms the origins of the Malacca Sultanate (thus possessing substantial importance for the validation of elements of the Malay polity), the remainder of the work is principally devoted to the celebration of the history of that state during its hey-day and until its reduction to the Portuguese in 1511. Though, like all court literature, much concerned with high life and politics, it also succeeds in conveying in some measure the dust and bustle of fifteenth century south-east Asia's greatest port city. WRR

Sen, Samar (b 1916 Calcutta), Bengali poet. He received his MA in English at Calcutta University. He started his career as assistant editor of *Kabitā*, poetry quarterly, and translated into Bengali some works of Tolstoi and other Russian writers while in Moscow, 1957–61. He was editor of the leftist political journal, *Now*, and presently edits his own political journal, *Frontier*. Samar stopped writing poetry around the age of thirty. He now says poetry bores him. But during the years when he was writing and ever since then, his poetry has excited others. A Marxist philosophy is exhibited in his works. He wrote what is called 'prose-poetry' at a time when such poetry was still not accepted in Bengal as genuine literature. An anthology published by Tagore intentionally contains no prose-poetry; thus Sen's poetry was excluded. Since then his poems are found in almost every anthology of Bengali poetry. Works: *Kayeṭi kabitā* (Several Poems, 1937), *Tinpuruṣ* (Three Generations, 1944), *Samar Sener kabitā* (The Poetry of Samar Sen, 1954).

Trans.: P. Nandy, *The Complete Poems of Samar Sen* (Calcutta 1970); KMBP; BBV. SBMP; SHBL 374. CBS

Senāpati, Fakīrmohan (1847–1918), Oriya novelist and short-story writer, father of the Oriya novel. Son of a poor father, he had only basic education. He first worked as assistant of the supervisor of sail repairs in Balasore, then as a printer, journalist, minister. He translated the *Rāmāyaṇa* and the *Mahābhārata* (qqv) into modern Oriya, and wrote poetry and the first Oriya short stories. His best works, however, are his novels, mostly social in content with living figures of peasants, fishermen, weavers, servants and other representatives of the lowest strata. Such is his *Chamaṇa aṭhaguntha* (Six Acres and Eight Decimals) on the ageless conflict between the wealthy and the poor, told in a simple language full of vigorous colloquialisms, *Momu* (Maternal Uncle) and *Prāyaścitta* (Penance). *Lachma* is a historical novel on the Maratha raiders, and *Utkal bhraman* (Wanderings in Orissa) a travelbook in witty, lively verse.

Priyaranjan Sen, *Modern Oriya Literature* (Calcutta 1947). DZ

Senggono (20th century central Java), Javanese writer, critic and publisher, who popularized contemporary Javanese literature. He wrote studies on modern Javanese verse and the transition from traditional forms to the sonnet (see Subagijo), and exercised important influence on the development of Javanese literature; while classical works were mainly poetic (*tembang*), there were few prose works (*gantjaran*) until early 19th century, and the movement led by R. Ng. Ranggawarsita (qv) for the recognition of prose writing as literature was more rapidly successful than the introduction of new poetic forms. Javanese stories and novels drew on the chronicle tradition (see *Pararaton*, *Tantu Panggelaran*), folk tales and myths (*tjerita* and *hikayat*, qv). At the turn of the 19th century, novels found their readers; short stories in Javanese found a home in magazines, as anthologies of stories by one or more writers were rare in Indonesia. Senggono edited and published the first anthology of contemporary Javanese prose and verse, the debut of many of the finest writers. *Kemandang* (Echo, 1958) presented prose by Agrarini, Any Asmara, Basuki Rachmat, S. Dwiprasodjo, Hadi Kaswadi, S. G. Soekandar, Soemarno, S. Iesmaniasita (qv) and poetry by Liamsi, Moeljono Soedharmo, R. Noegroho, all born 1913–34. Senggono's own work deals with topical social and political questions; the migration of Javanese to Lampung on Sumatra, which roused public feeling, is the theme of his social novel, *Kembang Kantil* (Kantil Blossom, 1957). Senggono writes in colloquial Javanese (*ngoko*). EV

Setubandha (The Building of the Causeway), Māhārāṣṭrī epic by Pravarasena II Vākāṭaka (c410–440 AD), one of the finest Indian *kāvya* (qv) epics. The plot of the slaying of Rāvaṇa and rescue of Sītā is extracted from the *Rāmāyaṇa* (qv). Rāma, already in the far south of India with his monkey allies, receives news of his abducted wife in Laṅkā and prepares to attack. The central episode is the construction of a causeway to the island by the monkeys, a feat paralleled only by the difficulty of the battle which follows, where natural strength and a just cause eventually prevail over a better armed enemy. Pravarasena's *leitmotif* or 'mark' (*aṅka*) is 'devotion' (*anurāa*), loyalty in love and friendship. Though Rāma is an incarnation of Viṣṇu, he is humanized as much as possible and in his weakness and even despair he needs the devotion and leadership of his ally Sugrīva. The poem is characterized by heroic speeches and some rich descriptions of the mountain scenery. The climaxes are marked by long compounds.

Trans.: Goldschmidt (London 1880). AKW

Shahnon Ahmad (b 1933 Kampong Banggul Derpak, Sik, Kedah), Malay novelist and short-story writer. Educated in Malay and English, Shahnon was for many years a school-teacher, and more recently has been on the faculty of the Australian National University, Canberra. He began what has become a brilliant, if at times controversial and uneven, writing career in 1956, with the publication of short stories, often satirical of the self-important in the new Malay. They are about the largely urban, middle classes and are sometimes disapproved of by the critics and others for their frank and often sensational treatment of sexual themes. Many of the stories were subsequently collected in *Anjing-Anjing* (Dogs, 1964) and *Debu Merah* (Red Haze, 1965). From about 1963, he turned to more sympathetic treatment of larger themes, especially in relation to rural rather than urban life.

Between 1965 and 1969 he published no fewer than six novels. The first of these, *Rentong* (Burnt to a Cinder, 1965), explored social and personal relationships within a Kedah rice-farming village, with the central dramatic theme the conflict between two young men, representing in a manner the old and the new, the balance being held finally by the village headman, skilled in the calming of internecine dispute and restoring the harmony held desirable by tradition. A pleasant, often gently humorous, and self-contained story, *Rentong* was praised by the critics for its skilful handling of character and its realistic use of local dialect in the depiction of peasant society. It was followed by a completely different kind of work, a psychological novel in Western style, dealing once again with urban Malay middle-class life, and more particularly with the compelling and potentially destructive force of sexual desire. *Terdedah* (Agape, 1965) differs, however, from earlier short stories with similar themes in its attempt to work out with greater seriousness the implications of the human emotions encountered, and in its innovative use of interior monologue and psychoanalytical theory. In *Ranjau Sa-Panjang Jalan* (Obstacles along the Way, 1966), widely regarded as his finest novel to date, Shahnon returned again to village Kedah, presenting (at a somewhat deeper symbolic level than in the earlier *Rentong*) the struggles of a poor peasant family against the harshness of rural life itself, the inertia of tradition, and the self-interest of the land-owning class despite a façade of paternalism. Though possessing clear ideological undertones (or at least a passionate concern for more genuine leadership for the rural masses), the novel is less didactic than realistic, and portrays movingly the story of one family's tribulations.

Characteristically restless, Shahnon turned in his next novel, *Protes* (Protest, 1967), to the examination of religious themes, largely in the form of argument between the characters, and though the work is of some intellectual interest it has too little dramatic momentum, and the writing is somewhat arid, though technically well-handled. The remaining two novels published prior to 1970 are both political in content, *Menteri* (The Minister, 1967), and *Perdana* (Premier, 1969). *Menteri*, much the shorter of the two, deals in part with 'corruption' in politics and the bureaucracy, is bitterly satirical concerning constituted Malay leadership, and contains a remarkable section in which one of the characters finds himself, in dream, witnessing Malay subjugation to the Chinese in the year 1987, a section which has since been the subject of some literary controversy. *Perdana* is an attempt to come to grips with potentially one of the largest themes in contemporary Malay life, the post-war nationalist struggle and the achievement of independence. However, it is flawed by being too thinly disguised as an historical resumé of actual political events, and too little an artistic transmutation of the meaning of those years. WRR

sha'ir, Malay verse form of Arabo-Persian origin (Arabic *shi'r*, poetry or poem). Characterized by a uniform four-line stanza rhyming a-a-a-a, it is now thought to have originated c1600, probably with the Sumatran Sufi mystic Hamzah Pansuri, who used it extensively. *Sha'ir* are commonly didactic, discursive, or narrative, often running to several thousand stanzas in length. Early examples appear to have been confined in subject matter to Islamic theology but by the later 17th century the *sha'ir* was being used for rhymed histories (eg the *Sha'ir Perang Mengkasar*, Rhymed Chronicle of the Macassar War), the genre being further extended to popular tales and romances (eg *Sha'ir Ken Tambuhan*, Princess Ken Tambuhan; *Sha'ir Si Lindong Delima*, The Princess and the Pomegranate) and in the 19th century to reportage upon topical events (eg *Sha'ir Kampung Gelam Terbakar*, Ballad of the Kampung Gelam Fire, by the famous Abdullah bin Abdul Kadir, qv). WRR

Shamim, Muḥammad Iṣḥāq (b 1923), Baluchi poet writing also in Urdu, founder of the *Anjuman-e taraqqī-e Balūchān* (Association for the Progress of the Baluchis). His verses are imbued with national spirit and ardent devotion to his native country. He was the first to introduce regular *mushā'iras* (poetical competitions) in Baluchi. JM

Sharar, 'Abdu'l-ḥalīm (b 1860 Lucknow, where d 1926), Urdu journalist, novelist and popular historian. A prolific writer, he produced (and largely wrote himself) the periodical *Dilgudāz*, in which his most popular works appeared in serial form. They are quasi-historical romances extolling the bygone glories of Muslim civilization, generally to the detriment of contemporary Christendom. Numbers of these appeared between 1887 and 1907, including *Ḥasan aur Anjalīna*, *Manṣūr Mohanā*, and *Florā Florinḍā*. A supporter of the modernist movement of Sayyid Aḥmad K͟hān (qv), from whom he differed in his opposition to purdah, some of his tales, eg *Badru'n-Nisā kī Muṣībat* (1897), were written in furtherance of contemporary social aims. One, *Asrār-e Darbār-e Ḥarāmpūr*, is a sensational exposure of the depravities of court life in a fictitious princely state. His best historical work, *Guẕashta Lakhna'ū* (Past Lucknow, 1914–16), is a series of articles which make up a picture of the history and social and cultural life of old Lucknow.

CNI 122–32; SDUN 66–89; MSHUL 339–44. RR

Shibli Nu'mānī, Muḥammad (b 1857 Bindaul, d 1914 Azamgarh), Urdu historian, biographer, poet and literary critic. He received a traditional religious education, in 1904 became director of Nadvatu'l-'ulamā (Theological Academy) at Lucknow and in 1913 founded the Academy of Letters at Azamgarh. He worked out a programme of liberal reform of Islamic thought from within, proving through historical research that the early Islamic theologians had approved of rational philosophy. As author of a number of monographs on great figures of early Islamic history he laid the foundations for modern historical writing in Urdu. In his chief critical work *Shi'ru'l-'ajam* (Persian Poetry, 1908–18) in 5 volumes he examined Iranian literature mainly from the formal and philological aspect.

Trans.: Zafar Ali Khan, *Al-Farooq: Life of Omar the Great* (Lahore 1939, [3]1947).
Rustamji P. Bhajivala, *Maulana Shibli and Umar Khayyam* (Surat 1932); RSHUL 287–94; MSHUL 274–85. JM

Shinwārī, Amīr Ḥamza (b 1907 Lwaragi), Pashto poet and writer from the Khyber region in Pakistan. As a youth he was a *murīd*, ie a disciple of the local *sheikh* (local head of the mystical order). This left its mark on his verse, tending to Sufi symbolism. He wrote in Urdu at first, and later only in Pashto, mainly for the periodical *Pashtūn*; these articles were social and patriotic in theme. He is one of the organizers of Pashto literary life. He has been called the father of the Pashto *ghazal* (see Vol. III), which is free of the typical Persian poetic mannerism and themes. In 1941 he wrote the scenario for the first Pashto film, *Layla wa Majnūn*; his volume of poetry *Ghazawenē* (Awakening) appeared in 1956. JBe

Shwedaung Thihathu, Burmese writer, see **Yatana Kyemon.**

Si Mahōsot, Thai poet, see **nirāt.**

Si Prāt, Thai poet, see **Khlōng Kamsūon.**

Siddhānta, the Jain canon, see **Jain literature.**

siddhar, siddhas, see **cittar.**

Siddhicaran, Nepali poet, see **Śreṣṭha,** Siddhicaran.

Silva, John de (1854–1922), Sinhalese author of large numbers of musical plays which were popular in the early part of the 20th century but later fell into disfavour. CHBR

Silva, W. Abraham (1892–1957), Sinhalese author of novels and short stories; the first to gain wide popularity while using ordinary conversational language. CHBR

Sirisena, Piyadāsa (1875–1946), early Sinhalese novelist. His works are mostly protests against the tide of Westernism. His first and best-known novel was *Jayatissa and Roslin* (1906).

E. R. Sarathchandra, *The Sinhalese Novel* (Colombo 1967). CHBR

Śivadāsa, Sanskrit writer, see **Vetālapañcaviṃśatikā.**

Śivaśaṅkara Piḷḷa, Takaẓi (b 1914), Malayalam novelist. Trained in the law, Takaẓi has for most of his life devoted himself to writing. In his younger days he wrote verse, but soon realized that his real talent lay in the area of prose fiction. Considered by some to be primarily a short-story writer, the prolific Takaẓi has also written a large number of novels. All his work shows the influence, readily acknowledged, of the French 'realist' school. An early member of the Progressive Writers' Association (see *progressive writing*), Takaẓi has argued that a creative writer must be explicitly committed to the cause of social reform. His work, however, like that of Zola whom he greatly admires, has more lasting qualities than this might be taken to imply. His novels and stories have a great variety of theme and setting. Most of the best ones are set among the less fortunate sections of Kerala society. *Tōṭṭiyuṭe makan* (Scavenger's Son, 1947) tells of three generations of night-soil carriers, *Raṇṭiṭaṅṅaẓi* (Two Measures of Rice, 1948) of the harsh conditions of work of agricultural labourers and *Cemmīn* (Shrimps, 1956), his most famous book, of the poor fishermen of Kerala's coast. That Takaẓi's gifts are not restricted to descriptions of poverty is shown by *Eṇippatikaḷ* (Steps of the Ladder, 1966), a complex narrative of Kerala's political life.

Trans.: Narayana Menon, *Chemmeen* (London and New York 1962); M. A. Shakoor, *Two Measures of Rice* (Bombay 1967).
CNI 218–26; PNHML 133–5; 143–4; VISNM 33–42. REA

Śivasvāmin, Sanskrit poet, see **Buddhist literature.**

śloka (original meaning in Sanskrit, 'cry', 'praise', whence) 'verse' or 'strophe' in any metre, though the word has sometimes been used incorrectly for one metre in particular, the *vaktra* or *anuṣṭubh.* This popular error perhaps arose from the punning anecdote that the *śloka* was invented by Vālmīki (see *Rāmāyaṇa*), the 'First Kavi' (Bhavabhūti calls him), to express grief (*śoka*) at a tragic spectacle and thereby produce the 'compassionate' aesthetic experience (*Dhvanyāloka* I.5). The verse uttered by Vālmīki (*Rāmāyaṇa* I.2.14) happens to be in the *vaktra* metre. The original meaning of the anecdote, however, was that Vālmīki invented poetry, *padya*, ie verse in general, as Aśvaghoṣa (qv) tells us (*Buddhacarita* I.43). Since a *sloka* of the commonest metre, the *anuṣṭubh*, consists of 32 syllables, the term came to be used by scribes as a measure of length of the texts they copied, regardless of metres, and applied equally to prose. Thus the oldest extant recension of the Prajñāpāramitā, a prose text, is known as the 'Eight Thousand', meaning that it is supposed to contain 8,000 × 32 syllables. This unit of length is also called a *grantha*, 'knot', and the total is sometimes found in the colophons of manuscripts, serving as a basis for payment.

WHIL I, 61. AKW

smṛti (500 BC–500 AD), ancient Indian code of law. This Sanskrit term may be literally translated as 'Remembrance' and it refers to the code of social and religious law originally handed down orally (ie by 'memory') from generation to generation of human jurists and priests. In this it is to be contrasted with *śruti*, literally 'Hearing', which refers to the older, Vedic texts which are believed to have been 'heard' by revelation from divine inspiration. *Smṛti* purports to be a development and exegesis of *śruti*, than which it is more secular both in origin and in provenance, although both deal with the religious sphere of behaviour and may be subsumed under the term 'scripture'. The Hindu canon of sacred law as a whole is designated as *smṛti*, which may also be used to describe any one of the individual texts within that canon. Although some of these texts were probably originally composed as early as the time of Buddha, if not earlier, they have undergone such constant revision, incorporating the dissident views of various authorities, adjusting their provisions in order to accommodate new social developments, that it is extremely difficult to date a particular text with any certainty, although the broad chronological outlines of the canon as a whole are fairly clear.

Trans.: SBE Vols 2 and 4, *Sacred Laws of the Aryans* (G. Bühler), Vol. 7, *The Institutes of Vishnu* (J. Jolly), Vol. 25, *The Laws of Manu* (G. Bühler), Vols. 29 and 30, *The Grihya Sutras* (H. Oldenberg and F. Max Müller), Vol. 33, *The Minor Law Books* (J. Jolly).
P. V. Kane, *History of Dharmaśāstra* (Poona 1930–62). WOF

Soebagijo, Javanese poet, see **Subagijo,** Ilham Notodijo.

Somadeva (11th century Kashmir), Sanskrit poet, the author of the *Kathāsaritsāgara* (Ocean of the Streams of Story, between 1063–81). It is the best and the most popular version of the so-called Kashmiri recension of the lost *Bṛhatkathā* (see Guṇāḍhya). About 350 stories, fairy-tales and anecdotes are retold here in relatively simple and fluent verse, not overburdened with poetic images and word-play. The author was a skilful narrator, and though he obviously did not invent any story himself, he knew how to tell them to catch the listeners' attention and how to make full use not only of his poetic abilities but also his creative imagination. His book is also a rich source of information on the way of life in India at his time, on religions, castes, social relations, etc.

Trans.: C. H. Tawney, *The Kathá Sarit Ságara, or Ocean of the Streams of Story*, 2 vols. (Calcutta 1880–84); reprinted, with the addition of numerous notes, essays, etc, by N. M. Penzer, 10 vols. (London 1924–28).
J. S. Speyer, *Studies about the Kathāsaritsāgara* (Amsterdam 1908); WHIL III, 353–65. DZ

Sot Sarun, Cambodian writer, see **pralomlok.**

Śrautasūtra, Vedic ritual handbooks, see **vedāṅga** and **sūtra.**

Śreṣṭha, Siddhicaran (b 1912 Okhaldhunga, eastern Nepal), Nepali poet, has lived mainly in Kathmandu, where, throughout the whole of his life, he has been engaged in various literary activities. For seven years he was co-editor of the Nepali newspaper *Gorkhā Patr* and for a long time edited the literary magazine *Śāradā*. The language of his poetry is simple and colloquial and his work represents the first Nepali attempt at realism. Because of the revolutionary ideas contained in his poem *Varṣā* (Rain, 1940), he was jailed for five years and during the time of the Rāṇā régime much of his work was suppressed. So far he has published three volumes of verse. DJM

Sri (real name B. M. Srīkaṇthayya, 1884–1946), a professor of English and passionate lover of Kannada. He inspired a renaissance in Kannada poetry by his translations of English romantic lyrics in *Ingliṣ Gītagaḷu* (English Poems, 1926), introducing poets like Wordsworth, Shelley, Burns, and new metres and poetic diction to a new generation. His spirited prose-poems on the mother-tongue, his anthology of Kannada verse (*Kannaḍa Bāvuṭa*, A Kannada Banner, 1938), his experimental verse-adaptation of *Ajax* from the Greek to *Mahābhārata* (qv) characters in *Asvatthāman* (1930), as well as his personal presence and patriotic-literary lectures gave new life to Kannada poetry and Kannada studies. AKR

Śri Śri, Telugu poet, see **Śriniwāsarāw,** Śrīraṅgam.

Śriharṣa (1), Sanskrit dramatist, see Harṣa.

Śriharṣa (2) (late 12th century AD), Sanskrit poet, author of the *Naiṣadha-carita*, a lengthy and most elaborate *mahākāvya* on the story of the *Nalopākhyāna* (qv). JB

Srikaṇthayya, B. M., Kannada poet and translator, see **Sri.**

Śrinivāsa, Kannada writer, see **Veṅkatesa Ayyangār.**

Śriniwāsarāw, Śrīraṅgam (b 1910 Visakhapatnam), Telugu poet. Śrī Śrī, as he is popularly known, wrote his first poem at the age of seven and first novel at the age of nine. Graduating in 1931, he never held any stable job. For some years now he has been working as a cinema script-writer. His sixtieth birthday was celebrated throughout the State. He heralded the beginning of a new school of poetry in Telugu literature in the mid-fifties, known as *abhyudayakawitwam* (progressive poetry, see *progressive writing*), and in 1970 became the first president of the newly formed Revolutionary Writers' Association (*Wiplawa racayitala saṅgham*). At a time when contemporary poetry preferred a highly romantic approach to life he was the only poet to champion the cause of the downtrodden in short and suggestive poems of great vigour and beauty. He has also the distinction of having brought the beauty of spoken Telugu into the writing of great poetry. According to one critic 'He took the Telugu world of letters by storm, compelling even diehards to acknowledge his astounding mastery of diction and metre.' Although a committed writer devoted to a Marxist transformation of society, and a leader of the militant group of young poets, he has written poetry which transcends the bounds of purely committed writing with a universal appeal and lasting significance. His poems have been translated into English, Russian, Czech and Hindi. His book of poems, *Khaḍgasṛṣṭi* (Creation of/by the Sword, 1966), won him the Lenin Prize in the USSR.

Trans.: K. V. Ramana Reddy, *Sri Sri Miscellany*. A Collection of English writings (Vijayawada 1970). BhK

Śriraṅga, Kannada playwright, see **Rangācārya,** Ādya.

Śrivāstav, Dhanpatrāy, Hindi writer, see **Premcand.**

śruti, see **smṛti.**

Subagijo, Ilham Notodidjo (b 1924 Blitar), Javanese journalist, poet and writer. He studied at Djakarta Arts Faculty and the Moslem University, Jogjakarta. He edited *Api Merdeka*, *Djiwa Islam*, *Panjebar Semangat* and *Tjrita Tjekak*, and wrote for many other periodicals active in the fight against Holland 1945–49. Shortly before World War II Subagijo and R. Intojo set in motion the transition from traditional Javanese poetic forms to more modern ones, eg the sonnet. While modernization progressed in Indonesian literature from the twenties, in Javanese literature it was a generation late, for here poetic tradition was based on highly cultivated classical forms; the *kakawin* (see Kanwa), *matjapat* and *kidung* had undergone changes as early as late 18th-early 19th century, but new forms were slow to take root; to this day poets use the old forms to a much greater degree than in Europe (see Iesmaniasita). Free verse, the sonnet and other new forms found poets and readers in Javanese only in the thirties, to a larger extent. Subagijo's poetry (*Gelenging tekad*, United, 1949) and stories treat patriotic themes, the struggle against colonialism, and the ideals of freedom. His prose uses a laconic journalistic style, and his heroes react resolutely to extreme situations. Both in poetry and prose he uses colloquial Javanese, while some journalistic and political writings are in Indonesian. EV

Subandhu (c first quarter of 7th century AD), Sanskrit prose writer, author of the *Vāsavadattā*, an ornate euphuistic romantic tale. If, as is probable, the *Vāsavadattā* mentioned by Bāṇa (qv) is Subandhu's work, he may have been a near-contemporary of Bāṇa, since other arguments indicate that he cannot be dated very much earlier. It should be noted that the heroine Vāsavadattā is not the famous queen of the same name in the legend of King Udayana which recurs in many Sanskrit works (see, eg, Harṣa). Possibly both the plot and the name of the heroine are due to the invention of the author, but this remains uncertain. The plot itself is a simple love-story, which is related at enormous length. In his use of elaborate and lengthy compounds, interminable sentences with epithet piled upon epithet, abstruse double-senses, and a vocabulary bristling with rare words and meanings, Subandhu rivals or even surpasses Bāṇa in this genre of difficult and complex prose-*kāvya*.

Trans.: L. H. Gray (New York 1913).
KHSL 307–13; DHSL 217–25. JB

Subrahmanya, Bharati C., Tamil poet, see **Pārati,** Cuppiramaṇiyam Ci.

Śūdraka (perhaps 3rd-4th centuries AD), Indian dramatist. Nothing is known of his life; in the prologue of his only known play, *Mṛcchakaṭikā* (The Little Clay Cart), he is introduced as a king, but he has not yet been identified by solid historical proofs. His name, if not a mere soubriquet or pseudonym, suggests a low social origin (its literal meaning is 'little *śūdra*'). His drama is undoubtedly one of the most excellent and interesting of Indian dramas. The author has probably rewritten the four preserved acts of Bhāsa's (qv) *Daridracārudatta* and completed the play, which is a love story of the impoverished Brahmin Cārudatta and the courtesan Vasantasenā, with the political motif of a palace revolution added as a means to restore the hero's fortune. In many respects, the drama deviates from the rules governing dramatic creation in ancient India, and for this reason has never been valued highly in India. Its dramatic and aesthetic qualities, however, the vivid portrayal of not only the hero and heroine but also of minor characters, witty dialogue, skilful heightening of dramatic tension, well balanced by lyrical and humorous interludes, make it a real gem of Indian literature. Last but not least, the *Mṛcchakaṭikā* is a rich source of information for a student of social life in ancient India.

Trans.: H. H. Wilson, *Select Specimens of the Theatre of the Hindus* (London 1827); J. A. B. van Buitenen, *The Little Clay Cart*, in *Two Plays of Ancient India* (New York and London 1968).
G. V. Devasthali, *Introduction to the Study of Mṛcchakaṭikā* (Poona 1951); G. K. Bhat, *Preface to Mṛcchakaṭikā: The Little Clay Cart* (Ahmedabad 1953); WHIL III, 224–32. DZ

Śukasaptati (Seventy [Tales] of the Parrot, c12th century AD), Sanskrit collection of tales and anecdotes. The merchant Madanasena, before leaving for a business trip, asks his parrot to prevent his wife from being untrue to him; the clever bird does it by narrating a story to the wife every time she wants to meet her lover. The tales are often frivolous, with a thin veil of morality expressed in didactic verses accompanying the prose narratives. The book was early translated into Persian and became known under the title of *Tūtīnāme* (see Vol. III). Several recensions in Sanskrit are a testimony to the popularity of the book.

Trans.: R. Schmidt, *Die Śukasaptati. Textus Ornatior* (Stuttgart 1899).
WHIL III, 377–82. DZ

Sunthọn Phū, Thai poet, see **nirāt** and **Phra Aphaimanī.**

Surāngkhanāng, K. (pseudonym of Kanhā Khīengsiri, b 1911 Bangkok), Thai writer. Of noble family, she was educated in English and French; a teacher of Thai, she even taught the royal princesses for a time. She displays profound social consciousness, portraying the negative side and the defects of modern society in a realistic way. One of her famous novels, for example, deals with the deplorable life of a prostitute, *Ying khon chūa* (The Prostitute, 1937); it was so successful that it was filmed. Her writing shows a sensitive power of observation. Some of her novels are strongly moralistic, like *Bān sāi thọng* (The Golden Sand House, 1955) and *Thāng sāi plīau* (The Lonely Way, 1950).

Trans.: *The Grandmother*, in: *Thai Short Stories* (Bangkok 1964).
GLUTR 83–4, 111–14. US

Sūranna, Piṃgali (16th century), Telugu poet, author of *Kalāpūrṇodayamu* (1585 AD). It is a comedy of errors, in which the celestial trouble-maker, Nārada, causes impersonations of two heavenly lovers, Raṃbhā and Nalakūbara. The counterfeit of each falls in love with the true of the other. JRM

Sūrdās (b c?1480), Hindi poet. According to unsubstantiated traditions of the Vallabha sect, he was a contemporary of Vallabha; after joining Vallabha's sect he lived in the district of Braj, near Mathura. Sūr is one of the earliest exponents of Kṛṣṇa devotionalism (see *bhakti*) in medieval Hindi literature. His huge *Sūrsāgar*

(Ocean of Sūr's Verse), an adaptation of the *Bhāgavata Purāṇa* (qv) into Braj Bhāṣā verse, dwells on the tales of Kṛṣṇa's childhood in Braj and especially on the love he inspires among the village herdgirls (*gopīs*). The devotee is encouraged to find the same love for Kṛṣṇa in his heart as did Kṛṣṇa's foster parents. The herdgirls' love, though presented in predominantly physical terms, is an allegory of the soul's love for the divine. Sūr's songs show a compelling mastery of rhythm and a natural grace of language which, with his recurrent theme of devotion to Kṛṣṇa, make him one of the finest poets in Hindi literature.

Trans.: Ch. Vaudeville, *Pastorales* (Paris 1971). RSM

Suri, Maṇikyacandra, Gujarati poet, see **pada.**

sūtra ('thread', then 'a short rule', 'aphorism'), Sanskrit formula expressing the meaning in the smallest possible number of words. Literary works consisting of such aphorisms, also called *sūtras*, arose for practical reasons; a condensed summary of knowledge in *sūtra* form was easy for students to learn by heart. The oral tradition among old Indian scholars required that these aphorisms were as short as possible. The grammarian Patañjali (qv) is often quoted, that when a *sūtra*-author saves half a short vowel he is as happy as if a son had been born to him. The aphorisms were learnt by heart and the teacher added an oral commentary. The commentaries as later recorded form a special type of literature. Commentaries on commentaries are not unusual. The *sūtras* were sometimes over-concise and could be explained in different, even contradictory, ways; this later gave rise to different schools (eg the branches of Vedānta explaining the *Brahmasūtras* of Bādarāyaṇa).

The *Śrautasūtras* and the *Gṛhyasūtras* are connected with Vedic ritual, the former with public rites, especially the fire sacrifice, new and full moon sacrifice, the seasons sacrifice, animal sacrifice and Soma sacrifice. The *Gṛhyasūtras* discussed everyday domestic ceremonies and those connected with the life of each individual (birth, name-giving, the first meal, cutting the boy's hair, introduction to the teacher, etc). The *Śulvasūtras* (connected with the *Śrautasūtras*) gave rules for building the sacrificial altar. The *Dharmasūtras*, explaining the *dharma* (rights, duties, ethics, etc) in a way continued the *Gṛhyasūtras.*

The *sūtra* style was used for all scientific disciplines, of which grammar, lexicography, philosophy, the science of law, politics, erotics, medicine, astronomy and mathematics were recognized in ancient India. In Buddhist canonical literature, the term *sūtra* (Pāli *sutta*) is used quite differently, and designates texts, many of them very long and discursive in style, being doctrinal discussions and dialogues purporting to contain the teaching of the Buddha (see *Tripiṭaka*). The Jaina canon also contains a number of texts named *sutta.*

A. Weber, *The History of Indian Literature* (London 1914); WHIL I, 268ff. JV

Śvetāśvatara-Upaniṣad, see **upaniṣads.**

Swaminath Aiyar, Tamil philologist, see **Cuvāminãta Aiyar.**

Syed Ahmad Khan, Urdu writer, see **Aḥmad K͟hān,** Sir Sayyid.

T

Tagore, see **Ṭhākur.**

Takdir, Indonesian writer, see **Alisjahbana,** Sutan Takdir.

Ṭālib 'Āmulī (b 1590 Mazandaran, d 1627 Ahmedabad), Indo-Persian poet-laureate of the Emperor Jahangir. His lyric *ghazals* (see Vol. III) abounding in unusual parallels and delicate metaphors, as well as his panegyrics in praise of the prophet Muhammad or the dignitaries of the court, are highly esteemed in India. His epic chronicle *Jahāngīr-nāma* narrates the events of the emperor's reign. His style is natural and far removed from the highly coloured artifices of his contemporaries. He was master of the miniature adventure novel in verse-form.

HIL 725–6. JM

Tan-Da (real name Nguyen-khac-Hieu, b 1888 Khe-thong, Son-tay province, d 1939 Hanoi), Vietnamese poet. After completing his studies he became a writer and journalist, editing *Huu-thanh* (Friendly Voice, 1921) and *An-nam tap chi* (Annam Revue, 1926). Besides poetry he wrote novels (which were more in the nature of collections of essays), theatrical plays, and translations. He wrote most from 1918 to 1928, and is acknowledged as one of the greatest Vietnamese poets of the early 20th century. He defended the rules of classical poetry against the criticism of the 'new poetry' school (see The-Lu). His work is permeated by sorrow, anxiety, dream and escape, but informed by ardent patriotism. His prose writing, as yet in no distinct genre, was the predecessor of the modern novel in North Vietnam, the first real Vietnamese novel appearing there in 1925. Works: poetry, *Khoi tinh con* (Lesser Loves, 1916); *Khoi tinh lon* (Great Loves); prose, *Giac mong con* (Little Dreams, I, 1917, II, 1932); *Giac mong lon* (Great Dreams, 1932, an autobiography); *The non nuoc* (Pledge to My Native Land, 1932); *Than tien* (The Devil of Money, 1921).

DNILVN 213–15. VV

Tantrākhyāyikā, ancient Indian collection of tales, see **Pañcatantra.**

tantras, Indian sacred books of the Śākta Hindu sect. They probably originated in Bengal, 5th–6th century, and spread to Assam and Nepal. These creations of the theologians are a mixture of philosophy and the occult, mysticism and magic, ritual and ethics. Usually in the form of a dialogue between the two gods, Śiva and Pārvatī, those in which the goddess asks questions and Śiva answers in the role of teacher being called *āgamas*, and those in which Śiva asks and Pārvatī is the teacher, *nigamas*. For the most part the authors were second-rate writers using barbaric Sanskrit, but the *tantras* are still very much in ritual use not only throughout India but in China and Tibet as well; they came here through Buddhism, into which they began to penetrate in the 7th–8th century. In Buddhism the *tantras* are the literature of the Mantrayāna and Vajrayāna, differing from the Śākta *tantras* by their elements of Buddhist thought and in many other respects. The Buddhist *tantras* fall into four groups: *kriyā-tantras* dealing with rites for the building of temples, raising of monuments, etc; *caryā-tantras* teaching the practical aspects of worship; *yoga-tantras* dealing with yoga-training; *anuttarayoga-tantras* discussing higher mysticism. For the most part they are unpublished, and are therefore little known in the West.

Trans.: H. G. Tattabhusan, *Kāmaratna Tantra* (Shillong 1928); A. Avalon, *Mahānirvāṇa-Tantra* (Madras 1953); D. L. Snellgrove, *The Hevajra Tantra*, 2 vols. (London 1959).
S. C. V. Bhattachārya, *Principles of Tantra. The Tantrasattva* (ed. by A. Avalon, Madras 1952). EM

Tantu Panggelaran (Genesis of the World, c15th century, east Java), an Old Javanese historical prose text, incorporating legends and myths, the anonymous work probably of a Śivaite hermit-monk. It opens with an account of the founder of the religious community in East Java. The myths are partly Indian, partly native, handed down for many generations by word of mouth. It is probably the earliest text to record native Javanese myths. At first popular in Java, later in Bali; the language is close to modern Javanese. The text gives the popular treatment of original and borrowed material, and shows the different ways in which court literature and folk literature treat ancient Indian themes. Among the most attractive myths are those of the origin of the island of Java and the first kingdom, the story of Śiva drinking all the poison in the world, Viṣṇu fighting the demon Rāhu for the nectar, the cause of regular eclipses of the sun and moon.

PLJ I, 119–23. EV

Taungdwin U Tha, Burmese poet, see **Yatana Kyemon.**

Taya, Dagoun (Htei Myain, U, b 1919 Thainku Myistan), Burmese poet, writer, literary critic and editor. He studied history and Burmese literature at Rangoon University, and was active in the student movement in 1936–40. In 1946–50 he edited the *Taya* literary magazine. He was active in the Union of Burmese Writers and in the Peace Movement, and was jailed by the military government in 1964–67. Taya started writing in the classical tradition, but was later influenced by *Khitsam* (see Zodji); he further developed its style and form. After the war he advocated a new type of people's literature aiming at socialist realism (*Sapeithis*, New Literature Movement). His short stories and novels are critical studies of the attitudes of the petty bourgeoisie in conflict with revolution. Works: poetry, *Sape u* (Spring Blossom, 1961); novels, *Myain* (1949) and *Tyapan yeisin* (Dew on Lotus, 1963); *Gandhalariz* (Travelogue on the People's Republic of China, 1951); autobiography *Dagoun Taya i Dagoun Taya* (1950); *Youppoumhlwa* (Profiles of Burmese Politicians and Artists, 1955), *Sapei Thabhotaya* (On Literature, 1967). DB

Tāyumāṉavar (18th century, born at Vēdāraṇyam), Tamil Śaiva devotee and poet. He was the author of *Tāyumāṉavar pāṭal.* His beliefs had their origin in Śaiva *siddhānta* (see *cittar*), but he differed from that philosophy in his approach to the dualism of the soul and the supreme spirit. His devotion to God as *Sacchidānanda* (Existence, Consciousness and Bliss) is noteworthy; he conceived of Him as a formless being pervading the whole universe, rather than as a particular deity.

JHTL 240–3. JRM

taẕkira, see Vol. III.

Teav-Ek (Tum-Teav), a romantic Cambodian love-story with a tragic end, which has long held a special place in Cambodian hearts. At least two written versions, in different metres and by different poets, are current today; both texts are 20th century, however. *Teav-Ek* has many features which are typical of the genre of Cambodian verse-novel. It is lengthy. It abounds in accounts of preparations for journeys and of the journeys themselves. It contains detailed descriptions of nature, as seen *en voyage*, and lyric passages describing the loneliness of the hero and heroine when separated from each other. Characteristically, too, the effect of *karma* (fate) is felt throughout the story. Certain features characteristic of the verse-novels whose stories are derived from India are lacking, however. Thus, there are no interventions of the gods or visits to heaven, no *apsaras* and no *garudas*. The essential appeal of the story lies in the human qualities of the characters and its tragic romanticism.

In verse-novels such as *Preah Chinavongs* and *Preah Laksanavongs*, Indian-derived stories which are well known from being performed as mimed ballet with recited and orchestral accompaniment, the characters are stereotyped royal personages, representing the male virtues of courage and wisdom or the female virtues of beauty and faithfulness. The characters in *Teav-Ek* are real people and, chiefly, ordinary people. Tum is a monk, who goes on a journey, selling lecterns, with his true friend and companion, Pech. They give performances of religious works, one reciting, one playing the musical accompaniment. Teav is the young girl with whom Tum falls hopelessly in love. Her mother schemes to prevent their alliance. When the Master of the monastery refuses permission for Tum to leave to court Teav, he disobeys, thereby starting the bad fate, which leads to the death of himself, of Teav and of her confidante. JMJ

Tenāli Rāmakṛṣṇa (17th century), Telugu poet at the court of Veṅkaṭapati Rāja. He was credited with much buffoonery at court and with jokes and humorous stories, but he also wrote a serious Vaiṣṇava work, *Pāṃḍuraṃgamāhātmyamu.* JRM

Thach-Lam (or Nguyen-tuong-Lan, b 1909, d 1943 Hanoi), Vietnamese writer of the *Tu luc van doan* group (see Nhat-Linh), author of stories published in the revues *Phong hoa* and *Ngay nay* and collected later into four volumes. He is considered one of the best writers of the group. Works: novel, *Ngay moi* (New Day, 1939); stories, *Gio dau mua* (The Beginning of the Monsoon, 1937); *Nang trong vuon* (Sunshine in the Garden, 1938); *Soi toc* (A Hair, 1942); *Ha-noi bam sau pho phuong* (36 Streets of Hanoi, 1943).

DNILVN 215. VV

Ṭhākur (Tagore), Rabīndranāth (b 1861 Calcutta, d 1941 Calcutta), Bengali poet, writer, playwright, painter, composer, reformer and philosopher, the greatest figure of modern Indian literature. He was the grandson of 'Prince' Dvārkānāth (1794–1846), friend and ardent follower of the 'Father of Modern India', Rāmmohan Rāy (qv), and the son of the philosopher Debendranāth Ṭhākur (1817–1905). The highly cultured home atmosphere of this leading Bengali family strongly influenced Rabīndranath, who started writing poetry in early childhood. After a year's stay in England, he took over the management of the family estates in East Bengal where he became familiar with the social and economic problems of the Indian village so often reflected in his writings. During the Partition of Bengal (1905), he joined the national movement, but was repelled by its overemphasis on purely political and nationalist aims. In 1912, he translated into English an anthology of his spiritual poetry, under the title of *Gitanjali*, and was the first Asian poet to be awarded the Nobel Prize (1913). The emotional shock of the First Great War, combined with the feeling of responsibility due to his exceptional position in world culture, turned him into an ardent propagator of the idea of friendship and cultural co-operation between all nations of the world, between East and West. In Santiniketan, he founded an international university (Viśva-Bhāratī), to serve this goal. He travelled widely all over the world, lecturing on his ideas and philosophy. The growth of fascism, however, and the deterioration of conditions in India as well as in the world at large, made him join the anti-fascist movement and turn his writings towards Man, his struggles and longings.

The main contribution of Rabīndranāth —or the *Gurudeb* (Godly Teacher), as his countrymen often call him—to world literature is his poetry. He was able to express in it the changing ideals of his contemporaries, the patriotic enthusiasm and optimism of the young bourgeois class in ascent; and, first of all, his enchantment with the beauties of Nature and the feeling of love; and, around the turn of the century, his original conception of God as the helpful and intimate friend of man, the lover and beloved of the human soul in one. It was this new religious tone, dominating his *Mānasī* (The Heart's Desire, 1890), *Sonār tarī* (The Golden Boat, 1893), *Naibedya* (Sacrifice, 1901), *Gītāñjali* (1910) etc, which, translated into English, won him his world fame. In later years, however, especially after 1930, these religious trends gave way, in his poetry, to purely humanist conceptions, striving after an expression of Man's and the Poet's place in life and the meaning of life, eg in *Punaśca* (Once Again, 1932), *Patrapuṭ* (Armful of Leaves, 1935), *Seṃjuti* (Evening Lamp, 1938), *Nabajātak* (Newly born, 1940), etc.

Most of Rabīndranāth's numerous dramas, such as *Ḍākhgar* (The Post-Office, 1912), *Muktadhārā* (Free Current, 1922) or *Raktakarabī* (Red Oleanders, 1924), are governed by the lyrical element and especially a symbolic cipher, which has prevented them from finding a constant place in the repertoires of Western theatres. Ṭhākur's prose fiction is large in extent and of great importance for the development of various prose genres and forms in modern Bengali literature. His novels are mostly social and psychological, often dealing with the conflict of the old and the new in Indian mentality and society. Thus his *Gorā* (1907) shows the untenability of orthodox Hinduism in the modern world, but also the weakness of narrow-minded modernist sectarianism. *Ghare-bāire* (The Home and the World, 1916) and *Cār adhyāy* (Four Chapters, 1934) reflect the Bengali political atmosphere and struggles in the first decades or our century. From the artistic point of view, however, Rabīndranāth was more successful in his short stories, four volumes of which were edited in *Galpaguccha* (A Bunch of Stories). They excel in interesting plots, often based on the author's first-hand experience (this is especially true of his stories from the countryside), their realistic treatment and narrative technique (internal gradation, sharp points and characterization). Ṭhākur was also among the first to introduce the colloquial form of Bengali into literature, both prose and poetry.

A substantial part of Rabīndranāth's writing is formed by his non-fiction, essays and articles (on subjects ranging from philology and the history of literature to astronomy and education), religious and philosophical treatises, autobiographical writings, (eg *Jīban-smṛti*, Reminiscences, 1912), travel books (*Rāśiyār ciṭhi*, Letters from Russia, 1931), political comments and correspondence. Many of these books were written in English, eg *Nationalism* (1917), *Sadhana* (1914), *Personality* (1917), *Creative Unity* (1922) and *The Religion of Man* (1930). They are an expression of Ṭhākur's philosophy of life, but show him often also as a keen observer and merciless critic of modern civilization and its inability to grant all people and all nations of the world a free development.

Rabīndranāth's activities never remained confined to writing. He was always trying to realize his ideals and reformist conceptions in practice as well. His Santiniketan school was a remarkable contribution to the modernization of education in India and his Sriniketan an interesting experiment in the field of modern agriculture and co-operative farming.

One of the basic features of Rabīndranāth's dynamic personality was his dialectic conception of life as a ceaseless stream of incessant changes to which man must adapt himself in order to keep pace with progress, both in private and public life. This conception was the main source of his youthfulness, even in old age, and of his ever new experiments in various fields. Thus he started painting when he was nearly seventy, invented new combinations of drama, music and dance (in his *nṛtyanāṭya*, dance-drama, such as *Caṇḍālikā nṛtyanāṭya*, 1938) and made various experiments in poetic techniques. From a broader point of view, Ṭhākur represents the culmination of the so-called Bengali Renaissance, the 19th century movement for a profound modernization of traditional Indian culture. Critics usually quote three main sources of his literary inspiration: the classical Indian cultural and philosophical heritage, the folk-literature of Bengal, and modern European, or rather English, literature, all of which he was able to harmonize and synthesize in his own work. His influence on contemporary and subsequent Bengali literature was very great.

Since 1913, Ṭhākur's books have been widely translated into many languages; some of his own translations into English may be considered second originals, eg *The Gardener* (1913), The *Crescent Moon* (1913), *Fruit Gathering* (1916), *Lover's Gift* (1918), etc.
English monographs on Rabīndranāth are too many to be quoted in full (see Pulinbihari Sen, *Books about Rabindranath Tagore*, The Visva-bharati Quarterly, April 1957). The most important are: E. J. Thompson, *Rabindranath Tagore, Poet and Dramatist* (London 1926); A. Aronson, *Rabindranath through Western Eyes* (Allahabad 1943); A. Chakravarti, S. K. Maitra, S. Sen and N. Ray, *Rabindranath* (Calcutta 1944), R. Chatterjee (ed.), *The Golden Book of Tagore* (Calcutta 1931), S. Radhakrishnan, *The Philosophy of Rabindranath Tagore* (London 1918). DZ

Than Sin, Maun, Burmese writer, see **Maun Tyi,** U Leti Pantita.

Thein Pe Myint, U (b 1914 Bhutalin), Burmese writer, politician and journalist; he studied at Mandalay College, Rangoon and Calcutta Universities and was active in student politics. Though he was a nationalist and Marxist, he never hesitated to follow his own line. He spent World War II in India, waged anti-Japanese propaganda, and later acted on behalf of the Anti-Fascist People's Freedom League. He lost his membership of the Central Committee of the Burma Communist Party in 1947 and was expelled from the party in 1948. He was jailed in 1948–49. In 1956–58 he became a Member of Parliament (National United Front). He travelled widely both in the East and West. He founded (1958) and edited (till 1964) *Botahtaung* (Vanguard) newspaper. All his short stories (1934 onwards) and novels reflect his close involvement with political and social questions; he uses his skill as a writer to shock, persuade and convince rather than to entertain. He was active in the Nagani Book Club (1936, see Nu, U), writing its first title *Hsaya Lun i ahtoupatti* (Biography of Thakhin Koujto Hmain). He became famous for the novel *Tek Bhountyi* (Modern Monk, 1936) attacking abuses in the monastic system and urging their reform. *Tekkhit Nathsou* (Evil Spirits of Modern Times, 1938) is a novel about the social consequences of venereal disease. Since then, in short stories, novels, travelogues, memoirs, biographies and essays, he has chronicled his own life and the political and social life of Burma, especially in *Sis atwin Khayijthij* (Wartime Traveller, 1953), *Ashei ka neiwun htwek thij pama* (As Sure as the Sun Rising in the East, 1958) and *Tjunto tyoumphu tho kambha* (The World as I've Seen it). AJA

Theippan Maung Wa, Burmese writer, see **Wa,** Theippam Maun.

The-Lu (b 1907 Hanoi), Vietnamese poet, leader of the 'new poetry' school. He attended the Ecole des Beaux-Arts in Hanoi and took part in activities connected with the anti-colonial rising organized by the Vietnamese National Party in 1929. He began writing in 1930, contributing to *Phong hoa* and *Ngay nay*, the reviews published by the *Tu luc van doan* group (see Nhat-Linh). His lyrics, written in clear popular language, sing of nature, love, and the poet's calling. He gathered a number of poets round him including Xuan-Dieu (qv), Huy-Can (b 1919), Nguyen-nhuoc Phap (1914–38), Dong-Ho (b 1906), Pham-huy-Thong (or Huy-Thong, b 1918), Luu-trong-Lu (b 1912) and others. This 'new poetry' school rejected the classical forms of Vietnamese verse and introduced free verse and all the poetic means current in modern French poetry. Since 1942 he has devoted himself to the theatre. He lives in Hanoi. Chief works: *Vang va mau* (Gold and Blood, 1934); *May van tho* (A Few Lines of Verse, 1935), and another volume of verse of the same name published in 1941.

DNILVN 121, 216. VV

Theragāthā and **Therigāthā** (Strophes of the Elder Monks and Strophes of the Elder Nuns), anthologies of the oldest autobiographical lyrics in India, both belonging to the *Tripiṭaka* (qv). *Theragāthā* comprise 1,279, *Therigāthā*, 522 *gāthās* or stanzas, divided into 21 and 16 chapters respectively (rising from one strophe). Both works are virtually anonymous, as the names of authors attached to the strophes (264 elders and about 100 nuns) cannot be historically verified. The poems reflect the sentiments and aspirations of members of the Buddhist Order. They portray the life in seclusion, sometimes with vivid illustrations of nature's splendour (missing, however, in the nuns' verses), the bliss of serenity, and a quiet joy of victory over mundane attractions. Dhammapāla's commentary on both works (probably 5th century AD) supplies the traditional framework of biographical legends concerning the persons to whom the *gāthās* had been ascribed.

Trans.: C. A. F. Rhys Davids, *Psalms of the Early Buddhists* (PTS I, 1909, II, 1913, in one volume 1964).
WHIL II, 100–13. IF

Thilawuntha, Shin (1453–1520), Burmese monk, poet, a rival of Rahtathara (qv), both being writers of poems in four of the five major genres. Most of his *pyo* (qv)—*Paramidawgan* (1491) and *Hsutaunggan* (Stories of Sumedha, the future Buddha, ?1498), *Buddhuppatti* (Life of the Buddha)—are expositions of Buddhism. Many Burmese scholars with strong religious leanings claim that he is a better poet than Rahtathara. His other *pyo* are *Taungdwin la* (Journey from Taungdwingyi to Ava), written in riddles, and the unfinished *Dhammapāla* (*Jataka*, qv, No. 441), 1520. Of his *mawgun* (qv), *Shisha Kandawbwè*

(1505) commanded attention from some of the later panegyric composers such as Ponnya (qv). He also wrote two of the earliest known prose-works on palm-leaf: *Parayana Wuthtu* (1511) and *Yāzawingyaw* (Celebrated Chronicle, 1520). HP

Thiphākarawong, Thai historian, see **Phongsāwadān.**

Thmenh Chey and other Cambodian folk-tales. The story of Thmenh Chey, a poor boy who, through wiliness, intelligence and daring, acquires the reputation of being the wisest person in the land and eventually becomes king, is a favourite in Cambodia, although other tales, such as *Chau Kambet Bantoh,* have a similar theme of a poor boy rising to become king. Another group of stories is concerned with appeals to the king to settle simple lawsuits involving stubborn men, which a mere judge cannot decide. A typical story of this kind tells of two men meeting on a bridge and neither giving way, or of four people trying to divide five objects and failing to share them equally. Many stories involve animals. Judge Hare is an outstanding character who regularly turns up just in time and, using his sharp wits, saves the right man or animal from a wrong judgement at law. Favourite narrative devices include: the extraction of a promise not to tell a secret and the inevitable telling of it; the placing of a character, usually a lover or a robber, under the house at night, where he overhears a secret as husband and wife talk in bed; the building up of tension when a lover is hidden in a pitcher into which boiling water is to be poured or in a coffin which is being nailed down. Farcical situations are much enjoyed. For example, a man is left hanging from a high branch, with another man clinging to his ankles, while the elephant which was to have saved them both marches on. The folk-tales, of mixed Indian, Chinese, Indo-Chinese and Cambodian origin, introduce people of all levels—poor men and their faithless wives, judges, pandits, ascetics, kings and ministers—and form the section of Cambodian literature which best reveals the spirit and humour of the people. JMJ

Ṭhombare, Tryambak Bāpūjī, Marathi poet, see **Bālkavi.**

Ṭiḷak, Bāl Gangādhar (called Lokamānya, 1856–1920), Marathi nationalist leader and journalist. Editor of *Kesarī* from which many of his leading articles have been published in book form in Marathi. Also *Gītā rahasya* (The Secret of the Gītā, 1901; translated by B. S. Suthankar, Poona 1935–36), *The Arctic Home in the Vedas* (1903), *Indian Unrest* (1919).

I. M. Reisner and N. M. Goldberg, *Tilak and the Struggle for Indian Freedom* (New Delhi 1966); M. D. Vidwans, ed., *The Letters of Lokamanya Tilak* (Poona 1966); S. Wolpert, *Tilak and Gokhale* (Berkeley 1962). IR

Ṭiḷak, Nārāyaṇ Vāman (1862–1919), Marathi nature poet and writer of Christian devotional verse, most of which was only published in collected form after his death. Odd translations as well as poems originally written in English can be found scattered in various places including Christian hymnals. IR

Timanna (16th century), Telugu poet at the court of Kṛṣṇadevarāya (qv). He composed the *Pārijātāpaharaṇamu* (about 1519). This tells the story of the predicament of the god, Kṛṣṇa, as a result of the jealousy between his two wives, Rukmiṇī and Satyabhāmā. As a result of the giving of a *pārijāta*-flower to the former, Satyabhāmā, enraged with jealousy, causes Kṛṣṇa to go to Indra's heaven and uproot his *pārijāta*-tree. Kṛṣṇa has to fight Indra's army and, along with Satyabhāmā, defeats it. JRM

Tin Aun, Banmo (b 1920 Pegu), Burmese writer, journalist, publisher and historian. After the 1936 student strike he left the University and worked for a timber company in Taunngu. In 1950–52 and from 1957 onwards he published the *Linjoun* Journal, Magazine and newspapers. A Marxist, he was jailed in 1952–56, in the late fifties and from 1965. He included passages on politics, philosophy, history and sociology in his early short stories and novels, eg *Bhoun Maun tajauk hte ye* (Hpon Maung Alone, 1947). *Thupountyi* (The

Rebel, 1952), inspired by J. Fučik's *Under the Gallows*, tells of the heroism of the entire nation; *Anjatra Tyekto* (Pauper Tyekto, 1953) is a social novel drawing attention to the miserable life of a youth from the lowest class of society. His later works, eg *Myain* (1957), are artistically more mature. For *Ma Ma Tyi* (1960) he refused the Sapei Biman Prize. *Tjunno* (Me, 1964) comprises autobiographical sketches on life and work. Historical works: *Myanma Naingam Thamain* (History of Burma, 1964), *Koulouni Khit Myanma Naingam Thamain* (History of Burma in the Colonial Period, 1964). Political works: *Hsoushelis Tika* (A Commentary on Socialism, 1962), *Hsoushelis Abhidhan* (A Dictionary of Socialism, 1964). Adaptations of G. B. Shaw, M. Gorky, etc. DB

Tin Tint, Burmese writer, see **Wa,** Theippam Maun.

Tiru. Vi. Ka., Tamil writer, see **Kaliyānacuntaram.**

Tirumūlar, classical Tamil poet, see **cittar.**

Tirumuṟai, collective name for the twelve Tamil books of Śaiva devotional poems, the work of the 63 *nāyaṉmār* (qv), gathered together by Nampi Aṇṭār Nampi. Most important are the first seven books, to which the name *Tēvāram* is applied. JRM

Tirupati Weṅkaṭakawulu (twin poets: Tirupati Śāstrī, Diwākarla, 1871–1920; Weṅkaṭaśāstri, Ceḷḷapiḷḷa, 1870–1950), Telugu poets and scholars. The two poets who called themselves by one name brought about a renaissance in Telugu literature after three hundred years of decadence. When native scholarship declined with the spread of English education, they revived a broad interest in Telugu literature by their writings, speeches, and other literary pursuits. They excelled in extraordinary feats of memory, seen in the performance of *śatāwadhāna*, where a hundred interrogators are given line by line a complete verse of four stanzas on a subject prescribed by each, the hundred verses finally repeated complete without missing a syllable. They toured all over Andhra to the remotest villages on a literary pilgrimage popularizing the beauty of Telugu poetry. They revelled in literary controversy in which large numbers of literati participated. They also translated many Sanskrit plays and adapted the *Mahābhārata* (qv) for the stage, in five plays of which *Pāṇḍawōdyōgamu* and *Pāṇḍawawijyamu* are still staged successfully. Weṅkaṭaśāstri, who survived his fellow poet by thirty years, was a great Sanskrit and Telugu scholar and a great conversationalist. He published many essays and travel sketches in beautiful modern spoken Telugu. He was awarded the title of 'Kalāprapūrṇa' (D.Litt.) by the Andhra University and was the first State poet nominated by the Government of the composite Madras State. The twin poets became the *gurus* of two successive generations of Telugu poets. Further important books: *Buddha caritra* (History of the Buddha, 1901); *Nānārājasandarśanamu* (Visit to the Courts of Princes, 1908); *Kathalu gāthalu* (Stories and Myths, 3 vols., 1953). BhK

Tiruttakkatēvar (10th century), Tamil poet. His *Cīvakacintāmaṇi*, an ambitious work, is historically the first of the great mediaeval Tamil epics. Though a Jain poem in philosophical outlook, it does not preach austerity and asceticism. The 13 cantos relate the love-conquests of the hero, Prince Cīvakaṉ, a perfect man, accomplished in all arts and sciences. He marries eight wives, is crowned king after conquering his father's enemy, and finally retires to lead an ascetic life. The narrative is interesting, the language sensuous, charming and rich, and the use of many metrical forms extremely skilful.

JHTL 146–9. KZ

Tiruvaḷḷuvar (c5th century AD), classical Tamil poet. Nothing definite is known about his life, though a number of legends mention him as the son of a Brahmin and a Pariah woman, living in Mylapore near Madras as a weaver. The work ascribed to him, *Tirukkuṟaḷ* (The Sacred Kuṟaḷ), comprising 1,330 skilful couplets (termed *kuṟaḷ veṇpā*), is called 'The Fifth (or Tamil) Veda' because of its depth of thought and the enormous influence it has always had on Tamil life and culture. For hundreds of years, this didactic work has been a moral guide, dealing with the three spheres of life, *aṟam* (ie *dharma*), 'ethical order', *poruḷ* (*artha*), 'social activities', and *iṉpam* (*kāma*), 'pleasure'. The fact that *vīṭu* (*mokṣa*) or 'deliverance' is not included shows how empirical and pragmatic Tiruvaḷḷuvar's ethics are. The work obviously does not direct man to ascetic negation of the world; on the contrary, it points out the noble beauty of social and family life, of work and activity, of love and children, though it does not deny the greatness of renunciation. It calls in strong terms for non-violence and for active participation in compassion and mutual assistance regardless of caste and creed. It was translated into many Indian and non-Indian languages (Latin, German, French, Russian, English).

Trans.: G. U. Pope, *The 'Sacred' Kurral of Tiruvaḷḷuva-Nāyanār* (London 1886).
JHTL 41–51. KZ

Tiruvātavūraṭikaḷ, see **Maṇikkavācakar.**

Tiruviḷaiyāṭaṟpurāṇam (16th century), probably the most famous of the Tamil *sthalapurāṇas*, tales of marvellous exploits of the deities at particular shrines. This one, by Parañcōtimuṉivar, describes the feats of the god Śiva as Somasundara at Madurai, one of the most famous temples in Tamilnad. It includes such well-known stories as the feeding of the insatiable dwarf, Kuṇṭōtaraṉ, and the re-instruction in grammar and rhetoric of the self-opinionated poet-president Nakkīrar. Another version of this *purāṇa* with the same title was written by Perumpaṟṟappuliyūr Nampi.

JHTL 211. JRM

Tivārī, Bhīmnidhi (b 1911 Kathmandu), one of the most prolific Nepali writers. So far he has published nearly forty volumes of poetry, short stories and novels. The themes of his poetry are extremely varied. His *ghazals* (see Vol. III), whose language and style are greatly influenced by modern Urdu writers, and his *bhajans*, are among the most remarkable of his compositions. He is, however, best known as a dramatist. His plays, which deal largely with the problems of modern urban life, have all been written in prose and their language reflects the modern speech of Nepal more closely than that of Bālkr̥ṣṇa Sama (see Sama) whom Tivārī has rivalled in this field.

DJM

Toer, Indonesian writer, see **Tur,** Pramudya Ananta.

To-Hoai (real name Nguyen-Sen, b 1920 Nghia-do, Hanoi), Vietnamese writer. Since 1943 he has been active in the Vietminh; after the August Revolution, he has been in charge of the official Vietminh organ *Cuu quoc* (National Salvation). Following the method of socialist realism, he is one of the first Vietnamese writers to describe the present life of the mountain minority people in North Vietnam. Works: novel, *Muoi nam* (Ten Years, 1957); stories, *Truyen Tay-bac* (Tales from the North-West, 1955); novella for children, *De Men phieu luu ky* (The Cricket's Adventures, 1941); film libretto, *Vo chong A-phu* (Mr and Mrs A-phu, 1960).

DNILVN 217. VV

To-Huu (real name Nguyen-kim-Thanh, b 1920 Phu-lai, Thua-thien province), revolutionary Vietnamese poet. Active in the Communist Party since 1937, he was held in prison from 1939 to 1942. Leader of the 1945 uprising in Hue, Secretary of the Central Committee of the Vietnam Workers' Party in Hanoi. His first poems were published in the Communist party press in 1937. His lyrics are endowed with revolutionary romanticism in the Gorkian sense. For To-Huu poetry means 'a beautiful form of revolutionary action'. His poems use various classical forms and metres, and achieve formal perfection. To-Huu is considered one of the best poets of the DRV. Chief works: *Tu ay* (Since That Time, 1959); *Viet-bac* (1954); *Gio long* (Hurricane, 1961).

DNILVN 217. VV

Tolkāppiyam (lit. 'The Old Kāvya'), the most ancient Tamil grammar extant (first two parts probably 3rd–2nd century BC, part III, 4th–5th century AD), ascribed to Tolkāppiyaṉār (a Brahmin seer named Tiruṇatūmākkiṉi), disciple of the sage Agastya. The work is more than a grammar: it represents an explicit systematization of classical Tamil culture. For Indian linguistics, it is as important as Pāṇini's (qv) grammar of Sanskrit, since it grows out of a different grammatical tradition. It consists of three books (*atikāram*), of nine chapters (*iyal*) each. The text has 1,612 *sūtras* (qv) of unequal length, some of them undoubtedly interpolations. The first part, *Eḻuttatikāram*, deals with the inventory, production and combination of sounds; the second part, *Collatikāram*, treats morphological, syntactical, semantic and etymological questions. *Poruḷatikāram*, or the book on 'subject-matter', is the prosody and rhetoric of classical Tamil and, in addition, it contains a wealth of sociological and cultural material. The grammar had an enormous influence, and its authority is unquestioned to the present day. As a single integrated work, it is first mentioned in Nakkīrar's commentary on Iṟaiyaṉār's (qv) *Akapporuḷ* (about 750 AD). However the first two parts were clearly composed in the pre-Christian era, while the third part must have been added later, since it contains allusions to later Sanskrit works. The grammar has seven commentaries, the most important being those ascribed to Iḷampūranar, Pērāciriyar and Nacciṉārkkiṉiyar.

JHTL 2–7. KZ

tonel, Indonesian theatrical form, see **sandiwara.**

Tongkat Warrant, Malay poet, see **Usman Awang.**

Toṭagamuva, Sinhalese poet, see **Rāhula, Śrī.**

To-van-Tuan, Vietnamese writer, see **Binh-nguyen-Loc.**

Traiphūm or **Traiphūmikhathā** (Three Worlds, 1345 AD), as far as is known, the oldest work in the Thai language. This Buddhist cosmography is based on Pāli sources listed at the beginning and end of the work, most of them non-canonical. The *Traiphūm* is thus an ingenious compilation and not an original work. In an Introduction and ten chapters it gives the Hindu–Buddhist view of the world: Hell, Heaven, intermediary worlds, continents. All that happens, life, death and the torments of hell, is subject to strict laws, and described in detail. It cannot be said how far the text corresponds to the original of 1345; the oldest manuscript dates from 1778, as most of the manuscripts were lost in the devastation of the ancient Thai capital, Ayuthayā (1767). KW

Tran-huu-Tri, Vietnamese writer, see **Nam-Cao.**

Tran-khan-Du, Vietnamese writer, see **Khai-Hung.**

Tran-te-Xuong (usually known as Tu-Xuong, b 1870 Vi-xuyen, Nam-dinh province, d 1907), Vietnamese poet. Although very talented, he was unable to pass the higher official examinations. His family lived in poverty, often in debt, while he led a gay life in Nam-dinh. He wrote much verse using various forms, the most marked characteristic being his satirical treatment of the decadent elements in the old society during the first phase of French colonization, and the parasites who made the most of it. He ridiculed the impotence of Confucian morality, bribery at examinations, the stuck-up native and colonial officials, the senseless pursuit of wealth, and any hypocrisy in human relationships. Fundamentally, however, he remained a passive observer, embittered by his own failures and lamenting that he was born at the wrong time. As a satirist he has an important place in Vietnamese literature.

DNILVN 105, 218. VV

Tripathi, G. M., Gujarati writer, see **navalkathā.**

Tripāṭhi, Sūryakānt, Hindi poet, see **Nirālā.**

Tripiṭaka (etymologically 'three baskets') means the Three Traditions or Three Collections of the words of the Buddha. All schools of Buddhism agree that after the Parinirvāṇa of the Buddha (486 BC) his followers met and rehearsed his (oral) teaching, so that, like the *Vedas* (qv), it could be preserved in enduring form. For about four centuries, as far as we know, the resulting texts remained purely oral, writing being current only for administrative and business purposes. To 'know' a text or doctrine presupposed memorizing it and writing appeared to serve no educational purpose. Nevertheless the *Tripiṭaka* was, or became, so extensive that ordinary student monks could not memorize the whole, nor did they need to since the essential doctrines were repeated in different texts. Thus we find a division of labour whereby students each learned one part, though a complete community of monks should between them possess the entire *Tripiṭaka.* The risks contingent on the death or dispersion of monks in times of famine or political upheaval eventually produced the realization that writing was a desirable form of insurance against loss. Meanwhile, however, the Buddhists had become divided into a score of schools, each with its own recension of the *Tripiṭaka* which was reduced to manuscripts (Bu-ston, Chos-ḥbyung), various Indian languages being used which had been current among the Buddhists of different countries (such as Pāli, or 'Paiśācī', in the west and south of India).

In the more original texts preserved by all schools, variation in readings seems not to have been serious from the point of view of doctrine, but every school seems to have added apocryphal texts which had become confused, in the oral tradition, with the authentic ones; there were also great variations of interpretation, the real cause of the division into schools. The subsequent development of the Mahāyāna added enormously to the apocryphal *Tripiṭaka.* Of the many *Tripiṭakas* of the schools, the Sthaviravāda (Theravāda) recension is extant in Pāli and is the only Indian version now available complete, most of the texts of the other early schools having been lost through the destruction of those schools in India. Extensive fragments of the Sarvāstivāda recension in Sanskrit exist and are in the course of being printed. Part of the Lokottaravāda *Vinaya* exists (*Mahāvastu,* qv, etc). The greater part of a Mahāyāna and Mantrayāna collection in Sanskrit is preserved in Nepal and further texts have been preserved elsewhere. In translation into non-Indian languages we have primarily the Chinese and Tibetan recensions or *Tripiṭakas.* (It may be noted that in Mahāyāna the old 'Three Traditions' became so distorted as sometimes to be broken into four or five as well as changed in content, but there is no space here to discuss these classifications, whilst the old title is still current.) The first is in the main a Mahāyāna collection, but also includes partial recensions of the original texts from some of the early schools (especially Dharmaguptaka, Sarvāstivāda, Mahāsāṅghika). The second is a Mahāyāna–Mantrayāna collection omitting most of the pre-Mahāyāna texts. By collation, it is now possible to reconstitute most of the original *Tripiṭaka* approximately as it stood before the division into schools. The Three Collections are the *Sūtra,* or Dialogues in which the Buddha expounded his doctrine (*dharma*) discursively, the *Vinaya* or Discipline of monastic organization and the *Abhidharma* or systematic philosophy extracted from the doctrine. The last was perhaps not propounded by the Buddha himself but only in the schools later, whose versions differ greatly in form, though its basis lay in certain *Mātṛkās* or Synopses of topics which appear original (common to all schools). The *Sūtra Piṭaka* is noteworthy for literature in the narrower, aesthetic, sense (see Buddhist literature of India). The 'Long' Dialogues of the *Dīrgha,* the first of its five subdivisions (*āgamas,* in Pāli, *nikāyas*), are especially fine examples of this style. The 'Minor' (*Kṣudraka*) subdivision became the bulkiest, being the depository for apocryphal texts of every kind (eg *Avadāna,* qv, *Niddesa, Paṭisambhidāmagga, Buddhavaṃsa, Cariyāpiṭaka*). In it, lyric and epic poetry predominated, contrasting with the prevailing prose of the other subdivisions. Its more original texts include the *Khaḍgaviṣāṇagāthā*, *Munigāthā*, *Arthavargīyāṇi Sūtrāṇi*, *Pārāyaṇa*, *Sthaviragāthā* (in Pāli, *Theragāthā*, qv) and perhaps parts of the *jātaka* and *Dharmapada* (*Dhammapada*) anthologies (qqv).

Trans.: Pāli recension by various scholars, now almost complete, PTS, Mahāyāna Sutras: *Sukhāvatīvyūha*, *Vajracchedika*, *Saddharmapuṇḍarīka* in SBE; *Sandhinirmocana* and *Vimalakīrtinirdeśa* by E. Lamotte (Louvain 1935 and 1962); *Laṅkāvatāra* by Suzuki (London 1932); *Hevajra* by Snellgrove (London 1959).

WIB 4ff, 201ff, Bibliography; A. K. Warder, Pali Metre (PTS 1967). AKW

Tripiṭaka in Cambodia. It is to the *Tripiṭaka* (qv) that Cambodia owes a major part of her literature, in the sense that, since Buddhism became the religion of the country at the end of the Angkor period in the 12th century, the Pāli Canon has been a vital source of inspiration. Under the heading of Buddhist literature four categories may be included. First, there is the Buddhist Canon in the form of Pāli texts which are preserved in Cambodian script both in manuscript form and, since this century, in published form. Second come the translations into Cambodian of such texts; a very large part of the Buddhist scriptures is translated and published. A third class of work connected with the *Tripiṭaka* consists of texts with commentary. A Pāli text, such as the *Āḷavakasutta*, is given, a few lines at a time, each small section being followed by a page or more of translation, explanation and teaching. The fourth section of what may be called Buddhist literature is composed of works on religious themes, such as the *Gatilok*, in which stories are told to illustrate morals, or the *Roeung Krong Subhamitra*, a *jātaka* (qv) retold in verse. Among poems composed for religious purposes one in particular deserves mention since it is the text of an inscription on stone at Angkor, dated 1701 AD. Although great reverence is felt for Buddhist beliefs and traditions and for the manuscripts themselves, the Cambodians have managed to impose, even upon translations, a character which is recognizably their own. In the *Vessantarajātaka*, for example, the lively conversation is extremely natural and in many details is a departure from the original. In addition to works of a religious nature, many works intended for entertainment, verse-novels, for example, and folktales, owe their origin to the *Tripiṭaka*. JMJ

Truong-vinh-Ky, Pétrus Jean-Baptiste (also Pétrus Ky, b 1837 Vinh-thanh, Ben-tre province, d 1898), Vietnamese writer and journalist. Of a Catholic family, he was a polyglot whose exceptional talent for languages attracted the attention of Catholic missionaries, who had him educated at mission schools in Cambodia and Malaya. Returning to South Vietnam in 1858 he was employed by the French military authorities as an interpreter during the first phase of the French conquest of Cochin China. In 1863 he travelled to France, Portugal, Spain and Italy. In 1865 the French authorities in Saigon put him in charge of the first Vietnamese newspaper *Gia-dinh bao* (Giadinh Paper) in which he collaborated with another well-known Catholic writer, Paulus Huynh-tinh-Cua (1834–1907), and others. In 1886 he worked with Paul Bert, the French High Commissioner in Hue. His work comprises over a hundred books, among the most important of which are his transcriptions of such classical works as *Kim-van-Kieu* (see Nguyen-Du and *truyen*), *Luc-van-Tien* (see Nguyen-dinh-Chieu) and others, from *chu-nom* characters into Latin script (*quoc ngu*), and his translations into Vietnamese of Chinese classics. Other works: *Chuyen doi xua* (Stories of Old Times, 1866); *Chuyen di Bac-ky nam at hoi* (Journey to Tonkin in 1876).

DNILVN 27ff, 220ff. VV

truyen, one of the most frequent poetical genres in Vietnamese, in both classical and folk literature; verse novel or verse romance, it may be several thousand lines in length. It was especially popular in the 18th and early 19th centuries. The traditional form consists of *luc bat* (qv) lines, not divided into strophes. The most famous *truyen* epic and the greatest work of Vietnamese literature is *Truyen Kieu* (see Nguyen-du). Besides a few works whose authors are known, like *Hoa tien* (Paper Decorated with Flowers), a love story by Nguyen-huy-Tu (1743–1790) given its final form in 1826 lines by Nguyen-Thien (1763–1818), there are a number of anonymous *truyen.* Analysis of their subject-matter, language and form places them mostly in the 18th century, but they are still widely read. Popular subjects are love triumphant, truth victorious in the face of treachery, honourable men getting the better of cunning villains (often villains highly placed at the royal court), sufferings of those to whom fate has been unkind, etc; the ending is most frequently a happy one.

Elements of Buddhist philosophy and ethics are characteristic of the novels, and supernatural forces affect the course of the plot; this latter feature is near to lacking only from *Truyen Kieu.* The best-known verse novels are: *Phan Tran* (954 lines), the love of a youth of the Phan family for a girl of the Tran family; *Nhi do mai* (Two-time Blossom in the Plum Orchard, 2,820 lines), the troubles of a young man whose family is persecuted by evil courtiers; *Quan am Thi-Kinh* (The Girl Thi-Kinh Who Became the Goddess Kwan-yin, 786 lines), the touching story of the sufferings and death of a girl wrongly accused; *Pham-cong, Cuc-hoa* (c4,000 lines), called after Pham-cong and his wife Cuc-hoa, a love story including adventures in foreign lands and in the Buddhist underworld; *Bich cau ky ngo* (Strange Meeting in Bich-cau, 648 lines), a story of a man married to a fairy; *Trinh-thu* (Virtuous Mouse), a moralizing allegory; *Tre coc* (The Catfish and the Toad), an allegory ridiculing inefficient mandarins; *Thach-sanh,* called after the young woodcutter hero whose courage, cleverness and nobility overcome all his enemies, winning him a princess for bride, and a powerful throne. This last novel is the closest to folk literature.

Trans.: M. Durand, *Than Tran, texte, traduction, commentaires* (Paris 1962).
DNILVN 58–61, 86–88, 89–100. VV

Tukārām (b 1608 Dehu, near Poona), Marathi poet, a contemporary of Śivajī, the great Maratha national hero; a low-born Śūdra like Nāmdev (qv). Of all the Maratha poet-saints, he is undoubtedly the greatest in popular estimation and his influence on the common people of Maharashtra is considerable. Tukārām's biography is comparatively well known, not only through Mahīpati's legendary account in his *Bhaktalīlāmṛta,* but also from a number of very remarkable autobiographical poems. Tragedy in the form of famine, the death of his first wife from starvation, extreme poverty, and the experience of the pettiness and cruelty of his co-villagers, especially of the haughty Brahmins, towards him because of his low caste, first led him to despair and then made him turn to God, who for him took the form of the merciful Viṭhobā of Paṇḍharpūr. Tukārām then devoted himself to His service and composed thousands of *abhaṅgas* or religious hymns in His honour. Tukārām's *abhaṅgas* are characterized by intensity of feeling, spontaneity and a delicate, almost feminine, charm. His best poems are simple outpourings of his heart, wounded by man's cruelty and loathing the ways of the world, but aflame with love for his ever-patient, ever-merciful 'Mother' Viṭhobā. He sometimes pictures himself as a child-bride longing to return to his mother's house, that heaven of peace.

Up to this day, Tukārām's songs live in the heart and soul of the people of Maharashtra, especially of the Maratha peasantry. The *Vārakāris,* fervent devotees of Viṭhobā, link his name with that of Dñyāndev (Jñāneśvar, qv), their prestigious, divinized Guru, as they cry and sing '*Dñyāndev-Tukārām!*' along their way to Paṇḍharpūr. Tukā, as he is more commonly called, is the ever-present companion and comforter of countless humble villagers of Maharashtra in their daily toils, as well as on the road to blessed Paṇḍharpūr.

J. A. Abbott, *Tukārām* (translation from Mahīpati's *Bhaktalīlāmṛta,* ch. 25–40, Poona 1930); J. E. Edwards, *Life and Teachings of Tukārām* (Poona 1922); N. J. Fraser and K. B. Marathe, *The Poems of Tukārām* (3 vols.,

Madras 1909–15); G. Deleury, *Psaumes du Pélerin* (French trans. of 101 poems, Paris 1956); AS 32–39; MPMS 18–21, 56–90 (English trans. of 75 poems of Tukārām); RPML 209–81; NHML. CV

tuḷḷal, a dance form of Kerala in which a solo male dancer narrates a story in verse with appropriate mime, gestures and dance movements. Two singers repeat the words of the principal performer and a drummer provides an accompaniment. See also Kuñcan Nampyār.

GSML 108-25. REA

Tulsidās (b probably 1532 Rajapur, d 1623), Hindi poet. A Brahmin, he lived most of his life in Banaras. His chief work, the *Rāmcaritmānas* (The Holy Lake of the Deed of Rāma, ?1574–77), is the greatest achievement of mediaeval Hindi literature. Written in the Avadhī dialect, it urges devotion (*bhakti*, qv) to Rāma, viewed as an incarnation of Viṣṇu, as the best means of salvation; it presents the chief figures of the traditional story, especially Rāma and his wife Sītā, as ideals of human conduct for the devotee. It combines its message of devotion to Rāma with approval of a monistic philosophical view after the fashion of the Sanskrit *Rāmāyaṇa* (qv), and accepts also much of the mythology of Hinduism involving Kṛṣṇa, Śiva and other gods. This eclecticism, the poet's skill, and the fact that it is a vernacular work have ensured its success, and it remains to this day the most influential single scripture among the Hindus of north India. Of a dozen other works the chief are *Kavitāvalī* (Collected Verses), *Vinayapatrikā* (The Petition to Rāma) and *Kṛṣṇagītāvalī* (Songs to Kṛṣṇa).

Trans.: W. D. P. Hill, *The Holy Lake of the Acts of Rām* (1952); F. R. Allchin, *Kavitāvalī* (London 1964), and *The Petition to Rām* (London 1966); Ch. Vaudeville, *Étude sur les sources et la composition du Rāmāyaṇa de Tulsī Dās* (Paris 1955). RSM

Tu-Mo (real name Ho-trong-Hieu, b 1900 Hanoi), Vietnamese poet. Of a poor family, he worked in the financial administration in Hanoi from 1918. He gained considerable popularity as a humorist and satirist, and in the 'thirties joined the *Tu luc van doan* group (see Nhat-Linh). It was then that he took the pseudonym Tu-Mo (Fat Batchelor), a witty play on the nickname of the satirist Tu-Xuong (Bony Batchelor) (see Tran-te-Xuong). From 1946 he was active in the anti-colonialist war on the side of the DRV and lives in Hanoi. Chief works: *Giong nuoc nguoc* (Against the Stream, 2 vols., 1934 and 1941) *Nu cuoi khang chien* (Smiles from the Resistance War, 1952).

DNILVN 222. VV

Tuñcatt' Eẓuttacchan, Rāmānujan (16th century), Malayalam poet. Though many legendary stories are attached to his name, little is known with certainty about the life of this most important figure in the history of Malayalam poetry. It is not sure that he was called Rāmānujan; Eẓuttacchan ('Father of Letters') is perhaps a title that was conferred on him; Tuñcattu is presumed to be a family name. Eẓuttacchan is important not only because of the supreme quality of his poetry, but because also his work marked the beginning of a period of devotional (*bhakti*, qv) and philosophical literature in Malayalam. His didactic purpose is sometimes felt to be too evident in his first major work, *Adhyātma Rāmāyaṇam*, which differs interestingly at many points from the Sanskrit *Rāmāyaṇa* (qv) on which it is based. His *Mahābhāratam* (qv) is more original. Much shorter than the Sanskrit epic, it has a greater unity, which it achieves by taking as central plot the story of the Pāṇḍavas and, in doing so, giving greater prominence to Kṛṣṇa. Several lesser works are attributed to Eẓuttacchan, with varying degrees of certainty.

Chelnat Achyuta Menon, *Eẓuttaccan and his Age* (Madras 1940); PNHML 63–78; GSML 68–78. REA

Tur, Pramudya Ananta (b 1925 Blora, Java), Indonesian writer. After attending his father's private primary school, he studied at the Radio Trade School in Surabaja and came to Djakarta in 1942. He took part in the 1945 Revolution and was imprisoned by the Dutch (1947–9). In 1950 he was awarded the Balai Pustaka Prize for his novel *Perburuan* (Pursuit). Having identified himself with the communist movement and the leftist *Lekra* (Institute of People's Culture), influenced deeply by his visit to Peking in 1956, he was imprisoned after the 1965 October events and deported to Buru Island. Tur is a writer of revolution; the majority of his themes are connected with the revolutionary fight against the Dutch, the British and the Japanese, and he has applied his first-hand acquaintance with both the battle-field and the prison in his novels and stories. His heroes escape the over-simplified black-and-white scheme; even when defeated, they become moral victors, never losing their human dignity (eg the novels, *Keluarga Gerilja*, A Guerilla Family, written in prison and published 1950, and *Mereka jang dilumpuhkan*, The Paralysed, 1951). His writings, especially short stories (*Tjerita dari Blora*, Stories from Blora, 1952; *Korupsi*, Corruption, 1954, etc) are characterized by lively and natural language, terse sentences and dynamic dialogues. Tur is undoubtedly one of the greatest Indonesian writers.

TMIL 163–80. MO

Tuwaang, Bagobo epic, see **darangan.**

Tu-Xuong, Vietnamese poet, see **Tran-te-Xuong.**

Tyāgarāja (1767–1847), Vaiṣṇava devotee and composer, born in Tamilnad of a Telugu-speaking family. His Telugu songs in praise of the Rāma incarnation of Viṣṇu are among the principal repertoire of classical south Indian music. He also wrote two musical dramas on Vaiṣṇava themes, *Prahlādabhaktivijayamu*, relating the tale of Narasiṃha's destruction of the demon-king Hiraṇyakaśipu, and *Naukācaritramu*, which tells of a prank of the young Kṛṣṇa. Boating on the Yamunā in company of the *gopīs* (milkmaids), he calls up a storm which nearly wrecks the boat. He is placated by their entreaties to save them all, and the whole is an allegory of the need of the human soul for God's grace and protection. Tyāgarāja's work is not especially significant in the history of Telugu literature *sensu stricto*, but he is of the greatest importance in south Indian music. JRM

Tyi, U, Burmese poet, see **Kyi,** U.

Tyin U, U, Burmese playwright, see **Kyin U, U.**

U

Uc-Trai, Vietnamese poet, see **Nguyen-Trai.**

Udbhaṭa (c850 AD), Indian literary critic, author of the *Kāvyālaṃkārasārasaṃgraha*, the only work of his to come down to us. Later writers refer to Udbhaṭa's commentary on the *Kāvyālaṃkāra* of Bhāmaha (qv), but this work has not yet been recovered. There is no doubt that Udbhaṭa also commented on Bharata's *Nāṭyaśāstra* (qv), probably, to judge from Abhinavagupta's (qv) remarks, on the whole text. This work, too, is lost. Fragments of his poem, the *Kumārasambhava*, are preserved in the *Kāvyālaṃkārasārasaṃgraha.* He may well have written other works (cf, eg, the comments of Indurāja, his 10th century commentator) but none have survived. The work we possess is divided into six chapters. Unlike most works on poetics, it begins with no benedictory verse and no introduction. It ends as abruptly as it begins, and this makes it probable that we have only a fragment of a much larger work. Udbhaṭa treats *rasa* (aesthetic experience) as a figure of speech, and says, rather strangely, that it can be conveyed by merely naming the emotion meant to be conveyed (*svaśabdavācya*). There exists no translation of the work at all, which is a pity, since many of the definitions and examples of figures of speech are original and deserve notice (their influence on the later tradition is manifest).

DHSP I, 72–3; II, 54–9. JLM

Ulloor, Malayalam scholar and poet, see **Paramēśvarayyar,** Uḷḷūr S.

Umāśankar Jośi, Gujarati poet, see **Jośi,** Umāśankar.

Uṇṇāyi Vāriyar, Malayalam poet, see **kathakaḷi.**

Upādhyāy, Ayodhyāsiṃh, Hindi poet, see **Hariaudh.**

upaniṣads, a comprehensive name for a comparatively limited number of older (±650–200 BC) Sanskrit texts which are more or less intimately connected with the *Veda* (qv). From the point of view of religion and philosophical thought they are highly important. Also the name for a great many treatises (some 200 of which are extant) of a more recent date and a sectarian character. These works are generally written in prose (with interspersed verses), but some are wholly in verse. The name *upaniṣad* has been variously explained; the more literal meaning, 'sitting at [the feet of a master] who imparts esoteric doctrines', is often replaced by 'mystic doctrines' or 'search for connections and correlations' and other explanations. The older *upaniṣads* are the earliest complete Hindu treatises which deal with philosophic subjects. Tentative, fluid, not rarely inconsistent and failing to reach any systematic or comprehensive codification, they reflect the struggling speculations of some generations of ancient teachers.

Although the cosmo-physical and ritualist ideas of the preceding *brāhmaṇas* (qv) are still prominent and legends and disconnected explanations of rites are intermingled with philosophical dialogue, their interest becomes increasingly anthropocentric. The recognition of a personal 'soul' (*ātman*), relating to a universal divine *ātman*, which is identified with the ultimate and fundamental principle of all existence, the Real (*Brahman*), is one of the main themes of one of the oldest *upaniṣads*. By mystically identifying one's own self with that One which is All, one has the All in control and becomes autonomous, free from death and sorrow. The celebrated formula 'That art thou!' contained in the *Chāndogya* was in later times regarded as the quintessence of monistic philosophy. The *Bṛhad-Āraṇyaka-Upaniṣad*, probably the oldest, consists of three divisions which were mechanically united. Among the subjects dealt with is a philosophical debate between a famous teacher, Yājñavalkya, and eight contestants, among them a woman. The nature of life eternal is discussed in the *Kaṭha-Upaniṣad*, relating the story of a youth, Naciketas, who visits Yama, the god of the dead and the only one who can give information on the beyond. The *Śvetāśvatara* bears witness to the spread of monotheistic tendencies in religious thought.

Trans.: R. E. Hume, *The Thirteen Principal Upanishads* (1934); S. Radhakrishan, *The Principal Upaniṣads* (1953).
WHIL I, 225–67. JG

upapurāṇa, see **purāṇa.**

'Urfi, Muhammad, Indo-Persian poet, see Vol. III.

Uroob or **Urūb,** Malayalam writer, see **Kuṭṭikkṛṣṇan,** P.C.

Usman Awang (pseud. Tongkat Warrant, b 1928 Kota Tinggi, Johore), Malay poet and short-story writer. One of the leading figures in the post-war literary movement *Angkatan Sasterawan 50* (characterized by its youth, political commitment and social idealism, and associated especially with the *Utusan* newspapers in Singapore, which Usman joined in 1950). Though known principally as one of the country's leading poets, he has made many other contributions to Malay letters, both organizationally (as Secretary of *Asas 50*, and President of *Pena*, the National Writers' Association, 1961–65) and as the author of numerous short stories, the novel *Tulang-Tulang Berserakan* (Scattered Bones, 1966), literary essays, and several plays. His verse is particularly noted for its passionate concern for the freedom of his people, peace, and social justice, expressed in an idiom almost always simple and direct but of great poetic subtlety. Two collections of poems have been published: *Gelombang* (The Long Wave, 1961), being poems 1946–60, and *Duri dan Api* (Thorn and Fire, 1967), 1961–66. Other works include collected short stories, *Degup Jantung* (Thuds the Heart, 1963), and a group of one-act plays under the title of the best known, *Tamu di Bukit Kenny* (Guest at Kenny Hill, 1968).

Trans.: SMB. WRR

Usmar Ismail, Indonesian playwright, see **Ismail,** Usmar.

Urramagyaw, Shin (1453–1542), Burmese monk and poet, contemporary and fellow monk of Thilawuntha (qv). Though a poet of great potential, he left only one poem of nine stanzas in the form of a *tawla* (see Rahtathara), which was enough to earn him literary fame. It is a noble work of devotional poetry, remarkable for sensitive observation and personification of nature. In it the whole universe, animate and inanimate, is represented, in elevated diction, as paying homage to the Buddha. It is great poetry in the context of the orthodox conceptions, but it lacks the human touch. HP

V

vacana (saying), free verse religious lyrics of mediaeval Kannada, spoken and sung by Vīraśaiva saint-poets. Vīraśaivism is a militantly reformist Śaivite religious movement, a protest against caste and priest, scripture and ritual, superstition and blind learning and for the experience of God. *Vacanas*, composed in colloquial, local dialects, were earthy and fresh in their images, though drawing on ancient Indian symbols and ideas. The *vacana* saint-poets were not pundits but artisans, weavers, ferrymen, washermen, etc. Four great *vacana*-poets must be mentioned, Basavaṇṇa (or Basavēśvara), minister of King Bijjaḷa (c1160), a saint in-the-world, usually considered the leader of the movement; Allama Prabhu, subtle, metaphysical, serene; Mahādēviyayka, joined to her Lord in physical and mystical love; Dēvara (or Jēḍara) Dāsimayya, direct, searing, often crude, who lived a century earlier (10–11th centuries).

Trans.: Nandimath, Menezes, Bhoosnurnath, Hiremath, *Śūnyasampādane* I–III (Dharwar 1965–); A. K. Ramanujan, *Speaking of Śiva* (Penguin Classics, 1972). AKR

Vættæve, author of *Guttilaya* (c1450), one of the finest of Sinhalese narrative poems. It tells the story of the *Guttila jātaka*, how an ungrateful pupil vied with his own master in a musical contest. Written in a melodious style, not over-ornate or lengthy, the poem holds the interest throughout as a story. Legend says that the author, a monk, was a pupil of Śrī Rāhula (qv). CHBR

Vaiticuvaraṉ (Vaitheeswaran, S.), modern Tamil poet, one of the representatives of the school of 'new poetry' (*putuk kavitai*). Apart from sharp poetic epigrams he writes powerful poems, re-interpreting traditional themes in a highly unconventional diction and style. Among his best poems are 'Thorn', 'Nature', 'Fireflies', contained in C. S. Chellappa's collection *Putuk kuralka* (New Voices, Madras 1962) and scattered in literary journals. KZ

Vajhī, Mullā (first half of the 17th century Golkonda), Urdu writer and court poet of the Quṭbshāhī rulers of Golkonda. His romantic *maṣnavī* (see Vol. III) *Quṭb-o-Mushtarī* (Polar Star and Jupiter, 1609) relates the adventures of a prince in love with an unknown Bengali princess (possibly the love of Sultan Muḥammad Qulī Quṭbshāh for the courtesan Bāghmatī), glorifying the charms of his native Deccan. His second work *Sab ras* (All Sentiments, 1635) in rhythmical rhyming prose is a free translation of an earlier Persian allegory. It explains various philosophical, ethical and mystic problems by personifying the parts of the human body and their qualities. The plot is thin and suffers from excessive didactic insertions; the narrative is prolix and verbose. The work has the distinction of being the first work of literary prose in Urdu.

RSHUL 38; MSHUL 49–50. JM

Vajradatta, ancient Indian poet, see **Buddhist literature.**

vākh, Kashmiri verse form, see **Lal Ded.**

Vali, Muḥammad (b 1668 Aurangabad, d 1744 Ahmedabad), Urdu lyric poet, who carried Urdu poetry from the Deccan to the north of India. In 1700 he came to Delhi, where he became a disciple of the Persian mystic and poet Sa'dullāh Gulahan. After living in Delhi, he gradually replaced the indigenous Indian elements in his erotic and mystical *ghazals* (see Vol. III), often ambiguous, by the traditional Persian style. He was a passionate lover of beauty in nature and people, and admired the Indian landscape, seasons, animals and festivals. His expression is simple, his verses spontaneous, his diction easy and melodious. He raised spoken Urdu to the level of a literary language and enriched it by taking over Persian figures of speech.

Trans.: Garcin de Tassy, *Les oeuvres de Wali* (Paris 1834).
RSHUL 41–4; MSHUL 56–65. JM

Vallabhadāsa, Sanskrit writer, see **Vetālapañcaviṃśatikā.**

Vallathol, Malayalam poet, see **Nārāyaṇa Mēnōn,** Vaḷḷattōḷ.

Vaḷḷuvar, classical Tamil poet, see **Tiruvaḷḷuvar.**

Vālmīki, Sanskrit poet, see **Rāmāyaṇa.**

Vāmana, ancient Indian writer on poetics, see **alaṃkāraśāstra.**

vār, Panjabi verse form, see **Gurdās Bhallā,** Bhāī.

Vāras Śāh (18th century), Panjabi poet, born and died at the village of Jandiala Sher Khan. His fame rests on his narrative poem of some 4,500 lines, *Hīr* (or *Hīr Rānjhā*), completed in 1765/6. The plot is drawn from a popular legend of the western Panjab: Rānjhā, the favourite youngest son of a landowner of Takht Hazāra, is forced by his jealous kinsfolk to leave home after his father's death. On his journey he meets Hīr, daughter of the Siāl chieftain Cūcak; they fall in love, and Hīr persuades her father to employ him as a buffalo-herder. They carry on an affair, until Hīr is married off to Saidā, of the Kheṛā clan of Rangpur. Rānjhā becomes the disciple of the great yogi Bālnāth, from whom he gains magic powers, and then comes to Rangpur to regain Hīr. At first Hīr's sister-in-law, Sahtī, frustrates his plans, but she is then won over and escapes with her lover together with Hīr and Rānjhā. They are captured by the pursuing Kheṛās and brought before the authorities, who, however, eventually grant Hīr and Rānjhā permission to marry. They return to their parental homes to prepare for this, but Hīr is poisoned by her kinsmen and Rānjhā then dies of grief. Although one of many, Vāras Śāh's treatment of this legend has become uniquely famous and popular and may fairly be described as the 'national epic' of the Panjab. The poem, containing some 600 rhymed stanzas of varying length, has few purely descriptive passages, being mostly in the form of dialogue, whose racy and immediate representation of Panjabi village speech has been the vital factor in securing its reputation. Its huge popularity has caused considerable corruption of, and accretions to, the original text, and it is unfortunate that the only English version, based on very inferior sources, does little justice to the original.

Trans.: C. F. Usborne, *Hir and Ranjha* (Karachi 1966). CS

Varatarācaṉ, Mu. (b 1912 Tiruppatur), Tamil writer. For several years Professor of Tamil at the University of Madras, and now Vice-Chancellor of the University of Madurai, Varatarācaṉ has made his mark both as a scholar and as a creative writer. His numerous books include works on linguistics, on literary theory and on classical Tamil poetry, biographies, discussions of social problems (in the form of letters, eg from a young man to his mother), essays, plays, short stories and novels. The latter, which form perhaps the most admired part of his work, are set more often than not in Madras and provide fascinating glimpses of life in that city. Main works: *Moḻi nūl* (1947, linguistics); *Ariñar Perṉārṭ Ṣā* (1948, biography of George Bernard Shaw); *Aṉṉaikku* (letters); *Ulaka pēreṭu* (1959, essays); *Mūṉṟu nāṭakaṅkaḷ* (1960, 3 plays); *Kuṟaṭṭai oli* (1956, short stories); *Karittuṇṭu* (A Piece of Charcoal, 1952) and *Maṇ kuṭicai* (The Mud Hut, 1961; novels).

REA

Varmā, Bhagavatīcaraṇ (b 1903 Safipur), Hindi writer. He was a lawyer in Kanpur and, since 1956, has lived as an independent writer. After his successful novel *Citralekhā* (1936) in which he discussed ascetic and lay morals in Hindu surroundings, he drew a panoramic picture of Indian politics about 1930 in *Ṭeṛe-meṛhe rāste* (Twisted Roads, 1946) and depicted the life of four generations of an Indian family in his monumental novel *Bhūle-bisre citr* (Forgotten Pictures, 1959). Besides several other novels, Varmā wrote short stories and socially committed poetry in Hindi and Urdu.

Trans.: Chandra B. Karki, *Citralekha* (Bombay 1957).
W. Ruben, *Indische Romane*, I (Berlin 1964), pp. 256–62; GHEH; AFMH. PG

Varmā, Mahādevī (b 1907 Farrukhbad), Hindi poet. She has spent most of her life in Allahabad, devoted to literature and women's education. Besides *rahasyavād* (qv) poetry, *Nīhār* (Mist, 1930), *Yāmā* (1939), *Dīp-śikhā* (Candle Flame, 1942), she wrote little masterpieces of socio-critical prose. IZ

Varmā, Vṛndāvanlāl (b 1889 Mauranipur, d 1969), Hindi writer, who was a lawyer in Jhansi. Influenced by Walter Scott he wrote a series of historical novels of which *Jhānsī kī rāṇī Lakṣmībāī* (L, the Queen of Jhansi, 1946) became very popular; it expresses a modern view of the Indian Mutiny (1857) as the first struggle for the freedom of India. In other novels, stage-plays and short stories he propagated Indian nationalism by depicting hard-working and dutiful leading characters and criticized the evil practices of Hindu society as the outcome of traditional attitudes of ritualism and laziness.

GHEH. PG

Vasubandhu (c4th century AD), Indian philosopher. The personality of Vasubandhu remains an enigma, because we have a variety of Buddhist philosophical works under that name, expressing the views of different schools. Buddhist tradition tends to the idea that one author wrote from different standpoints, which would harmonize at a higher level of abstraction; alternatively that his views evolved. One Vasubandhu was the brother of Asaṅga, the effective founder of the idealist Vijñānavāda. The *Thirty* treatise summarizing Asaṅga's philosophy is probably by this brother, as well as the polemic *Twenty* and the commentaries on Asaṅga's works. Commentaries on Mahāyāna *sūtras* may be by an earlier Madhyamaka writer. The much more original and philosophically-valuable *Abhidharma-kośabhāṣya*, a Sautrāntika critique of Sarvāstivādin *Abhidharma*, may be by a 5th century writer, yet some have supposed that the Sautrāntikas took up a position reconciling Mahāyāna and the early schools, the Pramāṇa School of Diṅnāga being a development of Sautrāntika rather than a retreat from Vijñānavāda. Now Diṅnāga was a pupil of a Vasubandhu, so that it might seem that three distinct philosophical subjects were studied by this group, who elaborated an idealist ontology, criticized *Abhidharma* and created a new epistomology.

Trans.: La Vallée Poussin, *Abhidharmakośabhāṣya* (Louvain 1923–31).
E. Frauwallner, *On the Date of the Buddhist Master of the Law Vasubandhu* (Rome 1951); WIB; WHIL II, 356–63. AKW

Vāsudēvan Nāyar, M.T. (b 1934), Malayalam novelist. Like many of his contemporaries, he shows less interest than the older generation of Kerala's writers in using his novels and short stories to promote social reform, and concentrates rather on the psychology of human behaviour. In recent years critics have begun to note poetic qualities of his novels. The bulk of his characters are Nairs (Nāyars), that is to say belonging to his own community. By way of experiment he has written one novel, *Aṛabipponnu* (Arab Gold, 1960), in co-operation with N. P. Muhammad. Main works: *Nālukeṭṭu* (The Nair Household, 1958); *Maññu* (Mist, 1964); *Kālam* (Time, 1969).

VISNM 53–6, 70–2. REA

Vasukalpa, ancient Indian poet, see **Buddhist literature.**

vāt (account, report, story), refers to various types of prose narratives in Old Western Rajasthani. The oldest *vāts* were composed by Jain *munis* as edifying tales. The bulk of *vāt* literature is composed of folk-tales, reflecting the customs, beliefs and culture of rural Rajasthan in a vivid manner. They are often interspersed with verses (of the *dohā* or *kavitta* type), according to the traditional manner of professional storytellers in northern India. A comparatively large number of *vāts* concern historical or semi-historical events and heroes, the latter being Rājput kings and nobles, and the theme being their heroic prowess. The *vāts* in old and modern Rajasthani constitute a considerable mass of literature, most of which is still unpublished. CV

Vātsyāyan, Hindi poet, see **Ajñeya,** Saccidānanda.

Vātsyāyana Mallanāga (c2nd–4th century AD), presumably a learned Brahmin, author of *Kāmasūtra* (The Textbook of Erotics), in which he systematized and codified the prevalent knowledge and theoretical assumptions on erotics, ie the culture of sexual life (*kāma*). Nothing is known about his life (except a few legendary anecdotes), but he preserved certain teachings and ideas of his predecessors, some of whom he mentions by name. Erotics formed part of the Hindu trinity of life-goals that aimed at a perfection of achievements in religious duties (*dharma*), material prosperity (*artha*) and a full satisfaction of physical urges (*kāma*). It was a recognized scientific discipline in India, treated in a dry, matter-of-fact style, and probably widespread among prosperous and world-oriented strata of society. The theory of sexual life with its social implications was also pursued by dramatists and poets who made abundant use of it in their works. Vātsyāyana's book contains a number of original observations and valuable data on private life of well-to-do people. Later works largely imitated its design and made little, if any, contribution of their own.

German trans., R. Schmidt (Leipzig 1897, 6th ed., Berlin 1920); English trans., Richard Burton—frequently inaccurate.
WHIL III, 620 ff. IF

Veda (lit. 'knowledge') is the partly preserved body of Ancient Indian religious literature, great in volume and very varied in content. It is composed in an older form of Indo-Aryan, the language of the Aryan peoples, which, perhaps in the 12th century BC, entered India from the north-west. After becoming the vehicle of literary expression for brahmanical society, this language gradually developed, in the second half of the 1st millennium BC, into Sanskrit. In a narrower sense, the term *Veda* applies to the basic collections of verses ('hymns') and formulae; in a wider sense it includes also the exegetical and liturgical texts associated with these. Moreover, the *Veda* is threefold (*Ṛgveda*, qv, *Yajurveda*, *Sāmaveda*) or (if the *Atharvaveda* is included) fourfold. The basic collections were, and incidentally still are, used for ritual purposes; the *hotar* priest and his assistants draw the material for their recitations from the *Ṛgveda-Saṃhitā*, the *adhvaryu* cum suis (the officiants entrusted with the manual acts) utilize the formula included in the *Yajurveda-Saṃhitā*, and the *udgātar* with his group perform their melodic recitations which, while drawn almost entirely from the *Ṛgveda*, were arranged in the *Sāmaveda-Saṃhitā*. The *Atharvaveda-Saṃhitā*, though in the course of time recognized as the fourth, is a collection of mostly magic hymns and spells, texts intended for the domestic ritual, speculative 'hymns' and *mantras* (qv) for atonement of ritual imperfections, to be used by the Brahmin priest supervizing the sacrificial acts and atoning the shortcomings of his colleagues.

With the inclusion of the *brāhmaṇas*, *āraṇyakas* and *upaniṣads* (qqv) associated with the *saṃhitās* this entire body of literature is traditionally considered to be *śruti*, ie eternal truth, formulated through a divine intermediary and 'heard' by inspired seers (*ṛṣis*) in hoary antiquity. The much debated chronological questions (a few texts except the latest works may date back to the 4th century BC) are therefore of little importance for the orthodox.

These works, in many cases very voluminous, were transmitted orally from teacher to pupil, a tradition which continued, despite the existence of written or printed texts (which, however, in some cases did not exist before the 10th century AD); in certain milieus, the tradition continues up to the present day. Although this literature was very carefully preserved, there arose local differences of tradition within each *Veda*, which in time gave rise to 'schools', or 'branches' (*śākhās*), which at one time were numerous, developing into different recensions. Little is known of them beyond those whose texts survive; nor is it possible precisely to date their rise or duration. Though authoritative in their own milieu, these collections were no canons in the proper sense of the term because there was no church or institution which could enact them as such. With the exception of the *Ṛgveda-Saṃhitā* they were subject to vicissitudes. Yet devout worshippers were convinced of their infallibility and effectiveness: if they were correctly understood and recited and the ritual acts correctly performed the sacrificer would gain control over the Unseen and earn worldly success and religious merit. Although the interpretation of large parts of this body of literature is, to a certain extent, facilitated by numerous quotations and by references in later texts to the earlier ones, the absence of reliable old commentaries is a serious disadvantage.

This literature is characterized by an hieratic style, often rigid in the prose texts, which has retained and developed many features of archaic oral literature (see also *Ṛgveda*). However, in the younger texts, it gradually loses its archaic grammatical form, to become, in the *sūtras* (qv, see also *vedāṅga*), very concise and aphoristic. Its importance for linguistics, historians of religion, of literature or of human culture in general, is unique. A good many of the myths and legends contained in the *brāhmaṇas* (qv), told in terse and straightforward prose, are jewels of archaic narrative art. Some of them, for instance the story of the marriage of the nymph Urvaśī and the mortal Purūravas in the *Śatapatha-Brāhmaṇa* (11, 5, 1), continued to attract the attention of later poets. The ritualistic demonstrations of the *brāhmaṇas* give a good insight into the pre-scientific art of argumentation, proceeding by means of analogy, similarity in quality, identity of number, (pseudo-)etymological explanations based on the conviction that name and thing are indissolubly connected, assumptions of special connections between acts and their purposes or effects, and so on. Many hymns of the *Ṛgveda* show deep feeling for nature, the most notable being the hymns to the goddess of dawn (*Uṣas*). The *Atharvaveda-Saṃhitā*, whilst abounding in perfect spells and incantations, introduces us also to sacrificial mysticism and ritualistic explanations of the universe and the basic categories of being. Like the ritual handbooks, especially those dealing with the domestic cult, it sheds much light upon the religion of the great mass of the people, which was different from the expensive and elaborate 'aristocratic' cult discussed in the *brāhmaṇas*. The *Kauśikasūtra*, belonging to the *Atharvaveda*, is a unique collection of magical rites and other ritual procedures requiring texts borrowed from the *Atharvaveda-Saṃhitā*. Giving a faithful impression of the philosophical discussions and the religious movements in the 6th–3rd centuries BC, the *upaniṣads* (qv) too rank high as literature.

To the Vedic schools which have survived belong, in the *Ṛgvedic* tradition, the *Aitareya* and the *Śāṅkhāyana*, each with a *brāhmaṇa* and other dependent texts; in the *Sāmaveda*, the *Kauthuma* and *Jaiminīya*. Of the *Atharvaveda* we possess the *Śaunakīya* and the *Paippalāda* recensions. As to the *Yajurveda*, there is the Black branch which includes prose explanations in *brāhmaṇa* style in their collections of *mantras* and *yajus* formulas (the latter being the short ritual formulae, as a rule in prose, used by the *adhvaryu* priest), and the White branch, so called because its *saṃhitā* does not intermingle formulae and explanations. To the White *Yajurveda* belong, inter alia, the *Vājasaneyī-Saṃhitā* and the *Śatapatha-Brāhmaṇa*, to the Black *Yajurveda* the *Kaṭha* and the *Taittirīya* schools. Of the last tradition we possess no less than six *Śrauta-* and six *Gṛhya-sūtras* (see *sūtra*), among them the voluminous works attributed to Baudhāyana and Āpastamba and the *Vaikhānasasūtras*, which, being most recent of all (c300 AD), have incorporated many non-Vedic elements. A considerable part of these works has been translated, and many have also been commented upon in the course of the last hundred years.

Trans.: W. D. Whitney and C. R. Lanman, *Atharvaveda-Saṃhitā*, 2 vols. (1905); W. Caland, *Das Śrautasūtra des Āpastamba*, 3 vols. (1921–8); H. Oldenberg, *The Gṛhyasūtras*, 2 vols. (SBE 1886–92, reprinted 1964); W. Caland *Vaikhānasasmārtasūtram* (1929) and *Altindisches Zauber-ritual* (part of the *Kauśikasūtra*, 1900); J. Gonda, *The Savayajñas* (part of the *Kauśikaśūtra* including hymns of the Atharvaveda, 1965). See also *Ṛgveda, brāhmaṇyas, āraṇyakas, upaniṣads*.
WHIL I, 52–310; H. von Glasenapp, *Die Literaturen Indiens* (1929, reprinted 1961); DHSL.
JG

vedāṅga. In ancient India it was the sacred duty of a Brahmin to hand down and teach the *Veda* (qv). The young Brahmins in their *guru*'s (teacher's) home did not however confine their attention exclusively to the *Veda* proper. As a result of considerable discussion on the interpretation of the *Veda* there gradually developed, probably between the 8th and 4th centuries BC, six subsidiary sciences, the so-called *vedāṅga* ('limbs of the *Veda*'). Belonging to the sacred tradition (*smṛti*) they are regarded as of human origin. They deal with scientific material and for mnemotechnical reasons are mostly aphorisms (*sūtra*-style, qv), partly in the versified didactic style of the ancient Indian scientific manuals. The learning necessary for the proper sacrificial employment of the *brāhmaṇa* portions of the *Veda* is *kalpa* ('ritual'). The general term denoting the handbooks on religious practice which emerged within the different Vedic schools is *Kalpa-sūtra*.

Kalpa-Sūtra comprises the *Śrauta-sūtras* (*sūtra* texts based on *śruti* or divine revelation), systematic guides for the use of the priests who had to execute the highly complicated great sacrifices each according to his own school, and the *Gṛhya-sūtras*, handbooks for rites in the home, such as birth ceremonies, name-giving, marriage, as well as the five daily sacrifices and some other rites. The *vedāṅga* called *śikṣā*, ie 'instruction (in recitation)', is mainly concerned with phonetics or correct pronunciation: in order to ensure the faithful transmission of the *Veda* the ancient teachers devised recitations of separate words of the texts (*padapāṭha*) and of words in pairs (*kramapāṭha*), and various other exercises for converting these analysed texts into the text of the Vedic bodies of literature. Besides, there are numerous smaller didactic works dealing with difficulties of pronunciation, etc. The *vedāṅga* called *chandas* discusses the Vedic metres and prosody. *Vyākaraṇa* (grammar), considered the foremost *vedāṅga*, was represented by a succession of older grammarians whose work culminated in, and was made obsolete by, the famous *Aṣṭādhyāyī* of Pāṇini (qv, ?5th century BC), which, although devoted chiefly to a later stage of the language, incorporated many features of Vedic. The *nirukta* (etymology) explains obscure words in the Vedic texts and studies synonyms and names of gods. Yāska (?5th century BC), commenting on a word list (*nighaṇṭu*) comprising such material, furnishes us with many illustrations, mainly from the *Ṛgveda*. The sixth *vedāṅga*, *jyotiṣa* (astronomy), deals with such knowledge of the heavenly bodies as was necessary to compile a calendar for sacrificial purposes (eg the position of the sun and moon at the solstices). JG

Veṅkatesa Ayyangār, Māsti or Śrīnivāsa (b 1891 Masti), pioneer and major Kannada short-story writer with over 50 books and a dozen volumes of short stories. His poetry, play and novels (*Subbaṇṇa*, a musician's life, *Cannabasavanāyaka*, on Mysore history), lectures and cultural-literary essays (*Vimarśe* 1–5, Criticism), are also important achievements. Realistic, humorous, wise, rooted in tradition and contemporary social detail, the stories depict themes and characters of great range, from tribals, village boys, and butter-milk sellers to Sultans, English art-collectors and epic characters. Artistic yet effortless, he created single-handed, in a steady output of nearly half a century, both a short-story form and a moving prose close to speech.

Trans.: N. Rama Rao, *Cennabasavanāyaka* (Mysore 1957); *Short Stories* (Bangalore 1943); *Subanna* (Bangalore 1943). AKR

Vēṇukōpālaṉ, Ti. Co. (**Venugopalan,** T. S.), modern Tamil poet. He is probably the best of the 'new poets'. His poems are penetrating, witty commentaries on modern problems and hitherto forbidden subjects, as well as metaphysical reinterpretations of traditional Hindu motifs, written with careful detachment and great formal skill. Some of his best poems are contained in C. S. Chellappan's anthology *Putuk kuralka* (New Voices, Madras 1962). KZ

Vetālapañcaviṃśatikā (Twenty-five Stories of a Demon), classical Sanskrit collection of stories of unknown date, set in an epic frame, with moralizing verses appended. The king is to bring a corpse possessed by a demon to an ascetic for a yogic ritual, without uttering a word, but has to repeat his performance twenty-five times, as he must always, under the threat of death, answer a question about a tale narrated by the demon, if he knows the answer. In the story, the demon, impressed by the king's perseverance, propounds a paradoxical question to which there is no possible logical answer. The king can therefore remain silent, and is thus able to accomplish his task. There exist at least five recensions of the collection, the oldest (in prose) being ascribed to Śivadāsa, another to Vallabhadāsa, and yet another preserved under the name of Jambhaladatta; two recensions in verse were incorporated into larger collections by Kṣemendra (see Guṇāḍhya) and Somadeva (qv) respectively. The stories may be of folk-origin, but their elaboration is marked by features characteristic of the *kāvya* (qv) style.

Trans.: M. B. Emeneau, *Jambhaladatta's Version of the Vetālapañcaviṁśati* (New Haven 1934); H. Uhle, *Die Vetālapañcaviṅçatikā* (Leipzig 1884); W. Ruben, *Die 25 Erzählungen des Dämons*. In *Ozean der Märchenströme*, I (Helsinki 1944).
WHIL III, 365–70. DZ

Vētanāyakam Piḷḷai, Samuel (1826–89), the author of the first novel in Tamil, *Piratāpa Mutaliyār carittiram* (The Life and Adventures of Prathapa Mudaliar, 1876). It is a curious mixture of realism and fantasy, with numerous digressions in which the author puts forward his views on political, social and moral questions. This and a second novel, *Cukuṇacuntari* (1887), were written after Vētanāyakam retired from his position as a district munsiff. Earlier he had published volumes of ethical and religious verses (*Nīti nūl*, 1859).

CNI 184–9. REA

Vidāgama Maitreya (15th century), Sinhalese monk of the *Mahānetraprasāda Mūla* (Fraternity) in the reign of King Parākramabāhu VI (1415–67), a leader of the puritan branch of the *sangha* (compared with Śrī Rāhula, qv, who dabbled in Mahāyāna beliefs and practices). His principal works are *Lōv ḍasaṅgarāva* (before 1446), one of the first poems learnt by the Sinhalese child, being a collection of 100 moral Buddhist maxims: and *Budugunālaṃkāraya* (1475), a versified account of the plague at Vesālī in the days of the Buddha and how it was stopped by the recitation of the *Ratana Sutta*; it is written in simple language and contains amusingly satirical attacks on Hindu practices. His other works are *Elu Attanagalu Vaṃsaya*, a prose version of a Pali historical work, and two small verse compositions, *Kavlakununiminimala* and *Dahamg ṭamālāva*. *Haṃsa Sandesa* (The Goose Message, c1460), is a counterblast by the school of Vīdāgama to the *Girā Sandesa* (Parrot's Message, see *sandesa*), which extols the school of Śrī Rāhula. There is however no indication of authorship. CHBR

Vidyācakravarti (13th century), author of the Sinhalese prose work *But Sarana*, and probably also of *Daham Sarana*. These contain a series of episodes from the life of the Buddha, told with vigorous narrative skill. Here the well-known *Vessantara jātaka*, the story of how the Buddha, in a previous incarnation, gave away his wife and children, is narrated at considerable length. CHBR

Vidyākara, ancient Indian critic, see **Buddhist literature.**

Vidyāpati, a Vaiṣṇava poet from the Darbhanga district of Mithila, situated between West Bengal and Bihar. His exact dates are still in dispute, though it is certain that he flourished well before the middle of the 15th century. His works were well enough known by the end of that century to have been read 'with pleasure' by Caitanya, the Bengali Vaiṣṇava saint born in 1486. There is a copper plate grant, deeding the village of Visfi, in Darbhanga, to him, and signed by the Rājā Siva Sinha; the grant is dated 1400 AD and is attested in a poem ascribed to Vidyāpati. But because the date on the copper plate is given in the Muslim Hijra era, a custom introduced only by the emperor Akbar at a much later time, and because the characters of the inscription do not conform to so early a date, the plate and the poem have been called forgeries by some scholars. In fact, very little is known with certainty about this very popular and skilful religious poet; there are legends that he on one occasion met with Advaita-ācārya, the *guru* (religious teacher) and trusted companion of Caitanya, and on another with the other great early Vaiṣṇava poet Caṇḍīdās (qv), but until Vidyāpati's dates are established, these will remain legends.

It is clear from Vidyāpati's poetry that he was learned in Sanskrit; his language and skill in using Sanskrit metres in Maithili attest to this, and there are eight works in Sanskrit ascribed to him. But he is known primarily as a poet of devotion (*bhakti*, qv), and his elegant verses on the love of Rādhā and Kṛṣṇa are sung today, in worship and from the concert stage. But it is sometimes difficult to ascertain which verses are actually his. It was the custom of poets of the period to close their poems with signature lines (*bhaṇitās*). But as was the case with Caṇḍīdās and perhaps other poets of great fame, later and lesser poets would often sign the names of their more distinguished predecessors to their own work. Thus the same poem turns up in two different manuscripts, one with the signature Vidyāpati, the other with the signature Sekhara. It might also have been that the poet's name was a title (*vidyāpati* means 'Master of true knowledge'), and that later poets assumed or were given this title. Historical uncertainties, however, cannot detract from the beauty and grace of many of the songs to which Vidyāpati's name is affixed.

Trans.: Deben Bhattacharya, *Love Songs of Vidyapati* (London 1963); E. C. Dimock, Jr and D. Levertov, *In Praise of Krishna* (New York 1967).
Sukumar Sen, *A History of Brajbuli Literature* (Calcutta 1935). ECD

Vidyāsāgar, Bengali writer, see **Bidyāsāgar,** Iśvarcandra.

Villa, Jose Garcia (b 1908 Singalong, Manila), Filipino poet writing in English. He first studied medicine, then switched to law. Even as a student, Villa wrote short stories and poetry and because of some controversial themes in his writing was expelled from the University of the Philippines. The same year, however, he won a prize for the best short story of the year. He then went to study in New Mexico and began publishing in American magazines. His poetry in prose won literary prizes both in the USA and the Philippines. Villa developed a new form of poetry, 'comma poems'. His craftsmanship and skill remains unchallenged among Filipino poets. Considered the greatest living Filipino poet, Villa is nevertheless criticized by some for being individualistic and not closely involved with real life and social problems. Works: poetry, *Many Voices* (1939), *Poems by Doveglion* (1941), *Have Come, Am Here* (1942), *Volume Two* (1949), *Selected Poems and New* (1958), *Poems 55* (1962), *Poems in Praise of Love* (1962); short stories, *Footnote to Youth* (1933), *Selected Stories* (1962). EH

Vinaya, see **Tripiṭaka.**

Vīr Singh, Bhāi (1872–1957), Panjabi writer. Born into a well-to-do Sikh family of Amritsar, devoted his life to furthering the ideals of the Singh Sabhā, the Sikh reformist movement, and later also politics, as well as to literature. His literary output was considerable, and the corpus of his writings embraces a wide variety of genres. In 1894 he founded the Khalsa Tract Society for the publication of Sikh reformist pamphlets, and in 1899 began the *Khālsā Samācar*, a weekly journal. The trilogy of short novels written at this period, *Sundarī* (1898), *Bijai Singh* (1899) and *Satvant Kaur* (1900) are glorifications of the Sikh past, important as the first examples of modern Panjabi prose fiction. A later novel, *Bābā Naudh Singh* (1921), has a more contemporary setting, but a similarly propagandist theme. Vīr Singh's concern with the Sikh past is also reflected in his editions of Sikh texts, including a *janamsākhī* (qv), and his three works of biography of the Sikh *gurūs*, based on traditional materials, *Kalgīdhar Camatkār*, *Gurū Nānak Camatkār* and *Aṣṭ Gurū Camatkār*.

His first published poem was the ambitious *Rāṇā Sūrat Singh*, a romantic epic of some 12,000 lines, remarkable for being in blank verse. He later turned to the composition of short lyrics, often mystical in tone and revealing a finely developed sense of the beauty of nature; he published eight volumes of these during the latter part of his life, from *Lahirāṃ de Hār* (1921) to *Mere Sāīāṃ Jīo* (1955). It is in these that his most important literary achievement is now seen to have lain. There can, however, be no doubt that Vīr Singh was the most important single figure in the modern Panjabi literature.

Trans.: Puran Singh, *Nargas, Songs of a Sikh* (London 1924).
J. S. Ahluwalia, *Tradition and Experiment in Modern Panjabi Poetry* (Jullundur 1960), pp 70–85; Harbans Singh, *Aspects of Punjabi Literature* (Ferozepore 1961), pp. 30–6. CS

Vīramāmuṉivar, Tamil poet, see **Beschi,** Constanzo.

Virudhachalam or **Viruttācalam,** Tamil writer, see **Putumaippittaṉ.**

Viśākhadatta, Indian dramatist. Nothing is known of his life and date, but he is assumed by some to have been a courtier of Candragupta II (376–415 AD). His play *Devīcandragupta* (The Queen and Candragupta) is known only in fragments, but his *Mudrārākṣasa* (The Minister's Signet Ring) is one of the best Indian dramas. It is semi-historical, dealing with court intrigue, during the reign of the last Nanda ruler, and the rise to power of Candragupta Maurya: it is centred around two rival ministers, Rākṣasa and Cāṇakya (or Kauṭilya), the former representing the loyalty and honesty, and the latter the wisdom and skill of an able statesman. The drama differs from other Indian plays by its complete lack of love element; apart from a few servants, there are no female characters in it. The plot is skilfully executed, with a mounting tension and lively dialogue.

Trans.: J. A. B. van Buitenen, *The Minister's Seal*, in *Two Plays of Ancient India* (New York and London 1968).
G. V. Devasthali, *Introduction to the Study of Mudrā-rākṣasa* (Bombay 1948); W. Ruben, *Der Sinn des Dramas 'Das Siegel und Rākshasa', Mudrārākshasa* (Berlin 1956); WHIL III, 232–7. DZ

Viśvanātha, Sanskrit writer on poetics, see **alaṃkāraśāstra.**

Vu-trong-Phung (b 1912 Hung-yen province, d 1939 Hanoi), Vietnamese writer of the realist school. Of a poor family, he worked first as a minor official and then tried to make a living by his writing. An opium addict, he died very young, of tuberculosis. In his short career as a writer (from 1931) he produced 15 books (novels, reportage, translations, short stories and plays). Although they contain satirical elements, his novels lay greater stress on the tragic than on the comic side of life. He was strongly influenced by Freudian ideas. Chief novels: *Cam bay nguoi* (Trap for Men, 1933); *Giong to* (Storm, 1936); *So do* (Luck, 1936); *Vo de* (The Broken Dyke, 1936); *Lam di* (Prostitution, 1939).

DNILVN 224. VV

W

Wa, Theippam Maun (Sein Tin, U, b 1899 Moulmein, d 1942 Gadahsijtyi), Burmese writer, essayist, dramatist and literary critic. He studied Burmese and Pāli at the Rangoon University and was active in the 1920 University Strike as a teacher in the Central National School, Rangoon (1920–1923). In 1927–29 he attended the Indian Civil Service course in Oxford. From 1929 he served in ICS in various places in Burma, and was shot by bandits in 1942. Wa was one of the founders of *Khitsam* (see Zodji) and an innovator in prose style. His short fictional works bordering on documentary give a realistic, somewhat critical picture of village life in 1929–36 as seen by the ICS official Maun Lu Ei (autobiographical character) on inspection tours. His descriptions of the uneducated, backward villagers point to the need for reforms. Under the pen-name Tin Tint he wrote plays sharply critical of the state of society. After 1936 he seems to have identified himself more with the official class and rejected the nationalist movement; his writing is then limited to the family life of Maun Lu Ei. Works: short stories in *Khitsam Poumpyin mja 1* (Khitsan Stories 1, 1934) and *Khitsam Poumpyin 2* (1938); *Oksphoud Tekkathoul Hmattam mja* (Oxford University Diary, 1935); *Sis atwin Neisin Hmattam* (War Diary, 1966); *Khitsam Yazawin yei mja* (Studies in History, 1935); *Sa* (Writings, 1966). DB

wajang, Javanese puppet theatre, originated probably in the early part of the Christian era. It was enriched in the course of time by Hindu mythology and philosophy, and later by Islamic thought. Both elements are apparent in the *wajang* subjects, while the structure and performance of the plays are of native origin. *Wajang* is stylized both in form and content. It flourished particularly in the kingdoms of central Java. *Wajang* has two basic meanings: theatrical performance, and puppet. The plays are performed either by puppets of several kinds, or by living actors pretending to be puppets. The oldest known types include *wajang kulit*, *wajang beber*, *wajang topeng*; c15th century new variants arose, some of which became independent genres, while others gave rise to new forms later (*wajang golek*, *wajang wong*). *Wajang kulit* is played with two-dimensional puppets, *w. golek* with three-dimensional, and *w. beber* uses painted scrolls, while *w. wong* and *w. topeng* are played by actors. Modern (20th century) forms, *w. Sulah* and *w. Pantja Sila*, devised for nationalist propaganda, failed to establish themselves.

The most important *wajang* personality is the *dalang*, who works the puppets and speaks. The traditional form and fixed plot provide the *dalang* with firm foundations for improvisation. He relies on his experience as an actor and on his intimate knowledge of the traditional plots. Hundreds of these plots have become fixed in the oral tradition of centuries; it was probably in the Middle Ages that they were recorded, together with rules for performance (*pakem*). Traditional *wajang* plots were absorbed, often in symbolic form, by the modern play (see *sandiwara*) in early 20th century. They can also be found in later genres such as *wajang wong* or the Javanese *ketoprak*. Treatment of *wajang* themes varies according to the type of performance, but all these types are marked either by native treatment of subjects of foreign origin (the Indian *Mahābhārata* and *Rāmāyaṇa*, qqv), or by Islamic themes such as the Menak cycle and native Javanese legends of Pandji, the sources on which the theatre throughout south-east Asia draws.

J. R. Brandon, *Theatre in Southeast Asia* (Cambridge 1967); C. Holt, *Art in Indonesia: Continuities and Change* (Ithaca 1967); W. H. Rassers, *Panji, the Culture Hero: A Structural Study of Religion in Java* (The Hague 1959); J. R. Brandon, *On Thrones of Gold: Three Javanese Shadow Plays* (Cambridge 1970). EV

Weṅkaṭaśāstri, Ceḷḷupiḷḷa, Telugu poet, see **Tirupati Weṅkaṭakawulu.**

Wickramasinghe, Martin (b 1891), doyen of living Sinhalese writers; author of novels and short stories, also of works of criticism. CHBR

Wirēśaliṅgam, Kandukūri (b 1848 Rajahmundry, d 1919 Madras), Telugu writer and social reformer. Telugu teacher by profession, Wīrēśaliṅgam was the first writer to use prose as a literary form and as an instrument of social reform in Telugu. An outstanding leader of the Brāhma Samāj movement in southern India, he used his literary talent to improve the lot of women in Hindu society by encouraging the re-marriage of widows and emphasizing women's education. He wrote in every genre of modern literature, the social novel, essay, children's literature, satire, autobiography, literary criticism; in addition, he extensively translated English poetry, plays, essays and novels. His collected works, published recently in 12 volumes, run into nearly 10,000 pages. In 1893 he was awarded the title Rao Bahadur by the British Government for his distinguished services to education and society. He edited two journals for the propagation of his views on education, literature, and social reform, one exclusively devoted to women's education. Although he dissipated his energies too widely to distinguish himself in any one form, he laid firm foundations for the growth of modern literature in Telugu. His militancy as a crusader of social reform was reflected in the prose style for which he became famous. His *Kawula caritra* (Lives of Poets, 1899), though incomplete, is the first authentic history of Telugu literature.

Trans.: J. Robert Hutchinson, *Fortune's Wheel* (London 1887), a social novel; A. Galletti, *Pleasures of Whirlgig* (Rajahmundry 1902). BhK

Wun, U, Burmese poet, see **Min Thuwun.**

X

Xuan-Dieu (b 1917 Trao-nha, Ha-tinh province), Vietnamese poet. He passed his childhood in Qui-nhon and studied in Hue and Hanoi, where he lives at present. One of the most prolific poets both before and after the 1945 Revolution, he played a significant role in the formation of modern Vietnamese poetry, new in content and form, *tho moi* (New Poetry, see The-Lu). Volumes of verse: *Tho tho* (Poems, 1938); *Gui huong cho gio* (The Incense Sent on the Breeze, 1945); *Ngon quoc ky* (The State Flag, 1945); *Hoi nghi non song* (Meeting of All the Land, 1946); *Me con* (Mother and Child, 1954); *Ngoi sao* (Star, 1955); *Rieng chung* (On the Personal and the Common, 1960); *Mui Ca-mau* (Cape Ca-mau, 1962); *Cam tay* (Hand in Hand, 1962). Besides verse he has published a volume of stories, *Phan thong vang* (The Gold Pollen of the Pines, 1939), and essays, reviews and notes.

DNILVN 151–3, 225. VV

Y

Yādav, Rājendra (b 1929 Agra), Hindi writer. He spent some years in Calcutta and lives now in Delhi. He is one of the leading pioneers of the *nayī kahānī* (qv), of strikingly modern literary techniques on themes from urban middle-class life, especially intellectuals, such as the novel, *Ek iñc muskān* (An Inch of a Smile, 1963). His best novel, *Sārā ākāś* (The Whole Sky, 1960), depicts the inside life of an orthodox Hindu family. Yādav also translates European literature (Chekhov, Turgenyev, Camus). Some stories: *Khel-khilaune* (Games and Toys, 1954); *Choṭe-choṭe Tājmahal* (Miniature Tajmahals); *Kināre se kināre tak* (From Bank to Bank, 1963). DA

yadu, Burmese classical verse-form of four-syllable lines (see *linga*), the only one with a fixed structure. It is a short poem (1–2 pages of a small book), usually of three stanzas, sometimes of only one or two. The three stanzas of the standard *yadu* were linked by making the final lines echo one another, and by making all the syllables of the first lines rhyme exactly. Unlike *mawgun* and *pyo* (qqv), *yadu* can be written on a wide variety of subjects, including giving edifying advice, and in praise of the king, but the greatest *yadu* are, in fact, love poems (see Natshinnaung). They express the writer's feelings of sadness and longing, aroused through separation from home or loved one, or by the contemplation of the changing seasons and the beauties of nature while journeying by river or through the forest. There are classical *yadu* of many moods; 'Parrot Messenger', 'Invocation to a Pagoda', 'Ranting at the Rain', 'Military Campaign', 'To my Sweetheart'. *Yadu* is also used in modern literature where its structure is looser and the themes are more varied. HP

Yājñavalkya, ancient Indian sage, prominent in parts of the *Śatapatha-Brāhmaṇa* and its appendix, the *Bṛhad-Āraṇyaka-Upaniṣad* (see *brāhmaṇa*, *upaniṣads*). His name has also been attached to a much later legal text, the *Yājñavalkya-smṛti* (see *dharmaśāstra*).

Yajurveda, one of the four books of the **Veda.**

Yamin, Muhammad (b 1903 Sumatra, d 1962 Djakarta), Indonesian writer and politician. A leading figure in the Sumatra youth organization while still at school; after completing his law studies he became chairman of the Gerindo nationalist party in 1932. A member of the People's Council 1938–42, after the revolution he held office in the ultra-left Murba party and in 1951 became a member of the Indonesian government. Yamin was one of the pioneers of modern poetry in Indonesia. His first volume of verse, *Tanah Air* (My Country), appeared in 1922, singing the praises of his native Sumatra. The second volume, entitled *Indonesia, Toempah Darahku* (Indonesia, Land of My Birth, 1929), a collection of ardently patriotic poems, used new literary forms and marked its author as a pioneer of modern poetry. Other works: novel, *Gadjah Mada* (1948); *Sedjarah Peperangan Diponegoro* (History of the Diponegoro War, 1945); *Revolusi Amerika* (The American Revolution, 1951).

TMIL 9–13. MO

Yāska, ancient Indian writer on etymology, see **vedāṅga.**

Yaśpāl (b 1903 Firozpur), Hindi writer, active in the terrorist trend of the nationalist movement and imprisoned for many years by colonial authorities. His stories and novels, mainly of urban middle-class life, attack all forms of social injustice, superstition and prejudice. His two-part social novel, *Jhūṭhā sac* (The Lying Truth, 1958–1960), is a broad vivid portrayal of the partition of India and the first decade of independence. Up to the end of the fifties he chose mainly burning social problems, in the sixties turning to intimate personal themes, eg the novel *Bārah ghaṇṭe* (Twelve Hours, 1963). Some short stories: *Jñāndān* (The Gift of Knowledge, 1943); *Khaccar aur ādmī* (Mule and Man, 1962); novels *Deśdrohī* (Traitors, 1942); *Manuṣya ke rūp* (Facets of Man, 1949). DA

Yatana Kyemon (The Precious Mirror), early Burmese fictional work written by Shwedaung Thihathu (?1708–?68), and completed by U Tha of Taungdwin. It is, according to some Burmese scholars, the earliest work embodying many of the features of a novel. Though similar in arrangement to the court plays by the Princess Hlaing (qv), it lacks the characteristic songs. It is quite different in its style and treatment of the theme from the religious stories by Thilawuntha (qv) or the stage-plays by Kyin U and Ponnya (qqv). HP

yātrā, a musico-dramatic genre of Bengali folklore, of uncertain origin. Since the Middle Ages, its main subjects are stories of Hindu gods and goddesses, especially Kṛṣṇa and his beloved Rādhā (*Kṛṣṇa-yātrā*). In the 18th and 19th centuries, new and even secular subjects were introduced. Main emphasis is put on songs, either without any dialogues or interspersed with improvised bits of prose. Women's parts are acted by boys and no scenic devices used. Highly emotional songs and sentimental episodes are the most characteristic features of *yātrās*, still performed today by professional and amateur groups. The performance takes place after sunset, often lasting till dawn.

SHBLL 724–43. DZ

Yi-tsing, ie **I-ching,** Chinese pilgrim to India, see Vol. III.

Yogeśvara, ancient Indian poet, see **Buddhist literature.**

Yūon Phāi, Lilit (The Conquest of Northern Thailand, a Poem in Lilit Metre), one of the oldest Thai poems, probably dating from late 15th century. Neither date nor author are known. It is a poem in praise of King Trailōkhanāt (1448–88) who besieged and took Chīengmai, the capital of northern Thailand, describing the campaign. Tilok, ruler of Chīengmai, had the governor of Chīeng Chūēn murdered; the latter's supporters called upon Trailōkhanāt for help. The conquest of Chīengmai put an end to hostilities between northern and southern Thailand for some time. The poetry is unusually musical and full of imagery, a masterpiece which is difficult for modern readers to understand. Much of the vocabulary is still unexplained. KW

Z

Ẓafar, Bahādur Shāh (b 1775 Delhi, d 1862 Rangoon), Urdu poet, and last Mughal king of Delhi. He acceded in 1837, reluctantly put himself at the head of the Revolt of 1857, and was exiled by the British to Burma in 1858. In poetry, he was the pupil of Ẕauq (qv), and later of G͟hālib (qv). His verse is mainly in the *ghazal* (see Vol. III) form; it has no great vigour or profundity, but expresses in simple, charming language a sad, calm resignation to the vicissitudes of life; it shows a marked sense of music and rhythm, and a special fondness for the longer metres.

Mahdi Husain, *Bahadur Shah II and the War of 1857* (Delhi 1958); RSHUL 96–7; MSHUL 208–9. RR

zarzuela, Filipino musical comedy, see **moro-moro.**

Ẕauq, Shaik͟h Muḥammad Ibrāhīm (b 1789 Delhi, where d 1854), Urdu lyric poet, panegyric of the Emperor Akbar Shāh II, who bestowed upon him the title 'K͟hāqānī-e Hind' (Indian Khāqānī, see Vol. III). An accomplished master of the *qaṣīda* (see Vol. III), he wrote polished odes on Indian aristocrats in simple, fluent and idiomatic language, avoiding Persianisms. He also composed popular musical *ghazals* (see Vol. III) and didactic quatrains containing moral teachings. His philosophical verses reflect the pessimism of his age.

RSHUL 152–6; MSHUL 165–72. JM

Zawgyi, Burmese poet, see **Zodji.**

Zēbu'n-nisā, Makhfī (b 1639, d 1702 Delhi), Indo-Persian mystic poetess, daughter of Emperor Aurangzeb. She spent 20 years imprisoned in Salimgarh fort. She hated the cold Islamic orthodoxy of her father and tried to weld Islam, Hinduism and Zoroastrianism together. Her *dīwān* shows traces of Sūfī pessimistic thinking and possesses a special Indian note. It is much read because it expresses convincingly the feeling of a suffering human soul.

Trans.: Magan Lal and J. D. Westbrook, *The Divan of Zeb-un-Nisa* (London 1913). HIL 729. JM

Zodji (Thein Han, U, b 1907 Phjapoum), Burmese poet, writer, dramatist, translator, leading literary historian and critic. He studied English, Burmese literature and history at the Rangoon University and librarianship in London and Dublin. Then he became a librarian at the Universities' Central Library, Rangoon. His poem *Pitauk Pan* (The Padauk Flower, 1929) is regarded as the first work of the *Khitsam* literary school. *Khitsam* (The Test of the Age) was born out of the conflict of the old literary tradition with the needs of modern times in the 1920's. Rejecting clichés and grandiloquent style, young authors from the Rangoon University tried to express themselves in a clear, understandable way. Ideas and feelings became more important than form, human experience more significant than traditional ideals. *Khitsam* helped Burmese literature to enter a new epoch and Zodji became its most progressive exponent. In his poetry he depicts Nature, having always Man and his fate in mind. A humanist, he believes that truth and strength must be sought among people, especially the poor, not in old books (story, *Pugam Zhei*, The Market of Pagan, 1934). In the drama *Shwei Maun Tham* (The Voice of the Golden Gong) he rejects expansionist wars and feels sympathy with the oppressed. He wrote realistic and romantic short stories, and liked historical themes. His latest poems, with mystical features and formal perfection, mark a new epoch in his work. Works: poems in the anthology *Khitsam Kabja mja* (Khitsan Poems, 1934), *Pitauk Shweiwa* (The Golden Padauk, 1951), *Beida Lam* (The Way of the Beida Flower, 1963); short stories in *Khitsam Poumpyin mja* 1 (Khitsan Stories 1, 1934), *Thoumpwinhsain Khitsam Sapei* (Trefoil of Khitsan Literature, 1955); literary history *Sapei Loka* (On Life and Letters, 1949), *Thakhin Koujto Hmain Tika* (On T. K. Hmain, 1956), *Yatha Sapei Aphwin* (On Fiction, 1963). DB

Ẓuhuri, Nūruddīn Muḥammad Ṭāhir (killed 1615 in south India), Indo-Persian poet and writer, master of the flowery Indian style of Persian prose. He lived at the courts of nobles in Iran, then became court poet first at Ahmadnagar, and later at Bijapur. His complicated panegyrics earned him fame as a poet, but he is noted more for his prose work, *Se naṣr* (Three Essays) written as an introduction to a book of Dakkhini songs composed by Sultan Ibrahim Ādil Shah II of Bijapur. The first abounds in metaphors derived from Indian musical tradition, the second praises the sultan, and the third discusses the court artists and their merits.

HIL 724–5. JM

LIST OF NATIONAL LITERATURES

BURMESE LITERATURE

Ananta Thuriya
Awbhatha, U
Hla, U, Luthu
Hlaing, Princess of
Hmain, Thakhin Koujto
Htin, Maun
Kala, U
Khin Hnin Ju
Kyi, U
Kyin U, U
Lat, U
Letwè Thondara
linga
Ma Ma Lei, Djanetjo
Maha Hswei
Maun Tyi, U Leti Pantita
mawgun
Min Thuwun
Mya Zedi
Natshinnaung
Nawade I
Nu, U
Padethayaza
Pi Mounin
Ponnya, U
pyo
Rahtathara, Shin Maha
Sa, U
Seinda Kyawthu
Taya, Dagoun
Thein Pe Myint, U
Thilawuntha, Shin
Tin Aun, Banmo
Uttamagyaw, Shin
Wa, Theippam Maun
yadu
Yatana Kyemon
Zodji

CAMBODIAN LITERATURE

Chbap Kram
Dhammarāja, Sri
Khmer inscriptions
pralom-lok
Ream Ker
Teav-Ek
Thmenh Chey
Tripiṭaka in Cambodia

INDIAN, PAKISTANI AND BANGLADESH LITERATURES

Ancient Indian literature

Abhinavagupta
alaṃkāraśāstra
Amaru
aṅga
āraṇyaka
Ārya Śūra
Aśvaghoṣa
avadāna
Avadānaśataka
Bāṇa
Bhagavadgītā
Bhāgavata Purāṇa
bhakti
Bhāmaha
Bhāravi
Bhartṛhari (1)
Bhartṛhari (2)
Bhāsa
Bhaṭṭa Nārāyaṇa
Bhaṭṭi
Bhavabhūti
Bhoja

Bilhaṇa	Nāgārjuna
brāhmaṇas	*Nalopākhyāna*
Buddhaghosa	*Nāṭyaśāstra*
Buddhist Literature of India	*Pañcatantra*
Dāmodaragupta	Pāṇini's Grammar
Daṇḍin	*Pātañjali*'s *Mahābhāṣya*
Dharmapada	*purāṇa*
dharmaśāstra	Rājaśekhara
dhvani	*Rāmāyaṇa* or *Vālmīki-Rāmāyaṇa*
Dīpavaṃsa	*Ṛgveda*
Divyāvadāna	Śaṅkara
Gaṅgeśa	*śāstra*
Guṇāḍhya	*Setubandha*
Hāla	*śloka*
Harṣa	*smṛti*
Hemacandra or Hemācārya	Somadeva
Hitopadeśa	Śrīharṣa
Jain Literature	Subandhu
jātakas	Śūdraka
Jayadeva	*Śukasaptati*
Kalhaṇa	*sūtra*
Kālidāsa	*tantras*
Kauṭilya	*Theragāthā* and *Therīgāthā*
kāvya	*Tripiṭaka*
Lalitavistara	Udbhaṭa
Māgha	*upaniṣads*
Mahābhārata	Vasubandhu
Mahāvastu	Vātsyāyana Mallanāga
Mahimabhaṭṭa, Rājānaka	*Veda*
mantra	*vedāṅga*
Mayūra	*Vetālapañcaviṃśatikā*
Milindapañha	Viśākhadatta
Murāri	Yājñavalkya

Assamese literature

Bezbaṛuā, Lakṣmīnāth	Mādhavadeva
Gosvāmī, Hemcandra	Śaṅkaradeva

Baluchi literature

Āzāt Jamāldīnī, 'Abdu'l-vāḥid	Hāshimī, Ẓahūr Muḥammad Shāh Sa'īd
daptar	Naṣīr, Gul Khān
Durrak, Jām	Raḥam 'Alī Marrī
Fāżil, Maulānā Muḥammad	Ṣābir, Qāżī 'Abdu'l-raḥīm
Haqqgū, 'Abdu'l-ḥakīm	Shamīm, Muḥammad Iṣḥāq

Bengali literature

Ālāol
Banaphul
Bandyopādhyāy (Banerji), Bibhūtibhūṣan
Bandyopādhyāy (Banerji), Māṇik
Bandyopādhyāy (Banerji), Tārāśaṅkar
Basu (Bose), Buddhadeb
Basu (Bose), Samareś
Bāul songs
Bidyāsāgar, Īśvarcandra
Cakrabarti (Chakravarty), Amiya
Caṇḍīdās
Caryā-padas
Caṭṭopādhyāy (Chatterji), Baṅkimcandra
Caṭṭopādhyāy (Chatterji), Śaratcandra
Dāś, Jībanānanda
Datta (Dutt), Michael Madhusūdan
Datta (Dutt), Sudhīndranāth
De, Biṣṇu
Gaṅgopādhyāy (Ganguli), Nārāyaṇ
Jasimuddin
kabiwālā
Kṛttibās
maṅgal-kāvya
Mitra, Dīnabandhu
Mitra, Premendra
Mukhopādhyāy (Mukherji), Subhāṣ
Nazrul Islām
Rāy (Roy), Bhāratcandra
Rāy (Roy), Rāmmohan
Sen, Samar
Ṭhākur (Tagore), Rabīndranāth
yātrā

English literature

Anand, Mulk Raj
Chattopadhyay, Harindranath
Chaudhuri, Nirad C.
Currimbhoy, Asif.
drama in English
Ezekiel, Nizzim.
Kailasam
Markandaya, Kamala
Moraes, Dom.
Narayan, R. K.
poetry in English
prose in English
Ramanujan, A. K.
Rao, Raja
Sarabhai, Bharati

Gujarati literature

arvācin kavitā
Jośi, Umāśankar
Kānhaḍade Prabandha
navalikā
navalkathā
pada
Premānanda

Hindi literature

Ajñeya or Agyey, Saccidānanda Hīrānanda Vātsyāyan
āñcalik upanyās
Aśk, Upendranāth
Baccan
Bhaṭṭ, Udayśaṅkar
Bihārīlāl
chāyāvād
Dinkar
Dvivedī, Mahāvīrprasād
Gupta, Maithilīśaraṇ
Hariaudh
Hariścandra 'Bhartendu'
Jainendrakumār
Jośī, Ilācandra
Kabīr
Kamaleśvar
Lallūlāl

Nāgar, Amṛtlāl
nayī kahānī
nayī kavitā
Nirālā
Pant, Sumitrānandan
Pāṭhak Śrīdhar
pragativād
Prasād, Jayśaṅkar
Premcand
Rāghav, Rāṅgey
rahasyavād
Rakeś, Mohan
Rāy, Amṛt
Sūrdās
Tulsīdās
Varmā, Bhagavatīcaraṇ
Varmā, Mahādevī
Varmā, Vṛndāvanlāl
Yādav, Rājendra
Yaśpāl

Indo-Persian literature

Auḥaḍī, Ṭaqī
Badruddīn Chāchī
Brahman
Dārā Shikōh, Muḥammad
Faiżī, Shaikh Abū'l-Faiż
Ḥasan Dihlavī
Kalīm Kāshānī, Abū Ṭālib
Nāsir 'Alī Sirhindī
Naẓīrī Nīshāpurī, Muḥammad Ḥusain
Qāni', Mīr 'Alī Shīr
Sarmad Kāshānī, Sa'īd
Ṭālib 'Āmulī
Zēbu'n-nisā, Makhfī
Ẓuhūrī, Nūruddīn Muḥammad Ṭāhir

Kannada literature

Aḍiga, Sopalakrishna
Bendre, Dattātrēya Rāmacandra or Ambikātanayadatta
Karanta, Kōṭa Śivarāma
Kārnād, Giriś
Kavirājamārga
Kumāravyāsa or Nāraṉappa of Gadugu
Pampa
Purandaradāsa
Puṭṭapu, K. V.
Rangācārya, Ādya or Śrīraṅga
Sarvajña
Srī
vacana
Veṅkatesa Ayyangār, Māsti or Śrīnivāsa

Kashmiri literature

Lal Ded
lol-lyric
Mahjūr, Ghulām Ahmad
Mahmūd Gōmī
Maqbūl Śāh
Parmānand

Maithili literature

Vidyāpati

Malayalam literature

Cantu Mēnōn, Oyyārattu
kathakaḷi
Kēśava Dēv, P.
Kṛṣṇa Piḷḷa, Caṅṅampuẓa
Kumāran Āśān, N.
Kuñcan Nampyār
Kuṭṭikkṛṣṇan, P. C.
Mādhava Paṇikkar, Kāvālam
Muhammad Baṣīr, Vaikkam
Nārāyaṇa Mēnōn, Vaḷḷattōḷ

Paramēśvarayyar, Uḷḷūr S.
Rāma Paṇikkar, Niraṇam
Rāman Piḷḷa, C. V.
Śaṅkara Kuṟuppu, G.
Śivaśaṅkara Piḷḷa, Takaẓi
tuḷḷal
Tuñcatt' Eẓuttacchan, Rāmānujan
Vāsudēvan Nāyar, M. T.

Marathi literature

Āgarkar, Gopāl Ganés
Āpṭe, Hari Nārāyaṇ
Atre, Prahlād Keśav
Bālkavi
Cipalūṇkar, Viṣṇuśāstrī
Deval, Govind Ballāḷ
Gāḍgīḷ, Gangādhar Gopāl
Gaḍkarī, Rām Ganés
Gokhale, Aravind Viṣṇu
Jñāneśvar or Jñāndev
Keśavsut
Khāḍilkar, Kṛṣṇajī Prabhākar
Khānḍekar, Viṣṇu Sakhārām
Kolhaṭkar, Śrīpad Kṛṣṇa
Māḍgūḷkar, Vyankateś Digambar
Marḍhekar, Bāḷ Sītārām
Nāmdev or Nāmā
Penḍse, Śrīpad Nārāyaṇ
Phaḍke, Nārāyaṇ Sītārām
Ṭiḷak, Bāl Gangādhar
Ṭiḷak, Nārāyaṇ Vāman
Tukārām

Oriya literature

Bhañj, Upendra
Dās, Sāralā
Senāpati, Fakīrmohan

Pali, see *Ancient Indian literature*

Panjabi literature

Ādi Granth
Bullhe Śāh
Dasam Granth
Farīd
Ghulām Farīd
Gurdās Bhallā, Bhāī
Hāsam Śāh
janamsākhī
Kādar Yār
Mohan Singh
Śāh Husain or Mādholāl Husain
Vāras Śāh
Vīr Singh, Bhāī

Pashto literature

'Abd ul-Karīm, Master
Aḥmad, Mawlavī
Aḥmadjān Khān Bahādur, Munshī
Shīnwārī, Amīr Ḥamza

Prakrit, see *Ancient Indian literature*

Rajasthani literature

Ḍholā-Mārū rā Dūhā
Kānhaḍade Prabandha
rāso
vāt

Sanskrit, see *Ancient Indian literature*

Sindhi literature

'Abdu'l-karīm of Bulrrī, Shāh
'Abdu'l-laṭīf Bhitā'ī, Shāh
Abrō, Jamāluddīn
Abū'l-Ḥasan, Miān
Adwani, Sir Bheeromal Mehrchand
Ayāz, Shaikh Mubārak
Bēdil, Qādir Baksh of Rohri
Girhōrī, Makhdūm 'Abdu'r-raḥīm
Hāshim, Makhdūm Maḥammad
Qādī Qādan of Sehwan
Qalīch Bēg, Mīrzā
Sachchal Sarmast

Tamil literature

āḻvār
Aṇṇāturai, C. N.
Āṇṭāḷ
Appar
Āṟumukam, Nallūr Kantappiḷḷai
Aruṇācalakavi
Aruṇakirinātar
Beschi, Constanzo Guiseppe
Campantar
Cāttaṉār
Cayaṅkoṇṭār
Cēkkiḻār
Cellappā, Ci. Cu.
cittar
Cuntaram Piḷḷai, Alappuḻai Perumāḷ
Cuntarar
Cuppiramaṇiya Aiyar, Varakaṉēri Veṅkaṭēcaṉ
Cuppurattiṉam, Kaṉaka
Cuvāmināta Aiyar, U. Vē
Eṭṭuttokai
Iḷaṅkōvaṭikaḷ
Iṟaiyaṉār
Irāmaliṅka Piḷḷai, Svāmi
Jānakirāmaṉ, Ti.
Jayakāntaṉ, T.
Kaciyappa Civāccāriyar
Kaliyānacuntaram, Mutaliyār Tiruvārūr V.
Kampaṉ
Kiruṣṇa Piḷḷai, Henry Alfred
Kiruṣṇamūrtti, R.
Maṇi, C.
Māṇikkavācakar
Mātavaiyā, Appavaiyā
Meyakaṇṭatēvar
Nakkīrar
Nālaṭiyār
Nālāyira[ttiviya]ppirapantam
Naṭēca Cāstiri, Caṅkēnti Mahāliṅkam
nāyaṉmār
Pārati (Bharati), Cuppiramaṇiyam Ci.
Pattuppāṭṭu
Pavaṇanti
Periyāḻvār
Pukaḻēnti
Putumaippittaṉ
Rajakōpālāccāri, Cakkaravartti
Rājam Aiyar, B. R.
Rāmāmirtam, Lā. Sa.
Tāyumāṉavar
Tirumuṟai
Tiruttakkatēvar
Tiruvaḷḷuvar
Tiruviḷaiyāṭaṟpurāṇam
Tolkāppiyam
Vaitīcuvaraṉ
Varatarācaṉ, Mu.
Vēṇukōpālaṉ, Ti. Co.
Vētanāyakam Piḷḷai, Samuel

Telugu literature

Appārāw, Gurajtāḍa Weṅkaṭa
Kr̥ṣṇadevarāya
Nannaya
Pedanna, Allasāni

Pōtana, Bammēra
Satyanārāyaṇa, Wiśwanātha
Śrīniwāsarāw, Śrīraṅgam
Sūranna, Piṃgali
Tenāli Rāmakṛṣṇa

Timanna
Tirupati Weṅkaṭakawulu
Tyāgarāja
Wīrēśaliṅgam, Kandukūri

Urdu literature

'Abbās, Khvāja Aḥmad
Aḥmad, 'Azīz
Aḥmad Khān, Sir Sayyid
Aḥmad, Naẓīr
Akbar Ilāhābādī
Ali, Ahmed
Amānat, Sayyid Āghā Ḥasan
Amīr Mīnā'ī, Munshī Aḥmad
Amman Dihlavī, Mīr
Anīs, Mīr Babar 'Alī
Ātish, Khvāja Ḥaidar 'Alī
Āzād, Muḥammad Ḥusain
Bēdī, Rājindar Singh
Chandar, Krishan
Chughtāī, 'Iṣmat
Dāgh Dihlavī, Navāb Mīrzā Khān
Dard, Khvāja Mīr
dāstāns
Faiż Aḥmad Faiż
Firāq Gōrakhpurī
Ghālib, Mirzā Asadullāh Khān
Ghavvāsī
Ḥaidar, Qurratu'l-'ain
Ḥālī, Khvāja Alṭāf Ḥusain
Ḥasrat Mōhānī, Sayyid Fażlu'l-ḥasan
Inshā, Sayyid Inshā'llāh Khān

Iqbāl, Muḥammad
Jigar Murādābādī
Jōsh Malīḥābādī
Jur'at, Shaikh Qalandar Bakhsh
Majāz, Asrāru'l-ḥaqq
Manṭo, Sa'ādat Ḥasan
Mīr Ḥasan
Mīr, Mīr Taqī
Mo'min, Ḥakīm Muḥammad Khān
Muḥammad Qulī Quṭb Shāh
Muṣḥafī, Shaikh Ghulām Hamadānī
Nāsikh, Shaikh Imām Bakhsh
Naẓīr Akbarābādī, Valī Muḥammad
progressive writing
Qāsimī, Aḥmad Nadīm
Rangīn, Sa'ādat Yār Khān
Rusvā, Muḥammad Hādī
Sarshār, Ratan Nāth
Sarūr, Rajab 'Alī Beg
Saudā, Mirzā Rafī'
Sharar, 'Abdu'l-ḥalīm
Shiblī Nu'mānī, Muḥammad
Vajhī, Mullā
Valī, Muḥammad
Ẓafar, Bahādur Shāh
Ẓauq, Shaikh Muḥammad Ibrāhīm

INDONESIA, see MALAY AND INDONESIAN LITERATURE

JAVANESE LITERATURE

Babad Tanah Djawi
Iesmaniasita, Sulistyautami
Jasadipura I, Raden Ngabehi
Kanwa
Pararaton
Prapañca
Ramayana Kakawin

Ranggawarsita, Raden Ngabei
Sedah
Senggono
Subagijo, Ilham Notodidjo
Tantu Panggelaran
wajang

MALAY AND INDONESIAN LITERATURE

Abdullah bin Abdul Kadir, Munshi
Al-Hadi, Sayyid Shaykh bin Sayyid Ahmad
Alisjahbana, Sutan Takdir
Anwar, Chairil
Apin, Rivai
bangsawan
Dharta, A. S.
hikayat
Idrus
Ishak bin Haji Muhammad
Iskandar, Nur Sutan
Ismail, Usmar
Jassin, Hans Baguë
Kajai, Abdul Rahim bin Salim
Mihardja, Achdiat Karta
Muis, Abdul
Pané, Armijn
pantun
Rusli, Marah
Samad Said, A[bdul]
sandiwara
Sejarah Melayu
Shahnon Ahmad
sha'ir
Tur, Pramudya Ananta
Usman Awang
Yamin Muhammad

NEPALI LITERATURE

Ācārya, Bhānubhakta
Bhaṭṭa, Motīrām
Devkoṭā, Lakṣmī Prasād
Maināli, Gurūprasād
Panḍyāl, Lekhnāth
Sama, Bālkr̥ṣṇa
Śreṣṭha, Siddhicaran
Tivārī, Bhīmnidhi

PAKISTAN, see INDIAN, PAKISTANI AND BANGLADESH LITERATURES

PHILIPPINES LITERATURE

Arcellana, Francisco
Balmori, Jesus
Baltazar, Francisco
Bulosan, Carlos
darangan
Gonzalez, Nestor Vicente Madali
Guerrero, Wilfrido Ma.
Hernandez, Amado V.
Joaquin, Nick
moro-moro
Polotan-Tuvera, Kerima
Rizal, José
Santos, Lope K.
Santos, N. Bienvenido
Villa, Jose Garcia

SINHALESE LITERATURE

Aligiyavanna
Devarakṣita Jayabāhu Dharmakīrti
Dharmasena
Dīpavaṃsa
Gonsalves, Jacome
Gurulugōmi
jātaka in Sinhalese
Kumāranatunga, Munidāsa
Mayūrapāda
Mihiripænne Dhammaratana
Parākramabāhu II
Parākramabāhu VI
Rāhula, Śrī
sandesa
Silva, John de
Silva, W. Abraham
Sirisena, Piyadāsa
Vættæve
Vīdāgama Maitreya
Vidyācakravarti
Wickramasinghe, Martin

THAI LITERATURE

Dǫkmai Sot
Khlōng Kamsūon, Khlōng Nirāt Nakhǫn
Khun Chāng Khun Phāēn
Mālai Chūphinit
nirāt
Phongsāwadān
Phra Aphaimanī, Ruang
Prachum Phongsāwadān
Pramūon Kotmāi Ratchakān thī nüng
Raden Landai
Rāmakīen, Phrarātcha niphon nai ratchakān thī nüng
Sathāpanawat, Srirat
Surāngkhanāng, K.
Traiphūm or *Traiphūmikhathā*
Yūon Phāi, Lilit

VIETNAMESE LITERATURE

Binh-nguyen-Loc
Doan-thi-Diem
Han-mac-Tu
Ho-bieu-Chanh
Ho-chi-Minh
Ho-xuan-Huong
Khai-Hung
Le-qui-Don
luc bat
Nam-Cao
Ngo-tat-To
Nguyen-cong-Hoan
Nguyen-dinh-Chieu
Nguyen-Du
Nguyen-gia-Thieu
Nguyen-Hong
Nguyen-Trai
Nguyen-Tuan
Nhat-Linh
Pham-Quynh
Phan-boi-Chau
Tan-Da
Thach-Lam
The-Lu
To-Hoai
To-Huu
Tran-te-Xuong
Truong-vinh-Ky, Pétrus Jean-Baptiste
truyen
Tu-Mo
Vu-trong-Phung
Xuan-Dieu

DICTIONARY OF ORIENTAL LITERATURES

VOLUME II

Literatures included in the present volume:

India, Pakistan and Bangladesh: Ancient Indian, Assamese, Baluchi, Bengali, Gujarati, Hindi, Indian literature written in English, Indo-Persian, Kannada, Kashmiri, Maithili, Malayalam, Marathi, Oriya, Panjabi, Pashto, Rajasthani, Sindhi, Tamil, Telugu, Urdu.

Nepali

Sinhalese

South-East Asia: Burmese, Cambodian, Javanese, Malay and Indonesian, Philippines, Thai, Vietnamese.

Literatures included in Volume I:

Chinese
Japanese
Korean
Mongolian
Tibetan

Literatures included in Volume III:

Ancient Near East: Akkadian, Aramaic, Assyrian, Babylonian, Carthaginian, Coptic, Egyptian, Hebrew, Hittite, Mandaic, Persian (Ancient and Middle), Phoenician, Sumerian, Syriac, Ugaritic.

Arab Countries: Arabic, Classical, Algerian, Egyptian, Iraqi, Jordanian, Lebanese, Moroccan, Palestinian, Sudanese, Syrian, Tunisian.

Turkey: Turkish, Turkic, Armenian.

Iran: Persian.

Afghanistan: Dari, Pashto.

Soviet East: Abkhazian, Armenian, Avar, Azerbaijan, Chukot, Circassian, Darg, Georgian, Kazakh, Kirghiz, Kurdish, Lezgian, Ossetian, Tatar, Tajik, Turkic, Turkmen, Uzbek, Yakut.